STRUCTURAL CHANGE IN BANKING

Michael Klausner
Lawrence J. White
Editors

NEW YORK UNIVERSITY SALOMON CENTER
Leonard N. Stern School of Business

BUSINESS ONE IRWIN
Homewood, Illinois 60430

This publication is designed to provide accurate and authoritative information in regard to the subject matter covered. It is sold with the understanding that neither the author nor the publisher is engaged in rendering legal, accounting, or other professional service. If legal advice or other expert assistance is required, the services of a competent professional person should be sought.

From a Declaration of Principles jointly adopted by a Committee of the American Bar Association and a Committee of Publishers.

Project editor: Karen J. Nelson
Production manager: Mary Jo Parke
Designer: Heidi J. Baughman
Printer: Book Press, Inc.

Library of Congress Cataloging-in-Publication Data

Structural change in banking / Michael Klausner, Lawrence J. White, editors.

p. cm.

Papers and discussion from a conference jointly sponsored by the New York University Salomon Center and the New York University School of Law and held on November 21-22, 1991.

ISBN 1-55623-600-X

1. Banks and banking—United States—Congresses. 2. Banking law—United States—Congresses. I. Klausner, Michael. II. White, Lawrence J. III. New York University Salomon Center.

HG2491.S78 1993

332.1′0973—dc20 92-41782

Printed in the United States of America

1 2 3 4 5 6 7 8 9 0 BP 9 8 7 6 5 4 3 2

CONTENTS

PREFACE

On November 21-22, 1991, the New York University Salomon Center in the Stern School of Business and the New York University School of Law jointly sponsored a conference on "Structural Change in Banking." The conference participants included academic researchers from the economics and legal fields, practitioners from banks and other financial services firms, and lawyers specializing in banking. We were the conference directors. We believe that the conference sessions generated a fruitful exchange of ideas on the fundamental problems of bank structure and the prospects for structural change. This book is the result of that conference.

We owe debts of gratitude in a number of directions. Chuck Muckenfuss, Martin Lowy, Jonas Prager, and Mitchell Berlin served as chairmen of the conference sessions; Muckenfuss also graciously agreed to be a last-minute substitute as a luncheon speaker and delivered an excellent talk. Mary Jaffier and her staff did their usual excellent job in making sure that the conference ran smoothly. Diane Belleville and her staff provided extra support in manuscript handling and preparation. Jim Cozby performed his magic in converting manuscripts into page proofs. And Ingo Walter, Director of the Salomon Center, and John Sexton, Dean of the Law School, offered encouragement and generous financial and organizational support for the conference.

Michael Klausner
Lawrence J. White

CONFERENCE PARTICIPANTS

Allen N. Berger, Senior Economist, Board of Governors of the Federal Reserve System

Mitchell Berlin, Assistant Professor of Finance, Stern School of Business, New York University

Charles W. Calomiris, Associate Professor of Finance, University of Illinois

Tamar Frankel, Professor of Law, School of Law, Boston University

Brian C. Gendreau, Vice President, J.P. Morgan & Co. Inc.

Gary Gorton, Associate Professor of Finance, Wharton School, University of Pennsylvania

William S. Haraf, Vice President, Citicorp

James P. Holdcroft, Jr., Executive Vice President, Republic New York Corp.

Emma C. Jordan, Professor of Law, Georgetown University Law Center

Edward J. Kelly, III, Partner, Davis Polk & Wardwell

Michael Klausner, Assistant Professor of Law, School of Law, New York University

Robert E. Litan, Senior Fellow, Brookings Institution

Martin E. Lowy, Counsel, Rosenman & Colin

Jonathon R. Macey, J. DuPratt White Professor of Law, School of Law, Cornell University

Geoffrey P. Miller, Kirkland & Ellis Professor of Law, School of Law, University of Chicago

Cantwell F. Muckenfuss, III, Partner, Gibson, Dunn & Crutcher

Leonard I. Nakamura, Senior Economist, Federal Reserve Bank of Philadelphia

George Pennacchi, Associate Professor of Finance, University of Illinois

Robert C. Pozen, Managing Director and General Counsel, FMR Corp.

Jonas Prager, Associate Professor of Economics, New York University

Sanford Rose, Principal, Oliver, Wyman & Co.

Kenneth E. Scott, Ralph M. Parsons Professor of Law and Business, School of Law, Stanford University

Steven D. Smith, Executive Director, GE Capital Corp.

Lewis J. Spellman, Professor of Finance, University of Texas

Gregory F. Udell, Associate Professor of Finance, Stern School of Business, New York University

Eugene N. White, Professor of Economics, Rutgers University

Lawrence J. White, Arthur E. Imperatore Professor of Economics, Stern School of Business, New York University

INTRODUCTION

BANK REGULATORY REFORM AND BANK STRUCTURE

Michael Klausner
Lawrence J. White

Banks in the United States differ from other financial institutions in two fundamental and closely related respects: They fund illiquid assets (loans) with liquid liabilities (deposits); and most of their liabilities are covered by federal deposit insurance. For reasons discussed below, one consequence of banks' adoption of this financial structure is the possibility of a depositor run on an otherwise solvent and healthy bank. Since 1933, however, deposit insurance has essentially eliminated bank runs. In addition, deposit insurance has insulated banks from the discipline of depositors and thereby exacerbated incentives for inefficient risk-taking. Such risk-taking is largely responsible for the thrift crisis of the late 1980s[1] and the more recent weakness in the commercial banking sector.[2]

In response to the thrift and bank failures of the last decade, academics and industry experts have proposed a wide range of deposit insurance reform proposals, some of which have already been enacted into law or adopted in regulations of the bank regulatory agencies.[3] Many of these reform proposals could have substantial impacts on the financial structure of banks, which in turn may impair the efficiency with which banks deliver services to customers.

Little attention, however, has been devoted to the relationship between the financial structure of banks and deposit insurance reform. In this introduction, we develop a framework of analysis that relates the issue of deposit insurance reform to bank structure and the provision of banking services. We examine how a bank's financial structure is related to the services the bank performs and how deposit insurance has preserved that structure at great social cost. We then examine how alternative reform measures could affect bank structure and the provision of banking services. Finally, we identify a set of empirical questions that must be addressed before one can confidently advocate one form of reform over another. The papers in this volume, originally presented at a conference sponsored jointly by the New York University Salomon Center and the New York University School of Law on November 21-22, 1991, address some of those empirical questions. Further work, however, remains to be done.

BANK FINANCIAL STRUCTURE, BANKING SERVICES, AND INSTABILITY

On the asset side of its balance sheet, a typical bank predominantly holds illiquid loans; and on the liability side, the bank primarily holds deposits payable on demand and short-term certificates of deposit. This structure, which is unique among financial institutions, is the source of many problems in the banking sector, but it may also be a source of banks' commercial appeal.

Banks provide two sets of services to their depositors. First, they pool depositors' funds and lend them out. These services are often referred to as "asset services." Second, banks make and receive payments on behalf of depositors, they allow depositors to make withdrawals from their accounts in the form of currency, and they stand ready to meet depositors' uncertain payment and currency needs. These services are often referred to as "liability services."

A bank's asset services offer two potential sources of efficiency compared to arrangements that savers and borrowers could make for themselves. First, a bank provides depositors with diversification that would be costly to obtain without an intermediary. Second, by centralizing credit analysis and loan monitoring, a bank exploits economies of scale in the collection and analysis of information, and it reduces the free-rider problem that would exist if many individuals were to make separate loans to a borrower. As a result, loans are made that otherwise would not be made. This service is most valuable for loans to borrowers for which information is not readily available, either at the loan approval stage or while the loan is outstanding.

The illiquidity of a bank's assets is thus a direct consequence of its asset services. The product of these services is a diversified portfolio of loans that cannot be evaluated easily by third parties.[4] This creates the classic "lemons" problem for the sale of a bank loan to a third party.[5] The asymmetry of information that exists between the bank and a potential buyer creates suspicion on the part of the buyer that the bank is asking too high a price for the loan. As a result, a market for bank loans is difficult to establish, and a high proportion of bank portfolios remains illiquid.[6]

Banks also offer efficiencies in liability services. The making of a payment involves three steps. The payor must access his or her funds, transport them to the payee, and ensure that the payee receives them. Because a bank holds assets corresponding to its depositors' claims, a bank implements a payment on behalf of a depositor by transferring its own funds to the depositor's payee (or the payee's bank) and simultaneously debiting the depositor's account. The depositor-payor is thus saved the trouble of initially obtaining his or her funds and transferring them to another party for transportation to the ultimate payee. Banks also achieve efficiencies in transportation (or, in the electronic era, communication) that few payors could achieve on their own. These efficiencies stem from the volume of payment transactions that banks process and from networking possibilities that arise as a result of repetitive transactions among payor and payee banks. Related efficiencies similarly allow banks to verify the receipt of funds by payees. Banks' efficiencies in providing currency to depositors, a relatively unimportant function today, stems simply from economies of scale in safes and related security devices.

Neither the processing of payments nor the provision of currency requires that banks offer liquid liabilities to depositors. A bank could offer only term deposits and stand ready to process payment or withdrawal requests when deposits mature. In addition to performing the mechanical task of processing a payment or conveying currency, however, banks also promise to meet any and all payment and withdrawal needs of their depositors, up to the amount of funds in their accounts. In this respect, the bank acts as an insurer against depositors' uncertain needs to make payments or obtain cash.[7] Without this service, risk averse savers would have to maintain excessive liquidity in order to be sure of having sufficient cash to meet unexpected payment needs, and payees would be less able to predict payment receipts.[8] To provide this payment-related service, a bank must offer liquid liabilities.

Asset services require a financial institution to hold illiquid assets, and liability services require it to offer liquid liabilities. Though banks currently offer these two sets of services together, they need not occur within the same institution. Indeed, nonbank financial institutions of various types provide each of these services separately. For instance, finance companies, insurance companies, and pension plans pool funds and make illiquid loans; and money market funds provide liability services.[9] However, finance company liabilities and insurance company liabilities, consisting of debt securities, insurance claims, and retirement benefits, respectively, are not as liquid as are bank liabilities. And money market funds' assets, consisting of short-term commercial paper and government securities, are not as illiquid as are bank assets.[10] Banks provide both asset services and liability services and, as a result, hold illiquid assets and liquid liabilities. To explain the historical persistence of the bank, therefore, one must identify some efficiency obtained by combining these two sets of services.

Whatever that efficiency was historically, it must have been great enough to outweigh the cost that depositor runs historically imposed on banks prior to the introduction of federal deposit insurance, which is discussed below. Runs are a direct consequence of banks' holding illiquid assets and liquid liabilities. If depositors have the right to repayment regardless of whether their bank can liquidate the necessary loans at fair market values, all depositors are at risk that the bank will have to liquidate at less than market value and, consequently, that the proceeds of those sales will be insufficient to cover all the bank's deposits. This creates an incentive for a depositor to withdraw funds any time he or she fears that others will do so in sufficient volume to overwhelm a banks' store of liquid assets and force sufficient below-market sales of illiquid assets to deplete its equity cushion. This is the dynamic of a bank run—the product of the inherent prisoner's dilemma among depositors who do not want to be last in line to make withdrawals. A run can occur regardless of the solvency of a bank on a market-value basis, although it may be more likely in the case of a bank whose solvency is questionable.[11]

A depositor run can entail several social costs. In the case of a run on a healthy bank, a valuable economic entity and its business relationships are destroyed. A run can also disrupt the availability of credit and reduce liquidity in the affected market. In addition, it can have a contagion effect by undermining faith in neighboring banks. At the extreme, it can undermine faith in the banking system as a whole, in which case widespread runs can cause a macroeconomic contraction. Furthermore, the mere threat of a run can impede a bank's ability to perform asset and liability services and to perform its role in the money creation process.

The nineteenth century and the first third of the twentieth century were marked by periodic bouts of bank runs. Policy responses to the run problem included state and federal regulation of banks' activities, investments, and liquidity, state-provided deposit insurance, and the creation of the Federal Reserve System as a lender of last resort. None of these public sector efforts, however, was successful in preventing bank runs. Voluntary coinsurance arrangements and other forms of voluntary cooperation among groups of state banks during the nineteenth century showed promise as responses to the run problem. Ironically, however, those arrangements were later undermined by state and federal laws that restricted banks' geographical expansion, thereby exposing them to localized risk and impeding their ability to monitor one another.[12] Following widespread bank runs and failures between 1930 and 1933, the federal government responded with federal deposit insurance.

DEPOSIT INSURANCE AND BANK FAILURE

With the federal government explicitly insuring a large proportion of bank deposits, and implicitly insuring essentially all deposits, depositors since 1933 have had no reason to start, or to fear, a run on a bank—even if the bank is insolvent—and, indeed, runs on federally insured banks have virtually ceased.[13] Deposit insurance has thus preserved the traditional bank structure. The elimination of the run problem and the preservation of this structure, however, have come at a high social cost.

Deposit insurance has substantially reduced the market's discipline over banks' investments and operations and dramatically skewed bankers' incentives to take risks. By charging banks a flat-rate insurance premium, federal deposit insurance provides a subsidy to bank risk-taking. To the extent that the bank regulatory agencies fail to control bank risk through administrative oversight, the federal deposit insurer, and ultimately the federal Treasury, bear the downside risk of banks' investments. Moreover, the economy as a whole bears the cost of misallocated investment.

Despite the potential for problems, the banking system exhibited remarkable stability from the mid-1930s until the late 1970s, and the federal deposit insurance funds experienced little loss. This stability was the product of three important factors: First, the national economy, and each of its major sectors, were relatively stable, avoiding serious bouts of inflation or recession. Second, nonbank financial institutions lacked the technologies that would eventually develop to allow them to provide services that banks traditionally provided; debt was predominantly illiquid and, for the most part, could be funded only by liquid savings. Third, federal and state legal restrictions protected banks from competition among themselves. This protection consisted of ceilings on deposit interest rates, as well as entry restrictions in the form of limits on intrastate and interstate branching and on the availability of new banking licenses. Banks thus operated in stable, protected markets. As a result, their franchise values were high, and the incentives of their shareholders and managers to take risks were low.

By the late 1970s, however, this formula for stability began to dissolve. The United States economy had become less stable, and individual sectors (e.g., agriculture, energy, real estate) became more prone to periods of boom and bust. In addition, the technologies of data processing and telecommunications began to allow the securities markets and nonbank financial institutions to offer services that competed with traditional banking services without the restrictions of the bank regulatory regime. Furthermore, state and federal governments removed some of the regulatory restrictions on local competition among banks. The result was increased competition for banks in unstable markets.

These phenomena had two effects on the banking industry. First, banks experienced declining franchise values, which tended to increase the incentives for bank managers and shareholders to take risks.[14] Second, to the extent that other financial institutions became more efficient than banks in providing traditional banking services, banks had a choice of either liquidating, shrinking, or developing a new clientele and new services.[15] As a consequence, many banks chose to begin serving a new clientele and to provide new services, and in doing so, they assumed risks with which neither they nor the bank regulators were familiar. The result was risk-taking on an unprecedented scale at the expense of the federal Treasury. There is a substantial question whether this option would have been available to banks if deposit insurance had not insulated them from market forces.[16]

The savings and loan industry was the first to experience shocks from the new environment. High interest rates in the late 1970s and early 1980s caused thrifts to experience large losses on their portfolios of long-lived, fixed-rate mortgages. Simultaneously, the advent of money market mutual funds, the securitization of residential mortgages, and the development of an active secondary market for these mortgage securities increased competition for thrifts in their primary lending and deposit markets. Federal and state legislation in the early 1980s provided S&Ls with some measure of relief by allowing them to engage in new types of lending and by phasing out deposit interest rate ceilings. Unfortunately, at the same time, state and federal regulators also reduced their vigilance in regulating the safety and soundness of these institutions.[17]

In this new environment, hundreds of thrifts took advantage of their new opportunities and expanded rapidly, with much of this expansion occurring in lending outside of their traditional field of residential mortgage lending. A combination of deliberate risk-taking, over-optimism, carelessness, incompetence, and venality—compounded by the fall in the price of oil in the mid-1980s and the removal of tax advantages for investments in commercial real estate—caused many thrifts to fail, with losses that bankrupted the thrift insurance fund and required substantial taxpayer contribution.[18]

Because the durations of their loans were shorter than those of thrifts, commercial banks were less affected by the interest rate spike of the early 1980s. Like thrifts, however, commercial banks had to compete with money market funds for deposits. In addition, losses on agricultural and energy loans in the early and mid-1980s, defaults on loans to third world borrowers, and losses on loans during the recession of 1990–91 exacted their toll on many banks. Further, as banks lost many of their high quality loan customers to the commercial paper market in the 1980s, banks turned increasingly to commercial real estate loans as a way to maintain loan volume and operating margins.[19] When the commercial real estate markets crumbled in the late 1980s, hundreds of banks crumbled with them, forcing large losses on the bank insurance fund. At the end of 1991, the Federal Deposit Insurance Corporation was authorized to borrow $30 billion from the Treasury to cover these losses, with the hope that future deposit insurance premiums would permit the repayment of this loan.[20]

In short, as of the early 1990s, banking is not the safe, stable industry that had required comparatively little political attention or analytical focus in the four decades between the mid-1930s and mid-1970s. The large sums required to deal with the thrift cleanup, plus the $30 billion in borrowing by the Federal Deposit Insurance Corporation, have been painful reminders that government deposit insurance has distorted the incentives of bankers, misallocated investment resources, and greatly increased the public's stake in the health of the banking sector.

DEPOSIT INSURANCE REFORM, BANK STRUCTURE, AND BANKING SERVICES

One aspect of deposit insurance that has received little explicit attention from commentators is the fact that it has preserved the traditional financial structure of banks through over fifty years of changing technology and market conditions. By ensuring the availability of funds to banks and effectively subsidizing their activities, the deposit insurance system has preserved the traditional bank regardless of its competitiveness in the current market. Prior to 1933 banks presumably offered efficiencies that outweighed the cost of their instability. There were essentially no other institutions that provided banking services. Since 1933, however, new technologies and new institutions have developed, and the relative efficiency of banks has not been tested in the market.

Such a test could be costly. If banks were stripped of deposit insurance and exposed to market forces, socially costly runs on healthy banks might occur. These runs would not necessarily indicate, however, that the traditional bank structure is inefficient. As discussed above, a bank run is a market failure that occurs as a consequence of the same structural form that allows banks to provide both asset and liability services. Deposit insurance is a response to the market failure that a run represents. The problem is that deposit insurance is a cure that may be (or may not be) more harmful than the illness. As a policy matter, we are faced with a choice between a banking sector potentially fraught with costly market failures in the form of bank runs or one that is dominated by a potentially costly intervention in the form of deposit insurance. There may exist middle ground, however, in a reformed deposit insurance system.

In discussions of deposit insurance reform proposals, little attention has been paid to the effect of reform measures on the financial structure of banks, or on the relationship between that financial structure and the provision of banking services. Our aim below is to frame such an analysis.

Deposit insurance reform proposals can be grouped into three categories. First, there is a set of proposals that would, directly or indirectly, remove insurance from deposits that fund illiquid assets. These relatively radical proposals include the total elimination of deposit insurance and various "narrow bank" regimes, which essentially limit the coverage of deposit insurance to deposits that are collateralized by liquid assets. The narrow bank proposal would retract deposit insurance to such an extent that it would no longer support the traditional bank structure. Deposit insurance would cover only deposits that fund liquid assets. Banks would have to finance illiquid assets with uninsured liabilities. The liquidity of those liabilities would be determined by market forces.[21]

A second group of reform measures would reduce the scope of deposit insurance but continue to have it cover deposits that fund illiquid assets. These proposals include reducing the current $100,000 coverage limit, changing the rules governing multiple accounts by a single depositor, and changing the rules governing pension plan deposits (bank insurance contracts or BICs). Under these rules, banks would have a choice of either shrinking or attracting uninsured funds, but their operations and financial structure would be otherwise unchanged.

The third group of reforms would preserve the near-complete coverage of deposit insurance, but introduce mechanisms that reduce inefficient risk-taking incentives and enhance regulatory oversight. This set of measures includes, for example, a requirement that banks use market-value accounting in reporting the values of their assets and liabilities, the use of risk-based insurance premiums, increased capital requirements, requirements that banks issue subordinated debt, and the recently enacted "prompt corrective action" and early closure rules. These reforms would not alter the financial structure of banks, although they would increase the banks' operating costs.[22]

The possible effects of deposit insurance reform on bank structure and on the provision of bank services are clearest in the case of the first set of reforms—the removal of deposit insurance from deposits that fund illiquid assets. Such a measure could lead to either of two extreme outcomes. First, traditionally structured banks could remain in existence and be vulnerable to runs. The extent of their vulnerability would depend on the success of private coinsurance or related arrangements banks might make. Second, banks in their traditional form may be so hindered by the threat of runs that they might fail in competition with other types of financial institution. If so, traditional banks would be replaced by mutual funds providing liability services, and finance companies providing asset services. The mutual funds would hold liquid assets, the finance companies would hold maturity-matched assets and liabilities, and the run problem would be nonexistent. Alternatively, a combination of these outcomes could occur. Some banks might fail to compete successfully, and nonbank financial institutions might gain market share in asset and liability services, but other banks might survive by minimizing the risk of runs and efficiently providing both asset and liability services. The survival of the traditional bank, in whole or in part, would depend on the existence of efficiencies created by providing these two sets of services together and on the effectiveness of private arrangements to alleviate the threat of depositor runs.

The possible effects of the second group of reform measures—leaving some bank deposits uninsured—would be less dramatic than the effects of the first set of reforms, but the differences are only differences of degree. The exposure of deposits of over $100,000, for instance, to the risk of a run would force traditionally structured banks to compete with other financial institutions for those funds. The result of this competition might be the shrinkage of the traditional bank sector and the growth of other forms of financial institution. The relative efficiency of the traditional bank structure, including its vulnerability to runs, would determine the extent to which uninsured deposits would remain in the banking sector. The degree of the run threat would then depend on the ability of banks to enter into private coinsurance arrangements and on the effectiveness of those arrangements.

Finally, the third set of proposals—those that would reform the deposit insurance system but retain its scope—would preserve traditionally structured banks and continue to allow them to operate free of the risk of depositor runs. Such reforms, however, could and presumably would increase the cost of banking and consequently reduce the size of the banking sector. Ideally, these reforms would eliminate the deposit insurance system's implicit subsidy of risk-taking and force banks to pay the social costs of their operations. If that is what they do, any adjustment in the size of the banking sector would present a painful transition problem, but no long-term inefficiency. It is likely, however, that deposit insurance reform will be imperfect. Regulatory burdens could well be imposed that increase the cost of banking and reduce the size of the banking sector either beyond the points that a hypothetical perfect market would establish or not far enough. Two important elements relevant to predicting the effect of these reforms, therefore, are how close a reformed deposit insurance system can come to the ideal and how efficiently other types of financial institutions would provide banking services as the banking sector contracts.

The impact of any of these three approaches to deposit insurance reform would be felt directly in the credit markets. The first approach would reduce the availability of bank credit substantially. The second and third approaches would probably reduce bank credit as well, but not to the same extent. Depending on the efficiency of nonbank lending, the credit gap left by banks might eventually be filled by other financial institutions and by lending through the securities markets directly to borrowers. Therefore, a central question that arises is whether nonbank sources of credit can efficiently replace bank lending.[23]

These reforms would be felt as well in the market for liability services. A reduction in the size of the banking sector would mean a reduction in the quantity of liquidity in the financial markets; fewer illiquid assets would be transformed into liquid liabilities in the hands of depositors. The impact of this change would depend on the extent to which the securities markets generate liquid liabilities and the extent to which money market funds make them usable for transactions. In the past, when banks were responsible for creating most of the liquidity in the economy, a reduction in the size of the banking sector would have meant a major reduction in liquidity. Today, however, with the existence of a large quantity of tradable short-term debt securities and money market funds that offer payment services, the outlook may be different. Further research on this question is surely warranted.

The first approach to reform could also leave traditionally structured banks vulnerable to depositor runs. Of course, if the withdrawal of deposit insurance results in the disappearance of traditionally structured banks (for instance, by having banks either hold only liquid assets or offer liabilities with maturities that match those of their assets), the run problem would not arise. But both the narrow bank proposal and the proposal to eliminate deposit insurance altogether anticipate that banks would maintain their current structure to the extent market forces allow. Similarly the incremental roll-back of deposit insurance reflected in the second set of proposals would permit traditionally structured banks to compete for acceptance in the market. Three additional questions thus arise. First, how effective can private coinsurance and other cooperative arrangements be in reducing the threat of a run? Second, is there any efficiency inherent in the traditional bank structure? And third, can the social cost of runs be reduced—for instance by altering some of the linkages among banks that can create a chain reaction of runs or failures?[24] Finally, before scaling back deposit insurance, in full or in part, one would want to know the potential of the less dramatic measures included in the third set of reform measures. That is, to what extent can deposit insurance be reformed without reducing the scope of insurance and what residual social costs would remain? These last two issues, which have received considerable attention elsewhere, are not addressed in this volume.[25]

THE CHAPTERS IN THIS VOLUME

The chapters in this volume address the questions identified above, although they make no attempt to do so exhaustively. Along with a relatively small existing literature on banking theory, bank structure, and bank reform, they represent the beginning of an attempt to bring theoretical and empirical analysis to bear on issues that are central to the task of reforming the U.S. bank regulatory system.

The first chapter in this volume, by Charles Calomiris, analyzes the stability of traditionally structured banks from a historical perspective. He provides substantial evidence from U.S. banking history and from the experiences of other countries that banks need not be as vulnerable to runs as is commonly believed. Calomiris demonstrates that, in the past, banks with large branch networks and those that entered into voluntary coinsurance and other cooperative arrangements with other banks dramatically reduced their vulnerability to runs. In contrast, unit banks and banks that did not become members of cooperative groups suffered serious runs, many of which resulted in failure, during each of the major historical periods of banking turmoil.

Calomiris further shows that the state deposit insurance systems of the nineteenth and early twentieth centuries ended in failure for reasons that mirror the problems of the current federal deposit insurance system. Nonetheless, in 1933, when Congress was presented with an explicit choice of deposit insurance or the elimination of legal restrictions on branching, Congress chose the former over the latter.

Calomiris's analysis provides reason for optimism that if deposit insurance were scaled back, and if the traditional bank is an efficient provider of financial services, private coinsurance arrangements among groups of banks could be established that would substantially reduce banks' vulnerability to runs. His analysis also demonstrates that the elimination of branching restrictions should accompany such a reform.[26]

In the second chapter, Leonard Nakamura explores a potential efficiency of the traditional bank—the possibility that a bank can glean information from a customer's checking account that is useful in evaluating the customer's creditworthiness for purposes of making and monitoring a loan. With the support of a wide array of data, Nakamura argues that this efficiency exists for small banks but not for large banks. This is due to the fact that large banks generally lend (and are best suited to lend) to large firms, which typically have multiple checking accounts and transactions that are too complicated for a single bank to monitor.

The implications of Nakamura's analysis for deposit insurance reform are complex. On the one hand, the efficiency of the traditional bank structure may be such that small banks can thrive in a market without deposit insurance. On the other hand, depending on the effectiveness of a bank's coinsurance arrangements, the threat of a run may be so great as to outweigh its efficiency relative to nonbank lenders. In either case, deposit insurance may be warranted, but only if the social costs created by deposit insurance are less than the value of those efficiencies.

In the third chapter, Gary Gorton and George Pennacchi explore how finance companies and other nonbank lenders provide asset services and how money market funds provide liability services. The development of the commercial paper market and other money markets over the last quarter-century has provided a source of liquidity that previously did not exist. Using the liquid assets generated by these markets, money market funds provide liability services that banks have traditionally provided. In addition, finance companies and similar nonbank lending institutions raise funds in these markets to finance their lending.

These two sets of institutions, however, are not entirely different from traditional banks. Money market funds hold portfolios of debt, just as banks do. There is a possibility, therefore, that in response to the failure of a large commercial paper issuer and uncertainty regarding others, shareholders of money market funds could redeem their shares in a panic similar to a bank run. Although the likelihood of their doing so and the effects of their doing so are less severe than in the case of a bank run, such a panic would be socially costly. Similarly, finance companies and nonbank lenders issue short-term callable bonds to finance their illiquid loans. Consequently, they too could experience panics similar to a bank run in response to the failure of a large borrower and uncertainty regarding other borrowers.

The question thus arises whether these institutions offer any improvement over the traditional bank. Gorton and Pennacchi address this question by analyzing whether there is any empirical evidence that panics have occurred in these new financial sectors, and they find no such evidence. They attribute the absence of run-like panics to improved information technologies that allow debt holders to determine with relative accuracy the riskiness of money market claims.

The implications of Gorton and Pennacchi's analysis for bank reform are twofold. First, if deposit insurance were scaled back or the regulatory burden on banks were increased, nonbank providers of asset and liability services may well fill gaps left by banks' exit from the market. On the other hand, the absence of panics among the debt holders of nonbank lenders may imply that technology now exists that would substantially alleviate the risk of runs on traditionally structured banks. They suggest, however, that an important ingredient in eliminating panics among nonbank debt holders is that these lending institutions are sufficiently large to allow for economies of scale in monitoring. This implies that legal barriers to increasing bank size, such as limits on branching, should be eliminated.

In the fourth chapter, Allen Berger and Gregory Udell explore the implications of securitization for banking. Securitization, they point out, takes two forms. In one form, a bank originates a loan that is ultimately held by another party. Berger and Udell term this "disintermediation-type securitization." In the other form, which they term "off-balance-sheet securitization," the bank retains the default risk of the loan through a standby letter of credit or similar device, but the funding is provided by a third party.

Disintermediation-type securitization is a means by which debt is held outside the banking sector. Through the securitization process, the securities markets rather than a bank or other intermediary are used to link lenders and borrowers. Improved data processing and telecommunications technologies have spurred dramatic growth in this type of securitization, which has led some commentators to speculate that the credit markets remaining for banks to serve are riskier than their traditional markets.

Berger and Udell present and empirically test a "monitoring technology hypothesis" to explain securitization, the implication of which is that the riskiness of banks' portfolios does not increase as a result of increased disintermediation-type securitization. In brief, they argue that banks have always lent to "information-problematic" borrowers and that as information technology improves two phenomena occur: First, some borrowers become informationally unproblematic and therefore gain access to the securities markets for borrowing; but second, other borrowers that previously could not borrow at all become suitable for bank lending. Off-balance-sheet securitization, in contrast, has no effect on bank risk or bank monitoring; it represents simply a rearrangement of the nature of the bank's claims.

The Berger and Udell analysis suggests that there will always be a demand for illiquid loans, but that the source of that demand will change as information technology changes. Consequently, there will always be a need for financial institutions to provide the asset services that banks traditionally have provided. Their analysis does not, however, address the question whether traditional banks or another type of institution should provide these services.

In the last chapter of this book, Tamar Frankel also examines the securitization process. She discusses how the securitization process offers banks the opportunity to target business niches and how the availability of securitized debt can enhance banks' flexibility in minimizing interest rate risk and in diversifying their portfolios. Finally, she explores the regulatory burdens on banks and cautions against the danger that financial regulatory regimes accumulated haphazardly over decades could place differential burdens on competing institutions and skew the outcome of competition among new financial technologies and institutions.

The papers in this volume, and the comments that follow each paper, provide a wealth of theoretical and empirical analysis that relates directly or indirectly to the issue of bank regulatory reform. Although more work remains to be done, the papers as a group suggest that financial services technology may have advanced to a point where our reliance on federally insured banks can at least be reduced.

NOTES

1. See White (1991).
2. See Barth, Brumbaugh, and Litan (1992).
3. In the discussion that follows, the term "bank" will refer to all depository institutions, including commercial banks, savings and loan institutions, savings banks, and credit unions.
4. Legal restrictions such as limits on a bank's geographical expansion through branching may impair the bank's ability to diversify its asset portfolio.
5. See Ackerlof (1970).
6. See the paper by Allen Berger and Gregory Udell in this volume. Although there is a market for the purchase and sale of certain types of bank loans, through securitization and through a small whole-loan market, most banks hold most of their loans in illiquid form until maturity. See Gorton and Pennacchi (1991).
7. See Diamond and Dybvig (1983).
8. To accommodate depositors' payment and withdrawal demands, banks must hold some fraction of their assets in liquid form. The amount of liquid assets they need is determined by the pattern of payments made and received and depositors' cash withdrawals. Thus, banks take advantage of the economies that arise from the pooling of large numbers of unpredictable flows of funds into and out of their depositors' accounts. Banks are assisted in performing this service by access to a liquidity lender

such as the Federal Reserve or other banks that participate in the inter-bank lending market.

9. Money markets today typically offer checking services through a bank.
10. Money market funds' assets must be marked to market on a daily bias. By contrast, most bankers claim that it is impossible to mark to market their loan portfolios.
11. See Diamond and Dybvig (1983).
12. See Charles Calomiris's paper in this volume.
13. Although federal deposit insurance has always had a nominal ceiling of coverage, the FDIC's actual practice has been frequently to dispose of insolvent banks through "purchase and assumption" transactions that have preserved all depositors' accounts regardless of size. Liquidations, which involve the loss of deposits over the specified ceiling ($100,000 today), have occurred infrequently. Fears of depositor losses did create a run by holders of large deposits in Continental Illinois Bank in 1984. The run on Continental Illinois had the potential to disrupt the financial markets severely. In response, the Federal Reserve assured not only holders of uninsured deposits but also nondeposit creditors of the bank and its holding company that their claims would be honored. To prevent future runs on large banks, the Federal Reserve and the FDIC, through their "too big to fail" policy, essentially provided insurance to large deposits in large banks. See Sprague (1986).
14. See Keeley (1990).
15. The services a bank could perform, and the efficiency with which it could perform those services, were and still are constrained by regulation.
16. For differing views on whether depositors can be effective monitors, see Randall (1989) and Gilbert (1990).
17. See White (1991, ch. 5).
18. The Tax Reform Act of 1986 removed tax advantages previously available to owners of real estate.
19. See Klausner (1991).
20. There are some observers who doubt that repayment will be possible. See Barth, Brumbaugh, and Litan (1992).
21. See, for example, Litan (1987).
22. For the most part, the Treasury Department's 1991 reform proposal consisted of a package of measures that fall into this category. See U.S. Treasury (1991); Financial Institutions Safety and Consumer Choice Act of 1991.
23. This question is relevant to the analysis in two respects. First, the efficiency with which funds can be aggregated and lent through nonbank channels relative to the efficiency of banks will determine the outcome of competition between banks and other institutions for uninsured funds. Second, it is possible that the threat of a run will so dominate the competition between uninsured banks and nonbanks that traditionally structured banks cease to exist. If that occurs, the efficiency of nonbank sources of credit will determine the size and nature of the credit gap left by banks' demise.
24. Reducing concentration of interbank lending would be an example of such a measure.
25. See U.S. Treasury (1991); Klausner (1991).
26. See Calomiris (1992).

REFERENCES

Ackerlof, George, "The Market for Lemons: Quality Uncertainty and the Market Mechanism," *Quarterly Journal of Economics*, 84 (August 1970), pp. 488–500.

Barth, James R., R. Dan Brumbaugh, Jr., and Robert E. Litan, *The Future of American Banking*. Armonk, NY: M.E. Sharpe, Inc., 1992.

Calomiris, Charles W., "Getting the Incentives Right in the Current Deposit Insurance System: Successes From the Pre-FDIC Era," in James R. Barth and R. Dan Brumbaugh, Jr. (eds.), *Reform of Deposit Insurance and the Regulation of Depository Institutions in the 1990s*. New York: Harper Collins, 1992.

Diamond, Douglas W., and Philip H. Dybvig, "Bank Runs, Deposit Insurance and Liquidity," *Journal of Political Economy*, 91 (June 1983), pp. 401–19.

Financial Institutions Safety and Consumer Choice Act of 1991, S. 713, Congressional Record, 137, p. S3712 (daily ed. March 20, 1991), H.R. 1505, Congressional Record, 137 p. H1912 (daily ed. March 20, 1991).

Gilbert, R. Alton, "Market Discipline of Bank Risk: Theory and Evidence," *Economic Review*, Federal Reserve Bank of St. Louis, 72 (January–February 1990), pp. 3–18.

Gorton, Gary, and George Pennacchi, "Banks and Loan Sales: Marketing Non-Marketable Assets," National Bureau of Economic Research, Working Paper No. 3551 (1991).

Keeley, Michael, "Deposit Insurance, Risk, and Market Power in Banking," *American Economics Review*, 80 (December 1990), pp. 1183–1200.

Klausner, Michael, "An Economic Analysis of Bank Regulatory Reform: The Financial Institutions Safety and Consumer Choice Act of 1991," *Washington University Law Quarterly*, 69 (No. 3), pp. 695–768.

Litan, Robert E., *What Should Banks Do?* Washington, DC: Brookings Institution, 1987.

Randall, Richard E., "Can the Market Evaluate Asset Quality Exposure in Banks?" *New England Economic Review*, Federal Reserve Bank of Boston (July–August 1989), pp. 3–24.

Sprague, Irwin H., *Bailout: An Insider's Account of Bank Failures and Rescues*. New York: Basic Books, 1986.

U.S. Treasury, *Modernizing the Financial System: Recommendations for Safer, More Competitive Banks* (February 1991).

White, Lawrence J., *The S&L Debacle: Public Policy Lessons for Bank and Thrift Regulation*. New York: Oxford University Press, 1991.

CHAPTER 1

REGULATION, INDUSTRIAL STRUCTURE, AND INSTABILITY IN U.S. BANKING: AN HISTORICAL PERSPECTIVE

Charles W. Calomiris

INTRODUCTION

From the mid-1930s through the 1970s the fundamental institutional and regulatory features of the U.S. banking system were taken for granted as permanent and mainly beneficial by most policymakers and economists. Various aspects of the regulatory system (particularly reserve requirements and deposit interest rate ceilings) were blamed for inefficiencies in capital market allocation by banks and often were seen as an impetus for financial innovations in and outside of banking: for example, NOW accounts, and the growth of credit unions and money market mutual funds. But much of the regulatory structure was seen as benign or beneficial. Studies of economies of scale in banking seemed to indicate that unit banking restrictions had little economic impact on bank efficiency. The stability of the commercial banking system seemed to have been ensured by the regulatory "safety net," including federal and state deposit insurance programs that removed depositors' incentives to run on their banks in response to adverse economic news,

The author wishes to thank Michael Klausner, Geoffrey Miller, Eugene White, Lawrence White, and Gavin Wright for helpful comments.

and by regulations on bank operations—notably, the separation of commercial and investment banking, justified in 1933 as a means to prevent dishonest or reckless practices by banks.

In retrospect, the faith in the post-Depression regulated system's ability to deliver bank stability is understandable given the unusual calm of the period from 1934 to 1980. Systemic banking panics or waves of bank failures had become a distant memory, easily attributable to a primitive state of affairs prior to the supposed rationalization of banking brought by the Depression-era reform. This view was shattered by the agriculture and oil busts of the early-to-mid 1980s, along with the economy-wide thrift debacle and Eastern real estate collapse of the late 1980s and early 1990s. While systemic banking panics were avoided through the safeguards of federal deposit insurance, recent loan losses have produced bank and thrift failure rates and bank asset declines of Depression-era proportion. Indeed, the losses per deposit dollar due to bank and thrift failures in the last decade dwarf the losses of failed banks in the 1930s (Baer and Mote, 1991).

Understandably, the upheaval of the past decade has led to an increased willingness to examine possible flaws in the industrial organization and regulation of the banking sector. Increasing numbers of economists and policymakers seem willing to fault bank regulation for the recent spate of costly failures. Restrictions on intrastate and interstate branching, obstacles to takeovers of inefficiently managed banks, limitations on bank activities, inadequate supervisory authorities, and the perverse incentives created by the federal safety net—which ironically was designed to reduce the threat of banking system collapse—have all been faulted for the poor performance of recent years. The Treasury Department, the Federal Reserve, and Congress have proposed altering the traditional post-Depression regulatory framework to correct the purported flaws in the regulatory system.

The recent openness to regulatory reform has spawned new interest in the history of financial institutions and regulation. Financial history has an important role in the current policy debate for at least two reasons. First, the history of bank regulation and instability can help provide a variety of regulatory "experiments" from which to identify more clearly desirable regulatory reforms. In particular, in the search for new alternatives to the existing system of federal deposit insurance [which Golembe (1960), Golembe and Warburton (1958), and E. N. White (1982, 1983), argue was motivated by the desire to avoid the disruption of bank panics] policymakers will want to ensure that any new institutional arrangement designed to reduce the costs of deposit insurance does not do so by increasing the propensity for panics. Second, the history and political economy of regulatory policymaking can help us understand how undesirable policy decisions have been made in the past and, possibly, how to avoid them in the future.

This chapter provides evidence from financial history, primarily of the U.S., on the links between systemic instability of banking and the regulation of banks. The second section discusses the meaning of bank instability and provides a brief review of the literature on bank panics. The third section presents empirical evidence regarding the consequences of branching restrictions on bank instability. In the fourth section, I describe and attempt to explain the history of limitations on branching in the United States. In the fifth section, I review the history of bank liability insurance prior to the establishment of the FDIC in 1933 and its potential role as a stabilizing or destabilizing influence in banking. Finally, in the light of history I assess opportunities and pitfalls for regulatory reform.

BANKING INSTABILITY: DEFINITIONS AND SYSTEMIC DIFFERENCES

Banking instability—by which I will alternately mean a propensity for panic and a propensity for insolvency (to be distinguished below)—has differed widely across times and places. Despite the similarities across systems in the types of business undertaken and the contractual structure of banks (that is, illiquid loans as assets, and primarily liquid short-term or demandable deposits as liabilities), some banking systems have been more vulnerable than others. International comparisons of the incidence and costs of panics and bank failures, and comparisons across regulatory regimes within the U.S., clearly document differences in banking instability associated with different regulatory regimes. The central lesson of these studies is that instability is associated with some historical examples of banking that had common institutional characteristics; it is not an intrinsic problem of banking per se. With respect to bank panics, models that abstract from institutional features of banking and focus only on the liquidity and maturity transformation common to virtually all historical banking systems cannot explain the varying incidence of panics across different times and places.

I will argue that the single most important factor in banking instability has been the organization of the banking industry. Systems based on large, geographically diversified banks that engage in a variety of activities have been the least susceptible to panic, have had a lower overall incidence of bank failure, and have suffered smaller losses when banks failed. Moreover, cross-sectionally within any particular banking system, relatively large, diversified banks have been least likely to fail. Finally, while branch banking systems have not been completely immune to extreme shocks, and some have experienced panics, they recovered more quickly than did unit banking systems under comparable circumstances.

Before reviewing the specific evidence along these lines it is useful to distinguish the propensity for panic from the propensity for failure. While bank liquidations or receiverships typically increased substantially during panic episodes, this was not always the case; and, conversely, there were episodes in which many banks became insolvent without causing a bank panic. Panics involved contractions of bank deposits and lending by all banks and often culminated in the general suspension of convertibility of bank liabilities. Nationwide panics in U.S. history include 1819, 1837, 1839, 1857, 1861, 1873, 1884, 1890, 1893, 1896, 1907, and the three successive waves of contraction from late 1931 to early 1933.

Calomiris and Gorton (1991) review and evaluate the recent theoretical literature on bank panics in light of new evidence from the National Banking Era (i.e., 1863–1913). Calomiris and Schweikart (1991) and Moen and Tallman (1991) provide complementary analysis of the Panics of 1857 and 1907, respectively. The salient facts about panics during this period are the following: Few banks actually failed during panics, while sometimes practically all banks in the country (with some notable exceptions) were forced to suspend convertibility for some period of time (one to three months), during which their claims (notes or cashier checks) circulated at discounts (typically between 0.5 and 4 percent for New York City cashier checks during the National Banking Era). Prior to the Great Depression, panics unrelated to wars occurred at both business cycle and seasonal peaks, during which times bank leverage was high and the variance of "news" about the state of the economy was greatest. Observable adverse shocks of sufficient magnitude prompted panics. During the National Banking Era, if and only if commercial failures (seasonally adjusted) increased by more than 50 percent and stock prices fell by more than 7.9 percent, during any three-month period, then a banking panic immediately followed.

The banking collapse of the 1930s differed sharply from these earlier episodes. The runs on banks did not occur at a cyclical peak. They were the result of deflationary policies that sharply reduced the net worth of banks (Fisher, 1933, Friedman and Schwartz, 1963, Bernanke, 1983, Bernanke and James, 1991, and Hamilton, 1987). In the 1930s banks did not suspend convertibility to halt disintermediation, possibly because self-regulation was pre-empted by the control of the Federal Reserve System. The Federal Reserve banks did not provide an adequate lender of last resort (Gendreau, 1990) or a coordinated response to the deflationary shocks. As a result, an unprecedented number of banks failed.

The banking collapse of the 1930s is explicable as a grand blunder of monetary and bank regulatory policy by the Federal Reserve. But the search for explanations of bank panics prior to the 1930s is more challenging. Theoretical models of these bank panics must explain why observable aggregate shocks with small eventual consequences for the banking system should cause widespread disintermediation and suspension of convertibility. Theory must also explain the optimality of the dependence on demandable debt to finance bank loan portfolios, since maturity-matched debt or equity would eliminate the first-come first-served rule for depositors that makes a panic possible.

Recent models have provided such explanations for the occurrence of panics and for the existence of demandable-debt banking. Beginning with Campbell and Kracaw (1980), Diamond (1984), and Boyd and Prescott (1986), economists have developed models of banks as repositories of scarce information capital about borrowers and their investment opportunities. Banks specialize in screening and monitoring borrowers and thus have better information about the value of their own loan portfolios than do outsiders.

Recent empirical evidence has lent strong support to this view of the function of banks. James (1987) and James and Wier (1989) find that the response of firm valuation in stock markets to announcements of bank loans is positive. This result is in sharp contrast to findings that stock or bond issue announcements reduce the value of a firm (Myers and Majluf, 1984, Asquith and Mullins, 1986, Korajczyk, Lucas, and McDonald, 1990). The positive news of a bank loan has been interpreted as evidence that banks provide information about firms to outsiders through their willingness to grant loans and that the same is not true of equity or debt placed outside the banking system. Lummer and McConnell (1989) divide their sample of bank loan announcements into announcements of new loans, favorable renegotiations of old loans, and unfavorable renegotiations of old loans. Interestingly, renegotiations, rather than new loans, account for James' findings. That is, bank behavior provides information for other markets only after banks learn about their borrowers by having previously lent to them. James and Wier (1990) also find less underpricing of IPOs for firms with established borrowing relationships with banks. Other papers document the proposition that the costs of financial distress (renegotiation of debt) are reduced by close ties to banks (Sheard, 1989, Hoshi, Kashyap, and Scharfstein, 1990b, Gilson, John, and Lang, 1990, and Brown, James, and Mooradian, 1991). Finally, firms with close bank ties show less sensitivity of investment to current cash flow, an indicator of lower costs of external finance (Hoshi, Kashyap, and Scharfstein, 1990a, 1991).

This asymmetry of information inherent in bank lending makes bank loans illiquid, and it can lead to confusion about the incidence of shocks among banks, which can precipitate a bank panic. Gorton (1989) argues that because bank loans are not marked to market, depositors are unable to discover which banks are most likely to be affected by an observable adverse shock. Under these circumstances, even if depositors know that only a small subset of banks are likely to fail in response to an observable shock, they may find it advantageous to withdraw their funds temporarily until the uncertainty over the incidence of the shock is resolved. Event studies of the effects of one bank's difficulties on the returns of other banks indicate that the possibility for confusion regarding the incidence of shocks among banks may still be important in contemporary data (Aharony and Swary, 1983, Lamy and Thompson, 1986, Swary, 1986, Grammatikos and Saunders, 1990, Musumeci and Sinkey, 1988, R. Schweitzer, 1989, and Pozdena, 1991), although Wall and Petersen (1990) provide contrary evidence.

Given the possibility of confusion, why did not banks avoid costly panics by matching the maturity of their loans and liabilities? If bank liabilities matured at the same rate as loans, there would be no potential for confusion about shocks to cause runs on banks. Calomiris and Kahn (1991) and Calomiris, Kahn, and Krasa (1991) argue that despite the costs associated with demandable debt (that is, the potential for runs), this form of financing was optimal because of the discipline it placed on the banker during normal times, given the asymmetric information between depositors and their banker about the banker's behavior. It is also possible to argue that demandable debt provided benefits during banking panics. By prompting suspension of convertibility it provided an incentive for banks speedily to resolve uncertainty about the incidence of a particular shock (Gorton, 1989, and Calomiris and Gorton, 1991).

The circumstances that give rise to bank failures can be very different from those that cause panics. Bank failures can occur during nationwide downturns (including panic episodes) but may also be confined to specific regions or types of banking activity. High rates of bank failure in the Midwest during the 1890s sometimes coincided with panics (especially in 1893 and 1896) and sometimes not. The devastating agricultural bank failures of the 1920s coincided with an era of expansion in much of the economy. The observable shocks of the 1920s did not lead to a general run on banks because in each case the adverse shock was isolated to certain locations and sectors (primarily producers of grains, livestock, and cotton) and their banks.

The industrial organization of banking affected the propensities for panics and for nonpanic waves of bank failures. Systems composed of a small number of diversified large banks were less likely to fail. This also meant that there was less opportunity for panic, since the potential confusion about the incidence of failure risk was reduced. Moreover, coordination among banks was enhanced by limiting the number of banks in any system and thereby promoting mutual assistance during crises. Gorton (1985, 1989), Gorton and Mullineaux (1987), Calomiris (1989, 1990, 1991a), Calomiris and Schweikart (1991), and Calomiris and Gorton (1991) emphasize that panics could be averted, or their costs reduced, if banks could form a coalition to coinsure credibly against an observable shock to the system. If banks as a group agreed to bear the risk of any individual bank's default, then so long as depositors were confident of the solvency of the group, they would have no incentive to withdraw their funds. The mutual benefit of such coinsurance is the avoidance of the panic and the consequent disruption of commercial payments and credit.

The feasibility of such coordination depended crucially on the ability of banks to form successful coalitions, which depended in turn on the number and locations of banks. Coalitions had to be able credibly to guarantee support and to prevent free riding from individual banks on the support of the group. This required self-regulation and the enforcement of regulations by voluntary mutual monitoring among members. City clearing houses, like that of New York (which was organized in 1853), and systems with a small number of geographically coincident branching banks were quite successful at forming coalitions, establishing rules for participation in the coalition, and enforcing compliance. But systems of many geographically isolated unit banks could not do so. The costs of monitoring were higher, and the benefits to any member bank from monitoring a neighbor's actions were too diffuse given the large number of coinsurers. This explains why the United States, with its prohibitions on intrastate and interstate branch banking, has never developed a nationwide coalition of coinsuring banks, unlike many other countries.

I divide the evidence on the importance of bank market structure in the next section into evidence on the incidence of panics and evidence on the risk, incidence, and cost of bank failures.

BRANCH BANKING AND BANK PANICS IN THE UNITED STATES

With the exception of the first and second Banks of the United States, which operated from 1791 to 1811 and 1816 to 1836, respectively, there has been no interstate branch banking in the United States. Except for these two banks, prior to the establishment of national banks during the Civil War all banks were incorporated according to the laws of individual states and operated within the confines of those states. Banks were not free to establish any form of corporate entity they pleased, and the location and activity of a bank was defined by its charter. The earliest banks chartered in the North were unit banks, while those in the South as a rule either were chartered with the intent of establishing branches or soon were granted branching authority upon request. By the 1830s there were several states in the South (Virginia, North Carolina, Louisiana, Kentucky, South Carolina, Georgia, and Tennessee) operating substantial branch networks. The reasons for this initial difference and its persistence are examined below.

During the Panics of 1837 and 1839 branch banking enabled Southern banks to weather the storm of the credit crunch in international trade (which, according to Temin, 1969, produced the panics) remarkably well compared to their counterparts in the North. Evidence of cooperation among Southern banks within and across state lines is provided in Govan's (1936, pp. 15–19) analysis of the banks' response to the Panic of 1837. He finds that Southern banks suspended as a group in response to the exhortations of merchants who feared a drastic contraction of credit. The banks acted collectively to set the timing of suspension, the intended date of resumption, the rules governing the clearing of interbank transactions during the suspension, and rules limiting individual bank liabilities during the suspension. Similar coordination seems to have characterized the Panic of 1839 and seems to have helped to limit the incidence of bank failure during that panic. In the North during the Panic of 1839 suspension was less common and not coordinated among banks, and failure rates were higher than in the branching states of the South (Calomiris and Gorton, 1991, pp. 117–118).

Banks in states dominated by centralized urban control (Delaware, Rhode Island, Louisiana, and the District of Columbia) also coordinated suspension and avoided widespread failure during the Panic of 1839. Similarly, banks in the mutual-guaranty system of Indiana suspended together in 1837 and 1839 and avoided any failures during the panics. Like the branch banking South, city-dominated systems in the North were able to coordinate better because they involved a small number of geographically coincident banks. The Indiana system, though composed of unit banks spread throughout the state, was uniquely suited to coordination. The number of members was limited, the banks regulated one another through a collective board of directors, and they guaranteed each other's liabilities without limit. The board of directors had broad authority (including the right to close banks, regulate capital ratios, and restrict dividends) and had strong incentives to monitor and penalize violations. During its entire history, from 1834 to 1865, no member bank failed. Indeed, the stability of the system was so great that during panics after 1839 it was even able to avoid suspension of convertibility (Golembe and Warburton, 1958, Calomiris, 1989).

During the Panic of 1857, once again Southern banks and the mutual guaranty banks of Indiana and Ohio (which imitated Indiana's system in 1845) coordinated effectively, recovered their pre-panic asset levels relatively quickly and saw relatively few bank failures (Calomiris and Schweikart, 1991). As before, branching banks acted together to coordinate their own and other banks' behavior, establish interbank markets for clearing notes and checks, transfer funds, and enforce agreed upon rules during the panic. For example, within one week of the onset of the panic, banks in Charleston agreed to receive each other's notes and the notes of other South Carolina banks and Augusta and Savannah banks at par. In his discussion of the Panic of 1857, Hammond (1957, p. 712), along with many other observers, notes that the successful coordination of the Southern banks was not possible in states like New York, where many geographically isolated unit banks in the periphery were forced to act independently. Markets for bank notes reflected these differences in coordination through lower discounts on the notes of Indiana, Ohio, and Southern banks before and during the crisis (Calomiris and Schweikart, 1988, and Gorton, 1990).

The Panic of 1857 also saw the origin of crisis management among members of the New York City clearing house (Cannon, 1910, Gorton, 1985). Member banks pooled funds and issued joint liabilities, coordinated plans for maintaining credit to brokers and merchants, eventually suspended jointly, established the date of joint resumption, and after the panic organized the orderly flow of country bank notes (which had accumulated in New York City banks prior to the crisis) to enable the country banks to resume convertibility in a timely fashion. The successes of the New York City clearing house led to imitation in 1858 when Baltimore and Philadelphia banks established their own clearing houses.

Interestingly, formal clearing houses never developed in the branching South during the antebellum period. Understandably, the small number of branching banks had a lesser need to coordinate clearings and were able to respond to panics effectively without the formal rules and enforcement mechanisms of the clearing house. Similarly, clearing houses did not develop in Canada's branch banking system until 1887. As Breckenridge (1910, pp. 162–3) writes:

> The volume of transactions for settlement, of course, had always been smaller than what would be expected of a system of an equal number of banking offices, each under independent control. The settlement between two or between all the branches of the same bank, of course, would be effected in the books of that bank, and is so still, independently of the clearing house.

The large financing needs and the ultimate defeat of the South in the Civil War led to the insolvency of its banking system, which was called upon to bear much of the burden for the South's war finance. At the same time, the mutual-guaranty systems operating in Indiana, Ohio, and (beginning in 1858) Iowa ceased to operate, as many of their members converted to national bank charters (after 1863) in order to avoid the 10 percent federal tax on state bank notes. With the demise of Southern branch banks and Midwestern mutual-guaranty banks, and the decision by the Comptroller of the Currency to restrict branching by national banks, the only form of interbank cooperation that remained in place during the immediate postbellum era was the clearing house, which had spread to the major cities of virtually every state by the end of the nineteenth century. As Johnson (1910, pp. 10) writes in describing the Canadian branch banking system to an American audience:

> ...to the student of the history of banking in the United States there is little that is radically new in the Canadian system. He finds in it many of the practices and expedients that were found excellent in the United States in the first half of the nineteenth century, and is almost persuaded that but for the civil war what is now known as the Canadian banking system would everywhere be called the American system.

While useful in coordinating the actions of local banks in large U.S. cities, clearing houses were unable to establish a national organization to coordinate clearings or the banking system's response to panics. Given its unusual position as the reserve center for the nation's interbank deposits, New York City banks and their clearing house came to play an increasing role as the main originator of policy during the panics of the National Banking Era. The clearing house continued to pool assets and issue joint liabilities (clearing house loan certificates) during panics, which at first were used only for interbank clearings but by 1893 were being used as a cash substitute by the public.

The ability of the New York clearing house to act as a lender of last resort for the economy as a whole was limited by the amount of high-quality assets that its members could contribute to the pool as backing for its loan certificates and by its ability to distinguish good from bad risks in interbank lending outside its own organization. While the use of loan certificates may have been helpful in forestalling suspension in 1884 and 1890, larger disturbances (1873, 1893, and 1907) resulted in widespread disintermediation followed by suspension of convertibility. The uncertainty regarding the incidence of shocks, which gave rise to panics, could not be entirely resolved by coinsurance of risk within the banking system (as it was in many other countries, notably England's resolution of the Baring Crisis in 1890). Thus the resolution of panics in the United States required prolonged delays in the convertibility of deposits on demand.

International Evidence on Branch Banking and Bank Panics

International comparisons provide similar evidence on the role of branch banking, with its advantages of diversification and coordination, in reducing the incidence of panics. Bordo's (1985) useful survey of banking and securities-market panics in six countries from 1870 to 1933 concludes that "the United States experienced banking panics in a period when they were a historical curiosity in other countries." (p. 73) Bordo, like many others, notes the likely association between the unique unit banking system in the United States and its unique propensity for panics. But because the regulatory environment of any country differs from others along dimensions other than unit versus branch banking, it is difficult to attribute the relative stability of other countries to branching per se. To facilitate comparison, I will limit my discussion of other countries' banking systems to the English speaking world, which shared a legal tradition and many common institutional features. A more inclusive survey (including France and Germany) would corroborate the evidence presented here; Kindleberger (1984) provides an introduction to these literatures.

Scotland

Scotland's early banking system is usually held up as an example of a virtually unregulated system of branching banks, and its panic-free history is often attributed to its large number of branches. Banks in Scotland were free to branch as they pleased. By 1845 19 banks of issue operated 363 branches (L. H. White, 1984, p. 37). The Scottish Bank Act of 1845 restricted Scottish bank note issues to those outstanding at that date plus any additional issues backed 100 percent by specie reserves. This was less restrictive than the Peel Act of 1844, which was designed to shrink the note issues of English banks (see Hughes, 1960, Capie and Webber, 1985, p. 211). Both acts helped to consolidate the power of the Bank of England. After 1845, branch banking continued to flourish in Scotland, but Scotland ceased to be independent of the English system. Commenting on Scotland's panic-free history of branch banking, L. H. White (1984, p.143) quotes two observers (from 1845 and 1832, respectively) as claiming that "runs are the last things that would ever enter into the mind of any man who is acquainted with the history of banking in this country," and that "A run upon a bank, such as happens in England sometimes, or a panic, are terms the meaning of which is hardly understood in Scotland."

The difficulty in attributing the stability of the Scottish system to branch banking per se is due to other unique features of the early Scottish system. Scottish banks generally were unlimited liability banks (with the exception of three limited-liability banks); thus depositors and noteholders of banks enjoyed greater protection than that afforded by the capital of a limited-liability bank. Furthermore, Scottish banks could be formed by as large a partnership and capital base as they chose, unlike banks in England where restrictions limited the number of partners and the amount of bank capital (L. H. White, 1984, pp. 41–2). Finally, Scottish banks before 1845, unlike banks in the United States and elsewhere, faced no limitations on their note issues. In fact, within the British Isles Scottish bank notes often were brought into England and constituted a permanent component of the money stock, particularly in the Northern regions.

The right to issue bank notes was deemed especially important for allowing the branching network to expand. Withers et al. (1910, pp. 43–4) argue that the costs of holding "till money" in the form of specie or equivalently the notes of other banks was an important restriction to branching in other countries, but in Scotland banks were able to avoid this cost. Scottish banks (around 1910) held reserves (specie plus other banks notes) of less than 10 percent of their total liabilities (Withers et al., 1910, p. 46), which Withers et al. show is low by comparison to England and other countries. Munn (1981, p. 141) shows that from 1811 until the restriction imposed by the Scottish Bank Act, the ratio of specie to demand liabilities for each bank ranged between 0.5 and 1.6 percent. This confirms the view that, particularly in the early period of branch expansion, Scottish banks had a distinct advantage in the form of low till costs.

These features of the Scottish system raise a caveat for the purposes of comparison with the U.S. system. Before using the observed stability of early-nineteenth century Scottish banks to answer the counterfactual question: "How different would the history of panics have been during the National Banking Era in the United States if national banks had been allowed to branch?" one should control for differences in the regulation of note issues, which may have influenced the potential for expansion and therefore diversification of the branching system (see the extended discussion of Canada below) and also control for differences in extended liability. Both of these features enhanced the Scottish system's stability.

England

Unlike that of Scotland, England's banking system experienced panics in the eighteenth and early nineteenth centuries, but saw none after 1866. It is hard to know whether to attribute the end of panics to the transformation of the English banking system from one of mainly unit banks to one of mainly branching banks, or to changes in the Bank of England's approach to dealing with crises. Private unit banks operated in England prior to the creation of joint stock banks in 1826. Initial restrictions on joint stock bank operations in London (to benefit the Bank of England) were relaxed somewhat in 1833. By 1836, the 61 registered joint stock banks operated 472 banking facilities, and the trend toward branching continued in the ensuing decades. By 1870, 111 joint stock banks operated 1,127 banking facilities. For Britain as a whole in 1870, there were 378 banks operating 2,738 banking facilities (Capie and Webber, 1985, p. 576).

At the same time, changes were occurring in the Bank of England's role in managing crises, and it is hard to separate this effect on the propensity for panic from that due to expanded branching. The monopolization of new English note issues in the hands of the Bank of England after 1844 and the restrictions on the note-issuing powers of the Bank of England (a 100 percent specie reserve requirement) limited the banking system's ability to protect itself from panics and made the system's fortunes heavily dependent on the discretionary policies of the Bank of England and the government during crises. The government had to provide the Bank with a special letter during the panics of 1847, 1857, and 1866 allowing it to violate its 100 percent reserve requirement on notes in order to create liquidity. By the 1870s (especially with the publication of Walter Bagehot's *Lombard Street* in 1873) such a relaxation of the rules during crisis was expected, and the mature view of the Bank of England's role as a lender of last resort had been articulated, perhaps most eloquently by Bagehot:

> ...whatever bank or banks keep the ultimate banking reserve of the country must lend that reserve most freely in time of apprehension, for that is one of the characteristic uses of the bank reserve, and the mode in which it attains one of the main ends for which it is kept. Whether rightly or wrongly, at present and in fact the Bank of England keeps our ultimate bank reserve, and therefore it must use it in this manner.
>
> And though the Bank of England certainly do make great advances in time of panic, yet as they do not do so on any distinct principle, they naturally do it hesitatingly, reluctantly, and with misgiving. In 1847, even in 1866—the latest panic, and the one in which on the whole the Bank acted the best—there was nevertheless an instant when it was believed the Bank would not advance on Consols, or at least hesitated to advance on them. The moment this was reported in the City and telegraphed to the country, it made the panic indefinitely worse. What is wanted and what is necessary to stop a panic is to diffuse the impression, that though money be dear, still money is to be had... (p. 64).

Interestingly, Bagehot lamented England's peculiar reliance on one bank to manage lending during crises and preferred the Scottish multicentric approach:

> I shall have failed in my purpose if I have not proved that the system of entrusting all our reserve to a single board, like that of the Bank directors, is very anomalous (p. 66).
>
> ...the natural system—that which would have sprung up if Government had let banking alone—is that of many banks of equal or not altogether unequal size (p. 67).

After 1866, the Bank managed to preserve liquidity without deviating again from the provisions of the 1844 Act, perhaps, paradoxically, because of its known willingness to do so (Dornbusch and Frenkel, 1984, Dutton, 1984, Hughes, 1984, and Pippenger, 1984). In one of the more interesting examples of interbank coordination, during the Baring Crisis of 1890, the commercial banks of London bailed out the Baring investment banking house by agreeing jointly to insure against losses to its creditors (with the Bank of England backing up the private bank coinsurers). In so doing, the banks succeeded in dispelling uncertainty about the incidence of losses among their number from the Baring collapse, thus avoiding the threat of a bank panic. According to Eichengreen (1992), the Bank of England's increasing success in preventing panics during the late nineteenth and early twentieth centuries, and even in quelling disturbances outside its borders, was due in part to successful coordination across national boundaries with central bankers on the continent—something that set the mature classical gold standard of the late nineteenth century apart from previous and subsequent arrangements among central banks.

Canada

The comparison between the incidence of panics in the United States and Canada possibly provides the most convincing evidence of the efficacy of branching for reducing the risk of panic, since the two nations and their banking regulations were otherwise quite similar. Both countries are vast geographically. Neither country had a central bank in operation in the nineteenth century. The Bank of Canada began operation in 1935, although the government had a limited role as a lender of last resort beginning in 1907, which was expanded in 1914 and 1923, as is discussed in Bordo and Redish (1987). The trade and activities of the two nations were similar and interlinked. Johnson (1910, pp. 9–10) writes:

> Financially Canada is part of the United States. Fully half the gold reserve upon which its credit system is based is lodged in the vaults of the New York Clearing House. In any emergency requiring additional capital Montreal, Toronto, and Winnipeg call on New York for funds just as do St. Paul, Kansas City, and New Orleans. New York exchange is current and universal medium in Canada and is in constant demand among the banks. A Canadian wishing to invest in securities that may be quickly marketed commonly turns to the New York market for stocks and bonds. Yet the American banker visiting in Canada...finds himself in a land of financial novelties, for Canada has a banking system unlike any in operation in the United States at the present time. Twenty-nine banks, known as the "chartered banks," transact all the banking business of the Dominion. They have 2,200 branches, and each may establish

> new branches without increase of its capital stock. They issue notes without depositing security with the government and in such abundance that no other form of currency in denominations of $5 and above is in circulation. Notwithstanding the fact that the notes are "unsecured," their "goodness" is unquestioned among the Canadian people.

Indeed, given the close connections among the two financial systems it is remarkable that the Canadian system did not suffer panics when they occurred in the United States.

One difference between the U.S. and Canadian systems worth commenting upon was the elastic supply of bank currency in Canada. As in Scotland, Canadian banks were permitted to issue their own currency. Until 1908, national banks wishing to issue currency in the United States had to deposit government bonds in the Treasury and await delivery of their notes from the government. Canadian banks were allowed to issue their own notes, during normal times, up to the amount of unimpaired paid-in capital. After July 1908, they were also allowed to issue an additional amount equal to 15 percent of capital and surplus during the crop-moving season (October 1 to January 1). As with the 1908 Aldrich-Vreeland Act authorizing emergency currency issues in the U.S., emergency currency issues in Canada could be taxed. Unlike American banks in both the antebellum and postbellum periods, Canadian banks faced no reserve requirements on their note issues. Furthermore, the ceiling implied by paid-in capital was never a binding constraint on Canadian note issues (Johnson, 1910, Chart IV, after p. 66). The difference in the flexibility of the Canadian and United States currency stocks was widely noted historically (see, for example, Gage, 1906). Gage (1906) shows that the Canadian pattern was typical of other elastic-note-supply, branch-banking countries.

This differing flexibility in the supply of currency was noted by many contemporaries. As in Scotland and many other countries, banks' ability to issue notes in Canada likely reduced the specie reserves held by the banking system and facilitated branching. Conceivably, this could have reduced the propensity for panics to the extent that adding loans from especially thinly populated rural areas helped to diversify bank portfolios.

The option to issue notes also likely reduced the cost of providing credit in the form of an exchange medium for seasonal currency payments to agricultural workers (particularly in August and September). By accommodating credit needs in a liquid form, banks limited the seasonal fluctuations in interest rates in the periphery (see Breckenridge, 1899a, pp. 51–2, Gage, 1906, Eichengreen, 1984a, and Miron, 1986). It is difficult to separate the effects of branching and note issuing on credit cost seasonality. Branch banks—by virtue of greater diversification and greater potential for interregional and interbank coordination—should have had flatter loan-supply functions than unit banks in the United States irrespective of note issuing authority. That is, banks should have been able to bear seasonal increases in the loan-to-reserve ratio without charging as high a cost to borrowers because the risk to the bank of doing so would have been less in Canada than in the United States. The marginal contribution of note issuing authority on the effective supply of credit depends on how large was the substitutability between notes and deposits as exchange media on the margin. To the extent the only exchange medium acceptable to peripheral borrowers in August and September was currency, and currency was costly to import seasonally for this purpose, the supply of loans would effectively have been more inelastic seasonally (borrowers would have to pay a seasonal currency premium).

Regardless of its effects on seasonal credit cost or access of branches to remote areas, the ability to issue notes in and of itself seems not to have been an important determinant of panics in the United States or, conversely, a protection against panics in Canada (although one can strain to make such a connection, in theory, as a recent model by Champ, Smith, and Williamson, 1991, illustrates). During the antebellum period in the U.S. and in Canada, note issues were highly elastic but this did not prevent panics from occurring in both countries in 1837 and 1839 and in the U.S. in 1857.

Data on the cyclical elasticity of note supply under New England's Suffolk System show cyclical variation comparable to that shown for Canada in the nineteenth century. (For discussions of and data for Suffolk System note issues, see Root, 1901, p. 211, Mullineaux, 1987, p. 889, *Hunt's Merchants' Magazine,* 1840, vol. 2, pp. 137–42, and Calomiris and Kahn, 1990.) *Hunt's Merchants' Magazine* (1851, vol. 25, p. 467) provides data on note redemptions under the Suffolk System. From month to month, note redemptions often varied as much as 10 percent. Calomiris and Schweikart (1988) find similar cyclical elasticity for bank notes in the South. For example, in Virginia, outstanding currency fell from $14.3 million to $10.8 million from January 1854 to January 1855. By the following January, outstanding currency was $13.0 million. Under New York's free-banking system note supply also showed elasticity. For example, from September 1855 to September 1856, total outstanding currency of New York banks increased from $31.3 million to $34.0 million. Weekly returns of New York City, Boston, Pittsburgh, and St. Louis banks in 1858 as reported in *Hunt's Merchants' Magazine* (1859, vol. 40, p. 215) show large seasonal changes in note circulation. For example, in New York City, circulation increased nearly 12 percent from March 27 to May 8 and fell more than 6 percent from May 8 to May 29. In Indiana's mutual-guaranty banking system, outstanding note issues changed by more than 10 percent (from the beginning to the end of the year) 16 times in 27 years between 1835 and 1862, with 12 increases and 4 decreases (Golembe and Warburton, 1958, p. IV-11). Monthly changes also could be large for these banks, as shown in Harding (1898, pp. 279–81). From January to August, 1842, circulation fell 40 percent; from July to December, 1844, notes outstanding rose 14 percent. From 1845 to 1862, Ohio's insured banks varied their outstanding currency annually by more than 10 percent in 9 out of 17 years, with 7 increases and 2 decreases (Golembe and Warburton, 1958, p. VI-17).

The fact that elasticity of note issues was a common feature of many different regulatory regimes in the United States during the antebellum period did not prevent panics in the United States. This contradicts the view that panics were caused by inelastic supply of currency and large random currency-demand shocks, as Chari (1989) and Champ, Smith, and Williamson (1991) argue. Calomiris and Gorton (1991) and Calomiris and Schweikart (1991) show that panics were caused not by the scarcity of a particular form of medium of exchange, but by adverse economic disturbances that created confusion regarding the potential insolvency risk of commercial banks.

In summary, despite the advantages attributable to note issuing authority, it seems reasonable to attribute differences in the vulnerability of the U.S. and Canadian banking systems to panics primarily to the branching laws of the two countries, rather than to the elasticity of currency supply, or perhaps to the combination of branching and the elasticity of currency.

Canada's system allowed nationwide branching from its beginnings in the early nineteenth century. Ironically, at that time, it was following the banking doctrines of Alexander Hamilton to the letter (Breckenridge, 1910, pp. 7–8) and the precedent established in the United States by the Bank of the United States. Banks relied on coordination among a small number of banks (roughly 40 in the nineteenth century, falling to 10 by 1929) to resolve threats to the system. The Canadian Bankers' Association, formed in 1891, marked the formalization of cooperative arrangements that served to regulate failures of individual banks and mitigate their consequences for the banking system as a whole. The Bank of Montreal—the depository of most government funds, and the largest of the Canadian banks, with 20 percent of the banking system's assets in 1910—sometimes acted as a private lender of last resort, stepping in to assist troubled banks (Breckenridge, 1910, Johnson, 1910, Vreeland, et al., 1910).

Canada experienced no banking panics after the 1830s. During their history, Canadian banks suspended convertibility only twice, from May 1837 to June 1838 and from November 1838 to June 1939. Breckenridge (1910) describes these suspensions as of questionable necessity and mainly motivated as a defensive action to prevent large outflows of specie to the United States (which was the origin of the problem). The Canadian banks did not suspend during the Panic of 1857 and saw a reduction in their activities (presumably reflecting the large outflows of specie abroad). Still, no bank failed in Canada during or immediately after the panic.

During subsequent panics in the U.S., Canada followed a similar path to that of 1857, acting as a shock absorber for the difficulties originating in the United States. Inflows of Canadian bank notes, as well as specie, helped to offset contractions in the U.S. money supply attendant to panics. These contractions had little effect on Canadian banks. For example, in the Panic of 1907, banks reduced their lending temporarily and rapidly rebounded. Johnson (1910, p. 96) describes 1908 as...

> ...a breathing spell in Canadian industry and finance, but the bank returns show that there was no lack of confidence in the banks and that the floating capital of the country had not been seriously impaired.

Schembri and Hawkins (1988) argue that Canadian branches in the United States benefited from the relative stability of Canada's banks during panics in the United States. U.S. depositors transferred funds to these banks in times of trouble, viewing them as a safe haven.

Coordination among banks within Canada is nicely illustrated by the events of the Panic of 1907. The Sovereign Bank of Canada failed during the crisis, but without loss to its liability holders because of the intervention of other Canadian banks (led by the Bank of Montreal) who guaranteed its liabilities against loss. As the English banks had done during the Baring Crisis of 1890, the Canadian banks sought to eliminate any confusion regarding the incidence of loss among banks by standing together as a group, whose collective solvency was beyond question. The Canadian banks had done the same for the Bank of Ontario in 1906.

> On the evening of October 12 [1906] the bankers in Toronto and Montreal heard with surprise that the Bank of Ontario had got beyond its depth and would not open its doors the next morning. Its capital was $1,500,000 and its

> deposits $12,000,000. The leading bankers in the dominion dreaded the effect which the failure of such a bank might have. The Bank of Montreal agreed to take over the assets and pay all the liabilities, provided a number of other banks would agree to share with it any losses. Its offer was accepted and a representative of the Bank of Montreal took the night train for Toronto...the bank opened for business the next day with the following notice over its door: "This is the Bank of Montreal." (Johnson, 1910, pp. 124–5).

The Bank of Montreal did not always bail out failing banks. When smaller banks failed (never with any losses to noteholders, and usually with small or zero losses to depositors), the bank did not intervene (Vreeland, et al., 1910, p. 219, and Johnson, 1910, p. 127).

Over time, beginning in 1907, the government provided additional protection to the Canadian banking system, through authorization of loans of currency (Dominion notes) against collateral of worthy securities. Johnson (1910, p. 121) argues that the intervention was unnecessary in 1907 and did not occur at the request of the banks, who opposed it. Bordo and Redish (1987) conclude that the rise of the Bank of Canada as a Depression measure in 1935 was not the result of economic necessity, but of political expediency due to domestic and international political pressures.

There is some disagreement about the role of Canada's branching system in preventing the collapse of the system during the Great Depression. Haubrich (1990) argues that Canada's resistance to panics during the Great Depression prevented Canada's financial system from propagating the severe external shocks that buffeted it, in contrast to the U.S. banking collapse, which Bernanke (1983) argues was so instrumental in prolonging the Depression in the United States. Both countries saw a large decline in GNP from 1929 to 1933 (42 percent in Canada and 46 percent in the United States). Kryzanowski and Roberts (1989) recently have questioned whether the success of the Canadian banking system in surviving the Depression was due to branch banking and coordination, or alternatively as they suggest, to an implicit guarantee by the government that depositors would be protected from loss. While they provide some interesting evidence in favor of the likelihood that some attempt might have been made to protect Canadian banks in the absence of successful private intervention, there is room for doubt regarding their conclusions. It seems unlikely that Canadian depositors would have resisted running on their banks because of the *possibility* of government backing, the existence of which remains controversial even today.

Australia

The single exceptional case of a mature, relatively laissez-faire, nationwide branch-banking system that experienced a panic involving widespread bank suspension was the Australian banking collapse of 1893. But even here, the particulars of the experience hardly constitute an indictment of the potential efficacy of diversification and coordination through branching.

In the latter half of the nineteenth century Australia grew rapidly, with GDP rising at a rate of 5 percent per annum from 1860 to 1890. In the fifteen years prior to the crisis Australian banks' real assets tripled, as the banks moved away from traditional commercial lending to participate in the financing of the speculative land and construction boom (Pope, 1989). Throughout the period the banking sector was highly concentrated, with roughly half of the banking system's deposits residing in four of the 26 banks in existence. Despite this concentration (and despite the operation of a clearing house in Melbourne since 1867), the crisis caused half the banks in the country, operating nearly 1,000 branches, to suspend convertibility.

Coordination among banks did occur to some extent. The clearing house issued loan certificates during the crisis and thereby managed to reduce the specie needed for interbank clearings from 20 percent in 1892 to 5 percent during the crisis (Pope, 1989). But apart from this, there was no explicit interbank risk sharing to promote public confidence in the banking system, as there had been in Canada and Britain during financial crises.

Pope (1989) argues that part of the explanation for the lack of coordination among banks during the crisis was that some of the largest banks in the system did not perceive a great benefit to themselves from providing the necessary assistance to the failing banks. The logic of voluntary ex post mutual assistance requires that the assisting banks see a large negative externality from not providing such help. Pope (1989) claims that two of the larger banks in the country (the Australasia and the Union) entered the crisis in a relatively strong position and thus were unwilling to participate in a proposed mutual-assistance plan. Both had high reserve ratios, had not participated as much as other banks in financing the land boom, saw little threat to their own position from the run on other banks, and may have viewed the collapse of their competitors as an opportunity to expand their market share. The opposition of these two banks was sufficient to undermine the initial promises of mutual assistance among banks.

This interpretation suggests that the Australian case may not have been a "classic" panic (one involving substantial confusion about the incidence of the disturbance among banks). Indeed, Pope (1989) shows that available measures of balance sheet liquidity positions and risk exposure provide reasonably good predictions of which banks were forced to suspend during the crisis. This supports his view that banks could be distinguished vis-à-vis their exposure to the shock. Moreover, the lack of interest in collective action suggests that the long-run social costs of the panic, in terms of disruption to the potential provision of credit by the banking system as a whole, were likely to be small. The existence of a few large nationwide branching banks of unquestioned health eventually would have provided a substitute source of commercial credit supply for failing banks.

All 12 of the banks that suspended in April and May of 1893 were able to reopen within three months. The Federal Bank, which alone had failed in January and had been denied assistance by all the banks at that time, was the only bank unable to resume business. The banks that were able to resume did so with the help of their depositors, who cooperated in providing capital infusions to their banks and converting their demandable obligations into shares or long-term debt. The fact that the failing banks were able to come up with a plan and have the plan successfully adopted at a national scale so quickly suggests that there may have been substantial ex post "coordination benefits" from bank concentration after all.

In summary, the Australian banking collapse involved an unusual set of circumstances (a very large shock to fundamentals with different consequences for different banks), and this explains the large suspension rate and lack of coordination among Australian banks. Furthermore, the social cost of the Australian banking collapse was probably small compared, for example, with the numerous bank failures during the similar land bust of the 1890s in the United States (see Calomiris and Gorton, 1991). In the United States, there was systemic suspension of convertibility (suggesting more ex ante confusion about the incidence of the disturbance among banks), failing banks were not able to reorganize through a coordinated recapitalization financed by depositors, and failed unit banks were not easily replaced (due to the prohibition on entry that branch banking restrictions entailed—see Calomiris, 1990, 1991a, for related evidence on the role of branching in providing for replacement of failed banking facilities in the 1920s). Finally, the 1893 crisis was an isolated incident in the history of Australian banking. As one observer wrote in 1933,

> Perhaps the most remarkable feature of Australian banking since the crisis of 1893 is the almost complete absence of bank failures. No commercial bank, except the Federal Deposit Bank, which was a small bank in Queensland, has

> failed since the troublesome days of 1893.... As Australia is essentially an agricultural and pastoral country that suffers from prolonged drought, the almost complete absence of commercial bank failures since 1893 is truly remarkable (Jauncey, 1933, p. 30, cited in Chapman and Westerfield, 1942, p. 256).

The stability of the post-1893 banking system coincided with increased concentration of banking and expansion of access through an enormous increase in bank facilities. In 1912, there were 23 banks operating 2,064 facilities. By 1929 there were 16 banks operating 3,262 facilities.

Branch Banking and Diversification

As discussed above, diversification of individual bank assets is one of the key elements linking branch banking and a reduced propensity for bank panics. The benefits of greater asset diversification under branching appears in a variety of other indicators as well. For example, as noted above, seasonal smoothing of interest rates is enhanced (the loan-supply function is flatter) under branching; equivalently, increases in bank leverage and reserve ratios can be accommodated with smaller increases in interest rates charged borrowers when banks are well diversified. Another piece of evidence is the lower market discount rates on the bank notes of branching banks during the antebellum period (Calomiris and Schweikart, 1988, and Gorton, 1990). As noted above, both of these pieces of evidence can be interpreted in other ways. The elasticity of currency under the branch banking systems of Canada, Scotland, and other countries may have facilitated the smoothing of interest rates, in addition to the effects of asset diversification due to branching. The coordination benefits during panics from branching, rather than within-bank diversification per se, may have been important in lowering discount rates on notes.

In what follows I consider several other indicators of lower asset risk of branching banks, which I will argue are clearer indicators of asset risk differences. These include: the propensity for bank failure (during and outside of panic episodes) across different types of systems; the propensity for failure of different types of banks within the same system; the recovery of banking (number of locations and asset levels) in response to shocks across different types of systems; the role of banks in equalizing rates of return across different locations; the greater expansion of branch-banking systems into thinly populated areas; and the reserve holdings of banks in branching and nonbranching systems.

Bank Failures

Prior to the 1980s four national waves of bank failures occurred in the United States: the disastrous episodes of 1837–1841, 1890–1896, 1921–1930, and 1931–1933. Especially in the first three of these episodes, bank failures were closely linked to the type of enterprises banks financed. Banks with close links to international trade (Temin, 1969, pp. 142–5) or to infrastructure investment (Schweikart, 1988a) were hardest hit by the collapse of 1837–1841. In the 1890s banks that had financed the rapid land expansion "on the middle border" in Kansas and Nebraska suffered the highest risk of failure (Bogue, 1955, and Calomiris and Gorton, 1991, pp. 156–9). In the 1920s, the agricultural bust of the post-World War I period caused widespread bank failures in some states (those with many grain, cotton, and livestock producers, in particular), while leaving others unaffected (Calomiris, 1991a).

The activities of banks and the shocks that buffeted them were important factors in predicting failure propensity during these disastrous episodes, but regulatory factors were important as well. In particular, systems that permitted branching saw lower failure rates and losses than systems that did not. During the 1837–1841 period, Virginia and South Carolina (two Southern states with advanced private branch banking systems) saw no bank failures (Klebaner, 1990, p. 51).

Regrettably, this same pattern persists to the present day. Comparisons across states, using evidence from the agricultural crisis of the early 1980s, confirm that branch banking systems have suffered lower failure rates than others, controlling for other factors. Calomiris, Hubbard, and Stock (1986, p. 469) found that California had an exceptionally high rate of troubled agricultural loans during the early 1980s. As of 1984, 8.4 percent of California's agricultural loans were in nonaccrual status, compared to an average of 4.7 percent for the rest of the country. The agricultural loan delinquency rate for California was 13.1 percent, compared to a national average of 8.9 percent. Net charge-offs as a percentage of agricultural loans were 6.1 percent in California and 1.8 percent in other states. Despite these difficulties, California accounted for only 1 of 68 agricultural bank failures in 1985. The reason they weathered the storm so well is that most agricultural lending in the state comes from large well-diversified banks, which hold only 3 percent of their portfolios in agricultural production loans.

Laderman, Schmidt, and Zimmerman (1991) show that bank diversification is inhibited by unit banking. After controlling for a variety of other factors, they find that rural banks devote a significantly larger proportion of their loan portfolios to agricultural loans than do urban banks. When statewide branching is allowed, rural and urban banks' portfolios are much more diversified. Smith (1987) shows that branching restrictions increase failure risk for agricultural and nonagricultural banks by limiting the potential for diversification.

> ...banks in restricted-branching states are generally at greater risk of closure because of less diversified loan portfolios than are banks in statewide-branching states.....in restricted-branching states, the probability of closure of banks seems equally influenced by the share of loans in the commercial and industrial category and the share in the agricultural category....several of the financial ratio coefficients are statistically different between restricted-branching and statewide-branching states (p. 35).

Historical comparisons across countries provide similar evidence on the benefits of diversification through branching. L. H. White (1984, pp. 44–9) emphasizes the low failure rates of Scottish banks compared to their counterparts in England during the early nineteenth century. Chapman and Westerfield (1942, p. 257) write:

> The last two bank failures in Scotland were the Western Bank of Scotland in 1857 and the City of Glasgow Bank in 1878....The shareholders suffered seriously, but the depositors and noteholders were paid in full.

Johnson (1910, p. 127) makes a similar point about the mature Canadian system:

> Since 1889 six small banks have failed, but note holders have lost nothing and depositors very little. They were local institutions with few branches and their failures possess little significance in a study of the banking system as a whole.

Thirteen Canadian banks failed from 1868 to 1889. The available data indicate that the costs of these failures for noteholders were quite low (zero in the 11 cases where data are available); and in at least 8 of the 13 cases, depositors losses were essentially zero as well (Vreeland, et al., 1910, p. 219). During the period 1870–1909, when the failure rate for national banks in the United States was 0.36, the failure rate of Canadian banking facilities (banks and their branches) was less than 0.10 (Schembri and Hawkins, 1988). Comparing average losses to depositors over many years, Williamson (1989) finds an annual average loss rate in the United States of 0.11 percent, and in Canada, 0.07 percent. Perhaps even more telling, during periods when both economies were buffeted by substantial regional or economy-wide shocks (the agricultural bust of the 1920s and the drastic decline in GNP during the Great Depression), Canada's banks performed exceptionally well. E. N. White (1984a, p. 132) finds:

> In Canada, from 1920 to 1929, only one bank failed. The contraction of the banking industry was carried out by the remaining banks reducing the number of their offices by 13.2 percent. This was very near the 9.8 percent decline in the United States.... In spite of the many similarities with the United States, there were no bank failures in Canada during the dark years of 1929–1933. The number of bank offices fell by another 10.4 percent, reflecting the shocked state of the economy; yet this was far fewer than the 34.5 percent of all bank offices permanently closed in the United States.

Chapman and Westerfield (1942, p. 258) show that losses to depositors in Canada were typically confined to small banks, which "could not by any reasonable test be regarded as branch banks..."

Within the United States, failure rates were lower for large banks, particularly those that branched. This pattern is evident beginning with the first and second Banks of the United States. During the Panic of 1857, Southern branch banks all survived, while a handful of small Southern unit banks failed (Calomiris and Schweikart, 1991).

Of the 5,714 bank suspensions in the United States from 1921 to 1929, only 459 had capital in excess of $100,000. Large banks accounted for only 8 percent of all suspensions, though they comprised roughly 25 percent of the number of banks in operation (American Bankers Association, 1935, p. 33–6). States that allowed branching in the United States saw lower failure rates in the 1920s (measured either in bank numbers or bank deposits) than other states. In the six states with the most firmly established branch-banking systems by 1925 (California, Louisiana, Massachusetts, Michigan, New York, and Ohio), only 13 banks failed. The failed banks held only 0.03 percent of the total deposits of these states (E. N. White, 1983, p. 218–9).

The vulnerability of small banks to failure in the 1920s and 1930s has been documented by a number of other researchers, including Bremer (1935), E. N. White (1983, 1984a), and Calomiris (1991a). Prior to the general economic decline of the Great Depression, failures by large branching banks were virtually nonexistent. From 1921 to 1929, only 37 branching banks operating 75 branches were liquidated. More than two-thirds of these banks operated a single branch, and only 6 of them operated three or more branches (U.S. House of Representatives, 1930, vol. 1, p. 462). The failure rate for branch banks was roughly 4 percent for the entire period 1921–

1929. The bank failure rate for this same period for the country as a whole was upwards of 20 percent.

The states with long-standing branching systems were not particularly hard hit by the agricultural decline of the 1920s, which might explain their superior performance; but more detailed evidence on the incidence of failure confirms a link between unit banking and bank vulnerability. Regional comparisons confirm the view that the period prior to 1930 saw exceptional stability of branching banks even in the hard-hit "agricultural-crisis" areas of the country. Calomiris (1991a) identifies 32 states that were most affected by the agricultural bust of the 1920s. In 1924, the 32 agricultural-crisis states contained 1,312 of the 3,007 branching facilities in the country. State-by-state decompositions of failures by type of bank are not readily available; but even if all branching failures had been concentrated in these states during the 1920s, the annual rate of branch-bank facility failure would be only 0.85 percent. Overall failure rates for these states typically were several times as large (Calomiris, 1991a, p. 42 and Table 20).

In some cases, specific within-state comparisons of branch and unit banks are possible. In the states that prohibited new branching from 1924 to 1928 but allowed banks to continue to operate existing branches (Alabama, Arkansas, Indiana, Minnesota, Nebraska, Washington, and Wisconsin), the annual failure (disappearance) rate of branch banks was a remarkably low 0.02 percent. Using *The Bankers Encyclopedia* one can trace the presence or absence of banks from 1920 to 1929. In all cases, a careful review of entries revealed whether disappearances were due to acquisitions or to closings. Calomiris (1991a) traces the entries for the branching banks of three states, chosen because they experienced high rates of overall bank failure and had a small number of branching banks (making data collection easier) and because branching banks in these states were allowed to operate branches outside their home city. In Mississippi, all 24 branches in operation in 1920 were located outside their home banks' cities. The same was true of Arizona's 20 branches in operation in 1920. In South Carolina, 13 out of 15 branches operated outside the home city. These states, therefore, provide a useful measure of the potential advantages of statewide branching during a crisis.

Arizona permitted statewide branching throughout the period. In Arizona in 1920, 8 banks operated 20 branches. By 1929, 2 of these (each operating one branch) had been acquired by larger branching banks. One of the branching banks (operating one branch) failed. In the interim, three new branching banks had entered. The average annual failure rate for total branching facilities was 1.6 percent for 1921–1929, compared to 4.3 percent for Arizona's state-chartered banks as a whole.

Mississippi had allowed branching outside home cities, but later prohibited branching, except for the establishment of limited agency facilities within home cities. Nevertheless, the existing statewide branches were permitted to continue operating. During the 1920s none of the 10 branching banks operating 24 branches failed, while the average annual failure rate for state-chartered banks as a whole was 1.4 percent.

In South Carolina from 1920 to 1929, 4 out of 8 branching banks in operation in 1920 closed, but all of these were banks that operated a single branch, and 2 of the 4 operated branches within their home city. Thus of the 23 towns or cities in which branch-banking facilities were located, 19 retained their branch-banking facilities. This is important because the lack of available banking facilities in thinly populated areas (where virtually all branches were located in Arizona, Mississippi, and South Carolina) increases transactions costs in those locations and can inhibit the flow of capital to worthy enterprises located there. The overall failure rate of existing branching facilities in South Carolina was 2.9 percent, compared to a rate of 4.9 percent for all state-chartered banks. Entry into branching was especially strong in South Carolina in the 1920s, and entrants apparently learned the importance of establishing multiple branches. Two new banks—The Peoples Bank of South Carolina and the South Carolina Savings Bank—entered during the 1920s and established 18 and 9 branches, respectively, operating outside the banks' home cities.

The lessons of the high survival rates of branching banks during the 1920s agricultural crisis were not lost on bankers and policymakers. As Calomiris (1991a, Table 17) shows, in states where branching was allowed, it flourished and increasingly took the form of multibranch banks, where possible. Four of the eight states that had deliberately enacted deposit insurance plans as an alternative to allowing branch banking prior to the 1920s passed laws allowing branching by the end of the 1930s. By 1939, for the United States as a whole, 19 states permitted full branching and 17 allowed limited branching, compared to 12 statewide and 6 limited-branching systems in operation in 1924 (Chapman and Westerfield, 1942, pp. 126–30). Of the 18 states that permitted branches to exist early on, only 3 saw a reduction in the number of total facilities from 1924 to 1928. These reductions all occurred in states that prohibited the establishment of new branches, but allowed existing branches to be maintained (Georgia, Minnesota, and Washington). In all three cases, the reductions consisted of the departure (failure or closure) of a single bank. In all the other states that allowed branching to continue, but prohibited the establishment of new branches, the number of branches remained the same. In states that allowed new branching, branches uniformly increased at a rapid rate, often as the total number of banks declined, and branching thus came to constitute a much larger fraction of total banking facilities (Calomiris, 1991a).

Moreover, the recovery of total bank asset levels was higher for state banking systems that permitted growth in branch banking. Arizona, Kentucky, Louisiana, Michigan, North Carolina, Ohio, Tennessee, and Virginia all saw relatively high rates of asset recovery in the late 1920s relative to other states experiencing agricultural distress. These were also the states that experienced the largest increases in the average size of banks. South Carolina was the only exception to the rule, with negative asset growth over the 1920s. But despite its overall banking contraction, South Carolina witnessed a more than doubling of its branch banking facilities from 1924 to 1929.

More formally, Calomiris (1991a) regresses bank asset growth from 1920 to 1926, and 1920 to 1930, for a sample of 32 agricultural–crisis states, on a variety of control variables and branching dummies for limited and statewide branching. While the few degrees of freedom warrant a cautious interpretation, the branching indicator variables are both economically large and statistically significant, and they grow in importance with the longer time horizon. States that allowed branching enjoyed 40 percent higher growth in assets from 1920 to 1930, controlling for other differences.

In summary, evidence on the mortality rates and losses of failed banks indicate substantial advantages from branching. Branching also enhanced the banking system's ability to absorb weak institutions and to recover quickly from adverse shocks. It is worth noting that the examples of successful branching within the United States are all intrastate branching systems. A full nationwide system of banks would have done much better, as the example of Canada during the Depression illustrates. Indeed, at least two large branching banks (notably in the undiversified cotton-dependent economies of Georgia and South Carolina) did fail during the Depression.

Financial Integration and Diversification

In most countries, interregional capital flows are an important means of equalizing rates of return and providing diversification for capital providers. One way to examine whether nationwide branch banking facilitates diversification of banks' risk across regions is to ask whether branch banking systems do a superior job of equalizing interregional interest rates on loans.

There is a large literature on the question of capital market integration in the postbellum United States (Davis, 1965, Sylla, 1969, 1975, James, 1976a, 1976b, 1978, Eichengreen, 1984b, Snowden, 1987, Sushka and Barrett, 1984, and Binder and Brown, 1991). This literature seeks to explain the rate of convergence of rates of return across regions of the United States during the late nineteenth century. While there has been some disagreement about which factors contributed most to the convergence in rates of return over time, all authors agree that the disparities in regional rates of return were the result of branching restrictions combined with the increasing geographical dispersion of economic opportunities. Bodenhorn (1990) shows that similarly large interregional differences in bank lending rates did not characterize the antebellum period. The antebellum environment differed both in terms of superior bank organization (branch banks operated in the South and coordinated groups of mutual-guaranty banks operated in Indiana, Ohio, and Iowa) and in less geographical dispersion of economic activity. These factors may explain the greater integration of capital markets prior to the Civil War.

Interregional interest rate differences continued to be important in the United States throughout the late nineteenth and early twentieth centuries. Table 1–1 provides data on interest rates for first-class two-name commercial paper in various cities during the 1890s, collected and published by *Bradstreet's* and quoted in Breckenridge (1899b). The accuracy of these data has been questioned by James (1978, pp. 252–62). James (1978, pp. 16–9) provides alternative measures of interregional interest rate differentials, using estimated average bank loan interest rates, which show a greater degree of convergence by 1900 (the maximum interregional interest rate differential falls from a roughly 4 percent in the mid-1890s to 3 percent by 1900) than do those reported in *Bradstreet's*. In defence of the accuracy of the *Bradstreet's* data one can point to the appearance of reproductions of Table 1–1 in many contemporary academic and trade journals and books. These data were often used by proponents of branch banking to show the extent of segmentation of U.S. capital markets. If the data were grossly inaccurate, one would expect that their validity would have been questioned at the time. Regardless of whether one prefers the James or the *Bradstreet's* data, however, both indicate large, persistent interest differentials across regions in the postbellum period.

The commercial paper instruments priced in *Bradstreet's* were essentially default-free money-market instruments. Greef (1938, p. 56, footnote

TABLE 1–1
Average Rate of Discount on First-Class Two-Name Commercial Paper in 43 Cities of the United States, for the Years 1893–1897, as Reported Weekly in *Bradstreet's*

	Lower Rates—Percent					Higher Rates—Percent				
Place	*1893*	*1894*	*1895*	*1896*	*1897*	*1893*	*1894*	*1895*	*1896*	*1897*
Boston	5.27	2.76	3.19	4.92	2.99	6.60	3.77	4.84	6.29	4.03
New York	6.73	22.90	3.55	5.40	3.46	8.72	3.65	4.24	6.17	4.00
Baltimore	6.11	4.62	4.00	4.00	4.09	6.63	5.23	4.82	4.50	4.64
Hartford	6.09	3.43	4.06	5.72	3.70	7.16	4.32	4.61	6.67	4.27
Philadelphia	6.15	3.46	4.31	5.57	3.69	7.01	5.31	5.56	6.27	8.88
Providence	6.12	3.81	4.65	6.07	4.24	6.80	4.83	5.25	6.82	4.96
Cincinnati	5.88	4.60	4.83	5.61	4.12	6.96	5.44	5.61	6.17	5.17
Chicago	6.49	5.24	5.33	6.54	5.08	7.19	6.25	6.24	6.92	6.07
Pittsburgh	5.94	5.28	5.96	6.00	6.00	6.46	6.00	6.01	7.00	7.00
New Orleans	7.01	4.98	4.76	6.50	6.00	7.61	6.34	6.65	7.78	6.88
St. Louis	6.65	5.38	5.25	6.23	6.00	7.74	7.01	6.98	7.44	7.00
Portland, ME	6.00	6.00	6.00	6.00	6.00	6.00	6.00	6.00	6.00	6.00
Richmond	6.00	6.00	6.00	6.00	6.00	7.00	7.00	6.00	6.00	6.00
Buffalo	6.11	6.00	6.00	6.00	5.92	7.78	7.65	7.00	7.94	7.92
Memphis	7.48	5.98	5.38	6.25	5.42	8.03	7.96	7.86	8.00	7.42
San Francisco	7.11	5.80	5.94	6.00	–	8.48	6.78	6.32	6.00	–
Milwaukee	6.98	6.11	6.00	6.28	6.00	7.00	6.98	7.00	7.15	7.00
Indianapolis	7.15	6.69	6.00	6.00	6.00	8.00	8.00	8.00	8.00	8.00
Cleveland	7.00	6.88	6.00	6.00	6.00	7.00	7.00	7.00	7.00	7.00
Detroit	7.00	6.23	6.00	6.84	6.00	7.19	7.23	6.09	6.84	6.00
St. Paul	7.61	7.69	6.00	6.34	5.38	8.00	7.69	6.32	7.69	7.38
Nashville	8.00	7.65	5.96	6.00	5.75	8.00	8.00	8.00	8.00	6.53
Louisville	7.03	6.40	6.78	6.94	6.96	7.07	7.23	7.00	6.96	7.00
Minneapolis	7.57	6.98	6.50	7.21	6.25	8.00	7.82	7.84	7.96	7.40
Kansas City	6.90	6.26	6.53	8.00	6.84	8.00	8.00	7.86	9.57	8.48
St. Joseph	6.84	7.00	7.00	7.00	7.00	7.84	8.00	8.00	8.00	8.00
Charleston	7.13	7.00	7.00	7.00	7.00	7.84	8.00	8.00	8.00	8.00
Los Angeles	7.28	7.00	7.00	7.00	7.00	9.28	9.00	9.00	9.00	9.00
Duluth	7.96	7.01	7.00	7.38	6.90	9.00	7.88	8.00	8.26	8.00
Galveston	7.01	7.00	7.00	7.53	8.00	8.00	8.00	8.00	8.00	8.00
Mobile	7.78	8.00	8.00	8.00	8.00	8.00	8.00	8.00	8.00	8.00
Omaha	8.00	8.00	8.00	8.00	7.90	8.65	10.00	10.00	10.00	9.80
Savannah	8.00	8.00	8.00	8.00	7.96	8.80	10.00	10.00	10.00	9.96
Atlanta	8.00	8.00	8.00	8.00	8.00	8.03	8.00	8.00	8.00	8.00
Birmingham	8.00	8.00	8.00	8.00	8.00	9.46	10.00	10.00	10.00	9.88
Houston	8.00	8.00	8.00	8.00	8.00	8.00	8.00	8.00	8.00	8.00
Portland, OR	8.00	8.00	8.00	8.00	8.00	10.00	10.00	10.00	10.00	10.00
Salt Lake City	8.00	8.00	8.00	8.00	8.00	10.00	10.00	10.00	10.00	10.00
Little Rock	8.07	8.00	8.00	8.00	8.00	9.88	9.84	10.00	10.00	8.73
Dallas	8.78	7.57	8.42	8.92	8.00	10.38	9.15	10.00	10.00	10.00
Tacoma	10.00	9.36	9.00	9.00	9.00	11.69	11.00	11.00	11.00	11.00
Seattle	10.00	10.00	10.00	10.00	0.84	12.00	12.00	12.00	12.00	11.84
Denver	10.00	10.00	10.00	10.00	10.00	10.38	12.00	12.00	12.00	12.00

Source: Breckenridge (1899b, p. 7)

65) shows that during the 1880s and 1890s, when many other debts were in default, commercial paper default rates were trivial (0.2 percent from 1886 to 1892 in New York according to one estimate; 0.05 percent from 1891 to 1895 in New York, according to another estimate; 0.001 percent from 1897 to 1902 in Chicago, according to a third estimate). Commercial paper was uniquely liquid during banking panics (Greef, 1938, p. 57). During the Great Depression, default rates on commercial paper remained extraordinarily low (0.03 percent in 1931 and 0.02 percent in 1932, according to Greef, 1938, p. 309).

Clearly, the commercial paper market neither provided a means for interregional diversification (risky loans simply were not admitted to the market), nor a means for completely integrating the national capital market for riskless instruments (otherwise riskless rates of return would have been identical across regions). The large interregional differences in essentially riskless returns show that the elasticity of capital flows across regions in the United States was low. Commercial paper was purchased mainly by bankers, and commercial paper houses received their bridge financing from local banks. The reliance on local banks for funding limited the ability of the banking industry in the nation as a whole to channel funds elastically through the commercial paper market to their best use. The immobility of capital even in the riskless market likely reflected problems of delegated monitoring (Diamond, 1984, Calomiris and Kahn, 1991, Calomiris, Kahn, and Krasa, 1991). Local commercial paper houses were funded by local banks because banks made sure that they performed their duties as "delegated monitors" properly. The financing of commercial paper dealers was limited to local banks and was therefore constrained by local bank capital, because of problems of enforcing appropriate screening and monitoring of potential borrowers. Local bank capital was, in turn, limited by the capital of the local economy. A study of national banks by the Comptroller of the Currency in 1897 showed that out-of-state holdings of bank stock were limited. The largest out-of-state holdings were for the Western and Pacific regions, which had outsiders' holdings of less than 12 percent. Citing this evidence, Breckenridge (1899b, p. 10) concludes that "there is nothing which takes the place of branch banks. The local borrower is at the mercy of the local lender."

The exclusivity of the commercial paper market, combined with limitations on interregional financing of commercial paper, kept the commercial paper market small compared to total bank loans and discounts. For banks in the nineteenth century, the ratio of commercial bills to total loans and discounts never exceeded 3 percent and averaged 1.3 percent for 1892–1897 (Breckenridge, 1899b, p. 9). As late as the 1920s, the number of firms issuing single-name (open-market) paper in the U.S. and Canada never exceeded 2,754. In 1930, 1,674 firms issued open-market paper, of which only 292 originated in cities west of the Mississippi (Minneapolis, Dallas, Kansas City, and San Francisco), and only 9 originated in Canada. Firms in the textiles, foodstuffs, and metals industries accounted for 1,101 of the 1,674 firms. At the trough of the Great Depression, in 1933, only 548 firms issued open-market paper (Greef, 1938, pp. 246–8). Default rates remained low on commercial paper during the Depression because the quantity of short-term paper could fall quickly as default risk rose.

Data on interest rates for bank loans during the early twentieth century provide additional evidence of financial market segmentation. Riefler (1930, p. 79) reports data on prime commercial loans, interbank loans, and loans secured by stock or warehouse receipts for major cities in the United States at the end of 1926. The ranges reported in Table 1–2 are *not* the highest and lowest rates charged, but rather "the rates at which the bulk of the loans of each class are made by reporting banks." Thus some of the rates charged in these locations might have been higher or lower than indicated by the ranges reported here. Even at this late date, there were substantial differences in loan interest rates for these low-risk commercial loans. In all categories, the range of differences across cities within the United States was equal to or in excess of 3.25 percent. Even within cities, differences in rates were often between 1 and 2 percent. New York and Boston showed the lowest range of rates and among the smallest within-city range of rates, while El Paso, Helena, Spokane, Little Rock, Omaha, and Denver showed the highest maximum rates and wider ranges of rates within their respective locations. Riefler (1930, p. 95) also reports average rates charged on bank loans in selected cities for 1919–1925, which are reproduced in Table 1–3. Of course, all of these are *city* loans, so the comparable rates on loans in peripheral areas outside the high-interest-rate cities likely were even higher.

Riefler (1930, p. 80) argues that the rate differentials were not attributable to differences in risk:

> Fairly consistent differences are reported between the rates charged customers in different cities, but they apply to loans where the risk is constant as well as to those where differentials in risk can be inferred. Banks in the city of Chicago, for example, consistently reported higher rates for loans secured by Liberty bonds than did banks in the city of New York, yet Liberty bonds are

TABLE 1–2
Money Rates in Federal Reserve Bank and Branch Cities: Prevailing Rates Charged Customers during the Week Ending December 15, 1926

	Prime commercial loans	*Interbank loans*	*Loans secured by prime stock exchange collateral*		*Loans secured by warehouse receipts*	*Cattle loans*	*Range*
			Demand	*Time*			
Boston	4¾	4½	5	5	-	-	4½ - 5
New York	4½ - 4¾	4½ - 5	5	4¾ - 5	-	4½ - 5	4½ - 5
Buffalo	5 - 6	4¾ - 5	5 - 6	5 - 6	6	-	4¾ - 6
Philadelphia	4½ - 4¾	5	5	4¾ - 5	5 - 5½	-	4½ - 5½
Cleveland	6	5	6	6	-	5 - 6	5 - 6
Cincinnati	5½ - 6	5½ - 6	5½ - 6	6	6 - 7	-	5½ - 7
Pittsburgh	5 - 6	5 - 6	5 - 6	6	6	-	5 - 6
Richmond	5½ - 6	4¾ - 5½	4¾ - 5¼	5½ - 6	5½ - 6	-	4¾ - 6
Baltimore	5 - 5¾	5 - 5½	5 - 6	5½ - 5¾	5½ - 6	-	5 - 6
Atlanta	5 - 6	5 - 6	5 - 6	5 - 6	5 - 6	-	5 - 6
Birmingham	5 - 6	5 - 6	6	6	6	-	5 - 6
Jacksonville	4½ - 6	6	5 - 6	6	5 - 6	-	4½ - 6
Nashville	6	5½ - 6	5 - 6	6	5½ - 6	-	5 - 6
New Orleans	5½ - 6	5 - 6	5½ - 6	5½ - 6	5½ - 6	-	5 - 6
Chicago	4¾ - 5	5	5	5 - 5½	4¾ - 5½	5 - 5½	4¾ - 5½
Detroit	4½ - 6	5 - 6	5 - 6	5 - 6	5 - 6	-	4½ - 6
St. Louis	4¾ - 5½	5 - 5½	5 - 5½	5 - 5½	4¾ - 6	5½ - 6	4¾ - 6
Little Rock	5½ - 6	6	6	6 - 7	6 - 8	8	5½ - 8
Louisville	5½ - 6	5	6	5½ - 6	6	-	5½ - 6
Minneapolis	4½ - 5½	5 - 6	4¾ - 5½	4⅞ - 6	4¾ - 6	-	4½ - 6
Helena	8	6 - 8	8	8	6 - 8	6 - 8	6 - 8
Kansas City	5 - 5½	6	5	5 - 6	5 - 6	6 - 7	5 - 7
Denver	6	6	5½ - 6	5½ - 6	5½ - 8	6 - 8	5½ - 8
Oklahoma City	5 - 6	6	6	6 - 7	6	7 - 8	5 - 8
Omaha	4¾ - 7	6	5½	5½ - 6	5 - 7	7	4¾ - 7
Dallas	4½ - 6	5	6 - 7	5 - 7	6 - 7	6 - 7	4½ - 7
El Paso	8	6 - 7	8	8	7 - 8	6 - 10	6 - 10
Houston	5 - 6	5	5 - 6	5 - 6	5 - 7	6 - 8	5 - 8
San Francisco	5 - 5½	5 - 5½	5 - 6	5 - 6	6	-	5 - 6
Los Angeles	6	6	6 - 7	6 - 7	7	6	6 - 7
Portland	6	6	6 - 7	6	6	6	6 - 7
Salt Lake City	6	6	6	6	7	7 - 8	6 - 8
Seattle	6 - 7	6 - 6½	6 - 7	6 - 7	6 - 7	-	6 - 7
Spokane	6	6	-	6	7	6 - 8	6 - 8
Range	4½ - 6	4½ - 8	4¾ - 8	4¾ - 8	4¾ - 8	4½ - 10	-

Source: Riefler (1930, p. 79)

TABLE 1–3
Cities Having Highest and Lowest Annual Average Interest Rates on Six Major Types of Loans, by Years, 1919–1925

	Highest average rate for six types of loans		*Lowest average rate for six types of loans*		
Year	*City*	*Rate (%)*	*City*	*Rate (%)*	*Difference between lowest and highest*
1919	El Paso	7.82	New York	5.45	2.37
1920	El Paso	7.99	New York	6.22	1.77
1921	El Paso	7.92	New York	6.31	1.61
1922	El Paso	7.97	Boston	5.05	2.92
1923	Helena	8.00	New York	5.18	2.82
1924	El Paso	7.74	Boston	4.59	3.15
1925	El Paso	7.36	Boston	4.48	2.28

Source: Riefler (1930, p. 95)

just as secure for loans in Chicago as in New York.

Summarizing these and other related data, Riefler (1930, p. 82) writes:

> So far as rates customarily charged on the bulk of customers' loans are concerned, therefore, differentials between cities and between different types of collateral security appear as frequently and consistently in those cases where there is no difference in risk involved as in those cases where differentials in risk can be inferred to exist.

Riefler (1930, p. 94) explains within bank differences in interest rates as having at least as much to do with market power as with risk:

> ...good "risks" are not distinguished so much by the type of collateral upon which they borrow as by their importance to the bank, the size of their balances, the amount of business which they bring to it, and their ability to establish banking connections elsewhere. These are the qualities which induce rate concessions, and distinguish those borrowers who pay the highest and lowest rates at the same bank on the same type of loan.

The establishment of the Federal Reserve System, with its intent to unify the national market, was not successful because it had little effect on the industrial organization of banking. Peripheral regions continued to be isolated from the main sources of capital in the East, and local bankers continued to enjoy substantial monopoly rents in the lending market. In part, the failure of the Fed to integrate the national money market resulted from the costs of Fed membership (which kept small peripheral banks from joining the system) and the resistance to branch banking, which would have increased membership in the Fed and promoted interregional capital flows and local competition in peripheral areas (E. N. White, 1983, pp. 149–87).

The interest rate differentials reported in Tables 1–1, 1–2, and 1–3 are large in comparison to similar interest rate differentials within and across countries. Using data on interest rates, exchange rates, and bill of exchange prices, Calomiris and Hubbard (1989) show that the comparable real interest differential between London and New York from the 1890s on was bounded by 3 percent and averaged roughly 2 percent. Breckenridge (1899b, p. 6) also discusses international interest rate differences:

> ...as compared with an international system which hurries capital across frontiers and over seas, for the sake of differences of often less than one percent, it might better be said that the United States has nothing in the way of arbitrage apparatus for domestic purposes, in any worthy sense of the name.

By the criterion of tolerance for riskless interest rate divergence, one could argue that the Eastern United States was less integrated with the Western United States than it was with the rest of the world.

Studies of interest rate variation within other countries show similarly small differences in interest rates. Comparing the United States to the branch banking systems of Europe, Breckenridge (1899b, p. 5) writes:

> ...there is not one of the leading States of Western Europe in which this process of equalization between domestic discount markets is not already far advanced. Take whichever of these one may, it will be found that the price of capital in provincial cities varies in close and usual correspondence to the rates prevailing in the principal financial centers. In Germany, for example, there are no less than 260 towns where paper of a standard quality is discounted at precisely the same rate paid upon like securities in Berlin. In France there are more than 200 communities in which borrowers in good standing and credit can obtain loans on terms as favorable as those accorded in Paris. Similar conditions exist in Italy, Belgium, and Holland. In England again the country bank rate is seldom more than five or less than four percent in any part of the Kingdom, while in Scotland the banks of issue have agreed to charge, and do charge, identical rates at each of their thousand banking offices.

Gillett (1900, pp. 185–6) provides some additional information on interest rate divergence within other countries. Over the last 15 years of the nineteenth century, interest rates across regions in Denmark typically differed by less than 0.5 percent, while the level of interest rates varied within the range of 2.5 to 6 percent. In 260 peripheral towns in Germany and 200 towns in France interest rates were identical to those charged in Berlin and Paris, respectively. H. White (1902, pp. 53–4) claims that "the rate of interest in the smaller towns of the West [in Canada] is only 1 or 2 per cent. higher than in the large cities of the East on the same kind of loans." H. White may have been referring to the findings of a study in 1898 that found "the difference in interest paid by high-class borrowers of Montreal and Toronto and the ordinary merchants of the Northwest was not more than 1 or 2 per cent." (Chapman and Westerfield, 1942, p. 194). A similar study of Canadian interest rate differentials (cited by Willit, 1930, p. 185) also concludes that "so perfectly is this distribution of capital made, that as between the highest class of borrower in Montreal or Toronto, and the ordinary merchant in the Northwest, the difference in interest paid is not more than one or two percent." Johnson (1910, p. 92) writes that the "transference of funds from sluggish to active communities is the inevitable result of a system of branch banking and is the cause of the tendency of the rate of interest toward uniformity in all parts of Canada." Breckenridge (1899a, p. 55) concludes:

> If a substantial uniformity in the rate of interest, extending to hundreds of widely separated markets, has been established in each of these countries [Canada, England, Scotland, Germany, and France] by means of branch banking, the "theory" that like results will follow the sanction of this device by the United States is entitled to some respect.

The fact that comparisons of low-risk interest rate differentials in other countries are typically for bank loans rather than for commercial paper illustrates another peculiar consequence of the American unit banking system—the reliance on commercial paper. In particular, an exceptional characteristic of U.S. financial markets was the use of commercial paper rather than bank trade acceptances to finance interregional movements of goods. Only in the United States, two-name commercial paper, and later single-name paper, dominated the scene (Myers, 1931, pp. 47–52). As in many other areas of financial innovation in U.S. capital markets during the late nineteenth century (including innovations in life insurance, futures markets, mortgage securitization, and investment banking), the exceptional growth of the commercial paper market was an outgrowth, in part, of the failure of the U.S. banking system to provide an integrated national market for commercial credit.

Trade acceptances were defined by R. H. Treman (1919) as follows:

> A trade acceptance is a time draft drawn by the seller of merchandise on the buyer for the purchase price of the goods and accepted by the buyer, payable on a certain date, at a certain place designated on its face. (Quoted in Steiner, 1922, p. 113.)

In essence, a trade acceptance is "an acknowledgement of the receipt of goods and a promise to pay for the same at a fixed date and place" (Steiner, 1922, p. 114). Bankers' acceptances financing trade were secured by goods in transit.

The advantage of trade acceptances from the standpoint of the seller of goods is the reduction in the need for credit during the interim period between the time goods are produced and the time payment is received from the buyer. The legal liability of sellers for delivery of goods as promised (the "doctrine of implied warranties") encouraged sellers (or their agents) to maintain ownership of the goods while in transit and to obtain credit to finance the costs of shipment. The commonly used alternative to the acceptance to finance trade within the United States during the nineteenth century was the "open account" system, in which sellers transfer goods to buyers, grant temporary trade credit to buyers (often for more than a month), and finance the float with bank credit or commercial paper.

The absence of bankers acceptances in the nineteenth-century United States is especially strange given the high costs of credit in the periphery, especially during the crop moving seasons. If bank credit was relatively costly in the region of production (as Table 1–1 shows it often must have been), then a trade acceptance would be a useful means for the seller to obtain cheaper credit. The seller could trade his acceptance (say, on New York) for deposits in his home bank. The acceptance would also be a superior credit instrument to the extent that creditworthiness could be ascertained better by a local bank lending officer than by a distant merchant (Steiner, 1922, pp. 161–4).

Why then were trade acceptances so rare? One answer revolves around unit banking. The difficulty of a seller's obtaining credit from a distant unit bank could explain the disuse of acceptances. A local office of a nationwide branching bank, however, could provide the needed monitoring of the seller's goods and general creditworthiness, but provide delivery of the acceptance at another location. Interestingly, trade acceptances were used to a relatively large degree during the existence of the second Bank of the

United States, but not as much before or afterward in the pre-World War I era. (After World War I, acceptances became more common, under the sponsorship of the Federal Reserve System, which saw them as the means to fulfill the dictates of the "real bills doctrine.") From 1823 to 1834, trade acceptances on the books of the Bank of the United States increased from $1.9 million to $16.3 million, while commercial paper increased from $22.5 million to $33.7 million (Myers, 1931, p. 50). Myers (1931, pp. 49–50) quotes Biddle's testimony describing the connection between the second BUS and acceptances:

> The crop of Tennessee is purchased by merchants who ship it to New Orleans, giving their bills founded on it to the branch at Nashville, which furnishes them with notes. These notes are in time brought to New York for purchasing supplies for Tennessee. They are paid in New York, and the Nashville bank becomes the debtor of the branch at New York. The Nashville branch repays them by drafts given to the branch at New York on the branch at New Orleans, where its bills have been sent, and the branch in New York brings home the amount by selling its drafts on the branch at New Orleans; or the New Orleans branch remits.

Bodenhorn (1990, p. 37) finds that antebellum banks in the Southern branch-banking states of Tennessee and Kentucky, and in the mutual-insurance system of Indiana (a closely intertwined system of unit banks), had much higher holdings of trade acceptances than country (unit) banks in Pennsylvania. Comparable detailed data on bank asset holdings are not available for other states.

Similarly, in Canada's branch-banking system trade acceptances provided credit for transfer of goods from the point of production, freeing the seller from having to borrow on his personal credit to finance the transfer of goods to the buyer:

> Throughout the entire transaction, from the purchase from the farmer to the final sale to the eastern customer, the bank practically has title to all agricultural products which are being moved by means of its funds (Johnson, 1910, p. 48).

Clearly, unit banks would be unable to manage such transactions across regions.

Access to Remote Areas

One way in which branch banking facilitated bank diversification was by allowing banks access to thinly populated areas. Because of the relatively low overhead costs of establishing a branch office, branches could operate in locations where unit banks could not. This allowed expansion into new areas and activities and led to diversification of bank portfolios.

Calomiris and Schweikart (1988) show that in Georgia and Virginia during the antebellum period the locations of new branches closely followed the economic opportunities of the time. In Virginia, the opportunities included the rich grain-producing area of the Shenandoah Valley during the boom in the wheat market of the 1850s. In Georgia, new offices followed the expansion of cotton production westward. Both movements involved diversification of loans by reducing the coincidence of risks among bank borrowers (from weather, factor prices, and product prices).

Evanoff (1988) provides a detailed empirical comparison of entry into remote areas by branch and unit banking systems within the United States. He measures access by the number of banking offices per square mile at the county level in 1980 and controls for other factors, including population and income. The results are striking. Branching increases the number of banking offices per square mile by 65 percent in remote areas.

Root (1897, p. 10) makes the same argument less formally for the Canadian branching system. He provides a plot of banking facilities in Canada in 1897 and notes a substantial presence of branch banking offices in remote and thinly populated locations. Chapman and Westerfield (1942, pp. 342–3) point out that the number of persons per banking office in Canada in 1940 was 3,410, compared to 7,325 in the United States. They also show that even in the most sparsely populated provinces the number of persons per banking office was in all cases less than 4,230. The comparable number for rural unit-banking states was sometimes much larger. For example, if one uses census data on population in 1940 (from U.S. Department of Commerce, 1975, Part 1, pp. 24–37) and Federal Reserve data on the number of banks in 1941 (commercial banks plus mutual savings banks, as reported in Board of Governors of the Federal Reserve System, 1976, pp. 24–32), the comparable ratios are: Illinois, 9,500; Texas, 7,700; and West Virginia, 10,500.

Reserve and Capital Ratios

Temin (1969, pp. 73–7) was among the first to relate cross-sectional evidence on bank reserve holdings across regions in the United States to the riskiness of banks. He finds that in the 1830s banks in the Northwest held substantially higher ratios of reserves to liabilities than banks in other parts of the country. The largest difference was between the New England banks (with a reserve ratio of 0.06 in 1834), and the Northwest banks (with a reserve ratio of 0.46 in 1834). Temin argues that the reserve ratios in the Northwest had to be high to inspire confidence in the banks. In part, this reflected the perceived riskiness of banks' assets, as well as the absence of coordination among Western banks, which was present to a greater degree in the East, for example under New England's Suffolk System (see Calomiris and Kahn, 1990).

To the extent that branch banking reduced the riskiness of banks by allowing diversification in loans across locations it should have reduced banks' demand for reserves. In addition to reductions in bank-specific asset risk through diversification, interbank coordination (motivated by advantages of diversification across banks) could have reduced depositors' risk. As Calomiris and Kahn (1991) and Calomiris, Kahn, and Krasa (1991) argue, reserves may serve as "bonding" to reward monitoring by some depositors with a first-come first-served preference. To the extent branching reduces the costs of monitoring by other banks (through the creation of lower-cost monitoring and insurance arrangements among banks, as argued above), then branching could reduce the riskiness of deposits and the demand for reserves, independent of bank-specific diversification of assets.

Inferences about risk from comparisons of reserve ratios across banks are complicated by the need to adjust for other differences. For example, if one bank has a higher capital-to-asset ratio than another and a lower reserve-to-asset ratio, the riskiness of its deposits could be the same for a given riskiness of its assets. Thus, variation in asset risk due to location and variation in capital ratios (a substitute risk buffer for depositors) complicate drawing inferences about bank risk from reserve ratios. Nevertheless, there are a few relatively well-controlled "experiments" useful for isolating the effect of branching on bank asset risk through the window of reserve demand.

Large branching banks in Georgia in the 1850s had lower ratios of reserves to assets and lower capital-to-asset ratios than unit banks in Georgia. For example, in 1856 the four large branching banks had a capital ratio of 0.27 and a reserve ratio of 0.09, while all reporting banks averaged a capital ratio of 0.46 and a reserve ratio of 0.20 (Calomiris and Schweikert, 1988).

Comparisons across locations do not control for all relevant differences in regulations or economic environment. Nevertheless, such comparisons do provide some support for the proposition that branch-banking systems entail lower risk than do unit-banking systems. Gillett (1900, pp. 203–4) compares reserve ratios of national banks in the United States to those of British joint stock banks in the late nineteenth century. He finds reserve ratios of U.S. national banks were more than double their British counterparts.

The comparison between the United States and Canada is more revealing. Table 1–4 compares loan-to-asset and capital-to-asset ratios of Canadian banks and U.S. national banks in the various states for 1904, a relatively calm year before any substantial presence of branching within (postbellum) state-chartered U.S. banking. Using the loan-to-asset ratio (rather than the reserve-to-asset ratio) to control for the ratio of risky assets biases the results against finding lower asset risk for Canadian banks, since relatively unrestricted Canadian loans, and the complement of loans and reserves in Canada, were probably riskier. Securities other than national government bonds accounted for roughly equal shares of bank assets in the two economies (8 percent in Canada, and 9 percent for national banks), but

TABLE 1–4
Loan-to-Asset and Capital-to-Asset Ratios, U.S. National Banks and Canadian Banks, June 1904

	Loans / Assets	*Capital + Surplus / Assets*
Canada	0.73	0.19
United States	0.55	0.20
Alabama	0.53	0.24
Arizona	0.44	0.17
Arkansas	0.60	0.24
California	0.51	0.22
Colorado	0.38	0.12
Connecticut	0.52	0.35
Delaware	0.53	0.32
Florida	0.53	0.20
Georgia	0.64	0.27
Idaho	0.53	0.19
Illinois	0.57	0.16
Indiana	0.50	0.19
Iowa	0.61	0.20
Kansas	0.54	0.19
Kentucky	0.53	0.24
Louisiana	0.59	0.21
Maine	0.58	0.31
Maryland	0.53	0.23
Massachusetts	0.58	0.23
Michigan	0.61	0.18
Minnesota	0.61	0.20
Mississippi	0.61	0.26
Missouri	0.52	0.16

TABLE 1–4, concluded

	Loans / Assets	*Capital + Surplus / Assets*
Montana	0.62	0.20
Nebraska	0.53	0.17
Nevada	0.64	0.21
New Hampshire	0.45	0.27
New Jersey	0.54	0.26
New Mexico	0.55	0.21
New York	0.53	0.17
North Carolina	0.64	0.25
North Dakota	0.67	0.21
Ohio	0.57	0.21
Oklahoma	0.57	0.30
Oregon	0.45	0.16
Pennsylvania	0.53	0.23
Rhode Island	0.57	0.38
South Carolina	0.60	0.26
South Dakota	0.59	0.21
Tennessee	0.55	0.19
Texas	0.57	0.29
Utah	0.48	0.20
Vermont	0.46	0.34
Virginia	0.58	0.21
Washington	0.56	0.14
West Virginia	0.57	0.23
Wisconsin	0.61	0.17
Wyoming	0.61	0.21

Source: Board of Governors of the Federal Reserve System (1959, passim) and Johnson (1910, Appendix C)

Canadian banks held fewer government bonds and more of other investments. The comparison of national banks across states allows one to maintain constancy of the regulatory regime to identify state-specific environmental factors. Data are from Johnson (1910, Appendix C) and Board of Governors of the Federal Reserve System (1959, passim).

Table 1–4 shows that the capital ratios for American and Canadian banks were roughly comparable, but the American banks had much lower loan ratios. This is consistent with greater portfolio risk for American banks. That is, banks had to hold more "reserves" (broadly defined) to reduce depositors' risk in the American system for any given ratio of deposits to assets.

The introduction of branch banking in California was associated with a reduction in capital ratios and an increase in loan ratios for state-chartered and national banks, as shown in Table 1–5. Branching began in 1909. By

June 1928, 63 California banks were operating 826 branches (Board of Governors of the Federal Reserve System, 1929, p. 102). Fourteen of these were national banks (operating 478 branches), and 39 were state banks (operating 348 branches). National banks in California maintained the same loan ratio in 1928 as they had in 1904, but substantially reduced their capital ratio from 0.22 to 0.12. Over this same period, other banks in the United States maintained roughly the same ratios of loans-to-assets and capital-to-assets as in 1904. Data for the ratios of all member banks of the Federal Reserve System for 1928, which includes national banks and state member banks, are identical to the ratios of the national banks reported in Table 1–4 (Board of Governors of the Federal Reserve System, 1976, p. 72).

Under the provisions of the McFadden-Pepper Act of 1927 national bank branch locations were more restricted than those of state banks. Thus one might expect California's state banks to have achieved better diversification and therefore to have been able to maintain lower capital ratios and higher loan ratios than its national banks. Table 1–5 confirms that prediction. In 1928 state banks had capital ratios of 0.10 and loan ratios of 0.60, which represented a substantial improvement over their 1904 ratios of 0.19 and 0.57, respectively.

Summary

In summary, bank balance sheets provide ex ante evidence that branching banks were perceived as less risky, which complements the ex ante evidence on bank note discount rates of branching banks, the ex post

TABLE 1–5
Loan-to-Asset and Capital-to-Asset Ratios of California State and National Banks, June 1928

	State Banks	*National Banks*	*All U.S. Banks belonging to Federal Reserve System*
Loans / Assets	0.60	0.55	0.54
Capital + Surplus / Assets	0.10	0.12	0.19

Source: Board of Governors of the Federal Reserve System (1959, pp. 152–9) and Board of Governors of the Federal Reserve System (1976, pp. 72–3).

evidence on bank failures, and the other indicators of diversification discussed above. Taken together the evidence shows that unit banks were less diversified, more vulnerable to failure, less able to grow in the aftermath of adverse shocks, less efficient in their use of scarce bank capital and reserves, less able to provide credit at low cost during times of peak demand, less able to provide services in remote areas, less competitive in local markets, less able to transfer capital across regions, and less able to finance interregional commodities trade. It is no wonder that the unit banking system was so uncommon in the international history of banking. The main puzzle is why it persisted so long, despite its disadvantages, in the American banking system.

THE PERSISTENCE OF BRANCHING RESTRICTIONS IN U.S. BANKING

One can divide the question of why branch banking has been so limited in the U.S. experience into two parts: First, why did the U.S. system start with a system based primarily on unit banks (with the notable exception of the South); and, second, why did limitations on branch banking persist in many states, despite the obvious advantages (enumerated above) of liberalizing branching laws? Once one poses the question this way, the puzzling predominance of unit banking in the American experience can be analyzed *historically*. Rather than offering a disembodied "model" of the choice for unit banking, I will offer a model embedded in a "story"—a story in which the economic, legal, and political contexts in which banks originally were chartered and regulated combined with subsequent historical events to produce a particular (in retrospect, possibly a very inefficient) set of regulations. Before one can answer the difficult questions about governments' choices of industrial organization for banks, one must understand the context in which the controversies over branching arose.

A Brief History of Bank Chartering

The story of unit banking in the United States begins with the historical motivations that underlay the chartering of banks. In the beginning, of course, there were no banks in America. Colonial "commercial banking" was carried on as a part of general merchant enterprises, along with importing and exporting, insurance, and transport. While some colonials called for the formal establishment of banks to promote greater liquidity, land development, and commerce (notably, Franklin, 1729), there was substantial resistance to the chartering of banks in the colonies and in England. The corporate form based upon limited liability was viewed with great suspicion—sometimes it was seen as a means for avoiding responsibility for debts incurred—and the granting of such a corporate form was seen as a privilege of government to be used selectively, until the mid-nineteenth century. Moreover, money-issuing authority for banks was sometimes viewed as a means to government-sponsored inflation, which was feared by creditors. (For a review of the debates over the inflationary effects of early currency creation by governments and banks see Bullock, 1895, 1900, Davis, 1900, 1911, Nettles, 1934, Lester, 1939, Ernst, 1973, Hurst, 1973, Brock, 1975, McCusker, 1978, Smith, 1985a, 1985b, Wicker, 1985, Michener, 1987, 1988, Calomiris, 1988a, 1988b, and M. Schweitzer, 1989).

The first commercial bank in the United States, the Bank of North America, was chartered in 1781 by the Confederacy to help finance the Revolution, was opposed by some from its inception, and was forced to abandon its controversial national charter to take up business as a state-chartered bank, first in Delaware, and later (in 1787) in Pennsylvania (Hurst, 1973, p. 7). The history of the Bank of North America illustrates two important elements of the political and legal context of early bank chartering in the United States. First, the constitutional basis for chartering banks by the federal government was unclear and highly controversial. Second, bank charters granting the right to issue money and allowing limited liability for stockholders were not freely available to all who wanted them, but were seen as a privilege and as a tool of the state (and, possibly, federal) governments to be used to achieve specific, appropriate objectives.

Americans were free to sign contracts of indentured servitude, but they were not free to establish limited-liability corporations, in banking or in other areas. As Hughes (1976, 1991), Hartz (1948), Handlin and Handlin (1947), and many others emphasize, the legal system of the United States grew out of the mercantilistic colonial system, in which the guiding principle was the exchange of monopoly privileges (including charters, land grants, exclusions of competition, and licensing) for advantages to the government (including new sources of government revenue, and strategic military advances). This was a system for promoting expansion, but in a heavily controlled atmosphere, in which society's interests (as interpreted by the government) took precedence over individual gain and the freedom to contract in particular ways. In banking, in particular, government would decide which activities and places warranted the establishment of banks and would tax, regulate, and own substantial shares of the banks that were created.

Early state chartering of commercial banks differed greatly across states with respect to the scope of bank activities and assets permitted and required, bank capital requirements, collateralization of note issues, extended liability of directors and stockholders, and a host of other regulations, including those pertaining to branching (Sumner, 1896; Knox, 1900; Dewey, 1910; Redlich, 1951; Hammond, 1957; Fenstermaker, 1965; Rockoff, 1972; Schweikart, 1988a; Calomiris and Schweikart, 1988; and Bodenhorn, 1990). Prior to 1838 charters were typically granted by state legislatures upon special request. Even banks within the same state often faced very different regulations on their lending and financing.

The Panic of 1837 was a watershed in the history of bank chartering in the United States. The destruction of banks brought an increase in the demand for new banks and offered an opportunity to change the form of chartering throughout the country. In the North, the "free-banking" movement emerged as a means to allow entry into banking for anyone willing to abide by the terms of a common set of regulations. Following New York's example in 1838, some systems (primarily in the North) permitted free entry into banking. Banks under the free-banking laws of a particular state faced many regulations, including a 100 percent reserve requirement against note issues in the form of government bonds (see Rockoff, 1972, for the details of the different state laws). Despite the spread of free banking in the 1840s and 1850s, many banking systems (notably in the South) continued to rely on special chartering, requiring that applicants demonstrate a public need for new banks before granting a new charter.

As states established new charters for banks, they typically allowed older chartering forms to continue. For example, in Ohio in the 1850s there were four different types of banking institutions in existence: old individually chartered banks, and three newer types of bank charters, including free banks and insured banks. In New York, there were three chartered forms: insured banks (dating from 1829), limited-liability free banks, and banks with unlimited liability. Some bank charters were perpetual, some were limited in duration. In some cases, banks were chartered to promote specific projects, including canals, bridges, roads, and railroads (for example, the Manhattan Company of New York was chartered to provide water to New York City), while others had no specific mandate.

All chartering systems helped to finance their respective state governments. In some cases, states taxed banks; in others (notably Pennsylvania and South Carolina) governments owned substantial shares in the banks; and in still others (free banks) governments forced banks to hold their bonds as security for notes. Sylla, Legler, and Wallis (1987) report data on the share of state revenues from banks in the antebellum period. They show that in some states, banks were the main source of revenue. For example, from 1811 to 1860 the bank share of state revenue in Massachusetts varied between 37 and 82 percent, with a median of 66 percent. The trend over time was to rely increasingly on taxation and bond reserve requirements, rather than direct ownership or control, as the method of rent extraction for the government. As Schweikart (1988a) shows, in the South, the period from 1837 to 1841 was something of a watershed in this respect. The high failure rates and large losses of banks organized and owned by the state governments (which often were involved in specific—typically unprofitable—public works projects) encouraged a movement away from direct government control and ownership. Similar lessons from the panic and depression years of 1837 to 1841 motivated the free-banking movement in the North.

With respect to the national government, chartering was sporadic. Despite constitutional and political controversies surrounding the federal chartering of a nationwide bank, the Bank of the United States (BUS) was chartered in 1791. This bank was founded by Alexander Hamilton with specific purposes in mind: to facilitate the marketing of government debt, to facilitate the collection of government revenues, and to make loans to the government in times of need at subsidized interest rates. In addition to performing these services for the government (Calomiris, 1991b, pp. 70–1), the government also owned a substantial stake in the bank and profited greatly from it. The Treasury Department estimated that the earnings for the government from dividends and sale of stock (in 1796) from its interest in the BUS amounted to $573,580, representing a return on capital of 28 percent (U.S. Treasury, 1897, cited in Love, 1931, p. 31). The bank's 20-year charter was not renewed in 1811, and its absence was sorely felt by the government during the War of 1812. This led to the bank's rechartering in 1816. Subsequent controversy over whether the bank constituted a national monopoly, and disagreement between Biddle and Jackson over the details of the renewed charter, led to a confrontation and a Presidential veto of the rechartering of the bank, which was not overridden by Congress (contrary to Biddle's expectations). From 1836 until 1863 there was thus no federal government presence in the chartering of banks.

Initially, limitations on branching seem not to have been an important constraint on what bankers who received charters wanted to do. From the beginning, banks in the South operated branches (Schweikart, 1988a, pp. 52–7, 62, 76, 98–9, 102, 120, 125–7, 174, 179, 202–3, 262), and banks in the North did not (Redlich, 1951, p. 193), but there was little clamor in the North to allow or prohibit branching. It seems not to have been an important bone of contention (Chapman and Westerfield, 1942, pp. 59–60). Opposition to the second BUS has sometimes been identified with an early opposition to branching, per se, but this seems incorrect. As Martin (1974) and Schweikart (1988b) show, Jacksonian opposition to the Bank mainly was fueled by a desire to reduce the connection between bank lending and bank currency issuing and to curtail the Bank's monopoly power, not by an opposition to federal chartering or branching, per se (see also Duncombe, 1841). Indeed, the branching South was a Jacksonian stronghold.

Branching and Consolidation Controversy in the 1890s

After the virtual disappearance of branch banks in the South in the 1860s (due to Southern banks' financing the Civil War), branching was restricted in many Southern states relative to its status before the War. Interestingly, Southern state governments, which had generally favored branching in the antebellum period, showed less interest in it in the immediate postbellum period, although Southern branching grew in importance in the early twentieth century. Although it is often difficult to describe the extent to which branching was prohibited, since it often was prohibited by the discretionary actions of regulators rather than by legal rules, the presence of branches is a fairly good indicator of the freedom to branch. In 1900, for the United States as a whole, there were 87 branching banks operating 119 branches. Forty-eight of these banks were in the South (which I define to include the obvious candidates, as well as Kentucky, Tennessee, Oklahoma, and Texas), and each of them operated only one branch located in the city of its head office (Board of Governors of the Federal Reserve System, 1976, pp. 298–9).

In the North, there was no significant movement in favor of branching until the bank-consolidation/branching movement of the 1890s. Only then did major struggles ensue over whether state-chartered or national banks could operate branches. This was the era that saw the mobilization of special lobbying groups to oppose bank consolidation and branching in particular (notably, the American Bankers Association).

National banks from the beginning were prohibited from opening new branches (but allowed to operate existing ones upon change of charter from a state system). The first Comptrollers of the Currency gave the National

Banking Act a very narrow interpretation, arguing that it prohibited the establishment of branches. With minor and brief exceptions, this remained the policy of the Comptroller's office until the enactment of the McFadden-Pepper Act of 1927.

The consolidation/branching movement of the 1890s in the North had two important sources. One was the high rate of bank failures during the 1890s, which prompted consideration of the advantages of large, nationwide, diversified banks (Chapman and Westerfield, 1942, pp. 62–74). Bank stress would also play a dominant role in the dramatic merger wave in banking during the 1920s (Willit, 1930, pp. 125–30, 159–247, Cartinhour, 1931, Chapman, 1934, Chapman and Westerfield, 1942, pp. 109–15, and E. N. White, 1985). As before, unit bankers would react to the demand for consolidation and branching by lobbying to oppose it (and, in 1930, by establishing the Independent Bankers Association, to spearhead the opposition).

The second source of demand for bank branching and consolidation was the secular changes occurring elsewhere in the economy in the production, distribution, and management systems of corporations, which affected their borrowing needs. In the United States, particularly with the expansion of transcontinental railroads after the Civil War and the coming of the "second industrial revolution" of the latter quarter of the nineteenth century, the scale of firms and their financial requirements increased dramatically. Aside from the growth of firm size for technological reasons (for example, in the chemical and steel industries) the spread of the railroad and the associated extension of a firm's relevant "market" led to the emergence of the large-scale enterprise, with a managerial hierarchy and a complex nationwide distribution network for coordinating movements of factors and output (Chandler, 1977). These dramatic changes in the scale of corporate financing needs first appeared in the financing of railroads, which were the harbinger of the new wave of large-scale national industrial and commercial enterprises.

The demand for large-scale corporate finance affected the propensity for bank consolidation and branching in at least four important ways. First, there was the direct effect of the increase in demand by the bank's customers for large-scale loans. Limitations on the amount any bank was willing to loan (or legally could loan) to an individual customer favored the establishment of large banks. To some extent, the American banking system had participated in the financing of the railroads of the 1840s and 1850s, but these financings were on a smaller scale than those of the transcontinental railroads of the postbellum era, and they were not accompanied by the enormous increase in corporate scale and scope witnessed in the last quarter of the nineteenth century (Fishlow, 1965).

Second, because the fragmented unit banking system in the United States was ill-suited to finance the new corporate giants, and because of existing limitations on branching and mergers, competing methods of corporate finance arose that began to erode bank profitability, thus compounding bank distress and encouraging consolidation. The new markets for commercial paper and corporate stocks and bonds helped to motivate efforts by bankers to consolidate. Corporate finance prior to the 1890s was a local endeavor. As the demand for capital by large-scale firms grew, however, the credit system adapted, and competition on a national scale (for the business of a limited class of firms) became important. Part of that adaptation was visible within the banking system. Prior to the 1890s banks did not have formal credit departments with systematic procedures for evaluating creditworthiness (Lamoreaux, 1991a). Rather, they relied on informal knowledge of local borrowers in determining access to, and the cost of, credit. As banks turned outward in the 1890s, that began to change.

Financial innovations outside of banking were at least as important, and these allowed competitors of banks to gain a foothold in the credit market. As early as 1857, *Bradstreet's* printed the first rating book—a volume of 110 pages, listing 17,000 firms located in nine cities (Schultz, 1947, p. 57). The coverage of the various rating agencies increased over the latter half of the nineteenth century, and the data reported became more detailed and systematic, as the national and international markets for commercial paper and inter-firm trade credit grew. Growth in the commercial paper market was especially large from 1873 until the mid-1880s (Greef, 1938, p. 54), and the ability of commercial paper to remain safe and liquid during the panics of the 1890s led to its increasing use. The Mercantile Agency (the predecessor of Dun and Bradstreet's) opened 90 offices in the United States between 1871 and 1890. From 1891 to 1916, 115 new offices were opened, including 83 outside the borders of the United States (Foulke, 1941, pp. 294–5). As noted above, the United States was unique in its reliance on commercial paper for commercial and industrial finance of high-quality borrowers.

Another peculiarity of U.S. financial history that was an outgrowth of changes in corporate scale and branching restrictions was the development of securities markets and investment banking syndicates in the nineteenth century. In other countries, commercial banks financed firms, often owning equity as well as debt and often involving themselves in corporate decision making, as well as finance. Markets for corporate stocks, bonds, and commercial paper were virtually nonexistent. The Japanese keiretsu (Hoshi, Kashyap, and Scharfstein, 1990a, 1990b, 1991) and the similar German system dating from the nineteenth century (Riesser, 1911) provide examples of large-scale corporate finance within the banking system. In the United States in the 1890s, for the first time, investment banking houses (which previously had dealt almost exclusively in railroad securities issues and the financing of corporate reorganizations) began to market the common stock of other corporations on a national scale (Carosso, 1970, pp. 29–50). During this period New York became the preeminent center for investment banking, as investment banks relied increasingly on commercial banks as a source of funding, financed through the pyramiding of reserves in New York (due to New York's dominance as a commercial center). Ironically, the fragmented banking system would help to finance its own decline by fueling its main sources of competition in credit markets. The pioneering efforts in common stock flotations for relatively small firms were by Lehman Brothers and Goldman-Sachs, beginning in 1906 with the United Cigar Manufacturers and Sears, Roebuck flotations (Carosso, 1970, pp. 82–3).

Significant changes in corporate law helped to usher in the increasing reliance on large-scale enterprise and the growing attractiveness of corporate bonds and stocks, by clarifying and extending the protection afforded corporations in the law. Changes in attitudes toward incorporation, which had evolved over the previous century (Horwitz, 1971, 1977, 1985, Hurst, 1970), accelerated in the 1880s and 1890s, giving rise to what Sklar (1988) terms the "corporate reconstruction of American capitalism." In a series of cases beginning in 1886, for example, changes in the law of property and views of contractual liberty gave corporations rights similar to those of individuals, which served to protect large-scale corporations from arbitrary government disappropriation:

> ...the [Supreme] Court established a legal doctrine of substantive and procedural due process, which further elaborated the reformulation of liberty attached to corporate property. In effect, with the limited liability of the stockholder it combined the limited liability of the corporation in the face of the legislative and executive powers of government....It defined property to include the pursuit, and therefore the legal protection, of intangible value, or earning power...(Sklar, 1988, p. 49).
>
> ...the resort to the corporate form of enterprise based upon negotiable securities and limited liability as a mode of property ownership became

> increasingly more compelling in the United States than in Britain and continental Europe, and its extension to intercorporate combination a familiar routine. Protected in part by law and otherwise by executive policy, the property form matched inducement and need with effective and available market instrumentalities (p. 166).

Banks in the United States were forced as never before to compete with new forms of finance.

A third connection between the increased scale of corporate finance and the consolidation/branching movement also came from the growth of the securities market. Commercial banks played a crucial role as conduits of information and outlets for the marketing of securities flotations by investment-banking syndicates. This role dates back to Cooke's government bond syndication campaign of the 1860s, in which the initial links between Eastern investment bankers and commercial banks throughout the country were forged (Carosso, 1970, pp. 51–3). Benveniste and Spindt (1989) argue that a crucial feature of investment banking syndicates is that they collect information necessary to price new issues from the same parties who ultimately purchase the new issues. By combining the two, Benveniste and Spindt show, syndicates can minimize information costs by creating appropriate incentives for the collection and sharing of information within the coalition. This model seems well suited to understand the role of commercial bankers in early stock and bond flotations. They may have had special insights about individual firms' credit histories and about the types of securities their local customers were most interested in purchasing. The involvement of commercial bankers in underwriting and trust activities was a two-edged sword from the standpoint of the banking industry. It allowed them to share in the profits from the new financial innovations, but it also made them unwitting accomplices in the decline of banks as a source of direct finance. Banks that saw the possibility of participating more directly in underwriting of securities (at a higher level in the syndicate pyramid) and that saw potential economies of scale in trust activities and securities marketing (E. N. White, 1985) yearned to increase their size and their geographical range, which would enhance their role in the syndicate.

Fourth, and finally, the changes in the scale of corporate finance, and the consequent growth of investment banking, reduced the costs of arranging bank mergers, which encouraged banks to consolidate and branch. In addition to planning new securities issues and coordinating the marketing and pricing of the issues and the distribution of fees within the syndicate, investment bankers assisted in reorganizing the banking industry. By the turn of the century, bank consolidation in New England began, and investment banks played an important role in the process:

> At the urging of an organization of Massachusetts savings associations, which collectively owned more than 40 percent of Boston's bank stock, a syndicate of private bankers under the leadership of Kidder, Peabody & Company liquidated nine of [Boston's] national banks and consolidated their operations into an enlarged and reorganized National Shawmut Bank. A year later, the Industrial Trust Company, under the aggressive leadership of Samuel P. Colt, acquired two banks in Providence and seven others elsewhere in the state. Each of these consolidations triggered a number of smaller mergers in their respective locales. As a result, by 1910 the number of banks in Boston had fallen to 23, little more than a third of the 60 banks operating in the city in 1895.... Over the same period, the number of national banks in Providence fell from 25 to 9.... (Lamoreaux, 1991b, p. 549).

Lamoreaux (1991b, pp. 549–50) finds that the profits of the new merged banks were substantially raised by the mergers. In explaining the timing of the mergers in New England, Lamoreaux (1991b, p. 551) emphasizes the importance of the demand for credit by large-scale industrial enterprises, which

> may explain why private banking houses like Kidder, Peabody showed a sudden interest in merging national banks. The heightened level of activity in the securities markets may thus explain much about the timing of the merger movement in banking.

The concentrated holdings of stock in the national banks, and the adept management of Kidder, Peabody allowed stockholders to merge the banks, despite the frequent opposition of "entrenched" bank managers (especially in Massachusetts).

Despite all these motivations for consolidation and branching, major changes in industrial organization of banking from 1900 to 1909 were confined to a few states and banks, as Table 1–6 shows (Chapman, 1934, pp. 52–3, Board of Governors of the Federal Reserve System, 1976, pp. 298–9). National banks, as already noted, were prohibited from opening new branches, and prior to 1918 bank consolidation was only allowed after banks went through the costly process of asset liquidation (Chapman, 1934, p. 43). State banking laws also acted as a continuing impediment to consolidation or branching. In addition to requiring very large supernumerary majority votes by stockholders as a condition for merger, regulators in all states reserved for themselves the right to deny consolidations (Chapman, 1934, p. 46).

TABLE 1–6
Bank Mergers and Consolidations, by State, and Branching, 1900–1910

	Consolidations and Mergers[a]										
State Banks	*1900*	*1901*	*1902*	*1903*	*1904*	*1905*	*1906*	*1907*	*1908*	*1909*	*Total*
Arizona	–	–	–	–	–	–	–	–	–	1	1
Connecticut	–	–	–	–	–	1	–	1	–	–	2
Florida	–	–	–	–	–	1	–	–	1	–	2
Georgia	–	–	–	–	–	–	–	–	13	10	23
Idaho	–	–	–	–	–	–	1	1	4	–	6
Illinois	–	6	–	4	1	6	7	4	4	2	34
Indiana	–	–	1	–	1	–	1	1	1	1	6
Kansas	1	1	1	–	–	–	–	–	–	–	3
Louisiana	–	–	1	1	2	5	4	2	–	–	15
Michigan	–	–	–	–	6	–	2	4	7	4	23
Minnesota	–	1	1	–	1	–	3	2	5	9	22
Missouri	–	3	3	3	5	7	6	7	5	11	50
Nebraska	1	5	5	2	1	4	2	–	4	2	26
North Carolina	–	–	2	1	–	–	2	3	5	2	15
Ohio	–	–	–	–	1	3	–	–	–	–	4
Oklahoma	–	–	–	–	–	–	–	–	2	8	10
Oregon	–	–	–	–	–	–	–	–	4	–	4
Pennsylvania	–	1	2	4	3	4	1	1	1	1	18
Rhode Island	1	2	1	–	2	1	1	–	–	1	9
South Carolina	–	–	–	–	–	–	–	–	4	2	6
South Dakota	–	–	6	–	1	1	–	–	–	–	8
Texas	–	–	–	–	–	–	1	–	–	1	2
Utah	–	–	–	–	–	1	–	–	–	–	1
Washington	–	–	–	–	–	–	–	–	7	–	7
West Virginia	1	–	2	–	–	–	2	1	–	–	6
Wisconsin	–	–	–	2	5	2	1	–	–	–	10
Wyoming	–	–	–	–	2	–	–	–	–	–	2
Total											
All State Banks	4	19	25	17	31	36	34	27	67	55	316
All National Banks	16	22	25	20	32	33	22	27	30	25	252
Grand Total	20	41	50	37	63	69	56	54	97	80	568

Branching

	1900	*1905*	*1910*
State banks with branches	82	191	283
Number of branches	114	345	536
National banks with branches	5	5	9
Number of branches	5	5	12
All banks with branches	87	196	292
Number of branches	119	350	548

[a] Data are incomplete. See Chapman (1934, pp. 52–3) for a discussion.

*Sources:*Chapman (1934) and Board of Governors of the Federal Reserve System (1976, p. 297)

One way around restrictions on new branching or merging, which offered an alternative means to expand in size and geographical scope, was to form "chains" (more than one bank owned primarily by the same shareholders) or "groups" (banks owned directly by a bank holding company). While the degree of control and organization of chains and groups was not as great as that of branching banks, it certainly encouraged some joint decision making in lending, cooperation in marketing and trust activities, and interbank lending within the group on favorable terms. Chain banking developed considerably after 1890, and became displaced in importance by group banking by the 1910s. As Cartinhour (1931) and Calomiris (1991a) show, some of the states with the largest chain and group presence were unit banking states. The rise of chain and group banking in Minnesota was particularly dramatic. By 1930, chain and group banks controlled 30 percent of the banks and 66 percent of bank assets in the state (Cartinhour, 1931, p. 110). By 1929, for the United States as a whole, 10 percent of the banks, and 21 percent of bank assets, were in groups or chains (Cartinhour, 1931, p. 101). Roughly half of these entities were controlled by holding companies (Cartinhour, 1931, p. 103). Beginning in the 1930s, the number and assets of groups and chains began to decline, in part due to failures of individual members and to the replacement of these entities with branching banks (Chapman and Westerfield, 1942, pp. 328–9). Perhaps most importantly, regulation at the state and federal level began to be restrictive. The Banking Act of 1933 prevented the shares of any member bank of the Federal Reserve System from being voted by a group without a permit from the Board of Governors (Chapman and Westerfield, 1942, pp. 334).

Clearly, Sklar's (1988) spirit of "corporate reconstruction" that dominated the legal and institutional changes of corporate capitalism did not extend to banks. Government remained opposed to consolidation (through mergers or holding companies) and branching, with few exceptions. The state and federal governments' responses to increased demand for banking in rural areas, and to the bank failures in the 1890s, were to decrease capital requirements and thereby promote bank expansion through small, unit banks. For national banks, minimum capital requirements were reduced in 1900. Details of state policies are provided in James (1978, p. 230).

The limits on banks' participation in large-scale corporate finance due to restrictions on branching imposed large costs on the economy. We have already noted that local firms in peripheral locations faced high costs of external finance due to the scarcity of bank capital. The instability of unit banks and the lack of competition in rural areas also increased costs to these borrowers periodically when their local banks failed (Calomiris, Hubbard, and Stock, 1986). And all bank-dependent borrowers suffered from general contractions of credit at cyclical and seasonal frequencies (Miron, 1986, Calomiris and Hubbard, 1989).

By impeding the integration of the national market for capital, branching restrictions also imposed costs on large-scale firms, which had to rely on investment banking syndicates to finance their large fixed-capital investments. SEC data on the fees paid to investment bankers in the late 1930s (Butters and Lintner, 1945) and estimates of external finance costs derived from firms' responses to the taxation of retained earnings in 1936–1937 (Calomiris and Hubbard, 1991) both indicate that for publicly traded firms costs of external finance through securities issuances often averaged in excess of 20 percent of the value of the issue. The SEC data are a lower bound on financing cost since these fees do not include interest costs and losses to shareholders due to the undervaluation of stock issues, as discussed in Myers and Majluf, 1984, Asquith and Mullins, 1986, and Korajczyk, Lucas, and McDonald, 1990. Calomiris and Hubbard (1991) find that more than 20 percent of the firms in the economy in 1936 likely faced financing costs in excess of 25 percent. Similarly high investment banking fees seem to have characterized earlier years, although data on these earlier transactions are scarce. Brandeis (1914, p. 95) cites scattered evidence on the fees for common and preferred stock and for bonds that are quite similar to those reported for the 1930s. Brandeis views such high fees as prima facie evidence of monopoly power by the "money trust." While it is difficult to distinguish the extent to which the high costs borne by some U.S. borrowers resulted from compensation for information production or monopoly rents (for the former view, see De Long, 1991), in either case U.S. costs were unusually high compared to the "main bank" system of financing large corporate investment, like that employed in Germany to finance the second industrial revolution (Riesser, 1911, Tilly, 1966, Neuberger and Stokes, 1974, Kindleberger, 1984, pp. 122–9).

The contrast with the German system is striking. German joint stock banks, which came into existence after 1848, combined investment and commercial banking activities and exercised enormous control over the enterprises they financed. Enterprises typically borrowed from only one bank, and the degree of integration and information exchange between bank and firm management was unprecedented. As Neuberger and Stokes (1974, p. 713) write:

> Contemporaries who analyzed the role of the *Kreditbanken* were most fascinated by the intimate relations with the major German industrial firms. The origins of this intimacy are not at all mysterious. Such close relations were a natural outgrowth of the scheme according to which the banks arranged industrial financing. The policy of granting large credits for fixed capital against security of uncertain value was unusually risky so that measures to reduce risk must have been a matter of special concern. One simple expedient was the requirement that the borrower conduct all business through one bank (or in cases where a loan was made by a consortium, through the leading bank). If this rule was followed, a bank was guaranteed adequate knowledge of a firm's condition. A second measure was the requirement that bank officials be appointed to the supervisory boards of the firms to which credit was granted. The directorships ensured the banks a voice in policy-making in the industries they financed.

While Morgan's men in the United States performed a similar function in monitoring firm activities (De Long, 1991), German banks were able to internalize the costs and benefits of monitoring within a single entity and to avoid the complications and costs of marketing securities and coordinating information flows among thousands of syndicate participants. Unbelievably (by American standards) this internalization of costs and benefits in the German main bank system allowed large-scale industrial firms in Germany to borrow and finance large amounts of fixed capital on the same terms as merchants financing import and export trade. The form of finance was very short-term, which further facilitated the discipline of banks over firms, since it gave banks a useful threat (the withdrawal of funding) if firms deviated from the straight and narrow (Neuberger and Stokes, 1974, pp. 713–5). (For a theoretical discussion of the use of short-term debt as a disciplinary device, see Calomiris and Kahn, 1991, Calomiris, Kahn, and Krasa, 1991.)

Despite the costs of regulatory limitations in the United States, it took the disaster of the 1920s to prompt meaningful regulatory reform in branching. Even then, local special interests that opposed liberalization were protected, in part, by the continuing dominance of state law over federal in matters of industrial organization. Under the stress of the 1920s many states in all regions of the country, especially agricultural states that previously had resisted branching reform, liberalized their branching laws. (For a useful and compact description of state and federal regulatory changes on branching from 1910 to 1990, see Mengle, 1990.) Branching restrictions for national banks were also liberalized to conform more to the regulations prevailing in the various states. The National Banking System followed, rather than led, the procession to branch banking. The 1920s saw a reversal in the position of the Comptroller of the Currency, who now pressured Congress to relax branching regulation (Chapman and Westerfield, 1942, p. 95–7), due to concern over the loss of membership to the state chartering authorities, with their more liberal branching laws. But the initiatives of the Comptroller in the early 1920s were limited by the initially strong opposition of unit bankers (many of whom had disappeared by the end of the 1920s, or possibly lost the financial capability to influence their elected officials), and by a Supreme Court ruling in 1924 that gave state governments the right to restrict branching by national banks, if their banks were similarly limited and if Congress did not specifically legislate otherwise. In other industries, state laws that restricted trade were unconstitutional (through the "commerce clause"); in banking, however, commerce-clause protection was found not to apply, and state law ruled supreme.

Interestingly, the first attempt at meaningful reform for national banks occurred only after the Comptroller had received the assent of the American Bankers Association, as a result of its 1921 convention held in Los Angeles, which was apparently dominated by California banks.

> The...Comptroller...was encouraged to take a more aggressive attitude for branch banking by the fact that the National Bank Division of the American Bankers Association had at its Los Angeles convention, after extensive debate, resolved to request the Congress...to permit national banks to maintain and operate branches within a prescribed radius from the head office of such national bank in states in which state banks were authorized to have branches...(Chapman and Westerfield, 1942, pp. 95–6).

The approach advocated by Comptroller Crissinger in 1921 would eventually become codified in the McFadden-Pepper Act of 1927, but in 1922 Congress was not so disposed. Neither was the American Bankers Association, which reversed the position advocated at the Los Angeles convention and adopted a strong antibranching platform at its 1922 convention (Chapman and Westerfield, 1942, p. 97). When the Comptroller decided to push through the changes on his own authority, Congress rebelled, and the political heat that was generated was sufficient to drive him from office. The weakening of the opponents of branching and the demonstrated benefits of branch banking during the 1920s hastened the passage of the McFadden-Pepper Act in 1927 and led to further liberalization of national bank branch locations in the Banking Act of 1933.

After 1920, states also allowed greater consolidation through acquisition and merger (Table 1–7). The large number of unit bank failures and the relative success of branch-banking systems during the crisis years weakened opposition to branching and consolidation (Chapman, 1934, Chapman and Westerfield, 1942, E. N. White, 1985). From 1920 to 1930 the number of banks operating branches (and branches) increased from 530 (1,281 branches) to 751 (3,522 branches). The annual number of banks absorbed by mergers from 1910 to 1920 averaged 139. From 1921 to 1931, mergers increased steadily, averaging 467 per year and reaching a peak of 719 in 1931 (Chapman, 1934, p. 56).

TABLE 1–7
Consolidation and Branching, 1910–1931

	Chapman Series		*White Series*				
Year	*Number of Mergers*	*Banks Absorbed*	*Banks Absorbed*	*Total Assets ($ millions)*	*Branching Banks*	*Branches*	*Loans and Investments of Branching Banks ($ millions)*
1910	127	128	–	–	292	548	1,272
1911	119	119	–	–	–	–	–
1912	128	128	–	–	–	–	–
1913	118	118	–	–	–	–	–
1914	142	143	–	–	–	–	–
1915	154	154	–	–	397	785	2,187
1916	134	134	–	–	–	–	–
1917	123	123	–	–	–	–	–
1918	119	125	–	–	–	–	–
1919	178	178	172	650	–	–	–
1920	181	183	184	874	530	1,281	6,897
1921	281	292	250	710	547	1,455	8,354
1922	337	340	311	750	610	1,801	9,110
1923	325	325	299	1,052	671	2,054	10.922
1924	350	352	341	662	706	2,297	12,480
1925	352	356	280	702	720	2,525	14,763
1926	429	429	348	1,595	744	2,703	16,511
1927	543	544	477	1,555	740	2,914	17,591
1928	501	507	455	2,093	775	3,138	20,068
1929	571	575	529	5,614	764	3,353	21,420
1930	699	698	627	2,903	751	3,522	22,491
1931	706	719	635	2,757	723	3,467	20,681

*Sources:*Chapman (1934, p. 56), E. N. White (1985, p. 286), and Board of Governors of the Federal Reserve System (1976, p. 297)

Modeling the Political Economy of Branching Restrictions

From the standpoint of optimal-contracting models of banking, which assume frictionless bargaining (no transactions costs), freedom of contracting, and freedom to choose asset and liability composition optimally (as in, for example, the very simple visions of banking in Fama, 1980, or Diamond, 1984), the absence of large, multibranch banks is puzzling. Opportunities for the diversification of risk, coordination in response to shocks, and a superior allocation of capital across regions should have been irresistible to a competitive banking system, which would be governed by the principles of cost minimization of banks and utility maximization of depositors. From this perspective opposition to branching seems inexplicable on economic grounds and instead appears to be the result of irrational populist distrust of large, big-city bankers.

From the standpoint of the historical context in which banks were chartered in the United States, however, restrictions on branching and bank consolidation are less puzzling and can be understood as a rational economic strategy of some segments of the population. In a world where banks are a tool of the state, where their activities are deemed a proper subject for public debate and government control, where it is presumed that their supply should be limited and their income should be shared with the state in compensation for the granting of the privilege of limited liability, it is little wonder that the maximization of depositors' utility was not achieved.

Bank regulations, and branching laws in particular, clearly were determined in large part by the lobbying of special interest groups. Indeed, the mercantilist partnership between banks and government often gave the interests of existing banks special weight. For example, in Rhode Island and Massachusetts in the antebellum period bank supervisors explicitly stated that their opposition to branching was based on the concern that existing banks (sometimes in the country, sometimes in the city) might be damaged by allowing competition in their lending markets (Dewey, 1910, pp. 141–2). While in some states the demands of the 1890s prompted a move toward branching (for example, in New York in 1898—see Klebaner, 1990, p. 71), in other states the lobbying by unit bankers and farm interests successfully blocked branching. Indeed, the number of states specifically authorizing branching fell from 20 to 12 over the years 1896 to 1910 (Klebaner, 1990, p. 71), although several other states allowed branching without specific legislation.

Given the transactions costs of lobbying the government, only those with special interests (i.e., with a lot to gain or lose) will pay the price to express their opinion and influence policymakers. This explains why bank regulation seldom maximizes depositors' welfare and why borrowers heavily dependent on banks, and bankers, would be the dominant players in the political regulatory game. This perspective also helps to explain why once a banking system begins as a unit banking system (giving location-specific rents to particular unit banks), unit bankers would resist change and often were able to do so successfully. And this explains why the destruction of unit bankers or the reduction in their wealth (and hence, influence) in the 1920s (and again, in the 1980s and early 1990s) coincided with the relaxation of branching and consolidation restrictions. Indeed, these are common themes in the political history of branching (Cartinhour, 1931, Chapman and Westerfield, 1942, E. N. White, 1982, 1983).

Understanding the differences in regulatory structure across states and over time, however, is far more challenging than stating the truism that change was governed by dominant special interest groups. In what follows, I address what I think are the three most puzzling features of the regulatory differences across states and eras, relying on economic theory to construct conjectures of what might have governed particular groups' interests and on some empirical evidence to buttress these conjectures. The three puzzles are: (1) Why was branching initially a feature of Southern, but not Northern banking? (2) Why did some agrarian areas in the South embrace branching in the antebellum period and not in the early postbellum era? (3) Why was California a major exception to this rule—that is, why was consolidation and branching into agricultural areas in California not successfully opposed?

The answer to the question of why antebellum Northern bankers and bank-dependent borrowers did not push for branching, while Southerners did, seems to come down to the specific differences in the goals of the states and to the common mercantilist principle that connected bank chartering to these goals. As discussed above, bank charters were initially established to promote particular activities. In the North, the main growth opportunities, and the activities promoted by the government, were primarily financing commerce and industry in cities; in the South they were primarily financing the crop cycle and moving the crops to market. The differing nature of the activities affected the desirability of branching. The special advantages of branch banking in the rural South were well understood in contemporary discussions of banking (Schweikart, 1988a, Calomiris and Schweikart, 1988). These included enhanced intrastate and intraregional capital mobility, access to thinly populated areas, and the ability to move agricultural goods long distances easily through the use of trade acceptances.

Similarly, three agriculture-dependent states in the North—Indiana, Ohio, and Iowa—established successful mutual-guaranty systems, which as noted above approximated some features of branching systems (coordination of clearings and acceptance transactions, diversification of risk ex ante, and coordination in the face of disturbances, ex post). The main difference between these Northern states and their counterparts in the South was that, like the free-banking systems of the antebellum Midwest, entry was sharply limited in the Northern mutual guaranty systems, while it was not so limited in the South. In the three Northern systems, banks were not permitted to branch into each other's local markets, which Southern banks often did.

In the Northeast, the commercial and industrial lending by banks typically had a different purpose from that of bank lending in the South, and the absence of branches was not an important obstacle to the satisfaction of those goals. In her studies of New England's banks, Lamoreaux (1991a, 1991b) argues that early-nineteenth century banking was nicely adapted to the needs of local industry:

> At that time, scarcity of information and the modest scale of enterprise had combined to keep credit markets localized and financial institutions small....(1991b, p. 539).

According to Lamoreaux, New England bank managers, particularly in Boston and Providence, often ran banks as credit cooperatives to finance their own firms' needs for working capital. They would have had less interest in diversifying risk, since they were most interested in lending money to themselves.

Maryland provides an interesting case of a banking system that allowed, but did not take advantage of, branching. Maryland's banking system was modeled on the Scottish system. Like the Scottish system, it allowed free branching. Bryan (1899, p. 15) writes:

> This principle was introduced into Maryland in 1804, but it has received comparatively little development. No bank in Maryland has had more than two branches performing a regular banking business, and but a limited number have had branches at all; these were organized early....Perhaps on this account outlying agricultural districts were developed more slowly than they might have been under a system of branch banking.

Furthermore, attempts to charter a state branching bank on the Southern model specifically to channel resources to the countryside were debated in great detail and defeated several times from 1829 to 1837 (Bryan, 1899, pp. 83–5). Why was there so little private branching or support for a public initiative to organize an agricultural branch bank? Like other Mid-Atlantic coastal cities, Baltimore was a hotbed of commerce and industry, and its banks concentrated on financing these activities, rather than searching out opportunities in rural Maryland. For these purposes, from the standpoint of bankers, Baltimore entrepreneurs, and politicians, branches were not particularly necessary.

These conditions changed in the last third of the nineteenth century. Lamoreaux (1991a) shows that in New England as local industrial and commercial opportunities waned and the potential for profits in other regions increased (notably the Midwest and the low-wage South, as discussed in Gates, 1951, Johnson and Supple, 1967, and Wright, 1981), New England banks (and some industrialists) became more outward-looking and began channeling funds to borrowers in other regions. Banks evaluated creditworthiness with newly developed formal methods implemented by newly created credit departments. Now the profitable opportunities for Northeastern banks involved outward-looking participation in the financing of large-scale enterprise in the national capital market. These changes were also related to changes in the sources of banks' external finance (their increasing reliance on deposits), and a change in the relationship between banks' management and shareholders (Lamoreaux, 1991b, Calomiris, 1991c). Changes in the incentives of bankers—whose opinions were instrumental in shaping regulatory policy—which encouraged them to pursue opportunities in the burgeoning national capital market help to explain the timing of the relatively successful branching and consolidation movements in the postbellum North.

In addition to its advantages in helping move crops, branch banking provided other benefits to wealthy antebellum Southerners, who could gain from capital mobility in the South in ways that wealthy Northerners could not. Wright (1986) argues that the profit-maximizing strategy of Northerners was to increase the value of land and local capital and that this encouraged large expenditures on public works and local "boosterism." Wright argues that Southerners with large slave holdings, who were the dominant political force, had little incentive to invest in local public works; instead, they wished to augment the value of their main capital asset, which was slaves. Territorial expansion, and the ability to move slave labor to its highest use were the hallmarks of this strategy. One can see the promotion of branch banking in the South as an example of the pursuit of this interest. Branching promised greater mobility of capital and greater access to new, remote areas, as needed.

From this perspective, one can also understand why the Northwest opted for its mutual-guaranty and free-banking systems, rather than free-entry branching. Entry restrictions helped to create location-specific bank capital and thereby limited potential capital losses on local property values. Location-specific bank capital ensured that banks would not move on to marginally "greener pasture" at the expense of local businesses and farms. One can view this arrangement as a form of insurance of wealth (where the "insurance premium" is the inefficiency, potential for bank failure, and high costs of borrowing in the unit banking system). In the absence of Arrow-Debreu markets, or nationwide mutual funds that offered opportunities to diversify all systematic risk, as imagined in the frictionless capital asset pricing model, landowners saw location-specific bank capital as a way to tie banks' fortunes to their own. If their city or town received an adverse shock associated with a long-term negative revision in expectations regarding the profitability of investment there (say, an expected long-term decline in the terms of trade), local farmers and businessmen could be confident that their bankers would continue to lend to them, even on reduced collateral. The unit bankers had little choice. Branches of banks, facing those same choices, might simply close or at least sharply curtail their lending in that community.

Another related motivation farmers would have had for creating location-specific bank rents was a desire for "loan insurance." In addition to limitations on diversification of wealth holdings, to the extent that borrowers faced external finance constraints, their creditworthiness may have depended importantly on their level of wealth (Leland and Pyle, 1977, Stiglitz and Weiss, 1981, Myers and Majluf, 1984, Gale and Hellwig, 1985, Williamson, 1986, Bernanke and Gertler, 1990, Calomiris and Hubbard, 1990). Given that wealth—particularly in undiversified land—was highly volatile in value, middle-class landowning borrowers had an additional motive to "purchase" loan insurance by supporting unit banking. The desire to tie banks to local lending markets is also visible in more recent regulation, notably the Community Reinvestment Act of 1977. Out-of-state banks that acquire local banks must commit to continue making local loans and not merely use the acquired banks as sources of deposits.

These explanations do not imply that branching restrictions or the earmarking of loans to specific regions are "optimal," or even "second-best," for society as a whole. One can argue that branching restrictions were a way for early settlers to benefit at the expense of later settlement elsewhere in the state—a "beggar-thy-neighbor" regulatory policy supported by the agrarian middle class. In any case, welfare comparisons, which are relatively easy in a frictionless world, are much more difficult in a setting where the standard assumptions of welfare economics (including no costs of information or bargaining) do not hold. These costs, as already noted, are precisely what give rise to "incompleteness" in capital markets, which motivates the taste for unit banking.

In summary, the antebellum South favored branching because the dominant economic interests (wealthy slaveholders) benefited from it. High costs of financing the movement of crops over long distances through peripheral unit banks explains this in part. Additionally, in the South the dominant form of collateral in the antebellum period was slaves rather than land (Kilbourne, 1992); thus there was little advantage from "bonding" the banker to a particular locale. In the Northeast, branching restrictions were not an important constraint on the dominant economic class, composed of merchants and industrialists. Indeed, they benefited by the creation of charter rents to the extent they could use their control of banks to improve their own costs of credit. In the Northwest, the middle-class farmer (later the "populist") would carry the day. In the mutual-guaranty systems of Indiana, Ohio, and Iowa farmers received many of the benefits of branching, while retaining the advantages of location-specific bank capital. Other banking systems of the Northwest opted simply for unit free banks. None authorized free entry in the form of branch banks.

The Civil War brought an end to slavery in the South. The declining price of cotton, as well as the reorganization of labor and land allocation after the War, made the South much poorer than it had been (Ransom and Sutch, 1977, Wright, 1986). There was no longer a plantation elite with an interest in establishing branch banks to promote the efficient movement of capital or commodities. Indeed, one could argue that the wealthy landlords benefited by the lack of competition in finance, which facilitated the "debt peonage" of tenants (Ransom and Sutch, 1977, 148–70). Despite its own antebellum successes with branch banking, there was no powerful political constituency to push for branching in the immediate postbellum period.

Empirical Support

There is a great deal of qualitative evidence to support the generalization that "rural interests" have opposed the branching movement from 1890 to the present. But that opposition has not been uniform. For example, Illinois has had a long history of opposition to branching. In a 1924 statewide referendum, the public voted against permitting branching, two to one (E. N. White, 1982, p. 38, citing Bradford, 1940, p. 17). Similar opposition was present in many states prior to the 1920s, but some relaxed their regulations after the destructive 1920s and 1930s, while others did not. Other states with a large agricultural sector—perhaps most notably, California—favored branching long before the 1920s.

One way to verify the "insurance model" of the rural support for unit banking after 1890 is to see whether cross-sectional variation in the "taste" for branching is correlated with variables that should matter from the standpoint of the "insurance model." The greater the demand for land and loan insurance, the greater the support should have been for unit banking laws. A formal econometric study of this type is beyond the scope of this paper, but there are some facts that appear consistent with it.

Table 1–8 reports data on rural per-capita wealth in 1900 for various agriculture-dependent states. I divide these states into two categories: those that made progress toward relaxing branching restrictions by 1910, and those that did not. Interestingly, with the exception of California, with its very high rural wealth per capita, branching states tended to have much poorer farmers than states that prohibited (new) branching. This is true even controlling for the presence of the Southern states in each group (which were dominated by tenant farming and sharecropping). The median index of relative rural wealth for the branching states was 0.5 (1.2 for non-Southern states), while the states that prohibited branching had a median index of 1.4 (1.8 for non-Southern states). In the latter states, landowning farmers would have been able to lobby politicians more effectively and may have been more interested in protecting their accumulated wealth through the "land and loan insurance" provided by unit banking. Much more empirical work needs to be done, however, before one can interpret this tentative finding conclusively.

E. N. White's (1984b) study of the 1924 Illinois referendum on branching provides evidence consistent with the insurance model. He finds that the presence of banks increased the probability of opposition to branching at the county level and interprets this as evidence that the public was influenced by local unit banks' propaganda. That may be true, but another interpretation of this finding is that the existence of a bank is a proxy for wealth insurance by banks. According to this interpretation, relatively well-off agrarian communities in Illinois were more prone to have banks and to support unit banking. Future empirical work can distinguish between these two interpretations by close examination of county level data.

The case of California is somewhat anomalous from the standpoint of the model and the patterns shown in Table 1–8. California, however, was an unusual state in other ways. For example, the long distances within the state that commodities had to travel and the consequent benefits of coordination

TABLE 1–8
Rural Wealth and Branching Restrictions

	Rural Per Capita Wealth Index, 1900[a]	*Number of Banks with Branches, 1910*	*Number of Branches 1910*	*Ratio of Branch-Banking Facilities to Total Banking Facilities 1910*
	States Allowing Some Branching, 1910			
Alabama	0.3	6	17	0.07
Arizona	0.7	7	15	0.34
California	2.5	34	45	0.12
Florida	0.3	5	7	0.07
Georgia	0.3	15	17	0.05
Louisiana	0.5	3	3	0.03
Michigan	1.1	23	55	0.10
Mississippi	0.4	15	30	0.12
North Carolina	0.3	8	13	0.05
Ohio	1.3	22	39	0.05
Oregon	1.4	5	6	0.05
South Carolina	0.3	2	7	0.03
Tennessee	0.5	3	4	0.02
Virginia	0.5	18	37	0.13
Washington	1.2	8	12	0.06
Mean	0.8	–	–	–
Median	0.5	–	–	–
Mean (non-South)	1.4	–	–	–
Median (non-South)	1.2	–	–	–

TABLE 1–8, concluded

	Rural Per Capita Wealth Index, 1900[a]	*Number of Banks with Branches, 1910*	*Number of Branches 1910*	*Ratio of Branch-Banking Facilities to Total Banking Facilities 1910*
	States Not Allowing Further Branching, 1910			
Arkansas	0.4	3	3	0.02
Colorado	1.3	0	0	0.00
Idaho	1.0	0	0	0.00
Illinois	2.1	0	0	0.00
Indiana	1.4	0	0	0.00
Iowa	2.6	0	0	0.00
Kansas	1.8	0	0	0.00
Minnesota	1.6	0	0	0.00
Missouri	1.2	0	0	0.00
Montana	1.9	0	0	0.00
Nebraska	2.2	1	1	0.00
Nevada	1.9	0	0	0.00
New Mexico	0.6	0	0	0.00
North Dakota	2.1	0	0	0.00
Oklahoma	0.9	0	0	0.00
Pennsylvania	0.9	8	8	0.01
South Dakota	1.8	0	0	0.00
Texas	0.9	0	0	0.00
Utah	0.9	0	0	0.00
Vermont	0.9	1	1	0.03
West Virginia	0.6	0	0	0.00
Wisconsin	1.4	7	9	0.03
Wyoming	3.0	0	0	0.00
Mean	1.5	–	–	–
Median	1.4	–	–	–
Mean (non-South)	1.7	–	–	–
Median (non-South)	1.8	–	–	–

[a] The per-capita rural wealth index is the ratio of a state's share of national rurual wealth, as calculated in Lee et al. (1957, pp. 730–11), divided by a state's share of national rural population, as reported in U.S. Department of Commerce (1975, Part 1, pp. 24–37).

Sources: Lee et al. (1957), U.S. Department of Commerce (1975), and Board of Governors of the Federal Reserve System (1976, pp. 298).

of finance through a branching system may have appealed to wealthy farmers in the California interior, much as it had to antebellum Southern plantation owners. Moreover, the details of the history of California branching seem to provide some support for the model. Specifically, branching was permitted only after the acquiescence of powerful agricultural interests to entry by city banks, and this entry seems to have been the result initially of local distress and eventually of the benefits to this powerful group from allowing branching. Branching was subject to the approval of the State Superintendent of Banks, whose approval was subject to the influence of special interests.

The first branch of the Bank of Italy that A. P. Giannini opened (with the requisite permission of state regulators) was in San Jose. The Superintendent of Banks found that San Jose "needed" the bank's help in the face of the collapse of the local bank. In fact, the failing local banker, himself a large landowner whose family had relied on his bank for large land-backed loans for the past 30 years, visited San Francisco to suggest the acquisition of his bank by Giannini. This was a crucial ingredient in the Superintendent's willingness to have the branch open. Large landowners stood to benefit from the preservation of the bank's stock value and the preservation of the local economy, which depended on the bank. The small landowners, many of whom were Italians who knew Giannini from his childhood days in San Jose, also saw the entry by the Bank of Italy as a favorable change, since previously they had not been granted equal access to the bank, which was being run first and foremost in the interests of large local landowners (James and James, 1954, pp. 48–51.). Giannini realized that further expansion of branching required the support of the powerful land interests:

> Giannini realized that, unless his branches could do more for the California ranchers than existing unit banks were doing, there would be little excuse for the branches (James and James, 1954, p. 52).

Giannini's next acquisition was in Los Angeles in 1910, where, again, the "reason for the speed of this acquisition was the fact that the Park Bank [of Los Angeles] was not in good shape" (James and James, 1954, pp. 58–9). Other attempts at takeovers in Los Angeles by the Bank of Italy met with failure. "These deals fell through in a manner that suggests intervention by the larger banking interests of Los Angeles" (James and James, 1954, p. 59). Giannini acquired another Los Angeles bank in 1913, again only after a fight with local bankers.

Giannini's statewide branching campaign did not begin in earnest until 1916, as the Bank of Italy expanded into the Santa Clara, San Joaquin, and Napa Valleys. The wartime increase in demand, his previous successes and growing popularity, and the scarcity of sound institutions willing and able to finance the expansion, all helped Giannini to win over farmers, regulators, and politicians who otherwise might have been opponents to branching. Just as important was Giannini's adept handling of the financing of large movements of goods over long distances, a natural comparative advantage of branching:

> Valley farming is pretty big business. Many of the crops were perishable or semi-perishable; their movement had to be rapid; their handling and packing, skillful; and their flow to the distant consumer, flexible and constantly under control. Moreover, the principal markets lay as far east as Chicago and New York. Much of the barley harvest was sold on the London market; valley orchardists had long supplied Europe with a good part of her prunes; delta rice was shipped to Japan; and Cuba and Puerto Rico were regular customers for California beans (James and James, 1954, pp. 88–9).

Giannini also was able to enlist the strong support of the Italian community and of small farmers involved in farm co-ops, which the Bank of Italy strongly supported.

In summary, several factors combined to make Giannini the right man in the right place at the right time. Initially, he fought an uphill battle against other banks and entrenched landowners who did not welcome his competition. At first, it was bank distress that would allow acquisitions. But gradually, he was able to convince the powerful, and the not so powerful alike, that on balance they stood to benefit from branch banking. In another state, or even in California at another time, he may never have been able to overcome the obstacles to branching.

Giannini's experience and the data in Table 8 run contrary to the view that the populist agrarian support for unit banks came from poor farmers. Instead, it was established farmers with significant land holdings (and often interests in unit banks) who opposed competition from outside. Indeed, agricultural impoverishment (like the destruction of agricultural banks in the 1920s and 1980s) has been good news for branching. Fifteen states allowed expanded branching from 1920 to 1939. During the expansionary years from 1939 to 1979 only 4 states relaxed their branching laws. In the face of the agricultural crisis of the 1980s once again 15 states loosened restrictions on branching (Mengle, 1990, Calomiris, 1991a).

Explaining the Uniqueness of U.S. Unit Banking

Other countries have agricultural middle classes (notably Canada), yet the successful U.S. support for unit banking is unique. Why was the United States so different? The answer lies in the institutional and historical peculiarities of the American political experience: the protection of local interests ensured by federalism, the distinctly American method for allocating power among national legislators (which also gives disproportionate weight to regionally concentrated minorities), and the legal precedents established by the Supreme Court, which gave states great latitude in the chartering of banks.

By not extending constitutional protection to banking as an activity involving interstate commerce the Supreme Court opened the way to state regulatory prohibitions on bank activities across and within states. Throughout the nineteenth and twentieth centuries state banking authority was limited only by the increasing incursions of the federal government in chartering and regulating banks, which were justified constitutionally by appeal to the federal government's special role in regulating the money supply, and therefore banks, and not by appeal to any constitutional protection on banking activities under the commerce clause. In 1924 the Supreme Court further insulated state government control over banking by ruling that state banks could enforce branching restrictions against state and national banks alike within their borders (in the absence of specific contrary action by Congress). Through these rulings the Supreme Court ensured that the struggle over branching would be fought locally rather than nationally, unless Congress decided to intervene. This approach was codified by Congress in 1927.

The Court's and Congress's willingness to allow state governments to limit the activities of state and national banks within and beyond their boundaries gave locally concentrated special-interest groups a better forum for lobbying than the national arena where they would have been up against all the opposing interest groups in the national economy. Thus federalism's decentralization of legislative power, supported by some crucial Supreme Court rulings and the absence of action by Congress, helps to explain the unique success of unit bankers and their allies in the United States.

The American method for electing national legislators and the means of allocating power within Congress also have helped to constrain opposition to unit banking and to enhance the power of geographically concentrated minorities that opposed branch banking. In contrast to many countries' parliamentary systems in which the national performance of the party can determine which individual representatives hold office, the support of local constituents is a sufficient condition for election to Congress. This tends to enhance the power of geographically concentrated interest groups on politicians. Moreover, congressional committees control the agenda of Congress, and these committees are often dominated by representatives whose constituents tend to agree and feel strongly about the set of issues under the aegis of that committee. Thus representatives from pro-unit banking agricultural states have tended to dominate the congressional committees that control banking regulation. Other states' representatives "trade" influence over these committees for committee appointments in areas of greater concern to their constituents. Congressional "horsetrading" over committee appointments and votes have thus tended to stifle the advocacy of branch banking by the "silent majority" and have favored the power of regionally concentrated enclaves of support for unit banking.

THE ORIGINS AND EFFECTS OF PRE-FDIC BANK LIABILITY INSURANCE

Studies of the political history of deposit insurance legislation show that it was the desire to preserve unit banking and the political influence of unit bankers and their supporters that gave rise to the perceived need for deposit insurance, both in the antebellum period and in the twentieth century (Golembe, 1960). It was understood early on (through observing the successful operation of branch banks in the South and in other countries) that branching—with its benefits both of greater diversification and coordination—provided an alternative stabilizer to liability insurance. But unit banks and their supporters successfully directed the movement for banking reform toward creating government insurance funds. All six antebellum states that enacted liability insurance were unit-banking states. In the antebellum branch-banking South neither government insurance nor urban clearing houses developed. Similarly, the eight state insurance systems created from 1908 to 1917 were all in unit-banking states.

In evaluating the performance of the various government-created liability-insurance schemes, Calomiris (1989, 1990, 1991a) analyses which experiments failed or succeeded, and why. Deposit insurance in many cases destabilized historical banking systems, as recent theoretical and empirical analyses of banks and savings and loans suggest it has today. The failures of insurance systems seem mainly attributable to flaws in their design, rather than to insurmountable exogenous shocks.

Antebellum Successes and Failures

Detailed analysis of each of the antebellum bank insurance programs is provided in Golembe and Warburton (1958). New York's Safety Fund was the first, established in 1829, funded by limited annual contributions of members and regulated by the state government. Losses severely depleted the accumulated resources of the fund from 1837 to 1841 until, in 1842, it ceased to be able to repay losses of failed banks and thus ceased to provide protection to the payments system.

New York in 1838 created an alternative to the insured system through its free banking statute and allowed Safety-Fund banks to switch to that system. The depletion in membership of the insured system kept its losses small during subsequent panics. After 1840 Safety-Fund banks comprised a small and continually shrinking proportion of total banks or total bank assets. Losses were also limited by the 1842 restriction on coverage of member banks' liabilities to bank notes, thus excluding the growing liability base in deposits.

Ultimately, the small number of banks that chose to remain in the system and make continuing annual contributions to its fund did manage to repay in 1866 the obligations incurred some thirty years earlier; but this "success" was not anticipated in the intervening years (as shown by the high discount rates attached to failed member-banks' notes during the 1850s), and the fund did not protect current bank liabilities or the payments system ex ante, as it was intended to do.

Not only did the system fail to provide protection to the payments system, but it also suffered unusually large losses due to fraud or unsound banking practices. While a supervisory authority was established to prevent fraud and excessive risk taking, supervision was ineffectual, and fraud or unsafe practices were common. Ten of sixteen member-bank failures prior to 1842 (the period when insurance was still perceived as effective) were traceable to fraud or unsafe practices. Moreover, such problems were not detected until after they had imposed large losses on the fund.

The failure of the Safety Fund was not the fault of external shocks, severe as they were. In aggregate, banking capital was large relative to losses, and thus coinsurance among all New York banks would have been feasible. Rather it was the design of the insurance system that made it weak.

Upper bounds on annual premia prevented adequate ex ante insurance during panics, and ineffectual supervision allowed large risk takers to free ride on other banks. Finally, adverse selection caused a retreat from the system through charter-switching to the alternative free-banking system, once solvent banks realized the extent of the losses.

Vermont and Michigan followed New York's example and suffered its problems. In Vermont, banks were even allowed to join and depart at will. It took only two bank failures to cause the dissolution of that system; one failure was due to fraud, and the other was that of a bank that joined the system after that bank's prospects had deteriorated. Again, an incentive-compatible, broadly-based system could have provided coinsurance among banks, but adverse selection and poor supervision prevented this.

Michigan's system, created in 1836, collapsed because it (like the other two systems) depended for its resources on accumulated contributions to the collective fund, which would be used to support banks during a crisis. The Michigan system had no time to accumulate a sufficient fund prior to the Panics of 1837 and 1839 and thus was unable to provide protection.

Not all antebellum experiments ended so disastrously as these three. Indiana enacted a different sort of liability insurance plan in 1834, one based on the principles of self-regulation and unlimited mutual liability that would later be imitated by private clearing houses. The Indiana system did not suffer the supervisory laxity or membership retreat of New York and Vermont, nor the illiquidity of Michigan and New York. Coverage was broad-based, and there was no problem in attracting and keeping members. During its thirty-year history no insured bank failed. There was a suspension of convertibility in 1837 and again in 1839, but this was the last time banks were even forced to suspend. During the regional panic of 1854–1855 and the national Panic of 1857 all insured banks maintained operations and convertibility. During those same panics 69 of 126 nonmember, uncoordinated free banks failed in Indiana.

The Indiana system relied on bankers themselves to make and enforce laws and regulations through a board of directors and, importantly, gave it authority to decide when to close a bank. Unlimited mutual liability provided bankers the incentive to regulate and enforce properly. The Indiana system was imitated in Ohio and Iowa, with similarly successful results. Ohio's law granted its Board of Control even greater authority than Indiana's Board, allowing it virtually unlimited discretionary powers during a banking crisis, including the right to force banks to make loans to one another. Interbank loans were successfully used during the Panic of 1857 to avoid suspension of convertibility. The insured banks, it seems, even came to the assistance of nonmember banks during the Panic, as indicated by flows of interbank loans. Only one Ohio bank failed during the crisis, and it was not a member of the insured system. Iowa's system was in place for a shorter and more stable period, but its operation was similarly successful.

Like clearing houses, these three successful insurance schemes aligned the incentive and authority to regulate and made insurance protection credible through unlimited mutual liability among banks. Like Southern branch banks in the Panics of 1837 and 1857 these systems were able to minimize systemic disruption through a coordinated, incentive-compatible response. They were brought to an end not by insolvency, but by federal taxation of bank notes designed to promote the National Banking System.

The Second, Postbellum Wave of State Insurance

The eight deposit-insurance fund systems of the early twentieth century failed to learn the lessons of the antebellum experience; they repeated and compounded the earlier errors of New York, Vermont, and Michigan. Supervisory authority was placed in government, not member bank, hands, and often its use or disuse was politically motivated (Robb, 1921). Furthermore, the numbers of banks insured were many more than in the antebellum systems (often several hundred), and this further reduced the incentive for a bank to monitor and report the misbehavior of its neighbor banks, since the payoff from detection was shared with so many and the cost of monitoring was private.

During the halcyon days for agriculture, from 1914 to 1920, deposit insurance prompted unusually high growth, particularly of small rural banks on thin capital. The insured states grew faster, were smaller, and had lower capital ratios than their state-chartered counterparts in fast-growing, or neighboring states. Table 1–9 reports regression results that confirm the unusually high growth of state-chartered insured banks (controlling for other variables) relative to other agricultural states. A decomposition among voluntary- and compulsory-insurance laws reveals that the incentives to grow were especially pronounced in the compulsory-insurance systems (where the potential for cross-subsidization, or free riding through excessive risk taking, was highest).

When agricultural prices fell, insured banking systems suffered the

TABLE 1–9
Regression Results: Asset Growth of State-Chartered Banks[a]

Independent Variables	*Coefficient*	*Standard Error*	*Significance Level*
Dependent Variable: Growth in total assets of state-chartered banks, 1914–1920			
Intercept	0.101	0.465	0.829
National bank growth	0.681	0.147	0.000
(Reserve center) × (National bank growth)[b]	–0.132	0.060	0.038
Growth in land values, 1914–1920	0.555	0.333	0.107
Ratio of farm to nonfarm population	–0.283	0.654	0.669
Presence of voluntary or compulsory insurance	0.518	0.165	0.004
$R^2 = 0.670$			
$\bar{R}^2 = 0.607$			
Dependent Variable: Growth in total assets of state-chartered banks, 1914–1920			
Intercept	0.156	0.468	0.741
National bank growth	0.682	0.147	0.000
(Reserve center) × (National bank growth)[b]	–0.115	0.063	0.080
Growth in land values, 1914–1920	0.526	0.334	0.127
Ratio of farm to nonfarm population	–0.328	0.655	0.621
Presence of voluntary insurance	0.327	0.251	0.205
Presence of compulsory insurance	0.609	0.189	0.004
$R^2 = 0.683$			
$\bar{R}^2 = 0.607$			

[a] Asset growth is defined as the log difference of total assets. All variables are defined at the state level for a sample of 32 agricultural states.

[b] National bank growth in each state is used as a control for state-chartered bank growth. In reserve-center states, national bank growth may be larger, as it reflects growth of correspondent banks outside the state as well. To control for this difference, I interact national banking growth with an indicator variable for states with reserve centers.

Source: Calomiris (1991a).

highest rates of decline and failure among state-chartered banks in agricultural states (although the statistical significance of failure rate comparisons is sensitive to choice of data and controls for interstate comparisons—see Thies and Gerlowski, 1989; Calomiris, 1991a; Alston et al., 1991). All the insurance fund systems collapsed during the 1920s (American Bankers Association, 1933, Federal Deposit Insurance Corporation, 1956). Insured systems also saw greater delays in closing and liquidating insolvent banks, reminiscent of politically motivated delays that have occurred during the current thrift crisis (Calomiris, 1991a).

Comparisons of losses by failed banks, however, leave little doubt that the presence of insurance was associated with greater bank stress. North Dakota, South Dakota, and Nebraska—the three states that had long-lived, free-entry, compulsory deposit insurance, which provided the worst and most prolonged incentives for risk taking—experienced the most drastic losses by far among the state- and national-chartered systems. While several state-chartered systems experienced shocks comparable to those suffered by these three, in no other cases were the asset shortfalls of insolvent banks nearly large enough to threaten the capital of the banking system as a whole (Table 1–10). In contrast, banks in these states showed shortfalls of between 1.5 and 5 times remaining bank equity of state banks. In light of the differences in the failure experiences of insured and branch banking in the 1920s, it is little wonder that four of the eight states that previously had opted for deposit insurance were among those liberalizing their branching restrictions during this period.

The evidence of moral hazard and adverse selection problems in these antebellum and postbellum liability insurance plans provide a fortiori evidence of similar dangers in current federal deposit insurance. The state insurance systems of the 1920s limited interest paid on deposits, typically required ratios of capital to deposits in excess of 10 percent, and were funded by the accumulated contributions of members. By contrast, today's federal insurance does not restrict interest payments to depositors, requires a trivial proportion of capital to deposits, and is supported by the full faith and credit of the federal government. Thus today's financial intermediaries can maintain higher leverage and attract depositors more easily by offering higher rates of return with virtually no risk of default. From this perspective, the unprecedented losses of Texas banks and thrifts in the 1980s should come as no surprise (Horvitz, 1991).

TABLE 1–10
Estimated Asset Shortfalls of Failed Banks Relative to Remaining Bank Equity in "Severe-Failure" States

	National Banks						State-Chartered Banks						All Banks
	Deposits of Suspended Banks ($000) 1921–30[a]	Number of Liquidations Relative to Suspensions[b]	Size Ratio[c]	Rate of Asset Shortfall[d]	Estimated Shortfall[e]	Total Total Bank Equity ($000) June 1930	Deposits of Suspended Banks ($000) 1921–30[a]	Number of Liquidations Relative to Suspensions[b]	Size Ratio[c]	Rate of Asset Shortfall[d]	Estimated Shortfall[e]	Total Bank Equity ($000) June 1930	Ratio of Shortfall to Equity[f]
Arizona	1,256	0.67	0.83	0.50	349	3,815	15,056	0.80	0.06	0.09	65	8,496	0.03
Colorado	11,003	0.94	0.45	0.40	1,862	13,776	12,187	0.95	0.95	0.32	3,520	10,273	0.22
Georgia	16,538	0.84	0.09	0.49	613	39,064	46,318	0.75	0.70	0.56	13,618	39,805	0.18
Idaho	10,601	0.81	0.65	0.53	2,958	4,612	9,185	0.85	0.63	0.51	2,509	4,983	0.57
Iowa	55,984	0.79	0.50	0.31	6,855	35,750	138,995	0.75	0.66	0.46	31,649	74,935	0.35
Minnesota	28,338	0.97	0.59	0.42	6,812	69,387	80,634	0.77	0.47	0.52	15,174	38,417	0.20
Montana	16,287	0.87	0.44	0.66	4,115	9,999	31,361	0.89	0.47	0.48	6,297	9,947	0.52
Nebraska	13,695	0.80	0.94	0.56	5,767	26,083	78,093	0.85	1.04	0.65	44,872	27,760	0.94
North Dakota	17,438	0.84	0.80	0.55	6,445	9,210	45,199	0.92	1.05	0.83	36,240	9,695	2.26
Oklahoma	27,364	0.72	0.70	0.57	7,861	41,251	38,986	0.79	0.28	0.44	3,794	11,493	0.22
South Carolina	12,153	0.92	0.57	0.49	3,123	11,665	50,970	0.91	0.58	0.34	9,147	17,069	0.43
South Dakota	21,109	0.93	0.60	0.49	5,772	9,477	91,619	0.77	1.00	0.76	53,615	10,848	3.07
Wyoming	9,154	0.91	0.45	0.30	1,125	4,819	7,536	0.80	0.48	0.46	1,331	3,844	0.28

[a] Deposits are defined at the time of bank suspension.
[b] The number of bank liquidations relative to suspensions measures the proportion of suspended banks that were liquidated.
[c] The average size of liquidated banks is divided by the average size of suspended banks to produce this ratio.
[d] The rate of asset shortfall equals 1 minus the ratio of the value of liquidated assets to deposit liabilities.
[e] The estimated shortfall is the product of the preceding four columns.
[f] The all-bank ratio of shortfall to equity divides estimated asset shortfall for state and national banks by the equity of surviving banks of both types.

Source: Calomiris (1991a).

FROM HISTORY TO INFORMED POLICY

Notwithstanding political-economic explanations, which I have argued can help to explain bank regulation, the regulatory mistakes of American banking history are remarkable and unique. Is there any hope for undoing the mistakes of the past, which have produced a fragmented, unstable, and inefficient banking system? Can we learn usefully from history?

In principle, the lessons are straightforward: The U.S. should move to an uninsured, interstate branching system with broad powers for banks (for historical perspectives on the advantages of broad powers for banks prior to Glass-Steagall see Osterweis, 1932, Peach, 1941, E. N. White, 1986, and Kaufman and Mote, 1989a, 1989b). In practice there are many obstacles. Change is always less comprehensive than we would wish, and introducing "lessons from history" is more risky than one might expect. The problem in the openness to "learn" from history is the possibility one will learn incorrectly or too selectively. In the history of banking regulation in the United States policymakers have been perhaps too willing to learn from immediate history. Banking regulation has traditionally been forged in the crucible of crisis. Consider the following examples: the rechartering of the Bank of the United States in the aftermath of the War of 1812; the introduction of entirely new chartering forms (including free banking) as a means of rapidly increasing the number of banks in the 1840s; the creation of the National Banking System as a Civil War measure; the enactment of state deposit insurance plans and the Federal Reserve Act on the heels of the Panic of 1907; branching and consolidation reforms during the agricultural distress of the 1920s; and the creation of the FDIC and the separation of investment and commercial banking during the trough of the Great Depression. In each case, policymakers in the United States have seemed incapable or unwilling to look farther back than the last crisis, farther ahead than the next election, or beyond the borders of their own nation or state. In some extreme cases, like the Glass-Steagall Act, one can find little rational basis for Congressional action (E. N. White, 1986, Benston, 1989)

While this "knee-jerk" approach to bank regulation has offered great flexibility in times of need, it also has led to myopic and simplistic applications of the lessons of the past. These reactions often have lasting effects, given that important changes are infrequent. Consider the most important changes wrought in the 1930s. An alternative to deposit insurance as a means to stabilize banking—one that was understood and considered—was a movement toward nationwide branch banking. Why was it rejected? One explanation for the failure to move in that direction was the weakening of support for branching by an influential policymaker (Marriner Eccles, the Chairman of the Federal Reserve System) during the debate over the 1935 Banking Act. Doti and Schweikart (1991, pp. 133–34, 139–40, 171–72) argue that Eccles' change of heart regarding branching was attributable in part to his desire to constrain the growth of the Bank of America, possibly due to Eccles' personal dislike of A. P. Giannini (who would have stood to benefit greatly from the reform) or to Eccles' hope to maximize the influence of the Federal Reserve Board by maintaining a fragmented banking system. In the absence of a strong supporter of branch banking in the Roosevelt Administration, congressional hostility to branch banking faced no significant opposition. Once the crisis had passed, any real opportunity for branching reform had disappeared, as well. Eccles's support at a crucial juncture could have made a difference. The lessons of this episode seem to be that the window of opportunity for policymaking is often brief, and the guiding principles of policymakers during such opportune moments often may have little to do with the optimal allocation of scarce resources.

Not only has the accident of the Great Depression had a lasting regulatory effect through the inertia of policy, it has provided selective "lessons from history" that continue to exert a death grip on the imaginations of academics and policymakers, providing seemingly incontrovertible evidence of the inherent instability of banking and the need for constant government intervention to prevent a "melt-down." A better set of lessons would have been how preventable and unusually bad the Great Depression was, even from the jaundiced perspective of earlier American banking history; and more important, that the fragility of American banking has always been an artifact of a fragmented, inefficient, and uncoordinated unit banking system.

A similar sort of regime-specific tunnel vision continues to preoccupy much of the current literature on economies of scale and scope in banking. It simply does not make sense to reject the efficiency of a nationwide branching system, or the efficacy of relaxing Glass-Steagall (the economies of which could not possibly show themselves in today's regulatory environment) on the basis of failing to find large economies of scale or scope for today's banks because the gains from expanded powers and size may be highly regime-dependant (Litan, 1987, pp. 110–11, Brewer, 1989a, 1989b, Kaufman and Mote, 1989a, 1989b, Brewer and Mondshean, 1991). Here our own history and the experiences of other countries are a much better guide to the advantages of deregulation.

Which Lessons, Which Cures?

If reform is to be more modest, successful advocates must be selective in the enthusiasm with which they advocate particular reforms. Before suggesting a cure, or a triage ordering—even one informed by history—it helps to know which disease is likely to kill the patient first. There is much that is wrong with U.S. banking today, and there are many competing priority lists for which things to "fix" first. Which historical episodes are most relevant for the current declines and high failure rates of banks? Have banks taken on too much risk in the face of the perverse incentives of deposit insurance, as in the agricultural boom of the 1910s? If so, then a reform of bank capital regulations or a move to "narrow banking" might be sufficient to reverse the trend (for a discussion of the relative merits of these views, see Calomiris, 1991d, 1991e). In contrast, simply allowing bank consolidation or branching as a means to stability, without reforming deposit insurance, may be highly inappropriate in the current context, and may lead to even greater losses. As Boyd and Graham (1991) point out, in today's economy large banks do not seem less likely to fail, possibly because the incentives to take on risk (due to the mispricing of deposit insurance) are largest for these banks. Calomiris (1991d) suggests a means for simultaneously reforming (partly privatizing) deposit insurance and expanding bank branching and other bank powers while avoiding the potential problems of moral hazard due to mispriced deposit insurance.

But there may be bigger problems to address than insurance reform. While there is an accumulating body of evidence that deposit insurance has increased the risk taking and losses from failure of savings and loans (Barth, et al., 1989, Brewer, 1989b), there is little evidence of this as a cause of the current distress of commercial banks, with the significant exception of Texas (Horvitz, 1991) and possibly some large, low-capital, "too-big-to-fail" banks in the East.

Gorton and Rosen (1991) propose a different explanation for bank distress, which sees banks as a declining industry with entrenched management. Declining lending opportunities, a captive deposit base, and bank managements' unwillingness to shrink, according to their view, have reduced the portfolio quality of commercial banks. In the absence of a means for banks to be acquired more readily (thus disciplining managers) banks will continue to operate inefficiently and fail. The closest historical parallel to this case is banking in the 1880s and 1890s. Lamoreaux's (1991a, 1991b) discussion of the entrenchment of some New England bank managements in the 1890s and their resistance to profitable consolidation is informative. By limiting branching and consolidation in the 1890s and by allowing expansion through lowered capital requirements, bank regulation set the stage for the increased fragmentation and subsequent collapse of the next four decades.

Another pitfall from historical learning in bank regulation is the selective application of lessons, which can be counterproductive. For example, the current trend in bank consolidation is to allow within-state, rather than interstate mergers. In some states (notably California) this may reduce the number of competitors so much that the system becomes monopolistic. Aside from the inefficiency of creating monopoly, such a development would tend to reinforce the unfortunate incorrect association between large scale banking and bank monopolization that has plagued U.S. regulatory history for 200 years. If Bresnahan and Reiss's (1991) findings regarding competition in local retail service markets is applicable to banks, somewhere between 3 and 5 competitors in any local market is adequate for competition. Indeed, Shaffer (1991) applies a similar method to measure the extent of market power in the current highly concentrated Canadian branch banking system and strongly rejects its existence. Thus the concentration ratios for some statewide-branching systems as of 1979, reported in L. J. White (1986, p. 187), probably did not pose a great problem for competition. Within-state mergers with a prohibition on entry by out-of-state banks, however, now threaten to restrict the field in some states to one or two major banks or bank holding companies, and this is worrisome.

A final caveat to applying the lessons of the past is the mutability of the economic environment. For example, Gorton and Pennacchi (1991) suggest that the technology of banking has changed significantly in the last decade and that securitization of loans and loan sales indicate a reduction in the asymmetric information problem that gives rise to banking panics (which has motivated deposit insurance, or alternatively, bank consolidation and branching). To the extent that banks increasingly can diversify risk ex ante through loan sales and securitization, the historical problems of fragility and inefficient capital allocation associated with fragmentation in banking are reduced.

This reduction does not mean that restrictions on the industrial organization of intermediaries have become irrelevant. So long as there are some links between bank loan portfolios and bank customer bases, entry restrictions will continue to be important impediments to diversification. Despite the important growth of loan sales without recourse, I remain skeptical that loans of many small and medium scale industrial and commercial borrowers of commercial banks, and even those of some larger firms, can be sold without recourse to passive investors. For example, the recent empirical findings of Lummer and McConnell (1989), Gilson, John, and Lang (1990), and Brown, James, and Mooradian (1991) all point to a continuing role for financial intermediaries to manage renegotiations of debt in distress states (rather than simply to screen borrowers initially). In particular, bank recontracting of debt can provide signals to other debtholders as to whether they should force liquidation of the firm or accept a particular form of renegotiation. What is not clear from any of these studies is whether the benefits of bank control over recontracting might depend, at least for some firms, on bank ownership of loans. For some firms an impediment to loan sales may be the problem of delegating recontracting decisions to relatively informed bank agents who do not themselves own the loans. If this were the case, then for some firms and their banks it would be beneficial to allow bank diversification directly through new products and locations.

REFERENCES

Aharony, Joseph, and Itzhak Swary (1983). "Contagion Effects of Bank Failures: Evidence from the Capital Markets." *Journal of Business 56* (July), 305–22.

Alston, Lee, et al. (1991). "Why Do Banks Fail? Evidence from the 1920s." University of Illinois—Urbana working paper.

American Bankers Association (1933). *The Guaranty of Bank Deposits. New York: The Association.*

American Bankers Association (1935). *The Bank Chartering History of the United States. New York: The Association.*

Asquith, Paul, and David W. Mullins, Jr. (1986). "Equity Issues and Offering Dilution." *Journal of Financial Economics 15* (January/February), 61–89.

Baer, Herbert L., and Larry R. Mote (1991). "The United States Financial System." Federal Reserve Bank of Chicago working paper.

Bagehot, Walter (1873). *Lombard Street: A Description of the Money Market.* New York: Scribner, Armstrong.

Bankers Encyclopedia Co. *The Bankers Encylcopedia.* New York, semiannual.

Barth, James R., Philip F. Bartholomew, and Carol J. Labich (1989). "Moral Hazard and the Thrift Crisis: An Analysis of 1988 Resolutions." Federal Home Loan Bank Board Research Paper No. 160.

Benston, George J. (1989). *The Separation of Commercial and Investment Banking: The Glass-Steagall Act Revisited and Reconsidered.* Norwell: Kluwer Academic.

Benveniste, Lawrence M., and Paul A. Spindt (1989). "Bringing New Issues to Market: A Theory of Underwriting." Federal Reserve Board Finance and Economics Discussion Paper No. 39.

Bernanke, Ben S. (1983). "Nonmonetary Effects of the Financial Crisis in the Propagation of the Great Depression." *American Economic Review 73* (June), 257–76.

Bernanke, Ben S., and Mark L. Gertler (1990). "Financial Fragility and Economic Performance." *Quarterly Journal of Economics 105* (February), 87–114.

Bernanke, Ben S., and Harold James (1991). "The Gold Standard, Deflation, and Financial Crisis in the Great Depression: An International Comparison." In R. Glenn Hubbard (ed.), *Financial Markets and Financial Crises.* Chicago: University of Chicago Press, pp. 33–68.

Binder, John J., and Anthony T. Brown (1991). "Bank Rates of Return and Entry Restrictions, 1869–1914." *Journal of Economic History 51* (March), 47–66.

Board of Governors of the Federal Reserve System (1929). "Branch Banking Developments, June 30 1928." *Federal Reserve Bulletin* (February), 97–105.

Board of Governors of the Federal Reserve System (1959). *All Bank Statistics.* Washington, D.C.: Board of Governors.

Board of Governors of the Federal Reserve System (1976). *Banking and Monetary Statistics,* 1914–1941. Washington, D.C.: Board of Governors.

Bodenhorn, Howard N. (1990). "Banking and the Integration of Antebellum American Financial Markets, 1815-1859." Rutgers University Ph.D. dissertation.

Bogue, Allan G. (1955). *Money at Interest: The Farm Mortgage on the Middle Border.* Lincoln: University of Nebraska Press.

Bordo, Michael D. (1985). "The Impact and International Transmission of Financial Crises: Some Historical Evidence, 1870-1933." *Revista di Storia Economica 2*, 41–78.

Bordo, Michael D., and Angela Redish (1987). "Why Did the Bank of Canada Emerge in 1935?" *Journal of Economic History 47* (June), 405–18.

Boyd, John H., and Stanley L. Graham (1986). "Risk, Regulation, and Bank Holding Company Expansion into Nonbanking." *Federal Reserve Bank of Minneapolis Quarterly Review 10* (Spring), 2-17.

Boyd, John H., and Stanley L. Graham (1988). "The Profitability and Risk Effects of Allowing Bank Holding Companies to Merge with Other Financial Firms: A Simulation Study." In *The Financial Services Industry in the Year 2000: Risk and Efficiency, Proceedings of a Conference on Bank Structure and Competition*, pp. 476–514.

Boyd, John H., and Stanley L. Graham (1991). "Investigating the Banking Consolidation Trend." *Federal Reserve Bank of Minneapolis Quarterly Review 15* (Spring), 3–15.

Boyd, John H., Stanley L. Graham, and R. Shawn Hewitt (1988). "Bank Holding

Company Mergers with Nonbank Financial Firms: Their Effects on the Risk of Failure." Federal Reserve Bank of Minneapolis Working Paper No. 417.

Boyd, John H., and Edward C. Prescott (1986). "Financial Intermediary-Coalitions." *Journal of Economic Theory 38*, 211–32.

Bradford, Frederick A. (1940). *The Legal Status of Branching in the United States.* New York: American Bankers Association.

Bradstreet's. New York.

Brandeis, Louis D. (1914). *Other People's Money and How the Bankers Use It.* New York: Frederick A. Stokes.

Breckenridge, Roeliff M. (1899a). "Bank Notes and Branch Banks." *Sound Currency 6* (April), 49–56.

Breckenridge, Roeliff M. (1899b). "Branch Banking and Discount Rates." *Sound Currency 6* (January), 1–14.

Breckenridge, Roeliff M. (1910). *The History of Banking in Canada.* National Monetary Commission. 61st Congress, 2nd Session. Senate Document 332. Washington, D.C.: U.S. Government Printing Office.

Bremer, C. D. (1935). *American Bank Failures.* New York: Columbia University Press.

Bresnehan, Timothy F., and Peter C. Reiss (1991). "Entry and Competition in Concentrated Markets." *Journal of Political Economy 99* (October), 977–1009.

Brewer, Elijah (1989a). "Relationship between Bank Holding Company Risk and Nonbank Activity." *Journal of Economics and Business 41*, 337–53.

Brewer, Elijah (1989b). "The Impact of Deposit Insurance on S&L Shareholders' Risk/Return Trade-offs." Federal Reserve Bank of Chicago working paper.

Brewer, Elijah, and Thomas H. Mondschean (1991). "An Empirical Test of the Incentive Effects of Deposit Insurance: The Case of Junk Bonds at Savings and Loan Associations." Federal Reserve Bank of Chicago Working Paper WP-91-18.

Brewer, Elijah, Diana Fortier, and Christine Pavel (1988). "Bank Risk from Nonbank Activities." Federal Reserve Bank of Chicago Economic Perspectives (July/August), 14–26.

Brock, Leslie (1975). *The Currency of the American Colonies, 1700-1764: A Study of Colonial Finance and Imperial Relations.* New York.

Brown, David T., Christopher James, and Robert M. Mooradian (1991). "The Information Content of Exchange Offers Made by Distressed Firms." University of Florida working paper.

Bryan, Alfred C. (1899). "History of State Banking in Maryland." *Johns Hopkins University Studies in Historical and Political Science* (January), 1–144.

Bullock, Charles J. (1895). "The Finances of the United States from 1775 to 1789, with Especial Reference to the Budget." *Bulletin of the University of Wisconsin; Economics, Political Science, and History Series I*, 117–273.

Bullock, Charles J. (1900). *Essays on the Monetary History of the United States.* New York: Macmillan.

Butters, J. Keith, and John Lintner (1945). *Effect of Federal Taxes on Growing Enterprises.* Boston: Harvard University.

Calomiris, Charles W. (1988a). "Institutional Failure, Monetary Scarcity, and the Depreciation of the Continental." *Journal of Economic History 48* (March), 47–68.

Calomiris, Charles W. (1988b). "The Depreciation of the Continental: A Reply." *Journal of Economic History 48* (September), 693–98.

Calomiris, Charles W. (1989). "Deposit Insurance: Lessons from the Record." *Federal Reserve Bank of Chicago Economic Perspectives* (May/June), 10–30.

Calomiris, Charles W. (1990). "Is Deposit Insurance Necessary? A Historical Perspective." *Journal of Economic History 50* (June), 283–95.

Calomiris, Charles W. (1991a). "Do Vulnerable Economies Need Deposit Insurance? Lessons from U.S. Agriculture in the 1920s." In Philip L. Brock (ed.), *If Texas Were Chile: A Primer on Bank Regulation.* Washington, D.C.: The Sequoia Institute.

Calomiris, Charles W. (1991b). "The Motives of U.S. Debt-Management Policy, 1790-1880: Efficient Discrimination and Time Consistency." *Research in Economic History,* forthcoming.

Calomiris, Charles W. (1991c). "Comment on 'Information Problems and Banks' Specialization in Short-Term Commercial Lending: New England in the Nineteenth Century'." In Peter Temin (ed.), *Inside the Business Enterprise: Historical Perspectives on the Use of Information.* Chicago: University of Chicago Press, pp. 195–203.

Calomiris, Charles W. (1991d). "Getting the Incentives Right in the Current Deposit Insurance System: Successes from the Pre-FDIC Era." In James Barth and Dan Brumbaugh (eds.), *Reform of Deposit Insurance and the Regulation of Depository Institutions in the 1990s.*

Calomiris, Charles W. (1991e). "The BIS Capital Standards Proposal: Comment on Benston." In an untitled forthcoming volume, edited by James Barth.

Calomiris, Charles W., and Gary Gorton (1991). "The Origins of Banking Panics: Models, Facts, and Bank Regulation." In R. Glenn Hubbard (ed.), *Financial Markets and Financial Crises.* Chicago: University of Chicago Press, pp. 107–73.

Calomiris, Charles W., and R. Glenn Hubbard (1989). "Price Flexibility, Credit Availability, and Economic Fluctuations: Evidence from the United States, 1894-1909." *Quarterly Journal of Economics 104* (May), 429–52.

Calomiris, Charles W., and R. Glenn Hubbard (1990). "Firm Heterogeneity, Internal Finance, and 'Credit Rationing'." *The Economic Journal 100* (March), 90–104.

Calomiris, Charles W., and R. Glenn Hubbard (1991). "Tax Policy, Internal

Finance, and Investment: Evidence from the Undistributed Profits Tax of 1936-1937." University of Pennsylvania working paper.

Calomiris, Charles W., R. Glenn Hubbard, and James H. Stock (1986). "The Farm Debt Crisis and Public Policy." *Brookings Papers on Economic Activity 2*, 441–79.

Calomiris, Charles W., and Charles M. Kahn (1990). "The Efficiency of Cooperative Interbank Relations: The Suffolk System." University of Pennsylvania working paper.

Calomiris, Charles W., and Charles M. Kahn (1991). "The Role of Demandable Debt in Structuring Optimal Banking Arrangements." *American Economic Review 81* (June), 497–513.

Calomiris, Charles W., Charles M. Kahn, and Stefan Krasa (1991). "Optimal Contingent Bank Liquidation Under Moral Hazard." Federal Reserve Bank of Chicago Working Paper WP-91-13.

Calomiris, Charles W., and Larry Schweikart (1988). "Was the South Backward? North-South Differences in Antebellum Banking." University of Pennsylvania working paper.

Calomiris, Charles W., and Larry Schweikart (1991). "The Panic of 1857: Origins, Transmission, and Containment." *Journal of Economic History 51* (December), forthcoming.

Campbell, Tim, and William Kracaw (1980). "Information Production, Market Signalling and the Theory of Financial Intermediation." *Journal of Finance 35* (September), 863–81.

Cannon, James G. (1910). *Clearing Houses*. National Monetary Commission. 61st Congress, 2nd Session. Senate Document 491. Washington, D.C.: U.S. Government Printing Office.

Capie, Forrest, and Alan Webber (1985). *A Monetary History of the United Kingdom, 1870–1982, Volume I*. London: George Allen and Unwin.

Carosso, Vincent P. (1970). *Investment Banking in America*. Cambridge: Harvard University Press.

Cartinhour, Gaines T. (1931). *Branch, Group and Chain Banking*. New York: Macmillan.

Champ, Bruce, Bruce D. Smith, and Stephen D. Williamson (1991). "Currency Elasticity and Banking Panics: Theory and Evidence." Cornell University CAE Working Paper No. 91-14.

Chandler, Alfred D. (1977). *The Visible Hand: The Managerial Revolution in American Business*. Cambridge: Harvard University Press.

Chapman, John M. (1934). *Concentration of Banking: The Changing Structure and Control of Banking in the United States*. New York: Columbia University Press.

Chapman, John M. and Ray B. Westerfield (1942). *Branch Banking: Its Historical and Theoretical Position in America and Abroad*. New York: Harper and

Brothers.

Chari, V. V. (1989). "Banking Without Deposit Insurance or Bank Panics: Lessons from a Model of the U.S. National Banking System." *Federal Reserve Bank of Minneapolis Quarterly Review* (Summer), 3-19.

Davis, Andrew M. (1900). *Currency and Banking in the Province of the Massachusetts Bay.* New York: Macmillan.

Davis, Andrew M. (1911). *Colonial Currency Reprints. Boston.* Reprinted in New York by Augustus Kelley, 1970.

Davis, Lance E. (1965). "The Investment Market, 1870-1914: The Evolution of a National Market." *Journal of Economic History 25* (September), 355–93.

De Long, J. Bradford (1991). "Did J. P. Morgan's Men Add Value? An Economist's Perspective on Financial Capitalism." Harvard University working paper.

Dewey, Davis R. (1910). *State Banking Before the Civil War.* National Monetary Commission. 61st Congress, 2nd Session. Senate Document 581. Washington, D.C.: U.S. Government Printing Office.

Diamond, Douglas (1984). "Financial Intermediation and Delegated Monitoring." *Review of Economic Studies 51* (July), 393–414.

Dornbusch, Rudiger, and Jacob A. Frenkel (1984). "The Gold Standard and the Bank of England in the Crisis of 1847." In Michael D. Bordo and Anna J. Schwartz (eds.), *A Retrospective on the Classical Gold Standard, 1821-1931.* Chicago: University of Chicago Press, pp. 233–64.

Doti, Lynne P., and Larry Schweikart (1991). *Banking in the American West: From the Gold Rush to Deregulation.* Norman: University of Oklahoma Press.

Duncombe, Charles (1841). *Duncombe's Free Banking.* Cleveland: Sanford and Co.

Dutton, John (1984). "The Bank of England and the Rules of the Game under the International Gold Standard: New Evidence." In Michael D. Bordo and Anna J. Schwartz (eds.), *A Retrospective on the Classical Gold Standard.* Chicago: University of Chicago Press, pp. 173–95.

Eichengreen, Barry (1984a). "Currency and Credit in the Gilded Age." *Research in Economic History 3* (supplement), 87–114.

Eichengreen, Barry (1984b). "Mortgage Interest Rates in the Populist Era." *American Economic Review 74* (December), 995–1015.

Eichengreen, Barry (1992). *Golden Fetters: The Gold Standard and the Great Depression, 1919-1939.* Oxford: Oxford University Press.

Ernst, Joseph (1973). *Money and Politics in America, 1755–1775.* Chapel Hill: University of North Carolina Press.

Evanoff, Douglas D. (1988). "Branch Banking and Service Accessibility." *Journal of Money, Credit and Banking 20* (May), 191–202.

Fama, Eugene F. (1980). "Banking in the Theory of Finance." *Journal of Monetary Economics 6* (January), 39–58.

Federal Deposit Insurance Corporation (1956). *Annual Report.* Washington, D.C.

Fenstermaker, J. Van (1965). *The Development of American Commercial Banking, 1782–1837.* Kent, Ohio: Kent State University.

Fisher, Irving (1933). "The Debt-Deflation Theory of Great Depressions." *Econometrica 1*, 337–57.

Fishlow, Albert (1965). *American Railroads and the Transformation of the Ante-Bellum Economy.* Cambridge: Harvard University Press.

Foulke, Roy A. (1941). *The Sinews of American Commerce.* New York: Dun and Bradstreet.

Franklin, Benjamin (1729). "A Modest Inquiry into the Nature and Necessity of a Paper Currency." In Jared Sparks (ed.), *The Works of Benjamin Franklin, II*, p. 1840.

Friedman, Milton, and Anna J. Schwartz (1963). *A Monetary History of the United States, 1867–1960.* Princeton: Princeton University Press.

Gage, Lyman J. (1906). "Currency Reform a Necessity." *Moody's Magazine*, 457–67.

Gale, Douglas, and Martin Hellwig (1985). "Incentive-Compatible Debt Contracts: The One-Period Problem." *Review of Economic Studies* (October), 647–63.

Gendreau, Brian (1990). "Federal Reserve Policy and the Great Depression." University of Pennsylvania working paper.

Gillett, A.D.S. (1900). "Better Credit Facilities for our Rural Communities." *Sound Currency 7*, 183–208.

Gilson, Stuart C., Kose John, and Larry H. P. Lang (1990). "Troubled Debt Restructurings." *Journal of Financial Economics 27*, 315–53.

Golembe, Carter H. (1960). "The Deposit Insurance Legislation of 1933: An Examination of Its Antecedants and Its Purposes." *Political Science Quarterly* (June), 189–95.

Golembe, Carter H. and Clark S. Warburton (1958). *Insurance of Bank Obligations in Six States During the Period 1829–1866.* Washington, D.C.: Federal Deposit Insurance Corporation.

Gorton, Gary (1985). "Clearing Houses and the Origin of Central Banking in the U.S." *Journal of Economic History 45* (June), 277–83.

Gorton, Gary (1989). "Self-Regulating Bank Coalitions." University of Pennsylvania working paper.

Gorton, Gary (1990). "Free Banking, Wildcat Banking, and the Market for Bank Notes." University of Pennsylvania working paper.

Gorton, Gary, and Donald Mullineaux (1987). "The Joint Production of Confidence: Endogenous Regulation and Nineteenth-Century Commercial Bank Clearinghouses." *Journal of Money, Credit and Banking 19* (November), 458–68.

Gorton, Gary, and George Pennacchi (1991). "Banks and Loan Sales: Marketing Non-Marketable Assets." NBER Working paper No. 3551.

Gorton, Gary, and Richard Rosen (1991). "Overcapacity and Exit from Banking."

University of Pennsylvania working paper.

Govan, Thomas (1936). "The Banking and Credit System in Georgia." Vanderbilt University Ph.D. dissertation.

Grammatikos, Theoharry, and Anthony Saunders (1990). "Additions to Bank Loan-Loss Reserves: Good News or Bad News?" *Journal of Monetary Economics 25* (March), 289–304.

Greef, Albert O. (1938). *The Commercial Paper House in the United States.* Cambridge: Harvard University Press.

Hamilton, James (1987). "Monetary Factors in the Great Depression." *Journal of Monetary Economics 19* (March), 145–69.

Hammond, Bray (1957). *Banks and Politics in America from the Revolution to the Civil War.* Princeton: Princeton University Press.

Handlin, Oscar, and Mary F. Handlin (1947). *Commonwealth: A Study of the Role of Government in the American Economy, Massachusetts, 1774–1861.* New York: New York University Press.

Hartz, Louis (1948). *Economic Policy and Democratic Thought: Pennsylvania, 1776–1860.* Cambridge: Harvard University Press.

Haubrich, Joseph G. (1990). "Nonmonetary Effects of Financial Crises: Lessons from the Great Depression in Canada." *Journal of Monetary Economics 25* (March), 223–52.

Horvitz, Paul M. (1991). "The Causes of Texas Bank and Thrift Failures." In Philip L. Brock (ed.), *If Texas Were Chile: A Primer on Bank Regulation.* Washington, D.C.: The Sequoia Institute.

Horwitz, Morton J. (1971). "The Emergence of an Instrumental Conception of American Law, 1780–1820." *Perspectives in American History 5*, 285–326.

Horwitz, Morton J. (1977). *The Transformation of American Law, 1780–1860.* Cambridge: Harvard University Press.

Horwitz, Morton J. (1985). "Santa Clara Revisited: The Development of Corporate Theory." *West Virginia Law Review 88*, 173–224.

Hoshi, Takeo, Anil Kashyap, and David Scharfstein (1990a). "Bank Monitoring and Investment: Evidence from the Changing Structure of Japanese Corporate Banking Relationships." In R. Glenn Hubbard (ed.), *Asymmetric Information, Corporate Finance, and Investment.* Chicago: University of Chicago Press. pp. 105–26.

Hoshi, Takeo, Anil Kashyap, and David Scharfstein (1990b). "The Role of Banks in Reducing the Costs of Financial Distress." *Journal of Financial Economics 27* (September), 67–88.

Hoshi, Takeo, Anil Kashyap, and David Scharfstein (1991). "Corporate Structure, Liquidity, and Investment: Evidence from Japanese Industrial Groups." *Quarterly Journal of Economics 106* (February), 33–60.

Hughes, Jonathan R. T. (1960). *Fluctuations in Trade, Industry, and Finance: A Study of British Economic Development, 1850–1860.* Oxford: Oxford University Press.

Hughes, Jonathan R. T. (1976). *Social Control in the Colonial Economy.* Charlottesville: University of Virginia Press.

Hughes, Jonathan R. T. (1984). "Comment on 'The Gold Standard and the Bank of England in the Crisis of 1847.'" In Michael D. Bordo and Anna J. Schwartz (eds.), *A Retrospective on the Classical Gold Standard, 1821–1931.* Chicago: University of Chicago Press, pp. 265–71.

Hughes, Jonathan R. T. (1991). *The Governmental Habit Redux.* Princeton: Princeton University Press.

Hunt's Merchants' Magazine. New York: G. W. and J. A. Wood.

Hurst, James W. (1970). *The Legitimacy of the Business Corporation.* Charlottesville: University of Virginia Press.

Hurst, James W. (1973). *A Legal History of Money in the United States, 1774–1970.* Lincoln: University of Nebraska Press.

James, Christopher (1987). "Some Evidence on the Uniqueness of Bank Loans." *Journal of Financial Economics 19*, 217–35.

James, Christopher, and Peggy Wier (1989). "Are Bank Loans Different? Some Evidence from the Stock Market." *Journal of Applied Corporate Finance*, 46–54.

James, Christopher, and Peggy Wier (1990). "Borrowing Relationships, Intermediation, and the Cost of Issuing Public Securities." *Journal of Financial Economics 28* (November/December), 149–72.

James, John A. (1976a). "The Development of the National Money Market, 1893-1911." *Journal of Economic History 36* (December), 878–97.

James, John A. (1976b). "Banking Market Structure, Risk, and the Pattern of Local Interest Rates in the United States, 1893–1911." *Review of Economics and Statistics 58* (November), 453–62.

James, John A. (1978). *Money and Capital Markets in Postbellum America.* Princeton: Princeton University Press.

James, Marquis, and Bessie R. James (1954). *Biography of a Bank: The Story of Bank of America.* New York: Harper and Brothers.

Jauncey, L. C. (1933). *Australia's Government Bank.* London: Cranley and Day.

Johnson, Joseph F. (1910). *The Canadian Banking System.* National Monetary Commission. 61st Congress, 2nd Session. Senate Document 583. Washington, D.C.: U.S. Government Printing Office.

Kaufman, George G., and Larry Mote (1989a). "Glass–Steagall: Repeal by Regulatory and Judicial Reinterpretation." Federal Reserve Bank of Chicago working paper.

Kaufman, George G., and Larry Mote (1989b). "Securities Activities of Commercial Banks: The Current Economic and Legal Environment." Federal Reserve Bank of Chicago working paper.

Kindleberger, Charles P. (1984). *A Financial History of Western Europe.* London:

George Allen and Unwin.

Klebaner, Benjamin J. (1990). *American Commercial Banking: A History*. Boston: Twayne Publishers.

Knox, John J. (1900). *A History of Banking in the United States*. New York: Bradford Rhodes.

Korajczyk, Robert A., Deborah Lucas, and Robert L. McDonald (1990). "Understanding Stock Price Behavior Around the Time of Equity Issues." In R. Glenn Hubbard (ed.), *Asymmetric Information, Corporate Finance, and Investment*. Chicago: University of Chicago Press, pp. 257–78.

Kryzanowski, Lawrence, and Gordon S. Roberts (1989). "The Performance of the Canadian Banking System, 1920-1940." In *Banking System Risk: Charting a New Course, Proceedings of the 25th Annual Conference on Bank Structure and Competition*. Chicago: Federal Reserve Bank of Chicago.

Laderman, Elizabeth S., Ronald H. Schmidt, and Gary C. Zimmerman (1991). "Location, Branching, and Bank Portfolio Diversification: The Case of Agricultural Lending." *Federal Reserve Bank of San Francisco Economic Review* (Winter), 24–37.

Lamoreaux, Naomi R. (1991a). "Information Problems and Banks' Specialization in Short-Term Commercial Lending: New England in the Nineteenth Century." In Peter Temin (ed.), *Inside the Business Enterprise: Historical Perspectives on the Use of Information*. Chicago: University of Chicago Press, pp. 154–95.

Lamoreaux, Naomi R. (1991b). "Bank Mergers in Late Nineteenth-Century New England: The Contingent Nature of Structural Change." *Journal of Economic History 51* (September), 537–58.

Lamy, Robert, and G. Rodney Thompson (1986). "Penn Square, Problem Loans, and Insolvency Risk." *Journal of Financial Research 9* (Summer), 167–83.

Leland, Hayne, and David Pyle (1977). "Informational Asymmetries, Financial Structure, and Financial Intermediation." *Journal of Finance 32* (May), 371–87.

Lester, Richard A. (1939). *Monetary Experiments: Early American and Recent Scandinavian*. Princeton: Princeton University Press.

Litan, Robert E. (1985). "Evaluating and Controlling the Risks of Financial Product Deregulation." *Yale Journal on Regulation 3* (Fall), 1–52.

Litan, Robert E. (1987). *What Should Banks Do?* Washington, D.C.: The Brookings Institution.

Lummer, Scott L., and John J. McConnell (1989). "Further Evidence on the Bank Lending Process and the Capital-Market Response to Bank Loan Agreements." *Journal of Financial Economics 25* (January), 99–122.

Martin, David (1974). "Metallism, Small Notes, and Jackson's War with the B.U.S." *Explorations in Economic History 11* (Spring), 227–47.

McCusker, John J. (1978). *Money and Exchange in Europe and America, 1600–*

1775: A Handbook. Chapel Hill: University of North Carolina Press.

Meinster, David R., and Rodney D. Johnson (1979). "Bank Holding Company Diversification and the Risk of Capital Impairment." *Bell Journal of Economics 10* (Autumn), 683–94.

Mengle, David L. (1990). "The Case for Interstate Branch Banking." *Federal Reserve Bank of Richmond Economic Review 76* (November/December), 3–17.

Michener, Ronald (1987). "Fixed Exchange Rates and the Quantity Theory In Colonial America." *Carnegie-Rochester Conference Series on Public Policy 27* (Autumn), 233–308.

Michener, Ronald (1988). "Backing Theories and the Currencies of Eighteenth-Century America: A Comment." *Journal of Economic History 48* (September), 682–92.

Miron, Jeffrey A. (1986). "Financial Panics, the Seasonality of the Nominal Interest Rate, and the Founding of the Fed." *American Economic Review 76* (March), 125–40.

Moen, Jon, and Ellis W. Tallman (1991). "The Bank Panic of 1907: The Role of Trust Companies." Federal Reserve Bank of Atlanta working paper.

Mullineaux, Donald J. (1987). "Competitive Moneys and the Suffolk Bank System: A Contractual Perspective." *Southern Economic Journal* (April), 884–97.

Munn, Charles W. (1981). *The Scottish Provincial Banking Companies, 1747–1864.* Edinburgh: John Donald.

Musumeci, James, and Joseph Sinkey (1988). "The International Debt Crisis and the Signalling Content of Bank Loan-Loss-Reserve Decisions." University of Georgia working paper.

Myers, Margaret G. (1931). *The New York Money Market: Origins and Development.* New York: Columbia University Press.

Myers, Stewart, and Nicholas Majluf (1984). "Corporate Financing and Investment Decisions When Firms Have Information That Investors Do Not Have." *Journal of Financial Economics 13*, 187–221.

Nettles, Curtis P. (1934). *The Money Supply of the American Colonies Before 1720.* Madison: University of Wisconsin Press.

Neuberger, Hugh, and Houston H. Stokes (1974). "German Banks and German Growth, 1883-1913: An Empirical View." *Journal of Economic History 34* (September), 710–32.

Osterweis, Steven L. (1932). "Security Affiliates and Security Operations of Commercial Banks." *Harvard Business Review 11* (October), 124–31.

Peach, W. N. (1941). *The Security Affiliates of National Banks.* Baltimore: Johns Hopkins Press.

Pippenger, John (1984). "Bank of England Operations, 1893–1913." In Michael D. Bordo and Anna J. Schwartz (eds.), *A Retrospective on the Classical Gold Standard, 1821–1931.* Chicago: University of Chicago Press, pp. 203–27.

Pope, David (1989). "Free Banking in Australia Before World War I." Australian National University working paper.

Pozdena, Randall J. (1991). "Is Banking Really Prone to Panics?" *Federal Reserve Bank of San Francisco Weekly Letter 91-35* (October 11).

Ransom, Roger L., and Richard Sutch (1977). *One Kind of Freedom: The Economic Consequences of Emancipation.* Cambridge: Cambridge University Press.

Redlich, Fritz (1951). *The Molding of American Banking: Men and Ideas.* New York: Hafner Publishing.

Riefler, Winfield W. (1930). *Money Rates and Money Markets in the United States.* New York: Harper and Brothers.

Riesser, Jacob (1911). *The Great German Banks and Their Concentration, in Connection with the Economic Development of Germany.* Translation of third edition. Washington, D.C.: United States Government Printing Office.

Robb, Thomas B. (1921). *The Guaranty of Bank Deposits.* Boston: Houghton Mifflin.

Rockoff, Hugh (1972). "The Free Banking Era: A Re-Examination." University of Chicago Ph.D. dissertation.

Root, L. Carroll (1897). "Canadian Bank-Note Currency." *Sound Currency 4* (May), 1–16.

Root, L. Carroll (1901). "Twenty Years of Bank Currency Based on General Commercial Assets." *Sound Currency 8* (December), 209–32.

Schembri, Lawrence L., and Jennifer A. Hawkins (1988). "The Role of Canadian Chartered Banks in U.S. Banking Crises: 1870-1914." Carleton University working paper.

Schultz, William J. (1949). *Credit and Collection Management.* New York: Prentice Hall.

Schweikart, Larry (1988a). *Banking in the American South from the Age of Jackson to Reconstruction.* Baton Rouge: Louisiana State University Press.

Schweikart, Larry (1988b). "Jacksonian Ideology, Currency Control and Central Banking: A Reappraisal." *The Historian* (November), 78–102.

Schweitzer, Mary M. (1989). "State-Issued Currency and the Ratification of the U.S. Constitution." *Journal of Economic History 49* (June), 311–22.

Schweitzer, Robert (1989). "How Do Stock Returns React to Special Events?" *Federal Reserve Bank of Philadelphia Business Review* (July/August), 17–29.

Sheard, Paul (1989). "The Main Bank System and Corporate Monitoring and Control in Japan." *Journal of Economic Behavior and Organization 11*, 399–422.

Sklar, Martin J. (1988). *The Corporate Reconstruction of American Capitalism, 1890–1916: The Market, the Law, and Politics.* Cambridge: Cambridge University Press.

Smith, Bruce D. (1985a). "Some Colonial Evidence on Two Theories of Money: Maryland and the Carolinas." *Journal of Political Economy 93* (December),

1178–1211.

Smith, Bruce D. (1985b). "American Colonial Monetary Regimes: The Failure of the Quantity Theory of Money and Some Evidence in Favor of an Alternate View." *Canadian Journal of Economics 18* (August), 531–65.

Smith, Hilary H. (1987). "Agricultural Lending: Bank Closures and Branch Banking." *Federal Reserve Bank of Dallas Economic Review* (September), 27–38.

Snowden, Kenneth A. (1987). "Mortgage Rates and American Capital Market Development in the Late Nineteenth Century." *Journal of Economic History 47* (September), 671–91.

Steiner, William H. (1922). *The Mechanism of Commercial Credit: Terms of Sale and Trade Acceptances.* New York: D. Appleton.

Stiglitz, Joseph E., and Andrew Weiss (1981). "Credit Rationing in Markets with Imperfect Information." *American Economic Review 71* (June), 393–410.

Sumner, William G. (1896). *A History of Banking in the United States.* New York: Journal of Commerce and Commercial Bulletin.

Sushka, Marie E., and W. Brian Barrett (1984). "Banking Structure and the National Capital Market, 1869–1914." *Journal of Economic History 44* (June), 463–77.

Swary, Itzhak (1986). "Stock Market Reaction to Regulatory Action in the Continental Illinois Crisis." *Journal of Business 59* (July), 451–73.

Sylla, Richard (1969). "Federal Policy, Banking Market Structure, and Capital Mobilization in the United States, 1863–1913." *Journal of Economic History 29* (December), 657–86.

Sylla, Richard (1975). *The American Capital Market, 1869–1914.* New York: Arno Press.

Sylla, Richard, John B. Legler, and John J. Wallis (1987). "Banks and State Public Finance in the New Republic: The United States, 1790–1860." *Journal of Economic History 47* (June), 391–404.

Temin, Peter (1969). *The Jacksonian Economy.* New York: W. W. Norton.

Thies, Clifford F., and Daniel A. Gerlowski (1989). "Deposit Insurance: A History of Failure." *Cato Journal 8* (Winter), 677–93.

Tilly, Richard H. (1966). *Financial Institutions and Industrialization in the Rhineland, 1815–1870.* Madison: University of Wisconsin Press.

Treman, R. H. (1919). *Trade Acceptances, What They Are and How They Are Used.* New York: American Acceptance Council.

U.S. Department of Commerce (1975). *Historical Statistics of the United States: Colonial Times to 1970.* Washington, D.C.: U.S. Government Printing Office.

U.S. House of Representatives (1930). *Branch, Chain, and Group Banking.* Hearings Before the Committee on Banking and Currency, 71st Congress, 2nd Session. Washington, D.C.: U.S. Government Printing Office.

Vreeland, Edward B., John W. Weeks, and Robert W. Bonynge (1910). *Interviews on the Banking and Currency Systems of Canada.* National Monetary Commission. 61st Congress, 2nd Session. Senate Document 584. Washington, D.C.: U.S. Government Printing Office.

Wall, Larry D. (1987). "Has Bank Holding Companies Diversification Affected Their Risk of Failure?" *Journal of Economics and Business 39* (November), 313–26.

Wall, Larry D., and David R. Petersen (1990). "The Effect of Continental Illinois' Failure on the Financial Performance of Other Banks." *Journal of Monetary Economics 26* (August), 77–100.

White, Eugene N. (1982). "The Political Economy of Banking Regulation, 1864–1933." *Journal of Economic History 42* (March), 33–40.

White, Eugene N. (1983). *The Regulation and Reform of the American Banking System, 1900–1929.* Princeton: Princeton University Press.

White, Eugene N. (1984a). "A Reinterpretation of the Banking Crisis of 1930." *Journal of Economic History 44* (March), 119–38.

White, Eugene N. (1984b). "Voting for Costly Regulation: Evidence from Banking Referenda in Illinois, 1924." *Southern Economic Journal*, 1084–98.

White, Eugene N. (1985). "The Merger Movement in Banking, 1919–1933." *Journal of Economic History 45* (June), 285–91.

White, Eugene N. (1986). "Before the Glass–Steagall Act: An Analysis of the Investment Banking Activities of National Banks." *Explorations in Economic History 23* (January), 33–55.

White, Horace (1902). "Branch Banking: Its Economies and Advantages." *Sound Currency 9* (June), 51–64.

White, Lawrence H. (1984). *Free Banking in Britain: Theory, Experience, and Debate, 1800–1845.* Cambridge: Cambridge University Press.

White, Lawrence J. (1986). "The Partial Deregulation of Banks and Other Depository Institutions." In Leonard W. Weiss and Michael W. Klass (eds.), *Regulatory Reform: What Actually Happened.* Boston: Little, Brown, pp. 169–209.

Wicker, Elmus (1985). "Colonial Monetary Standards Contrasted: Evidence from the Seven Years' War." *Journal of Economic History 45* (December), 869–84.

Williamson, Stephen D. (1986). "Costly Monitoring, Financial Intermediation, and Equilibrium Credit Rationing." *Journal of Monetary Economics 18* (September), 159–80.

Williamson, Stephen D. (1989). "Bank Failures, Financial Restrictions, and Aggregate Fluctuations: Canada and the United States, 1870–1913." *Federal Reserve Bank of Minneapolis Quarterly Review* (Summer), 20–40.

Willit, Virgil (1930). *Selected Articles on Chain, Group and Branch Banking.* New York: H. W. Wilson.

Withers, Hartley, R. H. Inglis Palgrave, and others (1910). *The English Banking System.* National Monetary Commission. 61st Congress, 2nd Session. Senate Document 492. Washington, D.C.: U.S. Government Printing Office.

Wright, Gavin (1979). "Cheap Labor and Southern Textiles Before 1880." *Journal*

of Economic History 39 (September), 655–80.
Wright, Gavin (1986). *Old South, New South.* New York: Basic Books.

COMMENT

Edward J. Kelly, III

I agree with Professor Calomiris's conclusions about the reasons for the instability in the U.S. banking structure and believe that his paper makes an important contribution to the ongoing debate about bank structural and regulatory reform. I also concur in his view that the best banking system would be one composed of uninsured banks with broad powers authorized to operate freely interstate. Unfortunately, as Professor Calomiris suggests, the unwillingness of policy-makers to look farther back than the last crisis, farther ahead than the next election, or beyond the borders of their own states presents a serious obstacle to achievement of a more rational, stable system.

Professor Calomiris clearly makes a compelling case for focusing on unit banking as a central problem in the U.S. structure. The history of banking in this country is littered with efforts to deal with the flaws and instability inherent in unit banking.

Clearly, unit banking was a major culprit in the wave of bank failures that plagued the country in the 1920s and early 1930s. Thousands of one-town, one-crop banks fell prey to their lack of geographic, portfolio, and product diversification. Unfortunately, as Professor Calomiris points out, policy-makers failed to recognize that this lack of diversification was at the core of the crisis and, instead, identified the rise of investment banking, which itself was a consequence of unit banking, as the culprit. This misperception led to the adoption of Glass-Steagall and other "reforms," which more than 50 years later continue to impede the development of a more rational and stable system.

In my view, the thrift crisis can be seen as another symptom of the inhibitions on geographic and product diversification imposed by U.S. banking law. There are limits inherent in the thrift franchise, which created a vulnerability to failure. But, as they did in the 1930s, policymakers today blame thrift failures on the drive to evade those limits through diversification. Admittedly, some of the efforts by thrift managers to diversify were imprudently conducted, but it is misguided to identify diversification as the cause of thrift failures. The imposition of further limits on thrift product diversification is likely, in fact, to exacerbate thrifts' problems.

Interestingly enough, the issues of geographic and product diversification have become more closely linked in the policy debate today. The insurance agents have been among the most adamant opponents of interstate branching and have demanded severe restrictions on banks' insurance powers as the price of interstate branching.

If unit banking, and more broadly inhibitions on diversification, are so clearly at the root of instability, why are they so difficult to overcome? As Professor Calomiris correctly suggests, the entrenched interests supporting limited banking franchises are hard to root out. Moreover, federalism and the traditional dual banking system in the U.S. contribute to the difficulty of implementing a more rational structure. But I believe the fundamental problem is identified in the following passage from Professor Calomiris's paper:

> From the standpoint of the historical context in which banks were chartered in the United States, restrictions on branching and bank consolidation are less puzzling. In a world where banks are a tool of the state, where their activities are deemed a proper subject for public debate and government control, where it is presumed that their supply should be limited and their income should be shared with the state in compensation for the granting of the privilege of limited liability, it is little wonder that the maximization of depositors' utility was not achieved.

In today's environment, one need only substitute "federal deposit insurance" for "the privilege of limited liability" to establish the continuing validity and applicability of this statement.

The existence of federal deposit insurance has resulted in the continued treatment of banks as public utilities and prevented the banking industry from persuasively arguing, as a political matter, that it should be free to pursue geographic and product diversification. The "benefits" of federal deposit insurance are cited by all opponents of reform as a basis for limiting, rather than expanding, the banking franchise. The securities industry argues that the subsidies implicit in federal deposit insurance justify a bar to bank entry into the securities business or, at a minimum, severe uneconomic restrictions on relationships between insured banks and securities affiliates. The real estate and insurance industries make similar arguments. In a different, but related vein, federal deposit insurance keeps alive those small banks that have been among the most ardent opponents of interstate branching. Although the link between federal deposit insurance and inhibitions on geographic (as opposed to product) diversification may be attenuated enough to permit the forces supporting interstate branching to prevail ultimately, recent experience suggests that this is by no means a foregone conclusion.

In my view, there is a need to address the central issue of federal deposit insurance and, if necessary, sever any link between deposit insurance and product and geographic diversification. Only at that point will banks be liberated from the "public utility" mentality that has prevented substantial progress to date.

There are encouraging signs on this front. In the debate over banking legislation in 1991 proposals emerged that would have given banks the freedom to diversify in exchange for giving up federal deposit insurance. Moreover, there was increased interest in proposals involving genuinely risk-based deposit insurance premiums and private reinsurance of risks assumed by the FDIC. Such proposals provide a market basis for deposit insurance and, to some extent, undermine the argument that deposit insurance is a subsidy that requires severe restrictions on the activities of the recipients.

Of course, there would be risks associated with permitting certain banks to forego insured status in exchange for greater freedom. The regulators, in particular, may be concerned about their ability to regulate such entities and, if necessary, to protect them. This concern highlights the division among separate agencies of the functions of a "central" bank in this country. While the Federal Reserve is the lender of last resort, it has no power to make equity or quasi-equity investments in troubled banks. That role is reserved for the FDIC. To the extent that a bank had no ties to the FDIC and the FDIC were unable to assist such a bank, concerns about the government's inability to intervene quickly in a troubled situation with potential systemic implications are justified.

But the fact is that uninsured banks with broad powers and the authority to operate freely across state borders would be likely to be more stable than their insured counterparts today. Given their uninsured status, such banks would be subject to stringent market discipline and would be likely to face liquidity problems long before they became insolvent. Accordingly, it is unlikely that uninsured banks would deteriorate into the financial "black holes" that are so common in the banking and thrift industries today. Moreover, it is certainly a matter of detail to construct a regulatory structure suitable to ensuring adequate prudential supervision of uninsured banks.

In short, I believe that eliminating the political complications associated with insured status may be the only way for banks to achieve the authority to diversify freely. This may not provide a solution for the industry as a whole, but it could be an important step for certain banks. Ultimately, it could mark out a path for the rest of the industry, and policy-makers, to follow.

COMMENT

Geoffrey P. Miller

Charles W. Calomiris' paper, "Regulation, Industrial Structure, and Instability in U.S. Banking: An Historical Perspective," represents a valuable contribution to the history of American financial institutions. Calomiris focuses specifically on the structural features that have affected the growth and development of the American banking industry over the years. And, although he does not answer all the questions, he at least has made substantial progress. No account of U.S. banking history will be able to ignore Calomiris' impressive contributions.

Although Calomiris focuses on a number of different topics in this paper, his major interest is on the history of branch banking. Drawing on extensive empirical research, Calomiris convincingly argues that banks organized in branch-banking structures have historically tended to be more stable and to experience fewer disruptions from runs and panics than unit banks. This is in itself an important finding, both for the light it sheds on the history of the U.S. banking industry and for its implications as regards the present crisis in American banking.

Although Calomiris does not emphasize the point, it is possible to extend the trajectory of his findings to reach the inference that the recent problems in U.S. banking may have stemmed, in part, from a banking system that was extremely poorly structured, with more than 10,000 banks—approximately 20,000 in the early 1920s—and many thousands of thrift institutions. The banking crisis of the 1980s, like the banking crisis of the 1930s, can plausibly be characterized as fundamentally a structural crisis: The rash of failures between 1986 and 1991, like the rash of failures between 1929 and 1933, may well have represented a form of consolidation in an industry that was notoriously inefficiently structured. It is probably not a coincidence that our sister nations, such as Canada, Japan, and Germany, all of which have a markedly more centralized banking structure, have not experienced anything like our banking catastrophe of the past few years.

Calomiris has presented a thoroughly documented case for the connection between stability in banking and branching, but he has not provided any single clear cut explanation for why this relationship existed. This isn't necessarily a defect in the paper, since branching might have contributed to bank stability in several different ways. It is useful, however, to sort out the different mechanisms posited by Calomiris to explain why branching might be correlated with stability in banking. These include:

1. Banks in branching states were able to achieve better interbank coordination, thus achieving an organized response to financial crises and panics that mitigated the severity of the disruption and facilitated more rapid recovery from the distortions that did occur.
2. Branching systems were able to provide a somewhat more elastic currency, softening interest rate fluctuations and thereby rendering banks in branching states less vulnerable to rapid economic fluctuations.
3. Banks in branching states were able to achieve better asset diversification through participation in geographically diverse credit markets.
4. Banks in branching states were able to grow larger than unit banks. These bigger banks may have been better able to withstand shocks and panics than small ones, even controlling for asset diversification. Calomiris does not speculate at length on the advantage bigger banks may have had in this regard, but surely economies of scale should be considered as one possible explanation, although, as Calomiris is aware, studies have failed to document significant economies of scale and scope in banking under the current regulatory regime.

In addition to these four potential advantages of branching structures recognized by Calomiris—better coordination, asset diversification, lower interest rate volatility, and size—the author might also consider the role of competition. Banks in branching states faced greater competition from other banks than banks in unit banking states. Presumably, the greater competition was likely to induce greater efficiency of operations, which might have provided protection in economic hard times. On the other hand, when competition is present, one would expect to see failures due to competitive forces. Accordingly, the significance of competitive factors is not clear cut, but might be something that would warrant further study.

In the remaining comments I would like to suggest a few areas that might merit further analysis in what is already an outstanding study.

1. Calomiris doesn't treat the effects of correspondent relationships. These were widespread in unit banking states and may have emulated the functions of branch banking to some extent. Data on the specific nature and extent of these correspondent relationships might provide some information as to whether correspondent banking provided a workable alternative to branch banking to any substantial extent.

2. Calomiris mentions the growth of chain and then group banking (bank holding companies) in the early years of the twentieth century, but he could do more with this observation. Like correspondent arrangements, these devices may have operated, to some extent, as quasi-branching structures. Bank holding companies, for example, provide some of the potential advantages of geographic diversification and centralized management that apparently characterized branch banking as opposed to unit banking structures.

3. Calomiris' important paper raises the obvious puzzle of how the United States got into the unit banking business in the first place. Calomiris rightly points to the influence of unit bankers as a potent special interest—aided and abetted, I should add, by their state bank supervisors. True, but this leaves open the questions of why that interest group was allowed to develop in the first place, and why its political force was not trumped by effective opposition from groups favoring liberalized branching. Calomiris speculates on these points by noting the impact of federalism and Supreme Court decisions, but I don't find these speculations persuasive. Supreme Court decisions can be overturned by Congress, and federalism considerations are ambiguous: While the U.S. federal system facilitated the development of in-state interest groups of small bankers who opposed branching, the competition between state and federal regulators for bank charters that characterized much of American banking regulation since the Civil War suggests that one or the other of these regulators might have tried to gain a step on the other—and thereby encourage charter conversions—by liberalizing branching rules, at least before the enactment of the McFadden Act in 1927 that placed national banks in rough parity with their state-chartered cousins as regards branching.[1]

Although Calomiris' explanations of the birth and persistence of unit banking are not entirely persuasive, they are thoughtful and interesting. This is an impressively documented and wide-ranging study, and it is sure to be influential both for future work in banking history and for considerations of regulatory reform options.

NOTES

1. The parity was not perfect in the original legislation of 1927, however, because national banks were not permitted, in the original McFadden Act, to branch their home cities. The Banking Act of 1933 rectified this imbalance by allowing national banks to establish branches outside anywhere within the state where a similarly situated state bank could branch, but even then national banks were not permitted to establish interstate branches. As a practical matter this potential advantage for state-chartered banks has not amounted to much because there has been almost no interstate branching by state-chartered institutions. The absence of interstate branching by such institutions is itself something of a puzzle, since a good argument can be made that another state could not constitutionally prohibit branching into that state by a state-chartered, nonmember bank located in another state. See Miller, "Interstate Branching and the Constitution," *Business Lawyer 41* (1986), p. 337.

COMMENT

Eugene N. White

Professor Charles Calomiris has provided us with a virtuoso survey of American banking history. This is a paper that should be read by every policymaker and economist interested in designing a new banking system. Many currently proposed reforms are based only on our recent disastrous experience and a few well-worn stylized facts of the past. What has been lacking is an interpretative study, which summarizes the large literature on banking history and speaks to our immediate concerns. Calomiris has performed this task and extracted the key lessons for policy.

His fundamental point, with which I wholly concur, is that basic problems of the American banking system arose out of the general prohibition on branch banking. Regulation attempted to find remedies to protect the soundness of thousands of small unit banks, but did not try to alter the industry's structure. The result has been an accumulation of regulation that has deformed the industry. The failure to correct this essential flaw in the system is the source of many of banking's problems. While I agree with Calomiris' general interpretation, my comments focus on his analysis of interregional interest rate differentials and the effectiveness of unit banks as a political interest group. To Calomiris' sweep of banking history, I would add a note on the role of bank examination and supervision.

INTERREGIONAL INTEREST RATES

The fear that has guided policy since the banking crises of the 1930s is that some economic shock could precipitate a panic and a collapse of the banking system, inaugurating a new Great Depression. What has been forgotten is that the panics of the 1930s were different from earlier ones. They were, ironically, the result of the Federal Reserve's inaction. Although it was established to promote stability, the Fed failed to act as a lender of last resort and permitted massive deflationary shocks to precipitate a banking collapse. In contrast, panics before 1914 resulted in comparatively few bank failures because coalitions of banks joined together to suspend convertibility and to increase interbank liquidity. These private market substitutes for a central bank were, however, limited by the central defect of American banking: the almost complete prohibition of branch banking and, consequently, large nationally diversified banks.

The absence of nationwide branching is a distinguishing feature of American banking compared to other countries. The most instructive comparison is to Canada, which has a similar economy but developed a nationwide banking system by the end of the nineteenth century. The relatively small number of Canadian institutions were able to coordinate their efforts in times of crisis and avoid panics—even in the absence of a central bank. While Canada's economic downturn during the Great Depression was no less severe than in the United States, the Canadian banking system's superior industrial structure prevented a financial crisis.

The key to branch banking's strength is diversification. Even with access to the money markets, banks could not diversify adequately because of the special character of bank lending. Calomiris provides extensive historical evidence to show that unit banks were particularly exposed to sectoral shocks because of their concentrated local lending. The thousands of small banks engendered by the state and federal prohibitions on branching were thus prone to failure. Compared to larger branching banks, their failure rates in normal and panic times were higher in both the nineteenth and twentieth centuries.

To back up his argument that unit banks failed to diversify and unify the capital market in the United States, Calomiris points to the behavior of interregional interest rates. He draws on the large literature on the integration of capital markets, which finds large, persistent interest rate differentials across regions in the post-Civil War period. These differentials appeared in commercial paper rates and the estimated rates of return on banks' earning assets (Davis, 1965). Calomiris argues that the failure to equalize interest rates on very similar instruments was the result of a low interregional elasticity of capital flows.

These continuing interest rate differentials may not be so easily explained. If one looks at a graph of the temporal movement in interest rate differentials and moves back in time from World War I to the Civil War, they widen significantly. The eye cannot help but extrapolate backwards—imagining that the differentials must have been wider before the Civil War. The surprise, discovered in recent work by Bodenhorn (1990 and 1991) and Bodenhorn and Rockoff (1992), is that markets before the Civil War were remarkably well integrated from the 1820s onward, measured either by open market rates of interest or rates of return from banks.

What is even more striking about this period is that there were no nationwide branch systems—with the exception of the Second Bank of the United States, which met its demise in 1836. The partial answer for this difference before and after the Civil War is that the war destroyed the physical, financial, and human banking capital in the South. However, this cannot be the complete story, and Calomiris needs to address this apparent paradox. Fortunately, the evidence on market integration does not carry the whole weight of the argument about the defects of unit banking.

POLITICAL INTERESTS

Given the importance of anti-branching regulation for shaping American banking and given the high costs that it imposed, the questions of why it was first adopted and why it endured are of great importance. To explain the difference between antebellum Northern unit and Southern branching systems, Calomiris points to regional economic differences. In the Northeast, banks' lending was concentrated on a small inside group of merchants and industrialists. The access to credit guaranteed by part-ownership led the business class to place a high value on obtaining a bank charter. Thus, each business community wanted its own bank. In the antebellum South, where long-distance finance to move crops was a necessity, branch banking's superior ability to move funds led to a more general adoption of branching systems.

While this story provides some insights, I do not find it particularly compelling. It rests too heavily on theory, and the historical evidence is rather slight. I think that the general adoption of unit banking, at least in the post-Civil War period, was more an historical accident. When the Comptroller of the Currency ruled in 1865 that national banks would henceforth be unit banks, it did not seem very important. The relatively small size of loans obtained by most businesses did not require large banks, and the minimum efficient scale of a bank may have been fairly small.

Once established, however, the unit banks formed a powerful lobby to protect their local monopoly powers from big city banks' competition. Still, it is necessary to explain why the unit banking regime was so durable. Why were rural areas so willing to accept unit banking that raised the cost of credit? Calomiris' explanation is that farmers wanted to keep their local banks for "loan insurance." This may sell the farmers short, and I think the economic theory of regulation can be used to explain unit bankers' success. Like so many other industries that have secured favorable regulation at huge cost to the public, bankers and their customers faced very different costs and benefits from a change in regulations. In a study of an unusual election in Illinois in 1924 on the issue of branching (White, 1985), I estimated a model of voting and found that in the face of a massive propaganda campaign by unit banking and a cleverly-worded referendum, the strongest *opposition* to continued unit banking came not from Chicago but from the underbanked parts of downstate. This is an area where one would expect there to be strong populist anti-bank sentiment or a high demand for "loan insurance."

The power of the unit bankers should, thus, not be underestimated. Garbed in populist rhetoric, their influence has shaped all banking regulation of the last one hundred years. Neither the Federal Reserve nor the FDIC were created in a vacuum. These institutions were designed not only to guarantee the safety of the banking system but also to protect its existing structure.

EXAMINATION AND SUPERVISION

While Calomiris has carefully examined the effects of regulation on banks, he is nearly silent on issues of bank examination and supervision. It is instructive to look at the practice of examination and supervision in the nineteenth century to gain some historical perspective on these activities. Under the national banking system, an examiner's task was to verify that a bank's books were correct and did not involve any shortage concealed by false entries, forced balances, or manipulation of accounts and that the bank complied with the letter of the law.

Thomas P. Kane, one long-time deputy comptroller, felt it important to draw a distinction between an examination and an audit. He wrote:

> Bank examiners, however, are not bank auditors. Unfortunately, the distinction between an examination and an audit is seldom recognized in the criticisms of examiners when banks suffer loses through dishonesty or other causes which have remained concealed for some time, undiscovered by the examiner through several successive examinations. A bank that may be thoroughly examined in one or two days could not be completely audited in less time than one or two weeks. (Kane, 1922, p. 308.)

This same official argued that every bank should receive a thorough audit at least once a year by accountants not connected with the bank and noted that many of the best banks have such audits. These audits helped to deter embezzlers, perhaps more than examinations. He candidly admitted that most failures were the product of accumulated dishonesty, adroitly concealed from the examiner. Poor management methods aided the potential embezzler by allowing him to conceal his handiwork.

Kane's account suggests that the smaller, less sophisticated institutions—the unit banks—were more dependent on the services of examiners to deter embezzlement. Larger institutions had more depth of management and better internal control procedures, including audits, which reduced the importance of examination. If there had been a nationwide system of branching banks, the need for a large external monitoring entity would have been reduced. Any losses uncovered by the managers or its auditors may also have been more easily absorbed by a large diversified institution.

It is worthwhile to emphasize again that bankers operated under very different incentives in this period and took more responsibility compared to bankers conditioned by the cocoon of New Deal regulations. Today, when an examiner challenges a bank's credits, some lengthy administrative procedures will ensue and end with a promise to address the problem. Before, if an examiner and a banker could not agree on whether a loan was good or bad, the examiner might suggest that the banker buy it himself. In this earlier period, shareholders were also more personally involved, having double liability for their shares. When they failed to administer sufficient oversight, they paid the price. One consequence of these different incentives was that many banks chose to liquidate voluntarily while they were still solvent rather than wait until the examiners closed them.

To conclude, whatever doubts or criticisms I have expressed about this paper, they should not be taken to detract from my general admiration of the paper, which sets forth the lessons from history for the current debate on how to reform banking.

BIBLIOGRAPHY

Bodenhorn, Howard (1990), "Banking and the Integration of Antebellum American Financial Markets, 1815–1859," Rutgers University Ph.D. dissertation.

Bodenhorn, Howard (1991), "Capital Mobility and Financial Integration in Antebellum America," mimeograph.

Bodenhorn, Howard, and Hugh Rockoff (1992), "Regional Interest Rates in Antebellum America," in Claudia Goldin and Hugh Rockoff, (eds.), *Strategic Factors in Nineteenth Century American Economic History*. Chicago.

Lance Davis, Lance (1965), "The Investment Market, 1870–1914: The Evolution of a National Market," *Journal of Economic History* (September).

Kane, Thomas P. (1922),*The Romance and Tragedy of Banking*. New York.

White, Eugene N. (1985), "Voting for Costly Regulation: Evidence from Banking Referenda in Illinois, 1924," *Southern Economic Journal* (April).

CHAPTER 2

COMMERCIAL BANK INFORMATION: IMPLICATIONS FOR THE STRUCTURE OF BANKING

Leonard I. Nakamura

INTRODUCTION

The banking system processes payments. To the alert banker, these payments are potentially immensely valuable bits of information that, properly understood, form a mosaic that can help make comprehensible the financial status of firms making and receiving these payments.[1] This information is particularly valuable in bank lending to smaller firms. The checking account of a small firm sheds a clear light on its revenues and expenses because the firm's cash flows are easily comprehensible and are typically documented completely within one account. By contrast, the checking account of a large, nationwide firm with thousands of employees is relatively uninformative, because the firm has a complicated cash flow dispersed geographically among many banks. Thus the finances of a smaller business are more fully

This paper reflects the views of the author and not necessarily those of the Federal Reserve Bank of Philadelphia or of the Federal Reserve System. The author thanks Larry White for extensive and valuable comments. He also thanks conference participants, particularly the discussants and Eugene White, and colleagues at the Federal Reserve Bank of Philadelphia, particularly Paul Calem, Loretta Mester, Sherrill Shaffer and James McAndrews, for helpful comments and Doug Robertson for excellent research assistance.

revealed to its banker through its bank account than those of a large business.

Recent theories about credit markets and banking have centered on information and information flows. The fundamental proposition is that information is crucial to bankers both in determining risk premiums that set the price of credit and in collecting loans, ensuring that lenders are repaid as much as possible within the terms of the loan contract. Moreover, information asymmetries—that is, the fact that borrowers know more about their businesses than lenders do—make comprehensible the ubiquity of the loan contract [Townsend (1979), Diamond (1984), Lacker (1990)]. At base, loan contracts are the simplest possible contract for lenders as long as they are fulfilled; they only become complicated when the borrower may fail to repay. As such, a loan is the form of outside finance requiring the least information.

Asymmetric information that banks possess about borrowers has been the foundation of modern theories of commercial banking that justify the "special" character of banks and the unique regulatory treatment that banks receive.[2] According to this analysis, banks are the best lenders because they can most easily monitor loans to maximize repayment in those cases where full repayment of the loan becomes doubtful. A seminal paper by Fischer Black (1975) offered an incisive analysis of banks' informational advantage. Black argued that banks have an informational advantage in lending to households because the banks have access to the household checking accounts.[3] Eugene Fama (1985) extended Black's analysis to firms in a paper that is worth quoting at length in this regard:

> "Black (1975) suggests that banks have a cost advantage in making loans to depositors. The ongoing history of a borrower as a depositor provides information that allows a bank to identify the risks to loans to depositors and to monitor the loans at lower cost than other lenders. The inside information provided by the ongoing history of a bank deposit is especially valuable for making and monitoring the repeating short-term loans (rollovers) typically offered by banks. Information from an ongoing deposit history also has special value when the borrower is a small organization (or individual) that does not find it economical to generate the range of publicly available information needed to finance with outside debt or equity.
>
> "Two facts tend to support these arguments. First, banks usually require that borrowers maintain deposits (often called compensating balances). Second, banks are the dominant suppliers of short-term inside debt. The inside debt or private placements offered by insurance and finance companies (which

do not have the monitoring information provided by ongoing deposit histories) are usually much longer-term than bank loans." (p. 38)

Although Fama's discussion suggests that banks' lending advantage applies to all types of borrowers at banks, I argue that the informational advantage of banks applies primarily to small- and medium-sized borrowers—and not large borrowers.[4] The information that banks derive from checking accounts of small and medium commercial firms is relatively complete and comprehensible while remaining exclusive. As I show below, many small commercial accounts transact between 50 and 300 credits and debits monthly, so that a lending officer can relatively easily grasp the contours of the customer's commercial activity.

Similar information on large borrowers is not nearly as comprehensive; large borrowers do business in many locations and, under current law, banks cannot branch widely enough to capture many large borrowers' full checking business. Moreover, even if banks could establish interstate branch networks, the complexity of large borrower's cash management would still limit the comprehensibility of its transactional information.

The hypothesis that checking account transactions give banks an edge in lending to small borrowers is what I call the "checking account hypothesis." While checking accounts are not the main source of information that banks use about their clients, they are the sole clear edge that banks have over nonbank lenders and that local banks have over out-of-state bank lenders. As a consequence of this informational edge, local banks are able to make better use of other information that any local lender could collect. This discourages competition from nonbank lenders. With larger borrowers, however, banks lack this edge and, as a consequence, have faced sharp competition from nonbank lenders. Thus, a corollary to my hypothesis is that small banks have a greater advantage vis-à-vis nonbank lenders than do large banks.

Banks' relative advantage in lending to small firms has important implications for the efficient scale of banks. The informational advantage that a loan officer has about a loan creates a credibility problem within the bank, which makes loans to small firms hard to administer. A loan officer may be able to attribute less risk to loans than they actually entail, causing too small a reserve to be set aside for loan losses and thereby showing higher profits than are appropriate. This problem is likely to be greatest in large banks. There is thus a managerial diseconomy of scale for loans to small firms. In theoretical terms, banks have an agency problem of the type first discussed by Jensen and Meckling (1976), caused by the outside owners having to monitor the behavior of the bank managers. Consequently, large banks have relied on large borrowers for much of their business, although this lending business has not been highly profitable. This helps to explain the relatively weak profitability of money center banks compared to smaller banks and the slow pace of the consolidation of the banking system.

The informational advantage that small banks have with small borrowers also carries with it a liability. This liability is that small banks' asset portfolios are illiquid. This is because there is a "lemons" problem: Any time a buyer knows less about the loan being bought than the seller, the buyer must be concerned that the seller is selling this particular loan because the seller knows that it is a worse than average risk.[5]

This problem associated with asymmetric information is at the core of the most coherent rationale for deposit insurance, articulated by Diamond and Dybvig (1983). They assume that bank loans are illiquid but that households prefer liquid assets. Depository intermediaries are able to transform illiquid loans into liquid transactions accounts because under normal conditions, the liquidity needs of the economy are highly predictable. However, this transformation is unstable: The belief that too many depositors will withdraw their deposits is self-fulfilling, since withdrawals force the liquidation of the illiquid assets, which reduces the value of a bank's assets and generates the failure of the bank that the depositors fear. Deposit insurance helps prevent these destabilizing panics.[6]

If loans are liquid, on the other hand, an unusual demand on the part of depositors to liquidate their deposits will be met simply by selling off the loans. This will be possible when large banks have no asymmetric information about their loans. If loans can be securitized or sold, then the thesis of loan illiquidity is false. In recent years, large quantities of loans have in fact been securitized or sold. But with the important exception of mortgage loans, these liquid loans have been those made by large banks (Gorton and Haubrich, 1988). Thus large banks have liquid assets and may not need deposit insurance.[7] Ironically, under the too-big-to-fail doctrine, large banks obtain more complete deposit protection than small banks.

The banking industry is often analyzed as if there were but a single type of bank. In practice, however, it is useful to distinguish between at least two archetypes: one, the money center banks that seek to compete nationally and internationally; and the other, the small, hometown banks of "Main Street." In considering the future of the banking system, we need to think through which theories, and which policy prescriptions, apply to each of the two kinds of banks. For example, although a large bank may be able to split loan and deposit functions under a "narrow bank" regulation without undue harm to either operation, a small bank may find the added administrative costs prohibitive. To take another example, large banks have recently been able to securitize a very wide variety of products, including commercial loans, auto loans, and credit card loans; by contrast, most small commercial banks have securitized only mortgages. Thus large banks have more liquid assets as a result of securitization, while small banks may find only a proportion of their portfolios have become more liquid.

Finally, large banks have easier access to capital markets than do small banks. In the short run, policies that require greater capital for banks may have the effect of raising borrowing costs for small borrowers and may have important local impacts on economic activity.

This paper begins by setting forth the theory of how banks gain and use information from checking accounts. I then present empirical evidence supporting the checking account hypothesis. Finally, the positive and normative implications of the hypothesis are presented.

THE THEORY OF BANK INFORMATION

Banks use information both to make commitments for new loans and to monitor existing loans. Banks obtain the information they use, in part, from the checking accounts of their loan customers (Black (1975), Fama (1985), Nakamura (1990a)). This information is particularly valuable in making decisions about troubled loans.

Let us take as an example a gas station that is the lone seller at a good intersection, earning above average returns due to market power.[8] One day, a rival opens up across the street, offering gasoline at a lower price. The incumbent gas station owner can choose to meet the price, staying in business but earning little profit, or to enter into a price war, with the victor able to charge higher prices thereafter. In the absence of debt, the gas station owner can be presumed to make this decision so as to optimize the value of the gas station. But with debt, some of the cost of losing the price war may be borne by the lender, while the profits from winning will go entirely to the station owner. Technically, the debtor is subject to moral hazard—the debtor may be induced by equity maximization to engage in behavior that harms the lender. If lenders know they cannot prevent such behavior, then they must raise the risk premiums they charge on loans. In this way, the borrower pays for the economic costs of moral hazard through higher interest rates.

An informed lender may be able to prevent or limit suboptimal risky behavior on the part of troubled borrowers, by declaring the loan in default due to covenant violations (Berlin and Loeys, 1988) or by using the threat of default to induce behavior that the lender prefers—a loan workout for example (Nakamura, 1990a). In particular, if the lender observes that the gasoline station's outlays for gasoline rise compared to revenues, the lender may be alerted to the existence of a price war. More importantly, the lender may be able to estimate the costliness of the price war and thus the probability that the station owner will win the war. Unless the probability of a victory in the price war is high, the bank may use the threat of foreclosure to prevent the price war or require the borrower to take other steps that shore up the loan.

It might be argued that the information in the bank account is easily transferred to nonbank lenders—in the example above, a nonbank lender could simply require the gas station owner to pass along bank statements or set up a lockbox to collect all checks sent to the gas station. However, there are several disadvantages to these procedures, which raise the costs of the alternative lender. First, the nonbank lender might not review the information in a timely fashion. The gas station may have committed itself to the price war before the statements are forwarded to the lender. Second, the information may be incomplete. A monthly statement may allow the gas station owner to hide actions taken to conserve cash during the price war, for example. Third, these procedures require a duplication of recordkeeping costs that the bank must incur in any case. Fourth, these procedures require that the confidential information in the checking account be passed on to an additional party. The bank and the nonbank lender must both be privy to it. This makes the information more public, which may make the gas station more vulnerable to defeat in the price war. Fifth, the gas station owner may delay sending the checking account information to the nonbank lender during the price war. Finally, the bank is privy to information about other checking accounts in the same locality, which may be useful in evaluating the borrower. For example, the bank may know something about the financial status of the other gas station owner.

Bank lenders thus have an advantage vis-à-vis alternative lenders in providing risky loans. As a consequence, banks are better able to price and administer loans. Moreover, by possessing superior information, a bank can maintain a portion of market power vis-à-vis the borrower: Potential competitors may be reluctant to bid business away from the bank, because the bank will allow the competitor to bid away borrowers who the bank knows are riskier, while the bank will compete vigorously to keep borrowers who are safer than they appear (Sharpe 1990). Banks in markets with free entry may earn smaller rents from their existing customer base if a reputation for low rates helps attract new customers. But in concentrated local markets, banks may well earn large rents. Market power derived from information thus leads to an expectation that banks as an industry may be able to earn monopoly rents that can pay for special industrywide taxes, such as interest-free reserve requirements (Fama (1985), James (1987)). The negotiations that typify loan workouts and default declarations are more easily conducted by a single lender than by a group of lenders. In general, with a single lender it is less costly to write loans with more restrictive covenants since these covenants can be renegotiated as needed (Berlin and Mester, 1991). Thus small banks are less likely to be lenders to large borrowers, even though small banks can syndicate large loans. This is because the practice of syndication changes the nature of the loan.

Information-based market power is a double-edged sword, because it makes the loans illiquid. Banks may thus need protection from unwarranted fears about bank safety. Banks themselves may be subject to moral hazard (Nakamura (1990b)), which may require special regulation and oversight. And banks may have limited access to capital markets. For these reasons banks may wish they had more liquid assets.

All these implications follow from the fundamental notion that banks are possessors of information about borrowers that is not common knowledge. The "checking account hypothesis" suggests that banks are the best monitors of small borrowers because they have access to important exclusive information on the finances of borrowers.

A key issue is how comprehensible and comprehensive the borrower's checking account is likely to be. A checking account that has relatively few deposits and debits per month will be relatively easy to interpret by a loan officer and will offer an important window into the borrower's business if it represents all of the borrower's business. On the other hand, if a checking account has a large number of deposits and debits, or if the borrower has multiple checking accounts with different banks, then the information contained in it will be harder to interpret and less informative.[9]

Branching regulations in the United States have effectively prevented the formation of nationwide banks. As a consequence, a bank is unable to provide full banking services to a firm with offices and factories scattered over a number of states across the country. Instead, corporate cash management has often involved multiple banking relationships, with cash ultimately being concentrated at a single location for financial management. In this case, no single bank has a complete picture of the firm's transactions.

This suggests that banks may be relatively easily replaced in the market for large loans by alternative financial institutions, because banks have no special informational advantage in lending to large borrowers. To the extent that large banks lend to relatively large firms, the former cannot rely on the Diamond and Dybvig argument to justify receiving deposit insurance.

Why then do large banks lend to large borrowers? If small borrowers are where the profits are, why don't large banks lend to small borrowers? The main reason is that there are managerial diseconomies of scale that are based on the type of informational asymmetries that we have found for small borrowers.[10] This informational asymmetry makes it harder within a large bank effectively to supervise lending to small firms, particularly at a geographic distance. The problem is that a bank's headquarters may not be able to assess whether loan officers at a distant branch or subsidiary are accurately classifying problem loans and adequately writing off risks in the portfolio. As a consequence, setting proper incentives for managers may be more costly and less efficient than if the branch or subsidiary were a bank functioning on its own.

Some large banks have grown through the amalgamation of small banks. Banc One, for example, until its recent acquisition of a large bank holding company in Texas, expanded primarily by acquiring small banks with strong market niches in the midwest. The banks that Banc One has acquired become part of a *multibank* holding company and preserve much of their identity as local lenders. However, there is some evidence that when local lenders are acquired by large multibank holding companies, they do less local lending. Gilbert and Belongia (1988) show that when rural banks, which tend to be small banks making small local, agricultural loans, are acquired by large bank holding companies, their portfolios become more diversified. This suggests that small scale lending by large banks may be relatively less efficient due to managerial diseconomies of scale.[11]

Another reason that large banks have lent to large customers is that earlier in the postwar period there was relatively little competition for the loan business of the largest firms. During the early 1950s, for example, Citibank was able to raise its domestic interest spread from 1.9 to 3.5 percent by increasing its corporate loans from 16 percent to over 40 percent of its domestic earning assets (Cleveland and Huertas (1985)). As a consequence, the annual real rate of return on Citibank stockholders' equity was

5.4 percent during these years. Since then, financial innovations, the growth and spread of knowledge about corporate finance, and improved electronic communication, recordkeeping, and computation have all contributed to reducing the profit margins from lending to large businesses. Large business lending in the United States has become close to the textbook paradigm of perfect competition. Thus large money center and regional banks have invested in a franchise that has increasingly paid small rents. It is thus not surprising to find, as Boyd and Graham (1991) do, that large banks have failed in disproportionate numbers in the 1970s and 1980s. Since most of their historical customer links are with large firms, it is difficult for large banks to increase their loans to small firms. If large banks attempt to invade the turf of small banks, they will generally find profits meager, precisely because of the "lemons" problem: The borrowers they will successfully pry away from small banks will generally be the riskier ones.

EMPIRICAL EVIDENCE

In this section I present empirical evidence that bears on the theory I have outlined. I begin by pointing out that large banks process a large number of large debits, which results in very high turnover rates. The average dollar at a money center bank turns over many times a day. Economies of scale in electronic funds transfers permit corporate treasurers to manage their cash actively. By contrast, turnover at small banks is much slower. I then examine commercial accounts at small banks and show that the amount of debit activity is relatively modest. This lends credence to the "checking account hypothesis" by showing that commercial checking accounts at small banks are readily comprehensible.

Turnover rates—the ratio of debits to deposits in checking accounts—give us some insight into the complexity of cash management at large banks.[12] They show striking qualitative differences between small banks and large banks. A dollar of deposits at a bank with assets of less than $1 billion, as can be seen in Table 2–1, turned over between 46 and 110 times a year in 1990—once or twice a week. By sharp contrast, large banks with assets greater than $1 billion had annual turnover rates of 511 to 1,764—roughly an order of magnitude greater. Large banks have turnover rates of 2 to 6 times *per day*.

Thus as we shift our focus from banks with deposits of $500 million to banks with deposits of $5 billion, the bank's processed debits rise from $5

TABLE 2–1
Annual Turnover Rates by Size of Bank*

	Bank Size							
Year	*1*	*2*	*3*	*4*	*5*	*6*	*7*	*Big NYC*
1980	100.5	62.5	127.4	200.2	323.4	592.1	NA	903.0
1981	50.2	92.7	116.9	296.6	304.2	659.7	1657.5	981.1
1982	107.0	95.6	141.5	398.4	317.7	785.0	1125.0	1178.1
1983	146.8	95.4	104.1	254.0	445.3	750.1	1528.7	1493.5
1984	72.9	94.0	127.5	273.8	421.9	980.6	1129.5	1613.9
1985	70.0	93.6	125.3	247.6	462.5	1024.2	1240.8	1693.2
1986	67.8	69.4	93.5	263.8	495.9	1134.3	1308.7	1881.1
1987	38.7	69.7	97.7	268.5	550.5	1470.6	1360.4	2171.7
1988	40.4	67.6	102.2	238.5	570.8	1473.0	1364.1	2348.9
1989	42.2	78.5	104.2	331.0	724.1	1401.5	1628.0	2954.7
1990	45.5	68.9	110.2	510.6	890.0	1430.6	1763.7	3630.8

Bank sizes:
1: Total assets < $ 100 million
2: $ 100 million ≤ Total assets < $ 300 million
3: $ 300 million ≤ Total assets < $ 1 billion
4: $ 1 billion ≤ Total assets < $ 3 billion
5: $ 3 billion ≤ Total assets < $ 10 billion
6: $ 10 billion ≤ Total assets < $ 30 billion
7: $ 30 billion ≤ Total assets

* Turnover = Debits/Deposits
Debits = Checks drawn, direct withdrawals, transfers
Deposits =Demand deposits of individuals, partnerships, corporations, states, and political subdivisions
NA = Not applicable

Source: Survey of Debits to Demand and Savings Deposits Accounts, Federal Reserve Board; Consolidated Report of Condition, Federal Reserve Board.

billion per month to $400 billion. This order-of-magnitude change does not occur when banks with $50 million in deposits are compared to banks with $500 million in deposits, or when $5 billion banks are compared to $50 billion banks. There is a qualitative change between banks under $1 billion or over $3 billion that is greater than for other size categories.

Also, interestingly, the increase in turnover rates among small and large banks has been diverging over time. In Table 2–2, banks are classified by asset sizes in 1980. Banks with assets of less than $1 billion in 1980 doubled their turnover rates by 1990. By constrast, the turnover rates of banks with assets of more than $1 billion roughly quadrupled. It thus appears that cash

TABLE 2–2
Percent Change in Turnover by Size of Bank*

From 1980 to	*Bank Size*						
	1	*2*	*3*	*4*	*5*	*6*	*Big NYC*
1981	15%	29%	34%	44%	26%	23%	9%
1982	38	45	58	98	54	51	31
1983	36	49	45	107	79	71	65
1984	44	60	57	123	95	93	79
1985	48	52	75	144	135	104	88
1986	36	41	92	158	164	120	108
1987	28	58	103	203	194	163	140
1988	22	62	107	203	201	181	160
1989	52	85	141	311	295	237	227
1990	102	78	142	383	400	270	302

Bank sizes:
1: Total assets < $ 100 million
2: $ 100 million ≤ Total assets < $ 300 million
3: $ 300 million ≤ Total assets < $ 1 billion
4: $ 1 billion ≤ Total assets < $ 3 billion
5: $ 3 billion ≤ Total assets < $ 10 billion
6: $ 10 billion ≤ Total assets < $ 30 billion
7: $ 30 billion ≤ Total assets

* Bank sizes as of 1980; note that there were no surveyed banks with more than $30 billion in assets as of that date.

Source: Survey of Debits to Demand and Savings Deposits Accounts, Federal Reserve Board; Consolidated Report of Condition, Federal Reserve Board.

management practices at small banks have changed less dramatically than at large banks.

What does a representative commercial checking account in a small bank look like? The best source of information is the Federal Reserve's Functional Cost Analysis program, which has data since 1971 on commercial checking accounts of participating banks. (The program is generally limited to banks with assets of less than $1 billion). Unfortunately, over the years the rate of participation in this part of the program has diminished dramatically, from 164 banks in 1971 to 15 in 1989, as participation in the program as a whole has fallen off from about a thousand banks to 206.

The general picture that emerges from Table 2–3 is that the average commercial checking account at a small bank has roughly 30-50 checks per

TABLE 2–3
Functional Cost Summary

	Bank Size											
	Deposits up to $50M				*Deposits $50M to $200M*				*Deposits over $200M*			
Year	*#*	*HD*	*D*	*TC*	*#*	*HD*	*D*	*TC*	*#*	*HD*	*D*	*TC*
1971	90	33.89	6.52	53.09	50	44.36	5.92	92.18	24	47.54	9.68	88.27
1972	67	30.26	5.66	46.36	50	47.89	6.89	103.24	25	46.04	6.55	86.45
1973	63	32.58	5.67	47.94	53	40.90	6.12	88.53	25	45.39	7.86	84.69
1974	48	28.59	5.28	43.47	43	50.87	6.98	88.26	28	40.30	5.95	83.82
1975	45	31.90	6.14	48.99	51	43.60	6.64	88.44	29	43.09	21.69	133.69
1976	50	28.69	6.10	50.61	51	48.52	7.90	91.91	31	45.42	6.96	119.77
1977	50	33.58	6.77	59.95	61	51.11	8.55	81.83	34	43.03	7.29	102.32
1978	33	24.98	6.51	44.05	47	51.27	7.33	88.19	22	49.21	8.23	138.68
1979	29	32.05	6.94	52.37	43	43.26	7.30	78.14	20	47.34	9.25	149.81
1980	24	32.11	7.61	69.04	30	49.52	8.64	81.65		NA		
1981	18	30.32	6.70	38.82	28	46.70	8.11	98.04		NA		
1982	17	40.86	9.30	61.06	26	54.23	9.72	99.22	11	89.37	9.69	131.35
1983	9	46.42	10.82	52.57	33	46.37	10.26	104.84	13	34.01	7.83	101.31
1984	11	39.82	7.67	64.13	33	49.47	8.94	88.70	8	46.34	9.44	89.98
1985	10	30.85	7.03	64.52	25	45.53	8.72	80.85	9	42.78	9.09	79.01
1986	7	35.89	5.14	22.26	25	51.02	8.39	91.58	9	47.10	9.22	56.99
1987		NA			20	50.10	11.15	106.46	5	40.02	8.50	55.52
1988		NA			16	43.84	9.51	87.94	5	39.90	5.50	52.88
1989		NA			8	34.81	8.59	67.31	7	37.26	10.05	51.79

\# = Number of banks in survey
HD = Home debits (debits against account per month)
D = Deposits per account per month
TC = Transit checks deposited per account per month
NA = Data not available

Source: Functional Cost Analysis, Federal Reserve Board Series, various years.

month written against it, receives between 50 and 100 checks, and has deposits about once or twice a week. The average balance is between $5,000 and $20,000.

Thus, by examining the 500 or so checks written annually against an average account, a bank loan officer can figure out the business's payroll, including salaries of key personnel, and the amounts paid for the business's supplies. By examining roughly 50 or 100 deposits, the bank loan officer can get a picture of the seasonal pattern of the business's receipts. Finally, by examining the thousand or so transit checks, the officer can identify the business's major customers.

Bank loan officers typically rely on summary data on a business's checking account when analyzing the profitability of the bank's entire relationship with the borrower. This alone gives the bank an edge over other lenders. Most loan officers and bankers spend the bulk of their time getting information about local businesses by calling on business executives in their service area. But the existence of detailed checking account data undoubtedly increases the candor of these conversations.

Cash management at small banks is relatively simple; at large banks it is much more complex. Even if a large bank performs all the banking services for a large firm, it would find the analysis of the data within the firm's accounts to be substantially more complex than for a small firm. But in general, large firms have multiple relationships with banks. A survey of large corporations, conducted in 1971 (Conference Board, 1971), shows how complex these relationships can be. Of 161 corporations, only 8 dealt with fewer than 10 banks. The majority dealt with more than 50 banks, with 59 dealing with more than 100. Subsequent surveys by Greenwich Associates confirm the complexity of large corporations' banking relationships. These multiple banking relationships are a natural extension of having to conduct a multinational business when banks are restricted from branching across state or country lines.

With these large businesses, a local bank has little or no monitoring advantage over an insurance company or an out-of-state bank that might compete to provide the loan. Thus, insurance companies, investment banks, and other financial intermediaries have been able to lend to large corporations, through private placements, commercial paper, and other types of loan facilities. And out-of-state banks have been able to establish loan production offices to lend to large businesses, even though they cannot offer checking services to these businesses.

In sharp contrast, small business borrowers typically depend primarily on banks within their local market areas for their general credit borrowing. One reason for local banks to specialize in lending to small businesses is that these businesses tend to use local bank facilities for checking. If checking facilities were not important for lending to small borrowers, banks could freely set up loan production offices where they could not establish branches, and branching restrictions would not limit bank lending to small firms.

Collateralized borrowing to small firms, such as mortgage borrowing, need not be local. Where standardized procedures that minimize the need to monitor the collateral can be established, nonbank financial intermediaries can lend to small businesses.[13] However, collateralized borrowing is limited by availability of the secure collateral that a borrower can provide. Moreover, the credit monitoring performed by banks may play a key role in the borrower's other relationships. Fama (1990) points out that most of a firm's contracts involve fixed future obligations that are contingent on the firm's viability. These contracts include labor contracts and supply agreements as well as formal debt contracts. The bank can then be viewed as a monitoring specialist that monitors on behalf of all these creditors.

Of small- and medium-sized firms (defined as firms with less than 500 employees[14]) surveyed in the 1988-89 National Survey of Small Business Finance, most used one bank, located within one mile of the firm (Elliehausen and Wolken, 1990). Indeed, ninety percent of all respondents obtained their checking services from a bank or thrift located within twelve miles of the firm.

My thesis is that the local bank checking account is an important source of information for loan monitoring. The National Survey shows that of the firms that had lines of credit, most received them from banks located close by—most within two miles of the firm. Thus the survey indicates that most borrowers give their checking account business to their local lender.[15]

Laderman, Schmidt, and Zimmerman (1991) provide tests that support the checking account hypothesis. They argue that banks located in rural (urban) areas should be more specialized in agricultural (nonagricultural) loans if they are located in states that restrict branching. If a bank cannot have branches, then a bank located in a rural area cannot have an urban branch, and vice versa. Such banks will thus be more restricted in their lending opportunities, if the checking account hypothesis is correct. If checking accounts were not important, then banks in states that restrict branching could establish loan production offices that are not branches and thereby achieve loan diversification. This test is particularly relevant because agricultural loans tend to be small.

They find that where branching is restricted rural banks do indeed specialize more heavily in agricultural loans and urban banks specialize away from agricultural loans. Further, when average farm size is smaller, rural banks tend to have portfolios more concentrated in agriculture. This lends further support to the proposition that checking account services are more important in monitoring loans to smaller firms.

In the presence of asymmetric information, local concentration may have two effects on lending. First, banks in concentrated markets will have relatively more complete information about their markets. The detailed information banks can glean from checking accounts will then be more meaningful and thus more profitable. Second, less competition implies higher profit margins. Since only local banks can provide checking account services, it is *local* concentration that should matter.

Hannan (1991) presents evidence that borrowers borrowing small amounts (less than $100,000) pay higher interest rates in concentrated banking markets. The estimated increase in interest rates from the least to the most concentrated markets are economically significant, ranging from 50 to 239 basis points depending on the time period and type of loan. There is some evidence that when larger amounts are borrowed interest rates also rise with concentration, but the magnitudes are smaller and estimates are more uncertain. He also presents evidence that local markets matter—i.e., that the metropolitan area a bank is located in has an important effect on the average loan rate.

In sum, where there are few banks in an area, small borrowers appear to pay higher interest rates. The effect is less clear for large borrowers, however, which is consistent with the proposition that larger borrowers are not as restricted to borrowing from local banks.

Preece and Mullineaux (1991a, 1991b) present evidence that banks do not have an informational advantage vis-à-vis nonbank lenders in lending to *large* borrowers. They examine announcements of loan agreements from the *Wall Street Journal* from 1980 to 1987 and find that both bank and nonbank loan agreements lead to excess stock returns for the borrowing firm. In fact, the excess returns are greater for nonbank loan agreements than for bank loan agreements. These findings are for large loans: The range of loan size is $2 million to $4 billion for banks and from $4 million to $150 million for nonbanks. The median bank loan is $50 million; a bank with assets of less than $5 billion would rarely be allowed to make a loan of this size, and it would be extremely rare for such a bank to lead the syndication of a loan of that size.

They also find that the excess returns are greater when the number of lenders is fewer. This suggests that flexibility of loan agreements is important in the value of new loans to borrowers. An alternative interpretation is that multilender loan agreements result in more information leakage, so that the value of multilender loan agreements is partially embedded in security prices before the agreements are made public. Either interpretation argues that loans made by a single lender are different from multi-lender loans.

Boyd and Graham (1991) present evidence that return on assets is higher for banks with asset size less than $1 billion than for banks with asset size more than $1 billion and that the same holds true for return on equity, although the latter evidence is less dramatic. Indeed, the evidence from return on assets is that banks with less than $100 million in assets had a greater return than banks with larger assets and, at least prior to 1983, banks with assets of less than $25 million had higher returns on assets than banks with assets of $100 million or more.

These results are particularly striking because cost studies for this same period showed economies of scale for banks up to about $50 million in assets (1984 data, in Humphrey, 1990). Thus banks with assets of less than $25 million were earning higher returns on assets despite (on average) having higher costs.[16]

Though small banks have an informational advantage in lending to small borrowers that larger banks do not have in lending to large borrowers, this advantage comes at a cost: The asymmetric information that small banks possess about borrowers makes these assets less liquid and also tends to limit these banks' access to capital markets. Indeed, the profit advantage of small banks is less evident when return on equity is considered, because small banks generally have higher equity-assets ratios than large banks. One rationale for this difference is that small banks have less access to capital markets and thus must hold greater capital as a hedge against losses. If small banks make loans with relatively more proprietary information, then capital markets may have a hard time distinguishing sound small banks' capital issues from "lemons."

Bernanke and Lown (1991) present evidence that bears on this question. In an analysis of the possibility that a lack of capital has reduced bank lending in the recent recession, Bernanke and Lown examine correlations between levels of bank capital prior to the recession and rates of growth of lending during the recession. Their results show that lower bank capital levels are associated with lower rates of growth of lending across states. They also examine individual bank data for the State of New Jersey, corroborating at the bank level the results at the state level. For our purposes, the key result is that weakly capitalized small banks (less than $1 billion in assets) appear to have contracted their lending relative to strongly capitalized small banks to a greater extent than have weakly capitalized large banks relative to strongly capitalized large banks.

My interpretation of the Bernanke and Lown results is that smaller banks face more imperfect capital markets than do large banks. The reason that smaller banks face more imperfect capital markets is, no doubt, twofold: The smaller size of capital issues at smaller banks causes greater relative transactions costs in capital markets, and smaller banks have greater information problems embedded in their portfolios than do larger banks.

The illiquidity of bank loans that is at the heart of the Diamond and Dybvig (1983) model of bank runs has been challenged by the existence of loan sales. If banks have asymmetric information about loans, banks will not be able to sell them. Indeed, Gorton and Haubrich (1988) have argued that the explosive growth of the loan sales market implies that loans are not illiquid. But loan sales have been largely restricted to very large banks that specialize in this market. The top twenty five banks in the loan sale market account for close to 90 percent of all loan sales (Table 2–4).

I have argued that all banks have a greater informational advantage in lending to small borrowers than to large borrowers. I have also presented evidence that *small* banks have higher rates of return on assets, but less

TABLE 2–4
Loan Sales by Banks with Most Loan Sales[a] (percent of all bank loan sales)

	1986 IVQ	*1987 IVQ*	*1988 IVQ*	*1989 IIQ*	*Bank Average Asset Size in Billion $ 1989 IIQ*
Top 10 Banks	59.8 %	77.9 %	91.6 %	84.7 %	$60.8
Top 50 Banks	77.8 %	87.6 %	93.2 %	94.0 %	$22.8

[a] Loans originated by the bank and sold or participated to others. Data include any loan made directly by the bank except residential mortgage loans, consumer loans, renewals or rollovers of loans previously sold with no new funds advanced, repos, and sales of loans reported as borrowings. Data are originally from Federal Regulatory Report of Condition.

Source: American Banker, "Top Numbers 1990," p. 34.

access to capital markets and less ability to securitize or sell assets. A key link between the two phenomena is that *small* banks lend to small borrowers and *large* banks to large borrowers. What accounts for this dichotomy? It is clear why small banks lend to small borrowers. Legal lending limits restrict small banks from making the large loans that large borrowers typically require. For example, national banks are forbidden to lend more than 15 percent of capital and surplus to a single borrower. In practice, this generally implies that a loan must be less than 1 percent of a bank's assets. On the other hand, large banks can, and do, make small loans. But these loans constitute a very small proportion of large banks' overall loan portfolios and a small proportion of all small loans.

Table 2–5 presents evidence that small banks make small loans and large banks make large loans. It presents data for 1988, taken from the Survey of Terms of Bank Lending, on the size[17] of commercial and industrial loans (including construction and land development loans but not mortgages) made by different size banks. A stratified sample of banks lists loans made during a specific week during a quarter. It can be seen that small loans (defined as loans of less than $1 million that are not part of commitments larger than $1 million) account for a large proportion of the loans banks with less than $1 billion in assets. Of course, banks with assets less than $100 million will generally not be permitted to make loans larger than $1 million. However, although loans of $1 million and more can be made by banks with assets of more than $100 million, in fact banks with asset sizes up to $1 billion devote most of their portfolios to loans of less than $1 million.

For banks with assets of more than $3 billion, loans of over $1 million overwhelmingly dominate their lending business. In fact, the portfolios of banks of asset size class 3 are far more different from those of asset size 5 than is true for the difference between banks of asset size 5 and 7.

I have argued that loans of $1 million and larger are relatively liquid.[18] Given this, Table 2–5 shows that banks with assets of $3 billion or more have loan portfolios that are relatively liquid. Thus these banks are unlikely to need deposit insurance in order to prevent panics. These banks will still need access to a back-up source of liquidity, however, such as a lender-of-last-resort, because it may take time to liquify the loan portfolio; the loans may be liquid but the market for them may lack immediacy and depth during a panic.

A second empirical issue is the extent to which small borrowers in fact turn to small banks for their borrowing. If large banks account for the bulk of small loans, then it would appear unlikely that they are inefficient lenders

TABLE 2–5
Loan[a] Size Distribution for Each Bank Size Category (percent), 1988

Bank Size	Loan Size 1	2	3	4	5	6	Loans < $1 million	Loans > $1 million
1	49%	24%	16%	5%	6%	0%	89%	11%
2	22	22	28	16	11	0	72	28
3	11	12	17	29	29	2	41	59
4	6	7	10	18	27	32	23	77
5	1	1	3	7	20	68	5	95
6	0	1	2	5	18	74	3	97
7	0	0	1	3	13	83	1	99

Bank sizes:
1: Total assets < $ 100 million
2: $ 100 million ≤ Total assets < $ 300 million
3: $ 300 million ≤ Total assets < $ 1 billion
4: $ 1 billion ≤ Total assets < $ 3 billion
5: $ 3 billion ≤ Total assets < $ 10 billion
6: $ 10 billion ≤ Total assets < $ 30 billion
7: $ 30 billion ≤ Total assets

Loan sizes[b]:
1: Loan size < $100,000
2: $100,000 ≤ Loan size < $300,000
3: $300,000 ≤ Loan size < $1 million
4: $1 million ≤ Loan size < $3 million
5: $3 million ≤ Loan size < $10 million
6: $10 million ≤ Loan size

[a] Loans are commercial and industrial loans greater than $1,000; includes advances of funds, takedowns under revolving credit agreements, notes written under credit lines, renewals, bank's portion of loan participation, commercial, industrial, construction, and land development loans; excludes purchased loans, open-market paper, accounts receivable loans, loans made by international division of bank, and loans made to foreign businesses.
[b] The loan size to which a loan is assigned is the larger of the actual loan amount or the commitment of which the loan is a part.

Source: Quarterly Terms of Bank Lending to Business, Federal Reserve Board.

to small borrowers.

The data in the Survey of Terms of Bank Lending represent a stratified sample of banks. We approximate the universe by expanding the banks of different asset sizes using the amounts of commercial and industrial loans (including in the definition construction and land development loans) from call report data. The data in Table 2–6 thus represent the proportion of loans of different sizes[19] made by banks of different sizes. Small banks (assets of

TABLE 2–6
Distribution of Banks Making Loans[a] for Each Loan Size (percent), 1988

Bank Size	Loan Size 1	2	3	4	5	6	Loans < $1 million	Loans > $1 million
1	45%	26%	14%	3%	2%	0%	27%	1%
2	23	28	29	13	5	0	26	3
3	16	20	23	29	17	0	20	8
4	12	17	21	27	24	12	18	17
5	3	6	9	17	28	39	7	33
6	1	2	4	8	16	29	3	23
7	0	1	1	3	8	20	1	15

Bank sizes:
1: Total assets < $ 100 million
2: $ 100 million ≤ Total assets < $ 300 million
3: $ 300 million ≤ Total assets < $ 1 billion
4: $ 1 billion ≤ Total assets < $ 3 billion
5: $ 3 billion ≤ Total assets < $ 10 billion
6: $ 10 billion ≤ Total assets < $ 30 billion
7: $ 30 billion ≤ Total assets

Loan sizes[b]:
1: Loan size < $100,000
2: $100,000 ≤ Loan size < $300,000
3: $300,000 ≤ Loan size < $1 million
4: $1 million ≤ Loan size < $3 million
5: $3 million ≤ Loan size < $10 million
6: $10 million ≤ Loan size

[a] Loans are commercial and industrial loans greater than $1,000. Includes advances of funds, takedowns under revolving credit agreements, notes written under credit lines, renewals, bank's portion of loan participation, commercial, industrial, construction, and land development loans. Excludes purchased loans, open-market paper, accounts receivable loans, loans made by international division of bank, and loans made to foreign businesses.
[b] The loan size to which a loan is assigned is the larger of the actual loan amount or the commitment of which the loan is a part.

Source: Quarterly Terms of Bank Lending to Business, Federal Reserve Board.

less than $1 billion) dominate the lending of loans less than $1 million: they account for over 72 percent of all such loans. Banks with assets of more than $3 billion account for roughly 10 percent of these loans. These results show that small borrowers do turn to small banks for their loans, buttressing the argument that managerial diseconomies of scale make large banks inefficient originators of loans to small firms.

In sharp contrast, small banks make few large loans; they account for only 12 percent of loans larger than $1 million. Banks with assets of $3 billion or more account for 71 percent of these large loans.

IMPLICATIONS FOR THE STRUCTURE OF BANKING

The propositions I have outlined shed light on three major sets of issues on the structure of banking. First, they suggest that the consolidation of the banking industry is likely to be slower than many observers have predicted. Second, the propositions suggest that publicly guaranteed deposit insurance may be an inappropriate form of government intervention for large banks and that the too-big-to-fail doctrine should not be an element of deposit insurance policy. And third, they suggest that narrow banking will tend to make lending to small firms less efficient and may harm the long-term growth prospects of the economy. I will take these arguments in order.

Consolidation

The forces in favor of consolidation of the banking industry are, in fact, rather weak. The key arguments in favor of consolidation are (a) that there are important economies of scale in banking, so that consolidation will result in lower cost, more efficient operation, and (b) that larger banks are able to diversify their asset portfolios and that small banks cannot, so that small banks must bear unnecessary risk.

The first argument derives its force from the claim that large firms have been able to achieve low cost operations in some key areas of banking through large scale. For example, during the 1970s Citibank developed an ability to process checks at very low cost (Cleveland and Huertas, 1985). Another example is credit card processing, for which there appear to be substantial economies of scale (Pavel and Binkley, 1987, and Ausubel, 1990).

However, a careful review of empirical studies of scale economies in banking (Humphrey, 1990) shows that economies of scale are important only for banks below $50 million in assets.[20] Moreover, if small banks do process information about borrowers more intensively than do large banks, the result will be higher interest earnings and lower loan losses for small banks. But these revenue enhancements do not appear as increased output in cost studies, whereas the small banks' more intensive information processing appears as an extra cost and thus as an inefficiency. Thus, these cost studies may be biased toward showing spurious diseconomies of small scale.

The other argument in favor of increasing the size of banks is to obtain greater portfolio diversification. It has been argued that small banks are inherently riskier than large banks because of their narrow lending base. A local economic slowdown—perhaps the failure or relocation of a single firm—might lead to a small bank's failure. Small banks can reduce their risk of failure by increasing their equity capital, but doing so results in a reduced return on equity.

If small banks perceive this as a crucial problem, they may choose to spread risk by merging into larger banks or bank holding companies. But this will be inefficient if (as I have suggested) there are significant managerial diseconomies of scale. An alternative and more efficient solution might be to develop financial instruments that hedge local geographical risk.

There are now increasing numbers of traded securities that reflect local geographic risk. These include securitized mortgages and loans, equities, and state and municipal debt. Combinations of these traded securities might be designed to reflect broad movements in regional markets. In this way the small banks might be able to hedge much of their local area risk while remaining independent.

In addition, it is possible that the special informational role of banks may uniquely cushion small banks from local shocks. The failure rate of large bank holding companies in Texas, for example, was greater than the failure rate of small banks. One reason for this may have been that small banks were able to earn higher returns from their close customer relationships to help cover their losses, because their local competitors were also weakened by the local shock; by contrast, large banks faced unwavering competition from (healthy) out-of-state banks. Again, in Texas funds from out-of-state banks were available but only for loans larger than $1 million.

If interstate branching legislation is ever enacted and if it makes opening or buying branches as simple as opening a fast-food or convenience-store franchise, then banks may establish branches to follow their multilocation customers so that national businesses will be able to do all their banking with a single bank. This could give loan officers for national firms the informational advantages that are now only available for local firms.

However, there are stumbling blocks that would reduce any positive impact that this reform might have. First, many firms use local banks at non-headquarters locations because these local banks are able to provide them with valuable local information and otherwise facilitate relationships with suppliers and customers in the local area (Beehler, 1978). This is not a role that a new branch can easily undertake. Second, even if a bank is the sole banker for a large firm, the cash flows of the firm may prove too complex for a loan officer to find meaningful. This is particularly true of multinational firms.

The current environment for bank regulation is one in which regulators have been very permissive about bank consolidation. In the past, mergers involving partners like BankAmerica and Security Pacific would have been unlikely to win regulatory approval. I believe that this change reflects a twofold attitude toward such mergers: first, that bank profitability is low and therefore concerns about market power are misplaced (and even that a little market power might be good for the banking industry); and second, that for large banks market competition is provided across state and national boundaries.

The analysis that I have presented suggests that this attitude is proper with respect to large borrowers. But it is not necessarily correct with respect to small borrowers. If large banks have managerial diseconomies of scale for small loans, then consolidation of the banking industry will tend to raise costs of borrowing for small firms. Recent studies, including Hannan (1991), Boyd and Graham (1991), Elliehausen and Wolken (1990), Sharpe (1991), and Calem and Carlino (1991), all emphasize the adverse effect of local market concentration on the interest rates of small loans and deposits. Thus market power may differ greatly depending upon the line of business.

Deposit Insurance

Publicly guaranteed deposit insurance has become a public issue, now that taxpayer funds have been used to protect depositors in insolvent savings and loans associations and may well have to be used to protect depositors in insolvent commercial banks. The checking account hypothesis has particular relevance to deposit insurance, as it provides strong support for the liquid-liabilities-and-illiquid-assets combination that is an important rationale for deposit insurance.

Publicly guaranteed deposit insurance coverage distorts the incentives of banks. An efficiently regulated banking system must find a means to minimize both the distortions caused by deposit insurance and the costs of runs or panics. The theory and data we have discussed imply that panics pose a threat primarily to small banks. This implies that deposit insurance may be crucial only to small banks and that regulations should be designed to minimize the extension of public guarantees to large banks.

Under the too-big-to-fail doctrine, however, uninsured depositors at large commercial banks are de facto fully insured. As a consequence, large commercial banks enjoy more complete deposit insurance protection than small banks. Yet the arguments laid out thus far show that, in fact, large banks may not need deposit insurance. The rationale that banks suffer from an illiquid asset portfolio and are therefore vulnerable to self-fulfilling runs, may not apply to large banks, since large banks have portfolios that are relatively liquid. Moreover, it appears that large banks could more easily make their accounting more transparent to the market, since their assets and liabilities are to a larger extent traded in secondary markets. Thus these large banks could more easily mark their portfolios to market, as mutual funds do, thereby reducing the role of regulators.

If there is a rationale for protecting large banks, it has to do with protecting the international payments mechanism and concerns about the functioning of the electronic payments networks, such as Fedwire and CHIPS. This suggests that these networks may require some kind of insurance scheme or reconciliation mechanism for large bank failures, but there may be little justification for folding this into the deposit insurance system.

The checking account hypothesis also suggests that large banks will face intense competition in the market for large loans and large firm finance. As a consequence, failure rates at these institutions are likely to remain high. Thus the cost of the too-big-to-fail doctrine is likely to increase, rather than diminish. Removing deposit insurance protection from large banks will tend to force these banks to raise additional capital or leave the banking business.

In sum, the development of financial markets has made large banks more liquid and thus less in need of deposit insurance. However, the same logic does not hold true for small banks.

Narrow Banking

One proposal for reducing the cost of deposit insurance is "narrow banking." In essence, commercial banks would split their operations into two pieces: a deposit bank and a lending bank. The deposit bank would be required to invest in risk-free assets, such as U.S. Treasury issues—in essence, a 100 percent reserve system. The lending bank would be allowed to invest in risky assets, such as commercial loans, but would have to fund these assets with uninsured deposits, debt, and equity.

In its broadest form, this proposal simply requires a bank to collateralize fully its insured deposits. Deposit insurance, in such a system, need only guard against outright fraud. This proposal can thus encompass a bank that maintains an ability to use information in deposit accounts in monitoring risky lending. In effect, however, the proposal would deprive small banks of deposit insurance, as it requires small banks to fund loans entirely from uninsured sources.

If small banks use uninsured deposits to fund their risky lending, then the small banks will still face the possibility of self-fulfilling runs. They will be in exactly the position of banks modelled by Diamond and Dybvig. On the other hand, if the small banks attempt to fund risky lending via capital markets, they will face capital market imperfections due to their asymmetric information about their loan portfolios. Narrow banking thus would raise costs for small banks and make finance more costly to small borrowers. If, however, the costs of deposit insurance to small banks are judged to outweigh the benefits of a system of many small banks, then narrow banking may be desirable.

An alternative might be to exempt small banks from a narrow banking requirement and to continue to supply deposit insurance to small banks. Under this system, "narrow" banks would pay a very small deposit insurance premium, just enough to provide insurance against fraud. Small banks exempt from narrow banking would pay a larger deposit insurance premium, but would benefit by being able to fund loans out of insured deposits.

SUMMARY

In this chapter, I have argued that large banks—defined as banks with more than $3 billion in assets—are different in kind from small banks. Large banks no longer hold illiquid assets as a large proportion of their portfolios and as such are not endangered by the self-fulfilling bank panics whose possibility justifies deposit insurance. This is because large banks no longer have an informational advantage in lending to large borrowers.

Large banks are, in fact, at a relative disadvantage in making loans to small commercial borrowers, because of managerial diseconomies of scale. The same information asymmetries that render small loans illiquid create agency problems within a large organization making such loans.

Large banks face sharp competition for lending to large firms; consequently, the prospects for large banks are uncertain. Only those large banks that are exceptionally agile and well-managed are likely to survive. Reducing deposit insurance protection, which would speed the winnowing of inefficient large banks, will likely increase the rewards to more efficient large banks and enable them to grow more rapidly. The first step in this direction should be the end of the too-big-to-fail doctrine.

Small banks, on the other hand, continue to need deposit insurance. Narrow banking would disproportionately increase their financing costs and would therefore increase the cost of funds for small firms that typically borrow from small banks.

NOTES

1. Information about households from personal checking accounts is useful in making consumer loans to those households, as is discussed by Black (1975).
2. In these models, banks act on behalf of depositors to monitor borrowers, a role known as delegated monitoring. This monitoring can take place for all loans (ex ante monitoring) in a mechanism formalized by Diamond (1984) or for loans that fail (ex post monitoring) in a mechanism formalized by Townsend (1979). We discuss below briefly why this leads to the bank's having illiquid assets. Diamond and Dybvig (1983), also discussed below, formalize why deposit insurance may be the optimal regulatory response to a bank's having illiquid assets and liquid liabilities.
3. The low cost of decentralized data services makes possible a fulfillment of Black's (1975) vision for consumer lending in "relationship banking." Rosenberg and Davidson (1988) argue that relationship banking can be built upon a foundation of computer-based customer profiles that "contain detailed information on a customer's current and historical relationship with the bank." (p. 31)
4. A number of economists and bankers have suggested this idea to me at seminars and in discussions, but Charles Jacklin was the one who convinced me.
5. George Akerlof originated this analysis, which is known technically as "adverse selection." Adverse selection can result in the complete failure of markets. For example, suppose banks wish to sell loans. The banks who hold loans know whether the loans are likely to be repaid or not. If the potential buyers cannot tell which loans are good or bad, then the sellers will maximize their profits by selling only those loans that are worth less than the selling price. But then buyers will refuse to buy. Reducing the price at which loans sell may not equate supply with demand, because as the price falls, the average quality of loans offered worsens.
6. According to this logic, there is no public policy rationale for deposit insurance as a means of preventing rational depositor runs. In a rational run, depositors withdraw funds from undercapitalized, risky banks. If such banks are viable, they will be able to withstand runs by liquidating assets, by raising equity, or by borrowing from other institutions using as security their liquid assets. A lender-of-last-resort with the power to issue currency may be necessary to ensure that the banking system as a whole has

adequate liquidity. If bank assets are liquid, then the lender of last resort need not bear the risk of the run, because the bank assets will be secure collateral.

7. This is incomplete evidence, as loans remaining in the portfolio may be less liquid than loans that have been sold and the liquidity of loans may rest on the bank's reputation for honesty rather than on the existence of public information about the quality of the loan (Berger and Udell, 1992).
8. I am indebted to Charles Jacklin for this example.
9. It might be argued that the bank has better information about large borrowers because the large number of transactions in the account provides more data points. However, for monitoring purposes, possession of complete information, rather than a sample of information, may well be crucial. In particular, during loan workouts, the bank typically forces a less risky business plan on the borrower (see Nakamura, 1990a); a borrower with multiple checking accounts may take actions with some other bank's checking account that are in violation of the agreement. Joseph Haubrich (1991) has argued that the information that is crucial in *ex post* monitoring is information that rules out states of nature, rather than information that simply changes probability distributions. Having the universe of data, rather than simply a sample, is more likely to rule out states of nature.
10. Gorton and Rosen (1991) argue that management problems such as these are endemic in banking. Mester (1991) finds empirical evidence of management problems at mutual, but not stock, savings and loan associations. See Mester (1989) for an overview of theory and empirical work in this area. Formally, my argument requires two elements: an "agency" problem in which managers can gain by hiding information from owners, and a scale argument that the degree of the inefficiency varies with the length of the firm's managerial hierarchy. The latter argument is made in a more general context by McAfee and McMillan (1989).
11. There are alternative interpretations of this result. It is possible that the rural banks have a lower cost of funds as a consequence of becoming part of the large bank holding company and that the response of agricultural loans to the decrease in cost of funds is less than that of other loans. It might also be the case that the rural bank is diversifying by swapping loans with other members of the bank holding company.
12. Unfortunately, the available data on turnover do not distinguish between commercial accounts and personal accounts. We do have some data on the proportion of commercial checking accounts and personal checking accounts at a sample of banks. Functional Cost Analysis data from the Federal Reserve Board, which unfortunately pertain only to small banks, show that as bank size rises from under $50 million to over $200 million, the proportion of commercial checking accounts as a share of checking accounts remains relatively unchanged. If this can be extrapolated to larger banks, this implies that the difference in turnover is due to more activity in commercial checking accounts at larger banks.
13. Nonbank lenders, according to Elliehausen and Wolken (1990), play important roles in lending to small businesses in leasing and motor vehicle loan markets.
14. More than three fourths of the firms surveyed had fewer than 10 employees and sales of less than $1 million.
15. One reason that the lending office may be located somewhat farther away than the checking office is that the borrower may go to the main branch of the bank for a loan,

while maintaining the checking account at the nearest branch.

16. For a more pessimistic view of the prospects for small banks, see Shaffer (1989).
17. Loan size is determined by the maximum of the actual loan amount or the loan commitment of which it is a part. The idea is that a large borrower may take down a small part of a large commitment, but we do not wish to categorize this as a small loan.
18. Note that these results are also qualitatively true if we believe that only loans larger than $3 million are liquid.
19. Loan size is classified by the maximum of the loan amount or the dollar amount of the commitment under which the loan is made.
20. One reason why economies of scale may not appear is that managerial diseconomies of scale may offset the gains from technical economies of scale. Humphrey (1990) emphasizes small banks' cost studies. Cost studies that focus on large banks often show modest economies of scale, but these disappear once loan quality is taken into consideration (Hughes and Mester, 1991).

REFERENCES

Ausubel, Lawrence M. (1991), "The Failure of Competition in the Credit Card Market," *American Economic Review 81* (March) pp. 50–81.

Bank for International Settlements (1989), *Payment Systems in Eleven Developed Countries* (third edition). New York: Bank Administration Institute.

Beehler, Paul J. (1978). *Contemporary Cash Management*. New York: John Wiley.

Berlin, Mitchell, and Jan Loeys (1988). "Bond Covenants and Delegated Monitoring," *Journal of Finance 43* (June), pp. 397–412.

Berlin, Mitchell, and Loretta Mester (1991). "Debt Covenants and Renegotiation," Federal Reserve Bank of Philadelphia working paper no. 90-16/R.

Bernanke, Ben S., and Cara S. Lown (1991). "The Credit Crunch," Princeton University mimeograph.

Black, Fischer (1975). "Bank Funds Management in an Efficient Market," *Journal of Financial Economics* 2, pp. 323–39.

Boyd, John H., and Stanley L. Graham (1991). "Investigating the Banking Consolidation Trend," Federal Reserve Bank of Minneapolis *Quarterly Review* (Spring), pp. 3–15.

Calem, Paul S., and Gerald A. Carlino (1991). "The Concentration/Conduct Relationship in Bank Deposit Markets," *Review of Economics and Statistics* (May).

Caskey, John P. (1991). "Pawnbroking in America: The Economics of a Forgotten Credit Market," *Journal of Money, Credit and Banking 23* (February), pp. 85–99.

Cleveland, Harold van B., and Thomas F. Huertas (1985). *Citibank, 1812-1970*. Cambridge, MA: Harvard University.

Conference Board, The (1971). *Cash Management*. New York.

Diamond, Douglas B. (1984). "Financial Intermediation and Delegated Monitoring," *Review of Economic Studies 51* (July), pp. 393–414.

Diamond, Douglas B., and Philip H. Dybvig (1983). "Bank Runs, Deposit Insurance and Liquidity," *Journal of Political Economy 91* (June), pp. 401–19.

Elliehausen, Gregory E., and John D. Wolken (1990). "Banking Markets and the Use of Financial Services by Small and Medium-Sized Businesses," *Staff Studies 160*. Washington, DC: Board of Governors of the Federal Reserve System.

Fama, Eugene F. (1985). "What's Different About Banks," *Journal of Monetary Economics 15* (January), pp. 29–40.

Fama, Eugene F. (1990). "Contract Costs and Financing Decisions," *Journal of Business 63* (January), Part 2, pp. 71-92.

Flannery, Mark J., and Dwight M. Jaffee (1973). *The Economic Implications of an Electronic Monetary Transfer System*. Lexington, MA: Lexington Books.

Gilbert, R. Alton, and Michael T. Belongia (1988). *American Journal of Agricultural Economics 70* (February), pp. 69–78.

Gorton, Gary, and Joseph Haubrich (1988). "The Loan Sales Market," University of Pennsylvania mimeograph.

Gorton, Gary, and Richard Rosen (1991). "Overcapacity and Exit in Banking," University of Pennsylvania mimeograph.

Greenwich Associates (1987). *Greenwich Reports*.

Hannan, Timothy H. (1991). "Bank Commercial Loan Markets and the Role of Market Structure: Evidence from Surveys of Commercial Lending," *Journal of Banking and Finance 15* (February), pp. 133–49.

Haubrich, Joseph G. (1991). "Imperfect State Verification and Financial Contracting," Federal Reserve Bank of Cleveland mimeograph.

Hughes, Joseph P., and Loretta J. Mester (1991). "A Quality and Risk-Adjusted Cost Function for Banks: Evidence on the 'Too-Big-to-Fail' Doctrine," Federal Reserve Bank of Philadelphia, Working Paper No. 91–21.

Humphrey, David B. (1990). "Why do Estimates of Bank Scale Economies Differ?" Federal Reserve Bank of Richmond *Economic Review 76* (September/October), pp. 38–50.

James, Christopher (1987). "Some Evidence on the Uniqueness of Bank Loans," *Journal of Financial Economics 19*, pp. 217–35.

Jensen, Michael C., and William H. Meckling (1976). "Theory of the Firm: Managerial Behavior, Agency Costs and Ownership Structure," *Journal of Financial Economics 3* (October), pp. 306–60.

Lacker, Jeffrey M. (1990). "Collateralized Debt as the Optimal Contract," Federal Reserve Bank of Richmond Working Paper No. 90-3.

Laderman, Elizabeth S., Ronald H. Schmidt, and Gary C. Zimmerman (1991). "Location, Branching, and Bank Portfolio Diversification: The Case of Agricultural Lending," Federal Reserve Bank of San Francisco *Economic*

Review (Winter), pp. 24–38.

McAfee, R. Preston, and John McMillan (1989). "Organizational Diseconomies of Scale," California Institute of Technology mimeograph.

Mester, Loretta J. (1989). "Owners versus Managers: Who Controls the Bank?" Federal Reserve Bank of Philadelphia *Business Review* (May/June), pp. 13–23.

Mester, Loretta J. (1991). "Agency Costs among Savings and Loans," *Journal of Financial Intermediation 1*, pp. 257–78.

Nakamura, Leonard I. (1990a). "Loan Workouts and Commercial Bank Information: Why Banks are Special," Federal Reserve Bank of Philadelphia mimeograph.

Nakamura, Leonard I. (1990b). "Reforming Deposit Insurance when Banks Conduct Loan Workouts and Runs are Possible," Federal Reserve Bank of Philadelphia Working Paper No. 90-30.

Pavel, Christine, and Paula Binkley (1987). "Cost and Competition in Bank Credit Cards," Federal Reserve Bank of Chicago *Economic Perspectives 11* (March/April), pp. 3–13.

Preece, Dianna, and Donald J. Mullineaux (1991a). "Monitoring, Contractual Flexibility, and the Capital Market Response to Loan Agreement Announcements," University of Kentucky mimeograph.

Preece, Dianna, and Donald J. Mullineaux (1991b). "Some Evidence the Loan Contracts, Not Banks, Are Unique," University of Kentucky mimeograph.

Rosenberg, Richard E., and Robert C. Davidson (1988). "A Technological Approach to Retail Banking," *The Bankers Magazine 171* (September/October), pp. 30–33.

Shaffer, Sherrill (1989). "Challenges to Small Banks' Survival," Federal Reserve Bank of Philadelphia *Business Review*, (September/October), pp. 15–27.

Sharpe, Steven A. (1990). "Asymmetric Information, Bank Lending and Implicit Contracts: A Stylized Model of Customer Relationships," *Journal of Finance* (September), pp. 1069–88.

Sharpe, Steven A. (1991). "Switching Costs, Market Concentration and Prices," Board of Governors of the Federal Reserve System mimeograph.

Townsend, Robert M. (1979). "Optimal Contracts and Competitive Markets with Costly State Verification," *Journal of Economic Theory 21*, pp. 265–93.

COMMENT

Brian C. Gendreau

In his paper Leonard Nakamura examines what I believe to be one of the most important issues in banking: whether banks obtain information from their borrowers' checking accounts that enhances their ability to make and monitor commercial loans. He argues that they do, but that they obtain useful information only from the accounts of small and mid-sized borrowers. He then explores the implications of this thesis for public policy, particularly toward large banks, which (he argues) lend principally to large borrowers.

Casual observation strongly suggests that an important link does exist between checking accounts and commercial loans. The vast majority of commercial banks in nearly all countries, after all, offer both products. But I think it would be premature to conclude that the link is the information that banks obtain through access to their borrowers' checking accounts. It may be that banks offer both checking accounts and loans because other economies of scope exist in offering the two products jointly. A bank that offers borrowers both checking accounts and commercial loans, for example, can use the same branch, sales personnel, and computer to service both products. Thus, even if a bank were unable to reduce its marginal credit monitoring costs by examining its borrowers' checking accounts, it might still find that offering the products jointly was less expensive. Gilligan, Smirlock, and Marshall (1984) present econometric evidence that loans and deposits are joint products and that banks' incremental costs are lowered by servicing both loan and deposit accounts, though other researchers have not found evidence of statistically significant economies of scope in offering both products.

Other economies of scope aside, the paper's central argument is still compelling. Credit officers at banks do have access to information from borrowers' checking accounts, and some do use that information to monitor their borrowers' creditworthiness. (I know because I saw loan officers doing it at the mid-sized midwestern bank that gave me my first job after graduating from college.) And it is not difficult to understand why the information would likely be of little value in monitoring the creditworthiness of a large corporation, some of which have accounts in scores of banks nationwide.

Once one accepts the proposition that banks can overcome the asymmetric information problems involved in lending to small- and mid-sized borrowers—but not large borrowers—by examining their checking account activity, the implications for public policy are profound. The paper spells out three. First, the "too big to fail" doctrine should be scrapped. Much of the rationale for extending near-100% de facto deposit insurance to banks is that their assets consist mainly of illiquid loans that cannot be sold promptly and economically to meet a deposit run. One reason why many kinds of loans are illiquid is that information about them is asymmetric: Banks typically know more about their borrowers than do outsiders, including potential buyers, in part because they can monitor the borrower's checking account. But if large banks have no special ability to obtain information from their borrowers' checking accounts, they are no longer "special" institutions and do not warrant government protection.

The assumption behind the paper's first policy prescription is that large banks hold mainly loans made to large borrowers and that those loans can be sold easily to meet a deposit run. I do not fully agree, for reasons I shall outline below. Nonetheless, I concur that the asset portfolios of some large money center banks are becoming more liquid and a reduction in federal safety net support for those institutions is possible.

The point is perhaps best illustrated in the accompanying chart, which shows the degree to which thirteen large American banks and five U.K. merchant banks are engaged in liquid, wholesale asset and liability markets. The U.K. merchant banks are included because they are an example of depository institutions that function in wholesale markets without full government safety net support: The U.K. merchant banks make loans and accept deposits (their deposits are included in the U.K.'s monetary aggregates), do a corporate finance business, and are engaged in securities

CHART
Loan Concentration and Reliance on Large Deposits—13 Large U.S. Commercial Banks and 5 U.K. Merchant Banks

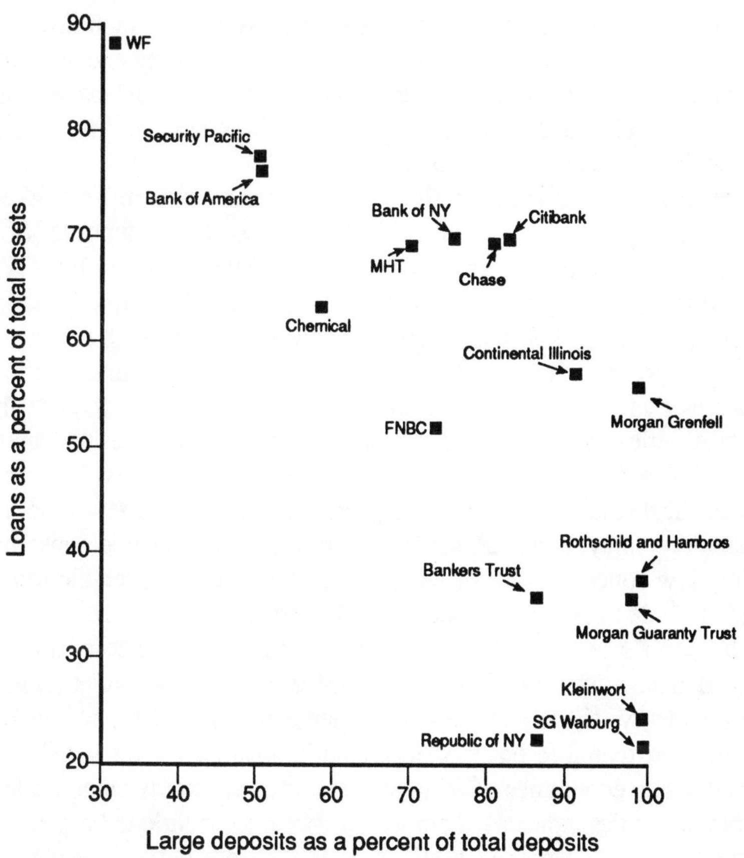

Source: IBCA and Federal Financial Institutions Examination Council bank holding company reports (1990 figures).

activities such as underwriting Eurobonds; but rating agencies such as IBCA Banking Analysis Ltd. do not believe that government support for the merchant banks would be automatic in the event of an insolvency. The vertical axis of the chart measures loans as a percent of total assets, while the horizontal axis measures large deposits as a percent of total deposits. Large deposits are defined for American banks as domestic CDs with a denomination of $100,000 or more plus foreign deposits, most of which are large-denomination deposits raised in the Eurocurrency markets. All U.K. merchant banks' deposits are assumed to be large, wholesale deposits. The farther down and to the right an institution's location is on the chart, the more likely the institution is to be a "wholesale" institution: Such firms tend to be involved in securities underwriting, dealing, and trading and as a result invest a relatively large portion of their portfolios in assets such as securities and interbank deposits rather than loans; such firms also tend to raise the bulk of their funds in the money markets.

It is apparent from the chart that large American banks differ markedly from one another in the composition of their assets and deposits. Some clearly dedicate a large portion of their assets to loans and rely heavily on small-denomination deposits for their funding. But at least five American banks have relatively low loan exposures and a relatively high reliance on wholesale deposits, and three of those banks have loan exposures and funding sources that are more akin to the U.K. merchant banks than to their brethren American banks. Moreover, the trend is for the wholesale banks to become less involved in lending: The banks with the smallest loan exposures had substantially larger loan exposures as recently as a few years ago. U.S. banking policy, however, has not yet recognized that some banks have relatively low concentrations of loans, are therefore less vulnerable to runs, and may be able to operate without federal deposit insurance.

The paper's second policy implication is that the absence of an information advantage for large banks weakens the case for consolidation in the banking industry. If we assume (1) that large banks lend mainly to large borrowers and therefore have no information advantage over small banks and (2) that any economies of scale are exhausted at a fairly small scale (as econometric studies indicate), there would appear to be little to be gained by merging banks into larger institutions. It is far from clear, however, that large banks lend mainly to large borrowers: Small banks often buy participations in loans to large borrowers, while several large money center and regional banks are making a sustained effort to attract and keep a retail and mid-market banking business. Moreover, even if large American banks are today engaged mainly in lending to large borrowers, it does not follow that they would continue to do so following consolidation. Most large banks in Canada, Japan, and Europe, for example, lend to small- and mid-sized borrowers as well as to large corporate borrowers. Finally, many of the loans over $1 million described in the paper as "large" would not necessarily be considered particularly big loans by American money center or regional banks: A loan of that size could easily be a credit to a mid-sized development company about which outsiders have relatively little information.

The author is on firmer ground, in my view, in his third policy implication: Narrow banking will make banks less efficient. The logic is straightforward: If access to checking accounts helps banks avoid losses on risky loans, then separating the lending and checking functions—as envisaged in some narrow bank proposals—will make banks less efficient and lead to higher loan losses. Whether the amount of information gleaned from a borrower's checking account can lead to a material gain in efficiency and reduction in loan losses is an open question. But it is worth noting that, with the exception of "nonbank banks" created to take advantage of the pre-1987 loophole in the Bank Holding Company Act, no bank has chosen willingly to organize itself as a narrow bank. Moreover, the parent companies of some "nonbank banks" that either do not accept demand deposits or do not make commercial loans have supported legislation that would allow them to own a full service bank. The implication is that the cost involved in being unable to offer checking accounts and commercial loans jointly is not trivial—which is consistent with the author's central thesis—though again the concern could be the loss of economies of scope of the more traditional sort.

To my knowledge Leonard Nakamura's paper is the first to explore explicitly the connection between checking account information and the ability of banks to overcome asymmetric information problems in lending. I hope it serves as the catalyst for more research. Policymakers, bankers, and academics alike would benefit from better knowledge of what makes banks "special" and why it justifies their unique regulatory treatment.

REFERENCE

Thomas Gilligan, Michael Smirlock, and William Marshall, "Scale and Scope Economies in the Multi-product Banking Firm," *Journal of Monetary Economics 13* (May /1984), pp. 393–405.

COMMENT

Steven D. Smith

Leonard Nakamura's hypothesis that community banks have an advantageous structure for serving the small businesses in their communities is intuitively appealing. Nevertheless, I have a number of reservations.

1. On an anecdotal basis, it appears that small banks' structure and form allows them greater success in lending to small businesses. They have the ability to develop strong client relationships and gain access to key officers and have the advantage of a local scale and focus. Large banks are more likely to use branches for consumer lending and deposit-taking activity. Large banks may be reluctant to court small business customers, since the latter rarely grow into large customers.

Nevertheless, Nakamura's data (in Tables 2–5 and 2–6) do not necessarily indicate that large banks are ineffective lenders to small businesses. After all, large banks do have many other lines of activities. Instead, their effectiveness in the small loan market should be judged against productivity and market share measures for branches or loan officers. This would be much harder to do; but it could tell us more about effectiveness.

2. Even if small banks are more profitable—as measured by return on assets—than large banks, this result need not be an indication that small banks are more efficient lenders to small businesses. It is, after all, return on equity that really matters. And "opaque" lenders like community bankers may still have difficulties funding themselves, which means that small businesses may well be paying too much for their loans.

3. The value of transactions (e.g., checking account) information is probably overstated. The structure of the lending arrangement is usually more important. There are numerous ways to manage the risk of an individual lending arrangement: Loan covenants are one way; asset-based lending provides another. If transactions data are vital, lock box facilities are possible. Also, by the time that transactions data are available to the lender, it may be too late!

4. Small banks' inability to diversify may leave them at a disadvantage vis-à-vis large banks that can diversify across a wider geographic and industry base. Small banks may get stuck in segments that are too narrow.

5. Consolidation of banking will be slow, but it is inevitable. But the reasons for and the mechanisms of this consolidation are likely to be different from those that are usually mentioned in these discussions. Community banks do provide an effective structure for originating and servicing loans to small businesses, and these banks will continue to be viable so long as local scale and focus matter, client relationships are valued, and small businesses remain an important sector of the economy. Big banks are unlikely to be the challenging force.

Instead, consolidation of lending is likely to be driven by *asset class* consolidation. Let us consider Nakamura's gas station example and contemplate the possible assets that might serve as the collateral for asset-based lending:

- commercial building and improvements
- storage tanks
- point-of-sale equipment
- data processing and accounting systems
- tools and parts
- truck fleet
- receivables
- inventory

Consequently, the small banks' relationship with small businesses may endure but at diminished magnitudes, as the narrowly focused asset-based lenders "cherry-pick" the borrowing possibilities. The end result will be greater consolidation, but in the hands of asset-based lenders.

6. Elimination of the "too big to fail" doctrine is certainly desirable. But Nakamura's call for the outright elimination of deposit insurance for large banks is impractical. Massive investments in consumer franchises would be threatened, and consumers and small businesses would lose access to services that they clearly desire; they would face higher costs and/or

poorer service from community banks that may not be focused to serve them. In the short-term, implementation of the "narrow" banking concept would make easier the end of the "too big to fail" doctrine and might even make it easier to remove deposit insurance from large banks.

7. Consolidation may well increase the choices for small borrowers. Many small businesses are currently "hostages" within local markets where lender concentration is high and lending spreads are wide. If consolidation is accompanied by more lenders crossing (current) regulatory boundaries, borrowers will have more choices.

8. Narrow banking may serve as a catalyst to provide more efficient funding mechanisms to small businesses. Narrow banking will challenge community bankers to tap new (and possibly cheaper) funding sources to overcome their burden of an opaque portfolio. Two possible sources of funds are risk-seeking mutual funds and partnerships with larger institutions.

The challenge will be to design a system that builds on the strengths of community banks while realizing the funding economies of large institutions. There are currently a number of examples of "partnership" structures between large and small institutions that are instructive: private label bankcards; mortgage banking; trust services; insurance. In each case, the local institution originates, while the large institution provides the funding.

This pattern suggests that in the long run community banks could look more like loan brokers and servicers and less like portfolio lenders.

COMMENT

Lawrence J. White

Leonard Nakamura's "checking account hypothesis" is an appealing one. He argues that lenders with access to the complete checking account information of their borrowers will be able to do a better job of monitoring losses to those borrowers.

An immediate corollary is that banks will have an advantage vis-à-vis nonbank lenders, since the former will have direct and immediate access to that checking account information. Further, he argues, small banks should have an advantage vis-à-vis large banks, for at least three reasons: First, the central management of large banks will have more difficulty in monitoring the actions of their loan officers with respect to small loans; they suffer a diseconomy of large scale. Second, the large borrowers that are the natural customers of large banks are likely to have multiple banking relationships, including multiple checking accounts, with multiple banks; consequently, no single lender has a complete picture of the large borrower's checking account information. Third, even if a large borrower deals exclusively with one bank, that large borrower's checking account transactions are likely to be too complex for the bank's lending officer to gain a coherent picture of the borrower.

Nakamura follows these theoretical arguments with evidence that tends to support his propositions.

There are some immediate implications of Nakamura's propositions for the structure of banking and financial markets. First, the future structure of financial markets is likely to continue to include small banks (though surely not as many as exist today); competition with large banks need not mean the complete demise of the population of small banks. Second, small banks will still face the problem of illiquid assets and liquid liabilities, so there will still be a role for a lender-of-last-resort; and because depositors may have difficulty evaluating the bank's assets, there will still be a role for deposit insurance. Third, antitrust officials should be skeptical of the claims by the executives of large banks of the efficiencies to be achieved from mergers.

I find Nakamura's propositions intriguing, and I am partially convinced. I do believe that there is a future role in the financial services market for the small lender that has good knowledge about its borrowers and can pay special attention to them, and that role may well be played by the small bank that can use its checking account information.

Still, there are some loose ends to Nakamura's arguments that make me uneasy. First, if up-to-date checking account information is so important, why don't *nonbank* lenders require that *they* receive it on a timely basis? Couldn't their receipt of this information undercut much of the advantage of the bank? Nakamura offers some arguments to the contrary, but I do not find them entirely convincing.

Second, I have difficulty with Nakamura's claim that the checking account activity of a large borrower, even if it is exclusively with one bank, is too complex to be comprehensible to the bank. More checking account activity may mean more complexity, but it is also means more observations and more degrees of freedom. The bank lending officer will simply need a more complex "model" to comprehend this more complex data set. The ability to deal with this greater complexity should not be beyond the capabilities of modern banks and their data processing facilities.

Third, if a bank can benefit by observing checking account activity of a borrower, shouldn't we see banks offering special inducements to larger borrowers to centralize their checking accounts with a single bank? I am not aware of such special efforts, and Nakamura does not mention any.

Fourth, the "checking account hypothesis" should apply equally well to consumer loans; indeed, it was first developed in the context of consumer loans. Consequently, banks should have a special advantage in extending loans to consumers who do their checking exclusively with that bank. And banks should be offering special inducements to link consumer loans (e.g., auto loans, personal finance loans, credit card loans) to such checking account exclusivity. This exclusivity requirement might be difficult to enforce and monitor; still, have banks tried? Again, Nakamura is silent.

Overall, Nakamura's "checking account hypothesis" has raised some intriguing possibilities as to the links between the asset and liability sides of banks' activities, and he has marshalled some interesting evidence. And I believe that his vision as to the future of small banks is probably correct. Still, I would be more convinced if we saw banks making a greater effort to obtain checking account exclusivity for their commercial and consumer borrowers and if we saw nonbank lenders making a special effort to obtain this checking account information. And in a world of fluid and rapidly changing technologies for financial services one should always be wary of predictions as to the future structure of those markets.

CHAPTER 3

MONEY MARKET FUNDS AND FINANCE COMPANIES: ARE THEY THE BANKS OF THE FUTURE?

Gary Gorton
George Pennacchi

INTRODUCTION

A rethinking of bank regulation must be predicated upon the recognition that technological change has altered the financial landscape to such an extent that the very idea of what constitutes a "bank" may have changed. This essay attempts to analyze some of these changes from a positive perspective. While we do not propose any specific policies, we stress that important economic forces are offering a vision of what banking may be like in the future. New policies should be consistent with these changes, rather than antagonistic to them. Designing new policies requires that we understand these changes better.

A commercial bank historically has been a firm that issues liquid debt and uses the proceeds to produce loans that play a special role in corporation

The authors would like to thank Kok-Hom Teo and David Hutchison for excellent research assistance and Mary Sue Hoban of IBC/Donoghue and Stephen Tulenko of Moody's Investors Service for providing data. They are also grateful for comments by Leland Crabbe, Mark Flannery, Michael Klausner, and Larry White.

finance. The basic change in banking on which we focus is the separation of lending from the issuance of liquid debt, the latter being performed primarily by issuing demandable (possibly insured) liabilities. In previous theoretical work [Gorton and Pennacchi (1990a)], we have discussed why these two activities would naturally and efficiently be combined in one institution, a bank. But, the combination of these two activities, historically, has been problematic. The difficulty is the problem of banking panics.[1] The loans that banks create are, in most cases, nonmarketable and, therefore, difficult for outsiders to value. Debt holders may, as a consequence of a change in the economic environment, have reason to believe that banks are riskier than before, but be unable to distinguish which banks are more or less risky. This creates the possibility of an information externality or "contagion" effect. That is, based on nonbank-specific aggregate information, depositors' assessment of the riskiness of all banks may change suddenly.[2] A banking panic can ensue in which depositors at all or many banks demand redemption of their deposits. The possibility of banking panics is the basis for deposit insurance and bank regulation.

Banking appears to be changing dramatically. In Gorton and Pennacchi (1990b) we documented recent changes in financial markets that are leading to a natural (i.e., not regulation driven) splitting, or unbundling, of the two basic functions of banks. This trend is important because the rationale for bank regulation depends on the possibility of panics for which a necessary condition is the combination of (nonmarketable) loan creation with demandable debt financing. To the extent these two activities can be separately produced in two sets of firms, regulation of these firms may be unnecessary, and regulation of commercial banks may have to be modified to address nonbank competition.

In this essay our goal is to explore whether the alternative set of institutions, some of which are providing loans and some of which are providing liquidity services, are prone to the same sort of information externalities that historically have caused panics for U.S. commercial banks. One possibility is that the splitting of loan and liquidity creation is motivated by the existence of costly bank regulation. If the splitting of the two activities is due to costly bank regulation, then it may well be inefficient. Moreover, the alternative institutions may well be prone to panics and, hence, require bank-like regulation. On the other hand, technological change may make the unbundling of the two activities into two different sets of firms not only efficient, but also less prone to panics.[3]

The alternative institutions of interest are nonbank lenders, including finance companies, insurance companies, and other types of lenders, and money market mutual funds, which are alternative providers of transactions services. In the last fifteen years the volume of "banking" activity provided by these firms has grown enormously; it appears that further growth is likely. In a less regulated world, it might grow even more. Should this growth be a source of concern? Are these firms similar to commercial banks, requiring regulation, or are they significantly different? These are the questions we address.

We begin the second section with a very brief review of our previous theoretical work, which explains how nonbanks can provide banking services by splitting traditional banking into two sets of firms. In the third section we consider money market mutual funds (MMFs) as an alternative source of liquidity. We describe how the market works and then turn to the questions of whether panics are possible or likely when liquidity is provided by MMFs. We test for the presence of information externalities in this market. In particular, we ask whether there are significant declines in the quantity of MMF assets following an event that might lead shareholders to infer that the value of their fund will be lowered. We also consider whether these firms can be more successful in competing with bank liquidity products.

In the fourth section we turn to nonbank lending. We briefly describe nonbank lenders and consider whether loans made by these firms are substitutes for bank loans. To the extent that they are substitutes, are they difficult to value, like bank loans? A key issue for banks is that the issuance of demandable liabilities allows debt holders to monitor the performance of banks by the periodic *en masse* exercise of this redemption option (prior to deposit insurance). Since nonbank lenders, like banks, appear to create nonmarketable loans that may be hard to value, we inquire as to how debt holders of these firms can monitor their performance. This leads us to ask whether this industry could face panics. We test for the presence of information externalities of the type that caused panics in the banking industry.

The splitting of loan creation from liquidity creation is not so simple, however. A key link between the two activities is commercial paper. MMFs buy a great deal of commercial paper, and nonbank lenders issue large quantities of commercial paper. But historically, commercial paper has been "backed" by bank loan commitments. If nonbank lending depends on liabilities that are backed by banks, and MMFs are only willing to buy private securities with this bank backing, then the trend of nonbank competition in loan and liquidity creation may depend crucially on banks. In the fifth section we discuss this complication. The final section offers a brief conclusion.

BANKS AND NONBANKS: BACKGROUND

Banks are generally viewed as unique providers of loan creation (credit) services and unique providers of transactions (demand deposit) services. In providing these services, part of the alleged special ability of banks has to do with ability of banks to combine them. In this section we briefly review the theoretical arguments for how banks perform these functions. We then inquire as to how nonbanks can offer the same services when they are not combined.

Banks

Historically, bank loans have played a special role in corporate finance because bank loans entailed services that could not be replicated by marketable securities.[4] These services consist of monitoring borrowers' managements through covenant enforcement and the production of information about credit risk.[5] A key insight of the theoretical work is that performance of these services by banks requires that they bear the residual risk associated with nonperformance. Theoretically, if banks are fully diversified and can honor liabilities with probability one, they will perform; practically, the argument implies a minimum equity/debt ratio to ensure performance. The implication is that the loans cannot be resold (without recourse) because such a resale would leave the originating bank with no incentive to monitor or produce information. Bank loans, then, are nonmarketable; banks must hold the loans they originate until maturity.

On the other side of the balance sheet, banks produce liquidity services in the form of demand deposits and, to a lesser extent, certificates of deposit. The demand for these services arises because firms and consumers often need to liquidate assets at low cost to meet unexpected consumption needs. When there is some urgency to the transaction, an uninformed agent having to sell a risky security may unknowingly obtain a price that undervalues the security. This can occur when the buyer is better informed about the value of the security. A security with the property that its value was always known—e.g., it was riskless—would prevent these losses since there would never be a better informed agent on the other side of the transaction. Agents, instead, would always be symmetrically informed because of the nature of the riskless security. The provision of liquidity services refers to the creation of securities that have this low-risk property. By issuing debt that is a claim on a diversified portfolio of loans, banks can create near-riskless securities, thus providing an attractive transactions security for uninformed agents. Historically, banks have been in the unique position of holding diversified portfolios.[6] Government insurance can further enhance the low-risk property of bank debt.

Banks can minimize the risk of their debt and, hence, maximize the value of their liquidity services, by issuing deposits that are either demandable or that have short maturities. In addition, the short maturity of this bank debt enhances the ability of debt holders to monitor banks. As discussed in Calomiris and Kahn (1991), if bank debt holders believe the risk of their bank has increased significantly, they can demand redemption or refuse to roll over their CDs. The threat of this action reduces the incentive of bank insiders to engage in activities that would harm depositors. But this option to demand payment, when combined with nonmarketable bank loans, creates the possibility of banking panics. Panics can occur when information of a bank failure or economic downturn leads depositors mistakenly to infer that their bank's risk has increased. These mistakes in assessing bank risk are likely due to the difficulty in valuing their bank's nonmarketable loans. The combination of nonmarketable loans and demandable debt is a necessary, but not a sufficient condition for the possibility of panics, a point demonstrated by the historical experience of other countries where the same combination has not resulted in panics.

Nonbanks

The theoretical rationale for banks is that it is efficient to combine the twin activities of creating nonmarketable loans and financing them with demand deposits that function as a medium of exchange. How, then, can competing firms, which provide either loans or liquidity but not both, be successful? Our view is that an important part of the answer is technological change.

If technological change results in lower costs of information production, then it may be possible to replicate bank products without having to combine them. Indeed, the loans created by nonbanks appear to have the same "special" features that bank loans have. Evidence that bank loans are "special" has been provided by James (1987) and Lummer and McConnell (1989), who show that the abnormal return on the stock of firms announcing the signing of a bank credit agreement, or renegotiated agreement, is positive and significant, whereas the abnormal response to announcements of other, nonloan, types of corporate securities is significantly negative or zero (see Smith (1986)). Bailey and Mullineaux (no date) examine the stock price response to firms announcing the signing of a loan agreement with a *nonbank* intermediary, such as a finance or insurance company, and find the same positive response that is found when firms announce the signing of a bank loan. The difference in the responses in the two cases is statistically insignificant. While nonbank lenders have been around for quite some time, they have not successfully competed with banks until recently (as we demonstrate below). Perhaps the reason that they can be successful now is that they are able to issue liabilities that allow their debt holders to monitor their performance without these liabilities' having to take the form of demand deposits. As Flannery (1991) has observed, lending institutions are relatively special in having a propensity to issue bonds with an embedded put option. Chatfield and Moyer (1986) report that 68 of the 90 putable bonds, in a sample they study, were issued by banking and other finance companies.

Since nonbank lenders create nonmarketable loans that are hard to value, their performance may be as difficult to monitor as the performance of banks. By issuing short-maturity or putable debt, such as commercial paper, they allow their debtholders potentially to behave like demand deposit holders of banks in that they, too, can monitor the institution's lending.[7] Though the debt of nonbank lenders is generally not payable on demand, much of it is commercial paper that has a short maturity. If the risk perceptions of nonbank debtholders change, these firms could have difficulty rolling over their commercial paper.[8] While the refusal to roll over debt might be better described as a "walk" (a gradual loss of funds) rather than a "run" on the firm, in principle a panic is possible in the case of nonbank lenders.

Technological change may have allowed putable bonds to be effective monitoring devices only recently. The reason is that market participants, apparently, have only recently learned how to price bonds with embedded options. In a study of callable bonds, Crabbe (1991) reports that for the period 1983 through 1988, the yield differences on callable and noncallable bonds were not statistically different. But, in 1989 and 1990, callable bonds sold at a significant yield premium over noncallable bonds. The ability of the market to price embedded options is particularly important if nonbanks are to be monitored by their debtholders. It appears that this ability is a fairly recent phenomenon.

Although it is difficult to demonstrate the existence of technological change, a large number of casual observations are consistent with this view. That there has been a reduction in information production costs is evidenced by the fact that new debt markets, such as the junk bond market and the medium-term note market, have opened.[9] Moreover, banks now sell a huge volume of commercial and industrial loans without recourse or guarantee.[10] In the case of such loan sales, Gorton and Pennacchi (1991) directly test for the presence of technological change and provide evidence for that hypothesis.

There is also evidence that nonbank producers of liquidity can more successfully compete with banks than before, although the presence of government insurance and government restrictions might hinder such competition. MMFs provide a competing method of liquidity creation. Because of the development of secondary markets for wholesale certificates of deposit, and the rise of the commercial paper market, MMFs can sell shares of diversified portfolios of near-riskless securities which, while not insured, compete with bank liquidity products.

A key question is whether the volume of privately created, near-riskless instruments is sufficiently large so that MMFs can compete with banks. As intermediaries, banks hold diversified portfolios. Can this feature be replicated by MMFs holding portfolios of privately created securities (and government securities)? In Gorton and Pennacchi (1990b), we argued that they could. This observation depends crucially on recent changes in corporate debt markets that have produced an explosion of near-riskless debt—in particular, commercial paper and wholesale CDs. Notably, the ratio of commercial paper to commercial and industrial bank loans was less than 10 percent prior to the 1960s, but by the end of the 1980s it exceeded 70 percent.

Since MMFs hold marketable securities, the values of their assets and liabilities are relatively easy to determine and their assets can be liquidated at relatively low cost. Therefore, a panic would seem to be less of a likelihood. But, the MMF contract provides for redemption on a first-come-first-served basis. Thus, MMF liability holders may still demand redemption *en masse*. The key question is whether they have any reason to do so.

MONEY MARKET MUTUAL FUNDS

A Description of Money Market Funds

Money market funds (MMFs) are the single most popular type of mutual fund in the United States, accounting for over 40 percent of all mutual fund assets. What distinguishes MMFs from other mutual funds are their investments in money market instruments characterized by low credit and interest rate risk. Most MMFs allow their shareholders to redeem shares by writing checks, thus providing transactions services similar to bank checking accounts. With the exception of a one year decline in 1983, the assets of money market funds have shown positive growth each year since their inception in 1972. As of October 1991, the assets of the 513 MMFs holding taxable securities totalled $461 billion, and the assets of the 288 MMFs holding only tax-exempt municipal securities totaled $89 billion.

MMFs can be categorized by the three types of clients they serve. Broker/dealer MMFs distribute fund shares through securities firms whose brokers then market accounts to the public. In contrast, general purpose MMFs distribute fund shares directly to the public. Finally, institutional MMFs specialize in selling shares to businesses and bank trust departments.

The assets of taxable MMFs consist of commercial paper (44%), Treasury bills and other short-term U.S. securities (22%), repurchase agreements (17%), domestic and Eurodollar bank certificates of deposit (13%), bankers' acceptances (.9%), and cash reserves (.4%).[11] Although the composition of assets varies from one MMF to another (e.g., some MMFs hold only Treasury securities), commercial paper is a significant proportion of most MMFs' assets. MMFs hold approximately one-third of all commercial paper outstanding.

As with other U.S. mutual funds, MMFs are regulated by the Securities and Exchange Commission (SEC) under the 1940 Investment Company Act (ICA) and its subsequent amendments. A mutual fund using the title of "money market" fund must meet the risk-limiting regulations given by rule 2a-7 of the ICA. Rule 2a-7, adopted in 1983, attempts to lower the volatility of the fund's net asset value per share by restricting the type of securities that a MMF can hold. Compliance with this rule allows a MMF to fix its price per share, which it usually sets equal to $1. The number of shares owned by a MMF investor then increases with the accrual of interest income.

To maintain this fixed share price, a MMF is permitted to use the "amortized cost" method of security valuation and the "penny-rounding" method of share pricing, rather than calculate its share price as the "marked-to-market" net asset value per share, the method required of other mutual funds. As an example of the amortized cost method, a security whose yield at time of purchase is 8% (annual simple interest) would be assumed to increase in value each day at the rate 8% × (1/365). Under the penny-rounding method, a MMF's share price can then be calculated by valuing its assets at their amortized cost value as long as this value does not deviate from its marked-to-market value by more than .5 percent. If this deviation exceeds .5 percent, the fund would be required to change its share price.

Fixed Share Price and MMF Stability

The great majority of MMFs choose to fix their share price rather than mark it to market. This suggests that the benefits of a constant share price exceed any potential costs. In this section, we attempt to identify these benefits and costs and discuss the question of MMF stability.

Relative to other mutual funds whose share price is permitted to fluctuate, a MMF's fixed share price makes redemption of its shares more convenient and allows the account to resemble a bank demand deposit account. This convenience comes from at least two sources. First, since a shareholder will usually realize no capital gain or loss when selling shares, the need for tax-related record keeping is reduced. Second, as long as a MMF can maintain a fixed price, a shareholder will be certain of her account's minimum balance, since rates of return will always be non-negative. In theory, this certainty may make MMF shares a better transaction medium because the need to hold precautionary balances is reduced. However, given the relatively low risk of a typical MMF's investments, the extra precautionary balances needed by a variable-price MMF shareholder are probably negligible. This suggests that the direct benefits of a fixed price are due mostly to simplified tax consequences.[12] Hence, one might expect that a tax law change that eliminated capital gains taxation of all MMFs might result in more variable price MMFs. However, there is another indirect benefit to a MMF's fixing its price: By fixing its price, a MMF can commit to following a safe investment strategy that is enforced by market discipline.

If MMF shareholders have some preference for share price stability (e.g., due to risk aversion or avoiding precautionary balances), it appears that MMFs that choose a fixed share price have greater incentives to follow low risk investment policies than funds that mark their shares to market. This is because it is more costly for fixed-price MMF portfolio managers to follow risky investment strategies than it is for portfolio managers of marked-to-market funds. These costs can be of two forms. First, excess volatility in the market value of a fixed-price fund's investments could lead to a loss of customers because of dilution of fund returns. Lyon (1984) shows that fixed-price valuation of MMF shares can lead to arbitrage opportunities by traders who buy (sell) MMF shares when this method undervalues (overvalues) shares relative to their marked-to-market value. He estimates that passive shareholders of institutional MMFs could be subject to losses of about 10 basis points per year due to this arbitrage activity. One would expect that passive shareholders would leave the more volatile funds that experience excessive dilution, so that fund managers will attempt to minimize portfolio risk.

Second, a fixed-price MMF portfolio manager would suffer a substantial loss in reputational capital if his fund was forced to "break the buck"—reduce the fund's share price below $1 following a greater than .5% decline in the marked-to-market value. To avoid this loss, portfolio managers have chosen to provide implicit insurance against a decline in the fund's price. There are numerous instances of parent firms and/or investment advisors that have purchased, at par, low-valued securities held by their MMF rather than reduce the fund's share price.[13] To minimize the cost of this implicit insurance, the fund managers will again have the incentive to follow low risk investment policies.

When a MMF is caught holding securities that significantly decrease in value because of default or interest rate risk, immediate action by the MMF to maintain its stability is crucial. The fund's directors must quickly decide whether to provide implicit insurance by having the fund's parent or portfolio manager buy back the low-valued securities at par, or to reduce the share price to less than $1.00. If action is delayed, investors may be uncertain that insurance will be forthcoming, leading to a desire to withdraw their shares prior to the fund's being forced to reduce the share price. If insurance is not to be provided, investors who immediately redeem their shares would benefit at the expense of the shareholders who remain in the fund after the share price is reduced. In this sense, "runs" on MMFs are possible. Fortunately, rule 2a-7 recognizes this problem and requires a MMF's board of directors to

> ...consider promptly what action should be initiated where the deviation between the amortized cost and the marked-to-market value exceeds one half of one percent, including whether to reduce the share price to less than $1.00 ("breaking a dollar").

Casual evidence suggests that a fixed price is critical to the possibility of runs. High-yield (junk) bond mutual funds have tremendously greater levels of credit risk but are able to function adequately following defaults of their securities due to their marked-to-market valuation.

To summarize, since most MMFs choose to maintain a fixed share price, the direct benefits of tax simplification, minimum balance certainty, and the indirect benefits due to superior investment incentives appear to exceed the costs of shareholder dilution or implicit insurance. Although price fixity creates the potential for runs, they can be circumvented by an immediate decision to provide implicit insurance or to lower the fund's share price.

Recent Efforts to Increase the Safety of MMFs

Several MMFs held the commercial paper of Integrated Resources and of Mortgage & Realty Trust, which defaulted in June 1989 and March 1990, respectively. While each of the MMFs voluntarily chose to provide implicit insurance, these events prompted the SEC to re-examine rule 2a-7. In February of 1991 the SEC issued new regulations that tightened the requirements that MMFs must meet to satisfy rule 2a-7.[14] These regulations include: (1) limiting a MMF's securities of any one issuer to no more than five percent of fund assets; (2) limiting the total amount of securities with less than the highest credit rating to no more than five percent of fund assets;[15] (3) limiting the securities of any one issuer with less than the highest credit rating to less than the maximum of $1 million or one percent of the fund's assets; (4) limiting a fund's average portfolio maturity to no more than 90 days. In addition, the SEC planned to examine all MMFs during 1991 to verify that they were complying with the securities laws and with their prospectuses. In the past, the interval between SEC examinations has been two to three years.

For the majority of MMFs, the above restrictions are not binding. MMFs had been reducing their holdings of lower-grade commercial paper well in advance of the effective date of the new SEC regulations.[16] In addition, between 1987 and 1989, the average maturity of MMF securities had a range of 31 to 50 days. As of October 1991, the average maturity was an unusually long 62 days.[17]

Regulators are clearly concerned about the link between commercial paper default risk and the safety of MMFs. In spite of rule 2a-7's precautions, there may still exist the threat of "runs" or other types of market dislocations that result from commercial paper default risk. We now turn to empirical evidence of the sensitivity of MMFs to commercial paper defaults.

MMFs, Commercial Paper, and Panics

In this section, we consider evidence of dislocations in MMF operations that coincide with defaults in the commercial paper market. A default in the commercial paper market could signal a general decline in commercial paper credit quality and could initiate two types of responses. First, risk minimizing MMFs might reduce their holdings of commercial paper, especially lower grade commercial paper. Figure 3–1 gives some evidence of this behavior. It indicates that over the past two years, a period of numerous commercial paper defaults, MMFs have reduced the proportion of assets invested in commercial paper and bank certificates of deposit.[18] In contrast, MMFs' proportional investment in U.S. government securities and repurchase agreements (which are most often collateralized by U.S. securities) have increased. But this reaction by MMFs is unlikely to be instantaneous. If MMFs choose to hold commercial paper to maturity, they may only gradually purge their portfolios of lower-quality paper. Thus, a second response could come about. Investors may choose to redeem their shares in MMFs holding lower-quality securities, switching funds to higher quality investments such as Treasury securities or to MMFs that invest only in U.S. government securities.

The potential flight to quality, initiated by either MMF management or and investors, suggests that yields on commercial paper will rise relative to that on government securities in the event of a commercial paper default. The size of this differential will depend on the perceived differences in credit quality. To examine whether yields on commercial paper respond to announcements of commercial paper defaults, we looked at the spread between the yields on commercial paper and Treasury bills—i.e., the default risk premium on commercial paper. The Federal Reserve compiles a weekly series on average three month maturity commercial paper yields and three month Treasury bill yields.[19] We used the commercial paper series as a proxy for the "typical" yield on commercial paper. We also obtained a list of commercial paper default dates from Moody's Special Report, "Defaults and Orderly Exits of Commercial Paper Issuers, 1972–90." The results of our analysis are given in Table 3–1.

The first column of Table 3–1 gives estimates and *t*-statistics from a regression of the commercial paper-Treasury bill yield spread on the current level of the Treasury bill yield and twelve dummy variables. These dummy

FIGURE 3–1
Proportion of MMF Assets

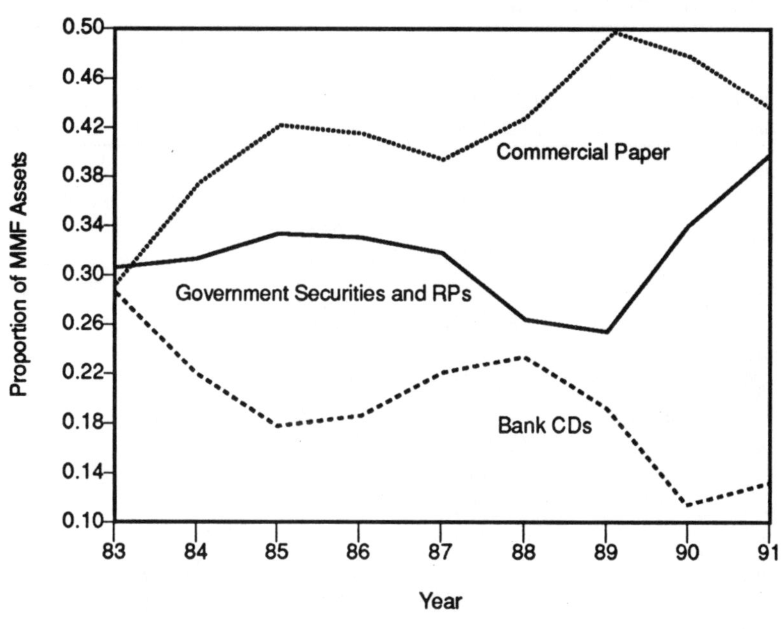

variables take the value of one during the week of a particular firm's default on commercial paper, and zero otherwise. Hence they represent the "abnormal" component of the yield spread associated with that particular week. The level of the Treasury bill yield was included as a right-hand side variable, since the level of market interest rates might be related to aggregate economic activity or risk and hence might explain some of the default risk premium on commercial paper. As can be seen from the first column, the level of T-bill yields is highly significant; the default risk premium increases when T-bill yields increase. However, with the exception of the 1982 default by Manville (which is significant at the 6 percent confidence level), in none of the other weeks in which a default occurred was there a significantly high abnormal default risk premium on commercial paper. In six of the twelve announcement weeks, the abnormal return was actually negative.

We then considered how a commercial paper default might influence the change in, rather than the level of, the default risk premium of commercial paper. The results are given in column two of Table 3–1. The one week

TABLE 3–1
Effect of Default Announcement on Three-Month Commercial Paper and Finance Company Paper Yields[a]—608 Weekly Observations, 11/10/79–6/28/91

Independent Variable	*Dependent Variable* (CP Yield −TB Yield)	Δ(CP Yield −TB Yield)	(FP Yield −TB Yield)	Δ(FP Yield −TB Yield)
Constant	.1232 (1.958)	−.00430 (−0.496)	.8610 (11.151)	−.0071 (−0.277)
TB Yield	.0814 (11.735)	−.0543 (−6.362)		
Δ(TB Yield)	−.0617 (−2.452)	−.5905 (−7.968)		
Manville 8/26/82	.8862 (1.892)	.1008 (0.473)		
Integrated Resources 6/15/89	.1141 (0.244)	.0319 (0.150)		
Wang 8/16/89	−.0604 (−0.129)	.1362 (0.639)		
Lomas 9/1/89	.0236 (0.050)	.1094 (0.514)	−.0024 (−0.004)	.0299 (0.048)
Equitable Lomas 9/12/89	.3081 (0.658)	.1408 (0.661)	.3213 (0.558)	.0772 (0.123)
DFC New Zealand 10/3/89	.3050 (0.651)	.1294 (0.607)		
Drexel 2/13/90	−.2868 (−0.612)	.1057 (0.496)		
Mortgage & Realty 3/15/90	−.4212 (−0.899)	.0574 (0.270)	−.3391 (−0.589)	.0466 (0.074)
Codec 4/1/90	−.2258 (−0.482)	.0794 (0.373)		
Wash. Bancorp 5/11/90	−.2333 (−0.498)	−.0525 (−0.246)	−.0311 (−0.054)	−.0279 (−0.044)
Stotler Group 7/25/90	−.3862 (−0.824)	−.0181 (−0.085)		
Polly Peck 10/05/90	.1063 (0.227)	−.0355 (−0.167)		
R^2	.196	.014	.064	.096

[a] *t*-statistics in parentheses

Sources: Federal Reserve *Bulletin*; and "Defaults and Orderly Exits of Commercial Paper Issuers, 1972–1990," Moody's *Special Report*, 1/91.

change in the spread between three month commercial paper and T-bills was regressed on the one week change in the level of the three month T-bill as well as the twelve default week dummy variables. A positive change in the T-bill yield is significantly related to a decrease in the commercial paper default premium. Although nine of the twelve abnormal changes in the spread are positive during the weeks of a commercial paper default, as theory would suggest, none of these abnormal changes is significantly different from zero. Hence, our results suggest that individual commercial paper defaults have little influence on the yields paid by other commercial paper issuers. This supports the hypothesis that commercial paper investors are able to discriminate between the risks of different issuers and that "contagion" effects from a default are not prevalent. In this sense, the market could be described as being "deeper" than in earlier years.[20] (Columns three and four of Table 3–1 are discussed below.)

In addition to our investigation of the effect of defaults on equilibrium commercial paper yields, we considered the effect of defaults on the level of MMFs' assets. If investors react to commercial paper defaults by redeeming their shares in MMFs holding commercial paper, an action that might be construed as a MMF "panic," we should observe a reduction in the typical MMF's assets.[21] In addition, we should observe an increase in the assets of MMFs that held only U.S. government securities. We tested these hypotheses using two time series: (1) the total assets of all taxable MMFs, excluding the assets of MMFs investing only in U.S. government securities; and (2) the total assets of taxable MMFs that invest only in U.S. government securities.[22]

The results of our statistical test for MMF panics is given in Table 3–2. We regressed the weekly change in the log of MMF assets on the three month and six month T-bill yields and the three month commercial paper yield, as well as their yields lagged one week. The three and six month T-bill yields and their one week lagged values were used as proxies for term structure effects that might explain changes in MMF assets. MMFs have relatively short durations (generally well below 90 days), so that changes in the steepness of the term structure may induce MMF asset flows. Since almost half of MMFs' investments take the form of commercial paper, the three month commercial paper rate was also included as an explanatory variable. Differences in the yield between commercial paper and T-bills, which could reflect differences in the yield between MMF shares and T-bills, might also affect the level of MMF assets. The remaining explanatory variables consist of the eleven dummy variables that take the value of one

TABLE 3–2
Effect of Commercial Paper Default Announcements on Changes in Money Market Fund Assets[a]—287 Weekly Observations, 12/31/85–7/02/91

Independent Variable	Dependent Variable: Δ ln MMF Assets	Δ ln GO MMF Assets	Δ ln MMF Assets	Δ ln GO MMF Assets
Constant	–.0061	–.0055	–.0056	–.0046
	(–1.695)	(–1.216)	(–1.497)	(–1.014)
TB3M	.0022	–.0106	–.0054	–.0145
	(0.465)	(–1.767)	(–1.116)	(–2.504)
$TB3M_{t-1}$	.0021	.0103	.0097	.0151
	(0.437)	(1.733)	(2.069)	(2.656)
TB6M	.0018	.0034	.0002	.0004
	(0.467)	(0.701)	(0.044)	(0.081)
$TB6M_{t-1}$	–.0087	–.0009	–.0032	.0004
	(–2.277)	(–0.180)	(–0.871)	(0.100)
CP3M	–.0161	–.0121		
	(–4.108)	(–2.445)		
$CP3M_{t-1}$	.0197	.0114		
	(5.365)	(2.457)		
Integrated Resources	.0048	.0024	.0061	.0018
6/15/89	(0.612)	(0.239)	(0.726)	(0.179)
Wang	.0078	.0046	.0059	.0030
8/16/89	(0.978)	(0.461)	(0.713)	(0.297)
Lomas	–.0040	.0069	–.0055	.0059
9/1/89	(–0.506)	(0.694)	(–0.657)	(0.590)
Equitable Lomas	.0020	–.0082	.0016	–.0089
9/12/89	(0.251)	(–0.814)	(0.187)	(–0.884)
DFC New Zealand	.0017	.0045	.0007	.0034
10/3/89	(0.215)	(0.451)	(0.090)	(0.341)
Drexel	.0021	.0055	–.0000	.0051
2/13/90	(0.261)	(0.544)	(–.004)	(0.508)
Mortgage & Realty	–.0008	.0028	–.0034	.0022
3/15/90	(–0.102)	(0.283)	(–0.414)	(0.216)
Codec	–.0078	–.0083	–.0093	–.0083
4/1/90	(–0.977)	(–0.831)	(–1.124)	(–0.827)
Wash. Bancorp	–.0116	–.0082	–.0115	–.0070
5/11/90	(–1.461)	(–0.818)	(–1.386)	(–0.699)
Stotler Group	–.0031	.0002	–.0036	.0006
7/25/90	(–0.386)	(0.016)	(–0.432)	(0.061)
Polly Peck	–.0031	.0108	–.0012	0.0118
10/05/90	(–0.393)	(1.077)	(–0.146)	(1.174)
R^2	.159	.097	.067	.075

[a] *t*-statistics in parentheses

Sources: IBC/Donoghue's *Money Fund Report;* Federal Reserve *Bulletin*; and "Defaults and Orderly Exits of Commercial Paper Issuers, 1972–1990," Moody's *Special Report*, 1/91.

during the week when a commercial paper default occurred, and zero otherwise.[23] Thus, the coefficient estimates of these variables represent the abnormal percentage change in MMF assets during the week that a particular commercial paper default occurred.

The first column of Table 3–2 gives the coefficient estimates and t-statistics of a regression where the dependent variable is the weekly change in the log of the assets of all taxable MMFs, excluding those funds holding only government securities. Evidence of a "panic" by MMF investors would show up as a negative coefficient for the default event dummies. Six of the eleven default event coefficients are negative, but none of them is significantly different from zero at the ten percent confidence level. Hence, there is little evidence that MMF investors withdraw funds following commercial paper defaults.

The second column in Table 3–2 gives estimates of the same regression except that the dependent variable is the weekly change in the log of the assets of all MMFs holding only government securities. Unlike the previous regression, we expect that evidence of a "flight to quality" would imply significant positive coefficients on the event dummies. Eight of the eleven point estimates are positive, but none is significantly different from zero at the 10 percent level. Thus, significant flight to quality behavior following commercial paper defaults is unsupported.

Columns three and four repeat the regressions in columns one and two, but leave out the yields on commercial paper as independent variables. We wanted to check that our results were not influenced by the possibility that commercial paper defaults might cause an increase in the risk premium on commercial paper (though this was not borne out in our previous tests) that could spuriously rob the event dummies of their explanatory power. However, we find that this modification does not affect our previous conclusions. MMF asset flows simply do not appear to be sensitive to commercial paper defaults.

MMF Transactions Services

In this section we document the current level of transactions services provided by MMFs and the possible impediments to these services. Table 3–3 compares the annual level of debits (or redemptions) to MMFs and various types of bank deposits for the years 1988-1991. The first half of the table indicates that the debits to Demand Deposits, ATS-NOW Accounts, and MMDAs each exceeds the debits to (redemptions from) MMFs. This is not due to a relatively smaller level of MMF shares since, over this time period, the assets of MMFs exceeded the balances in each of the aforementioned deposit accounts. As the second half of Table 3–3 indicates, the turnover in MMFs is significantly lower than each of the three checkable bank accounts. This is even the case for MMDAs that limit checks to three per month. Hence, MMFs seem to be under-utilized in terms of their potential level of transactions services.

Apparently, MMFs currently face a net disadvantage relative to commercial banks in providing transactions such as wire transfers and check clearing. In fact, the typical MMF appears to discourage checking services by setting a minimum check amount.[24] What might explain MMFs' unwillingness to provide transactions? Is it due to some inherent disadvantage in the structure of MMFs versus banks and/or some regulatory barriers that might potentially be reformed?

One disadvantage is that MMFs are restricted from access to Fedwire, the Federal Reserve's wire transfer facility. A MMF must arrange wire transactions through a commercial bank that acts as its agent. This lack of direct access could be an important deterrent to providing wire transfers for

TABLE 3–3
Debits ($ billions) and Annual Turnover of Bank Deposits and MMF Shares

	1991 Q1 Annualized	*1990*	*1989*	*1988*
Debits to				
Demand Deposits	$278,992	$277,400	$256,133	$219,709
ATS-NOW Accounts	3,610	3,342	2,910	2,477
MMDA	2,843	2,923	2,677	2,343
Savings Deposits	559	558	547	536
MMFs	1,500	1,320	1,055	899
Turnover[a]				
Demand Deposits	823.9	799.6	735.4	622.8
ATS-NOW Accounts	16.7	16.4	15.2	13.2
MMDA	7.4	8.0	7.9	6.6
Savings Deposits	2.8	2.9	2.9	2.9
MMFs	3.3	3.0	2.9	3.3

[a] Turnover data are averages of annualized monthly figures.

Sources: Federal Reserve *Bulletin*, September 1991; and *Trends in Mutual Fund Activity*, various issues, Investment Company Institute.

MMF shareholders, especially businesses and institutions. Since wire transfers account for approximately 82 percent of the dollar value of all transactions, this single regulatory restriction could explain the lion's share of the difference in turnover rates between MMFs and demand deposits.[25] A natural question to ask is, should financial intermediaries structured as MMFs be restricted from being members of a settlement system such as Fedwire?

A recent article by Goodfriend (1991) suggests that perhaps they should. He reasons that MMFs are inefficient, relative to banks, as providers of payments services. His first premise is that efficient clearing of payments between financial institutions will involve the granting of temporary credit rather than the insistence on instantaneous payment in reserves. This is because many payments between institutions cancel each other and thus net to zero over a finite interval of time. Hence, the costs of transferring reserves for each transaction can be avoided by delaying payment and instead granting temporary credit.[26] Because commercial banks (or any lending institution such as finance companies) have expertise in information-intensive lending, they can more efficiently evaluate the credit of other members of a payment systems clearinghouse. This enables them to extend credit to members of the clearinghouse at lower cost than can financial institutions, such as MMFs, that do not have this expertise in credit evaluation. Thus, it is argued, payments are best carried out by financial institutions that also have lending expertise. Goodfriend reasons that this economy of scope can explain why, historically, lending and payments settlement were combined in a single financial institution in the form of a commercial bank.

While the previous argument for combining credit and transactions services may have historical validity, we believe that the presumed economies of scope no longer hold in an economy with extensive money markets. As argued in Gorton and Pennacchi (1990), recent improvements in information technology that have led to the creation, by corporations, of liquid securities (e.g., commercial paper) allow alternative means of carrying out transactions. The newly expanded supply of money market instruments implies that equity-financed MMFs can provide redemption of shareholder account balances in the same way as the traditional levered bank redeems deposit account balances. Furthermore, a payments system based solely on financial institutions that are legally restricted to hold only safe money market instruments would make the need for the mutual credit evaluation of clearinghouse members superfluous. Because MMFs hold only marketable securities, their ability to make payments is observable. Furthermore, since they are equity financed intermediaries, rather than levered institutions,

MMFs cannot "fail" in the same sense as banks, making MMFs' risk of non-payment inconsequential. Hence, we would argue that a MMF-based payments system would actually be a safer, simpler, and more efficient method of providing transactions.[27]

Regarding the relative advantages of MMFs and banks in check clearing, a clear advantage of MMFs is that they can provide accounts with unlimited checking that are free from the 12 percent reserve requirement imposed on checkable bank accounts such as demand deposits and NOW accounts. This is likely to be a significant advantage for consumer checking accounts but not for businesses and institutions whose account balances are minimized by cash management systems. While this advantage is entirely due to regulation and is not inherent in the structure of MMFs, it might appear strange that MMFs do not attempt to exploit it. The explanation could again be MMFs' lack of direct access to Fedwire. As noted by Flannery (1988), most check clearing eventually involves a settlement of funds over Fedwire.

However, we believe the main barrier to MMFs' provision of transactions services, especially transactions services marketed to consumers and small businesses, stems from MMFs' greater constraints in pricing transactions services. Relative to banks, MMFs are at a disadvantage because they lack the ability to extract significant amounts of consumer surplus from their customers. MMFs cannot easily control the rate of return received by their customers. The following discussion develops this argument in more detail.

Recent empirical research indicates that banks exert significant market power in consumer deposit markets, especially for those deposits that offer transactions services, such as NOW accounts and MMDAs.[28] Moreover, because market power is found to be greater in geographic areas where bank concentration is higher, there is a spatial aspect to consumer deposit markets. It seems reasonable that consumers derive convenience from a bank's local presence. In part, close vicinity to a branch office makes converting deposit balances into currency more convenient. This local presence creates the potential for banks to exert local monopoly power.

Banks extract quasi-rents from the transactions services they provide to local consumers and small businesses by employing a relatively complicated system of pricing. Transactions services often consist of two complementary component services: (1) provision of a customer (deposit or MMF) account, normally having a positive balance and; (2) provision of check clearing, wire transfer, or ATM services that take the form of debit or credits to the customer's account. If a financial institution has market power in supplying these two services, it will consider their demand complementarity in its optimal pricing. There is ample evidence that, in practice, banks' optimal pricing of these two services takes rather complex forms. A typical pricing arrangement is one in which banks set a low interest rate (high price) on deposit accounts (i.e., an interest rate that is lower than if the account was a pure savings, non-transactions account) and a low price on actual checking, ATM services, and wire transfers.[29] Banks often provide free checking on NOW accounts and MMDAs (which is certainly a price below that which would equate marginal revenue to marginal cost for this service alone), because this increases customer demand for deposit balances on which banks extract surplus via a low interest rate. Besides "under-pricing" checking while "over-pricing" deposits, banks often offer numerous checkable accounts with different minimum balances necessary to earn interest or avoid account maintenance fees. This quantity-based, nonlinear pricing schedule further helps increase the profitability of transactions services. These various minimum balance levels aid in segmenting depositors by wealth levels, thereby allowing banks to engage in second-degree price discrimination.

On the assumption that banks' complicated system of pricing transactions services is one that maximizes profits, let us now consider whether MMFs can replicate this pricing structure. Evidence suggests that they cannot. The goal of the Investment Company Act of 1940 (ICA) was to establish a corporate structure for mutual funds that would protect the small investor. All mutual funds, including MMFs, must pass their asset returns, less reasonable management expenses and fees, through to shareholders. To help enforce this behavior, the 1970 amendments to the ICA strengthened the oversight ability of mutual fund directors, mandating that they be truly independent of the fund's investment advisor. These amendments also provided a mechanism by which the size of an advisor's fee could be challenged. In fact, a number of lawsuits alleging excessive fees have been brought against MMFs in the 1970s and 1980s.[30] Courts have judged the merit of these cases based on whether the advisor's fee was reasonable in light of the fund's costs. The profits of the advisor should not be excessive.

Because of these regulatory restrictions on MMFs, they are in a poor position to extract consumer surplus from their shareholders. Faced with the decision of whether or not to enter a particular local market for transactions services, a MMF is likely to find that its fixed costs of entry (e.g., establishing a branch network and an initial marketing campaign) cannot be offset by sufficient future quasi-rents. The parent firm of the MMF would be better off obtaining a bank charter and providing these transactions services through a bank that could extract rents using a less restricted system of insured deposit pricing. But while the supplier of these transactions services is better off operating as a bank rather than a MMF, it is unlikely that social welfare is increased.[31] Social welfare may well be augmented by requiring all providers of transaction services to operate in a MMF structure—i.e., as a narrow bank. However, from our preceding discussion, it seems clear that one cannot expect that simply opening this market to MMFs will lead to any significant entry. The spatial aspects of retail transactions services, which create monopoly rents that only banks can extract, will provide a deterrent.

NONBANK LENDING

In this section we first document the increasing importance of nonbank lenders, insofar as the data are available.[32] We then test for the presence of information externalities with respect to these lenders.

The Rise of Nonbank Lending

Commercial banks' share of the short-term nonfinancial corporate debt market has historically been high, almost 90 percent in the 1950s. This dominance was consistent with the theoretical and empirical arguments about bank loans' being a unique form of corporation finance. Banks' dominance, however, has eroded substantially.

Table 3–4 provides data on commercial banks' share of this market, together with the shares held by commercial paper and finance companies. Since 1960, the banks' share has dropped precipitously, while commercial paper and finance company shares have risen significantly. It is also notable that in this series (taken from flow of funds data) finance companies are rather narrowly defined, so that their share is probably underestimated.

Consumer lending displays a more complicated picture. Table 3–5 shows commercial banks' shares of the most important consumer lending categories. In the case of consumer installment credit, there is a slight (but statistically significant) upward trend in banks' share.[33] Banks, however, have lost market share in automobile loans.[34] Competition from finance companies is the main factor in this downward trend in banks' share of the automobile loan market. In the case of consumer revolving credit, banks show a downward trend, which is marginally significant.[35] But perhaps the

TABLE 3–4
Banks' and Other Lenders' Shares of the Short-Term Nonfinancial Debt Market[a]

Year	*Banks' Share*	*Commercial Paper Share*	*Finance Companies' Share*
1960	85.10	1.75	9.31
1961	84.37	2.41	9.23
1962	84.79	2.43	8.67
1963	85.31	1.82	9.39
1964	84.64	1.91	9.81
1965	85.70	1.12	9.55
1966	85.18	2.00	9.00
1967	84.66	3.40	7.98
1968	84.45	4.20	8.15
1969	83.07	4.50	9.02
1970	81.71	5.62	8.60
1971	82.37	4.78	8.86
1972	82.15	4.75	9.33
1973	81.34	4.97	9.59
1974	79.04	6.20	9.21
1975	77.43	5.19	11.03
1976	73.50	5.80	12.98
1977	71.95	5.95	14.62
1978	71.67	6.34	15.23
1979	69.32	8.32	14.34
1980	69.31	8.43	13.34
1981	65.67	10.72	12.53
1982	70.19	8.29	11.13
1983	69.25	7.47	11.83
1984	65.43	9.78	12.51
1985	64.34	10.95	13.26
1986	65.61	8.70	13.66
1987	63.12	9.74	15.27
1988	61.45	10.31	16.29
1989	59.59	11.73	16.05

[a] Excludes tax-exempt debt.

Source: Flow of Funds.

most significant finding in Table 3–5 is that since 1975 there are downward trends in the bank shares of all three categories of consumer lending.

That nonbank lenders have been successful at competing with banks for commercial and industrial loans, and for some categories of consumer lending, is also indirectly evidenced by the inability of banks to find profitable investment opportunities, as reflected in their realized rates of returns

TABLE 3–5
Banks' Share of the Consumer Loan Market

	Banks' Market Share of		
Year	*Consumer Installment Credit*	*Auto Loans*	*Revolving Credit*
1960	41.41	49.37	NA
1965	43.09	58.39	NA
1970	46.16	61.34	69.78
1975	49.16	58.15	81.98
1980	48.67	54.96	50.88
1985	46.55	44.23	61.18
1990	46.83	44.27	57.84

Source: Federal Reserve *Bulletin.*

on loans and assets, as compared with their charge-offs. Returns have fallen (almost continuously) over the 1980s, while charge-offs have continuously risen over the 1980s. Since the 1980s was not generally a period of recession, this pattern is difficult to reconcile with banks' finding profitable new opportunities to replace lost market share—e.g., with off-balance-sheet activities; see Gorton and Rosen (1991).

The Monitoring of Nonbank Lenders and Information Externalities

Above we briefly discussed how nonbank lenders may be monitored by outside debt holders. This was an issue because, historically, banks that create nonmarketable loans issue demandable debt. The fact that their deposits are demandable allows depositors to discipline bank managements by exercising their redemption option. Although the debt of nonbank lenders is not, in general, payable on demand, they issue significant quantities of putable bonds and commercial paper that allow debtholders (gradually) to withdraw funds if the perception of the lender's riskiness increases. A firm's inability to roll over its commercial paper has been described as an "orderly exit" from the commercial paper market rather than a "run."[36] However, this gradual withdrawal of funds by debtholders could provide a way of disciplining nonbank lenders that is similar to, though perhaps less disruptive than, bank runs.

Since nonbank lenders' loans are similar to bank loans, there may be an information asymmetry concerning their value. If nonbank lenders' debtholders cannot accurately value a firm's loan portfolio, they could panic in response to a mistaken perception that their firm's riskiness has increased. Hence, we need to consider whether nonbank lenders are exposed to panics, as banks were during the predeposit insurance era. This is a key issue considering the previously documented trend toward nonbank lending.

We address this question by testing for the presence of information externalities or "contagion" effects. The basic testing strategy is to examine the abnormal return on the stocks of a variety of nonbank lenders in response to the announcement of various types of defaults. We also consider the effect of these default announcements on the risk premium of finance company paper.

There are two reasons, however, why this information asymmetry might not be present. First, unlike most banks, most nonbank lenders have traded equity.[37] In order for equity to be traded, a firm must be large enough so that analysts find it profitable to produce information on the value of the firm. In countries such as Canada where there are a small number of large banks, there has not, historically, been a problem with banking panics.[38] One reason for this is that efficient stock markets do appear to be able to differentiate between banks with assets of differing value. In the U.S., branching restrictions have led to the existence of many small banks that do not have traded equity. Perhaps nonbanks could always compete, in the sense that there would be no information asymmetry due to their size, but markets could not value their putable debt and commercial paper until recently.

A second reason why nonbank lenders (as well as bank lenders) may not be subject to panics is that information asymmetries between outsiders and insider loan creators have recently been reduced. This would be consistent with the arguments in Gorton and Pennacchi (1991), who found evidence that bank outsiders could now observe the behavior of banks because of technological change; this, it was argued, explains the rise of the loan sales market.[39]

The use of event studies to test for the presence of information externalities in banking is not new. Swary (1986), using weekly data, examined the responses of other banks to the announcement of Continental Illinois' failure. He found significantly negative returns for questionable banks, liability-managed banks, and solvent banks. Wall and Peterson (1990) also use event study methodology to reexamine the Continental case and do not find Swary's results in daily data, though they do find some evidence consistent with concerns about bank panics.[40] Pozdena (1991), using different methods, finds evidence of contagion effects in U.S. banking.

One important issue concerning panics has to do with the timing of the shock—the failure of Continental Illinois in the above event studies. Even in the National Banking Era, 1865–1914, banks failed—sometimes even large banks—without triggering a panic or even detectable abnormal withdrawals from banks. During this period the crucial trigger of a panic was the coincidence of a shock with a business cycle peak. At that time, depositors would know that they would soon be dissaving and that this dissaving would take the form of withdrawing from their bank. The intertemporal terms of trade would then make risk perceptions of the banking system much more important [see Gorton (1988)]. This suggests that a bank failure *per se* is not as important as the external shock. We attempt to address this issue below.

Seven categories of nonbank lenders are considered in what follows. They are: (1) personal credit institutions; (2) short-term business credit firms (except agriculture); (3) miscellaneous business credit firms; (4) mortgage bankers and loan correspondents; (5) loan brokers; (6) financial lessors; and (7) financial services. We also consider the group as a whole. The categorization of nonbank lenders follows *Compustat*. Appendix 3–A1 lists the firms in each category that are included in our sample.[41] There are 52 firms in the sample in total.

We examine the stock price responses to four events. The first two events are the announcements of defaults by nonbank lenders: Lomas Financial, which announced a default on September 1, 1989; and Equitable Lomas Leasing, which announced a default on September 12, 1989. The two firms are legally separate entities, despite the similarity of their names. Appendix 3–A2 provides more detail about these firms. The two events provide an opportunity to examine the hypothesis that nonbank lenders face the same information externalities as banks. If there is little firm-specific information about the value of these firms' portfolios, because of the nature of loans, then there should be a significant negative abnormal return on the event dates because of the presence of information externalities.

We also examine the response of the nonbanks to the announced defaults of two other types of firms. The first is the announcement of the default, on March 15, 1990, of Mortgage and Realty Trust, a self-administered real estate investment trust. The second firm is a commercial bank holding company, Washington Bancorporation, which announced default on May 11, 1990. Mortgage and Realty Trust held mortgages, while Washington Bancorporation was a commercial bank holding company. Appendix 3–A2 provides some additional details about these firms. In each case, information about their defaults could potentially be used to infer that the value of nonbank lenders was lower than previously believed, if there is a significant information asymmetry.

Several considerations influenced our choice of events. First, we wanted to examine not only the potential impacts of defaults by nonbank lenders on other nonbank lenders, but also the defaults of other types of financial firms on nonbank lenders. Second, the events had to be as recent as possible, certainly in the 1980s, in order to have occurred during the period when banking was undergoing significant change. Finally, we mentioned above that, historically, panics were triggered when shocks occurred near business cycle peaks. The events we chose are all near the cyclical peak of July 1990.

Since each event date is common to all the nonbanks, there may be cross-sectional dependence in the abnormal returns if each nonbank is treated as an independent observation. [See Bernard (1987) for a discussion of this problem.] To avoid this problem, or at least minimize it, we form equally-weighted portfolios of the firms in each group and a separate portfolio for the entire sample of firms.

Our event study procedure is the standard one that relies on estimating the Capital Asset Pricing Model. [See Brown and Warner (1980)]. The market portfolio is taken to be the equally-weighted CRSP index. We use daily returns for the period that starts 100 days before and ends 100 days following the announced event, excluding the 41 trading days centered around the event date. Because there may have been some leakage of the default news, we include both the trading day before the announcement and the announcement day to calculate the two day cumulative abnormal return (CAR). In addition, because the estimated CAPM might be inaccurate, we check the calculation of the abnormal returns by simply subtracting the market portfolio from the return. In essence, this last procedure calculates the abnormal return where α is set to zero and β is set to one.[42]

The results are contained in Tables 3–6 and 3–7. Table 3–6 contains the results for the defaults by the two nonbank lenders, Lomas Financial and Equitable Lomas Leasing. Table 3–7 contains the results for Mortgage and Realty Trust and Washington Bancorporation. Both methods of determining abnormal returns result in approximately the same cumulative abnormal return, but in slightly different standard errors. The cumulative abnormal returns are significant in only one instance. The reaction of the stock returns

TABLE 3–6
Stock Price Reactions to Failures of Finance Companies[a]

	Failure of Lomas Financial		*Failure of* Equitable Lomas Leasing	
	(1) *2-day CAAR*[b]	*(2)* *2-day CAAR*[c]	*(3)* *2-day CAAR*[b]	*(4)* *2-day CAAR*[c]
1. Personal Credit Institutions	.0085 (.5216)	.0085 (.5077)	.0363 (2.0660)	.0363 (2.0000)
2. Short-Term Business Credit Firms	–.0416 (–.9503)	–.0416 (–.9092)	–.0247 (–.5508)	–.0247 (–.5248)
3. Miscellaneous Business Credit Firms	–.0370 (–.7629)	–.0370 (–.7348)	–.0287 (–.5824)	–.0287 (–.5588)
4. Mortgage Bankers and Loan Correspondents	.0026 (.0428)	.0026 (.0418)	–.0060 (–.0976)	–.0060 (–.0950)
5. Loan Brokers	–.0175 (–.2338)	–.0175 (–.2295)	–.0147 (.1943)	–.0147 (.1906)
6. Financial Lessors	.0379 (.4790)	.0379 (.4707)	–.0054 (.0685)	–.0054 (.0673)
7. Financial Services	–.0112 (–.1407)	–.0112 (–.1383)	.0134 (.1673)	.0134 (.1643)
8. All Above Firms	–.0066 (–.7255)	–.0066 (–.7262)	.0004 (.0429)	.0004 (.0433)

[a] *t*-statistics in parenthesis.
[b] Computed from CAPM estimates.
[c] Computed from $\alpha = 0$, $\beta = 1$.

on the portfolio of the personal credit institutions portfolio shows a *positive* response to the default of Equitable Lomas Leasing. In every other case, the response is insignificant. In fact, the *t*-statistics are so low that they would not be significant at very high *p*-values. It is difficult to explain the one instance of a significant, and incorrectly signed, result except to suggest that it is spurious.

TABLE 3–7
Stock Price Reactions to Failures of Finance Companies[a]

	Failure of Mortgage & Realty Trust		Failure of Washington Bancorp	
	(1) 2-day CAAR[b]	(2) 2-day CAAR[c]	(3) 2-day CAAR[b]	(4) 2-day CAAR[c]
1. Personal Credit Institutions	.0183	.0183	.0035	.0035
	(.1077)	(.1.0240)	(.2024)	(.1951)
2. Short-Term Business Credit Firms	.0088	.0088	–.0092	–.0092
	(.1038)	(.1036)	(–.0969)	(–.0968)
3. Miscellaneous Business Credit Firms	–.0037	–.0037	–.0033	–.0033
	(–.0412)	(–.0411)	(–.0332)	(–.0031)
4. Mortgage Bankers and Loan Correspondents	.0311	.0311	–.0300	–.0300
	(.3196)	(.3108)	(.2784)	(.2764)
5. Loan Brokers	.0177	.0117	–.0452	–.0452
	(.1094)	(.1086)	(.–.3830)	(.–.3806)
6. Financial Lessors	–.0158	–.0158	.0019	.0019
	(–.1434)	(–.1423)	(.0155)	(.0162)
7. Financial Services	–.0030	–.0030	.0021	.0021
	(–.0270)	(–.0268)	(.0018)	(.0175)
8. All Above Firms	.0063	.0063	.0031	.0031
	(.5630)	(.5623)	(.2955)	(.2941)

[a] *t*-statistics in parenthesis.
[b] Computed from CAPM estimates.
[c] Computed from $\alpha = 0, \beta = 1$.

A final test for contagion effects was performed using a time series of yields on finance company paper that is collected by the Federal Reserve. Similar to our earlier test using commercial paper, we regressed the three-month finance company paper–Treasury bill spread (the risk premium on finance company paper) on the contemporaneous three-month Treasury bill yield and four dummy variables. The dummy variables take the value of one during the week that one of the previously mentioned defaults occurred, and zero otherwise. As can be seen from the third column of Table 3–1, three of the four default events coincide with a negative, rather than positive, abnormal component of the risk premium. In all four default events, however, the abnormal component is statistically insignificant. Column four of Table 3–1 repeats this test, but instead uses the change in the risk premium, rather than the level. Again, there is no statistically significant evidence of an increase in the risk premium on finance company paper.

The main result of this section is that there is no strong evidence that nonbank lenders are subject to contagion effects that, historically, have affected U.S. commercial banks. We interpret this as evidence that these firms do not require government insurance or regulation in the way that banks may require.

THE BACKING OF COMMERCIAL PAPER: THE LINK BETWEEN LENDING AND TRANSACTIONS SERVICES

The U.S. commercial paper market is over a century old, but it expanded rapidly only after the 1966 credit crunch that resulted from Regulation Q's restrictions on the interest rates that could be paid on commercial bank CDs. Unable to raise sufficient funds at this time, banks actually encouraged their corporate customers to issue commercial paper for which the banks would provide back-up lines of credit (loan commitments). Why were these lines of credit necessary? A short answer is that they enhanced the marketability or liquidity of the paper. By providing borrowing firms with access to credit when their commercial paper matures, a bank provides a type of (limited) insurance to the holders of the maturing paper. With a back-up line of credit, the likelihood of the company's defaulting on its paper is reduced, making the paper a nearly riskless security. This makes commercial paper a much more attractive, tradable security for those investors who cannot evaluate the risk of the issuing company at low cost. Individuals and institutions that do not have expertise in information-intensive credit evaluation, but that have potential needs for liquidity, would prefer this security to unbacked paper.[43]

If a bank has the ability to enhance the marketability of commercial paper by guaranteeing that the issuer has sufficient funds to repay the maturing paper, one might expect that issuers would contract to have banks provide binding guarantees, such as an irrevocable letter of credit. However, this is usually not the case. The great majority of commercial paper issues are backed by lines of credit that give banks an escape clause.[44] The line of credit contract specifies that the bank is not obligated to provide credit if there is a "materially adverse change" in the borrower's condition. This vague phrase gives banks significant leeway in determining whether to fulfill their loan commitment and hence appears to reduce the value of the bank's credit enhancement. It might seem odd that use of this ambiguous contract is widespread.

A recent paper by Boot, Greenbaum, and Thakor (1990) gives a compelling explanation to this puzzle.[45] They consider a model in which a bank's value consists of both its financial capital and reputational capital. Financial capital is the bank's tangible net worth, while reputational capital reflects investors' beliefs about the bank's likelihood of honoring its guarantees, such as a back-up line of credit. The value of the bank's financial capital is known only to itself, and if it becomes too small, insolvency will prevent the bank from providing future guarantees to borrowers whose credit is known only by the bank. In this environment, it may be optimal for contracts to be ambiguous because it gives the bank the flexibility of reducing its reputational capital (by not fulfilling its guarantee) rather than its financial capital. In contrast, a precise binding contract would force a bank to reduce its financial capital, which could be extremely costly if it led to a high probability of the bank's insolvency. This model might explain the unusually high number of commercial paper defaults since 1989. Perhaps because of the recent weakness of many banks, they have become more inclined to invoke "materially adverse change" clauses, giving up their reputational capital rather than more of their financial capital.

While the weakened position of banks may have reduced the value of their back-up lines of credit and increased the risk of commercial paper, there are other market forces that may be leading to lower risk commercial paper. Prior to the 1970 Penn Central default, commercial paper was unrated. Now, over 99 percent of all commercial paper outstanding is rated. Moody's *Special Report* "Defaults and Orderly Exits of Commercial Paper Issuers," January 1991, documents a number of features regarding the commercial paper market. While a number of public issuers have defaulted since the early 1980s, only one issuer (Manville) had a prime rating at the time of its default.[46] Three issuers (Wang, Lomas Financial, and Equitable Lomas Leasing) were rated below prime at the time of default. Most of the other issuers were unrated. In addition, U.S. investors now appear to be more averse to lower rated and unrated commercial paper. The stock of unrated commercial paper fell from a high of $5 billion (0.7% of the total) in June of 1989 to $2 billion (0.2% of the total) in December of 1990. This aversion often forces companies experiencing a decline in credit worthiness to exit the commercial paper market well in advance of their failure.

Commercial paper issuers are also finding alternatives to less reliable bank lines of credit.[47] Internal sources of liquidity, such as a portfolio of marketable securities, will enhance an issuer's credit worthiness. Related to this is the market for collateralized commercial paper, where commercial paper holders are given a senior claim on a pool of receivables or other assets, often backed by a bank letter of credit. In addition, commercial paper issuers can seek irrevocable guarantees from non-bank sources, such as insurance companies or the issuer's parent company. This last alternative is worth emphasizing. While there are likely to be valid economic reasons for firms to continue to issue commercial paper that carries a third party guarantee, we see no reason why this third party need be an institution issuing government insured liabilities. Based on historical experience, lending institutions structured as insurance or finance companies appear to have the expertise needed to perform the role of a guarantor. A parent or affiliated company possessing known financial strength is also a candidate for this role, given its easy access to information regarding the issuing firm. The Japanese *keiretsu* could be broadly construed as an affiliation in which these guarantees are provided.[48]

CONCLUSION

In this study, we have reviewed theoretical arguments and examined empirical evidence regarding the stability of nonbank lending and nonbank transactions services. Our findings yield no evidence that these activities are prone to the type of information externalities that seemed to exist, historically, when these activities were combined. Improvements in information technology have likely been the primary cause of the rapid development of money markets, such as the commercial paper market. This new source of liquidity has made the MMF industry feasible. In addition, it has stimulated the growth in nonbank loan creation because nonbank lenders are now able to issue securities, such as commercial paper, that provide the beneficial incentives previously provided for only by demandable bank debt.

Given that information technology has altered the financial environment and allowed the separation of lending and transactions services, it should be no surprise that certain sources of financial instability have also been alleviated. In designing financial system reforms, it is imperative for policy makers to recognize the new possibilities created by this innovation.

NOTES

1. It is worth emphasizing that banking panics are not inherent to banking since many countries have not experienced banking panics despite the fact that the banking contracts are similar or identical to those in the U.S. The industrial organization of banking seems to be the crucial factor determining whether panics occur or not. Highly branched banking systems, with a small number of banks, are not prone to panics. See Calomiris and Gorton (1991) for a discussion.
2. In fact, in the six banking panics in the U.S. that occurred between 1865 and 1914, the panic began at business cycle peaks when depositors received information predicting a recession. Every time this variable reached a critical level there was a panic, and not otherwise. See Gorton (1988).
3. An issue we do not consider concerns the effect of this unbundling on monetary policy.
4. Empirical evidence that bank loans are unique in corporation finance is provided by James (1987), Lummer and McConnell (1989), Fama (1985), Hoshi, Kashyap, and Scharfstein (1990), Gilson, John, and Lang (1990), and James and Weir (1991).
5. The basic theoretical argument is that individual investors cannot produce these services because of free riding problems and the costly duplication of effort that would be entailed if investors individually undertook to perform these functions. The theoretical arguments are provided by Boyd and Prescott (1986), Campbell and Kracaw (1980), and Diamond (1984), among others. See Gorton and Pennacchi (1990b) for a discussion.
6. The theoretical arguments are provided by Diamond (1984) and Gorton and Pennacchi (1990a, 1989).
7. Though not payable on demand, the average maturity of U.S. commercial paper has been fairly short, between 20 and 30 days.
8. The inability to roll over commercial paper when the issuing firm's perceived risk increases is a common characteristic of the commercial paper market. It is referred to as "orderly exit" by Moody's. See Moody's *Special Report* on "Defaults and Orderly Exits of Commercial Paper Issuers," January 1991.
9. The junk bond market grew from $1.2 billion issued in 1980 to over $30 billion issued in 1986. See Asquith, Mullins and Wolf (1989). Medium-term notes grew from almost nothing to $34.9 billion issued in 1989. See Federal Reserve *Bulletin*, November 1986, and August 1990.
10. The outstanding volume was $258.7 billion in the last quarter of 1989. See Gorton and Pennacchi (1990c).
11. Figures are for August 1991 as published in "Trends in Mutual Fund Activity," Investment Company Institute.
12. Precautionary balances need not be an issue if MMF shareholders have access to a (separately structured) line of credit that operates in conjunction with their MMF. For example, Merrill Lynch's Cash Management Account (CMA) provides an Investor CreditLine Service that gives individual investors an automatic line of credit when balances in their CMA Money Fund accounts reach zero. Hence, overdraft checking is effectively provided. Merrill Lynch also provides a similar service for corporations and businesses called the Working Capital Management account.

    Note, also, that a constant share price is not a necessary condition for the feasibility of checking services. A number of variable share price bond mutual funds offer checking services.

13. Four MMFs were holding commercial paper issued by Integrated Resources when it defaulted on $276 million in June 1989. Ten MMFs were holding commercial paper of Mortgage & Realty Trust when it defaulted on $150 million in March of 1990. In each case, the fund managers re-purchased the defaulted paper at par. For example, Value Line Cash and Liquid Green Trust held $22.6 and $9 million, respectively, of Integrated Resources paper. Losses of approximately 60% of principal were absorbed by Value Line, Inc., the parent of Value Line Cash, and Unified Management, the investment advisor of Liquid Green Trust. An example of absorbed losses due to interest rate risk occurred in 1980. Institutional Liquid Assets, an institutional MMF, increased the average maturity of its $1.4 billion portfolio of government securities to over 70 days. Following a surge in interest rates, investors withdrew over $400 million in three days, resulting in a $2 million capital loss on the liquidated securities. This loss was covered by Salomon Brothers, the fund's distributor, and First National Bank of Chicago, the fund's advisor. However, there is one instance in which implicit insurance was not provided. In 1977, the shareholders of First Multifund for Daily Income, a small New York MMF, suffered a 7% decline in their holdings during a two day period following a surge in interest rates. The fund's advisor and directors were later sued by the SEC for lengthening the duration of the fund's portfolio beyond the limits set by SEC regulations. See Barron's "Never Say Never or, How Safe is Your Money-Market Fund?" March 26, 1990, and the "SEC is Accelerating Its Inspections of Mutual Funds," the *Wall Street Journal*, December 4, 1990.
14. See the *Federal Register*, Vol. 56, No. 39, February 27, 1991, pp. 8113–30, for the details of these new requirements.
15. A security is considered to have the highest rating if at least two nationally recognized statistical rating organizations (NRSROs) give the security their highest short-term rating. Currently, the SEC has designated five NRSROs: Duff and Phelps, Inc., Fitch Investors Services, Inc., Moody's Investors Service, Inc., Standard & Poor's Corp., and IBCA Limited.
16. See "Money Market Funds Shedding Lower-Grade Paper," the *Wall Street Journal*, October 22, 1990.
17. See IBC/Donoghue's, "Money Fund Report," for week ending October 8, 1991.
18. While time series data on the rating of MMFs' commercial paper holdings were not available, there is some casual evidence of a reduction in MMFs' holding of lower grade paper. See "Money Market Funds Shedding Lower-Grade Paper," the *Wall Street Journal*, October 22, 1990.
19. Over the 11/10/79 to 6/28/91 sample period, the mean of the three month commercial paper–T-bill spread was .825 (82.5 basis points). The spread had a weekly standard deviation of .516. While not reported here, some statistical tests were also performed using six month maturity commercial paper and Treasury bill yields. There were no significant differences in the results. We choose to emphasize the results using three month paper because of the greater volume of paper issued at this maturity.
20. In 1970 when Penn Central defaulted on $82 million of commercial paper, many commercial paper issuers had difficulty in rolling over their paper. At the time, commercial paper issues were unrated.

21. A panic could potentially arise because investors in the typical MMF may not know whether their fund is holding the particular commercial paper issue that has defaulted. While MMFs list their security holdings at the time of their quarterly reports, their exact holdings in between report dates are uncertain. However, this panic situation could be avoided if MMFs immediately announce whether they are or are not holding the defaulted paper. Those that hold the paper should also immediately announce whether they will provide implicit insurance or mark down their share price.
22. During this sample period, the assets of taxable MMFs, excluding funds holding only government securities, grew at a 13.6% annual rate (weekly mean = .0026), with an annualized standard deviation of 6.0% (weekly standard deviation = .0083). The assets of MMFs holding only government securities grew at a 22.1% annual rate (weekly mean = .0042), with an annualized standard deviation of 7.3% (weekly standard deviation = .0101). These time series were kindly supplied to us by IBC/ Donoghue of Holliston, Massachusetts. The data are listed in their weekly Money Fund Report over the period 12/31/85 to 7/02/91.
23. These regressions were also carried out with the eleven dummy variables taking the value of 1 in both the week when a default occurred as well as the following week. This was done to account for the possibility that a default event might induce an abnormal change in MMF assets not only immediately, but with a one week lag. This modification made no difference in our qualitative results.
24. A notable exception is the largest MMF, Merrill Lynch's Cash Management Account (CMA), with assets of approximately $29 billion. Note that the setting of a minimum check level is not due to any legal prohibition against charging a per check fee, as some funds do charge a fee. However, Baumol et al. (1990) state that the average MMF's minimum check size has declined since the introduction of bank Money Market Deposit Accounts.
25. See Berger and Humphrey (1990) for the volume of transactions provided by different payment mechanisms.
26. Goodfriend (1991) makes this argument in terms of savings from transporting commodity money reserves. In the current age in which payment takes the form of electronic debiting or crediting of a reserve account at a clearinghouse, it is not clear that significant savings result from delay of payment. Instantaneous payment may require an institution's maintaining a greater reserve account that otherwise. But if reserves can be held in the form of interest bearing securities (e.g., Treasury securities), as in the case of futures clearinghouses, the cost of holding greater reserves should not be significant.
27. While member banks of the private Clearing House Interbank Payments System (CHIPS) are at risk to each other for the extension of intraday credit, this is not the case for Fedwire. Similar to federal deposit insurance, the federal government guarantees "daylight overdrafts" on Fedwire. A number of academics and policy makers have expressed concern regarding the government's potential loss from bank payment-system failures. This exposure to losses would be largely eliminated (as it would be for deposit insurance) if member financial institutions were structured as equity financed MMFs.
28. See Berger and Hannan (1989), Hannan and Berger (1991), and Neumark and Sharpe (1991).

29. For example, see Davis, Korobow, and Wenninger (1987) and Davis and Korobow (1987), who report survey evidence on banks' consumer deposit pricing.
30. See Baumol et al. (1990, chapter 3). Investors have access to good information regarding a MMF's fees and expenses. A fee table must be included at the beginning of each fund's prospectus.
31. Given that the profit maximizing pricing of accounts balances is a non-linear function of the quantity of account balances (e.g., banks charge interest rates that vary by deposit level), suppliers are clearly worse off if they are restricted to a linear pricing schedule (e.g., MMFs must pay the same dividend per share irrespective of the number of shares owned by a MMF investor). As is discussed in Tirole (1988, p.149), however, restricting suppliers to a linear pricing schedule has ambiguous social welfare implications in general. However, a requirement that transactions be provided by MMFs not only requires linear pricing but also that pricing be fairly close to marginal cost (because of the ICA's excessive-fee restrictions). Hence, it is likely that social welfare would increase with this requirement.
32. The key data omission concerns lending by insurance companies. These lenders are not counted as finance companies by the government, and data have, so far, eluded us.
33. Using annual data from 1960 to 1990, a regression of banks' share on time has a coefficient of 0.189 and a standard error of 0.004.
34. Again, using annual data from 1960 to 1990, a regression of the auto loan share on time results in a coefficient of –0.492 with a standard error of 0.112.
35. The coefficient is –.821 with a standard error of 0.461, significant at the 10 percent level.
36. See Moody's *Special Report* on "Defaults and Orderly Exists of Commercial Paper Issuers," January 1991. Most firms issue commercial paper with overlapping thirty day average maturities. Hence, an inability to roll over their paper generally implies a gradual, but steady loss of financing.
37. The important exceptions are the wholly owned financial subsidiaries of other companies, such as Ford Motor Credit, Chrysler Financial, or GE Credit.
38. Canada's last banking panics were in the 1830s. Deposit insurance was passed in the late 1960s.
39. A third potential explanation for why nonbank lenders may not be subject to panics is that a substantial portion of their liabilities (e.g., commercial paper) is backed by lines of credit or third party insurance. We discuss this issue below.
40. As Wall and Peterson (1990) point out, the results do not imply that there are not information externalities in banking since the "too big to fail" doctrine is unobservable. The results are consistent with a lack of market discipline.
41. Firms without traded equity clearly could not be included.
42. Because of the cross-sectional dependence we report *t*-statistics. The *t*-statistics are calculated as follows: There are two trading days included in the calculation of the cumulative abnormal return (*CAR*). *AAR* is the average abnormal return over the period of 100 trading days prior to 20 trading days before the event date. The standard error is given by:

$$se(CAR) = [2Var(AR) + 2Cov(AR_t, AR_{t+1})]^{1/2}$$

where:

$$\text{Var}(AR) = \frac{\sum_{t-100}^{t-21} (AR_t - AAR)^2}{100}$$

$$\text{Cov}(AR_t, AR_{t+1}) = (\frac{1}{100})\sum_{t-100}^{t-21} [(AR_t - AAR)(AR_{t+1} - AAR)]$$

The formula captures first-order serial dependence among the average abnormal returns and adjusts the estimated standard error accordingly. The results are not sensitive to this.

43. Gorton and Pennacchi (1990a) provide the theoretical model that is the basis for this idea.
44. Rowe (1986) reports that as of May 1986 only 7.7% of commercial paper outstanding was backed by letters of credit or other irrevocable guarantees.
45. An alternative, though less than satisfactory, explanation is that current risk-based capital standards require banks to hold additional capital when they provide an unambiguous guarantee such as a standby letter of credit, though not when they provide a short-term line of credit. This explanation is inadequate, however, since the great majority of commercial paper issues were backed by credit lines prior to capital requirements on off-balance sheet guarantees.
46. Moody's states that well over 90% of commercial paper issues carry a prime rating.
47. See Moody's *Special Report*, "Alternate Liquidity for Commercial Paper Programs," November 1989.
48. See Hoshi, Kashyap, and Scharfstein (1990) for empirical evidence regarding the benefits of *keiretsu* affiliation.

REFERENCES

Asquith, Paul, David Mullins, and Eric Wolf (1989), "Original Issue High Yield Bonds: Aging Analyses of Defaults, Exchanges, and Calls," *Journal of Finance 44*, pp. 923–52.

Bailey, Dianna, and Donald Mullineaux (no date), "The Nonuniqueness of Bank Loans," University of Kentucky mimeograph.

Baumol, William J., Stephen M. Goldfeld, Lilli A. Gordon, and Michael F. Koehn (1990). *The Economics of Mutual Fund Markets: Competition Versus Regulation.* Boston: Kluwer Academic Publishers.

Berger, Allen N., and Timothy H. Hannan (1989), "The Price-Concentration Relationship in Banking," *Review of Economics and Statistics 71*, pp. 291–99.

Berger, Allen N., and David B. Humphrey (1990), "Market Failure and Resource Use: Economic Incentives to Use Different Payment Instruments," in David B. Humphrey (ed.), *The U.S. Payment System: Efficiency, Risk and the Role of the Federal Reserve, Proceedings of a Symposium on the U.S. Payment System Sponsored by the Federal Reserve Bank of Richmond.* Boston: Kluwer Academic Publishers.

Bernard, Victor (1987), "Cross-Sectional Dependence and Problems in Inference in Market-Based Accounting Research," *Journal of Accounting Research 25*, pp. 1–48.

Boot, Arnold W., Stuart I. Greenbaum, and Anjan V. Thakor (November 1990), "Reputation and Constructive Ambiguity in Financial Contracting," Indiana and Northwestern Universities mimeograph.

Boyd, John, and Edward Prescott (1986), "Financial Intermediary-Coalitions," *Journal of Economic Theory 38*, pp. 211–32.

Brown, Stephen, and Jerold Warner (1980), "Measuring Security Price Performance," *Journal of Financial Economics 8*, pp. 205–58.

Calomiris, Charles, and Gary Gorton (1991), "The Origins of Banking Panics: Models, Facts, and Bank Regulation," in Glenn Hubbard (ed.), *Financial Markets and Financial Crises.* Chicago: University of Chicago Press.

Calomiris, Charles, and Charles Kahn (1991), "The Role of Demandable Debt in Structuring Optimal Banking Arrangements," *American Economic Review 81*, pp. 497–513.

Campbell, Tim, and William Kracaw (1980), "Information Production, Market Signalling and the Theory of Financial Intermediation," *Journal of Finance 25*, pp. 863–81.

Chatfield, Robert, and Charles Moyer (1986), "'Putting' Away Bond Risk: An Empirical Examination of the Value of the Put Option on Bonds," *Financial Management 15*, pp. 26–33.

Crabbe, Lee (1991), "Callable Corporate Bonds: A Vanishing Breed," Division of Research and Statistics, Board of Governors of the Federal Reserve System working paper No. 155.

Davis, Richard G., and Leon Korobow (1987), "The Pricing of Consumer Deposit Products—The Non-rate Dimensions," Federal Reserve Bank of New York *Quarterly Review* (Winter), pp. 14-18.

Davis, Richard G., Leon Korobow, and John Wenninger (1987), "Bankers on Pricing Consumer Deposits," Federal Reserve Bank of New York *Quarterly Review* (Winter), pp. 6–13.

Diamond, Douglas (1984), "Financial Intermediation and Delegated Monitoring," *Review of Economic Studies 51*, pp. 39–44.

Fama, Eugene (1985), "What's Different About Banks?" *Journal of Monetary Economics 15*, pp. 5–29.

Flannery, Mark J. (1988), "Payments System Risk and Public Policy," in William S. Haraf and Rose Marie Kushmeider (eds.), *Restructuring Banking and Financial Services in America.* Washington, DC: American Enterprise Institute

Flannery, Mark J. (1991), "Debt Maturity and the Deadweight Cost of Leverage: Optimally Financing Banking Firms," University of Florida mimeograph.

Gilson, Stuart, Kose John, and Larry Lang (1990), "Troubled Debt Restructurings: An Empirical Study of Private Reorganizations of Firms in Default," *Journal of Financial Economics 27*, pp. 315–54.

Goodfriend, Marvin (1991), "Money, Credit, Banking, and Payments System Policy," Federal Reserve Bank of Richmond *Economic Review 77*, pp. 7-23.

Gorton, Gary (1988), "Banking Panics and Business Cycles," *Oxford Economic Papers 40*, pp. 751–81.

Gorton, Gary, and George Pennacchi (1989), "Security Baskets and Index-Linked Securities," National Bureau of Economic Research working paper no. 3711.

Gorton, Gary, and George Pennacchi (1990a), "Financial Intermediation and Liquidity Creation," *Journal of Finance 45*, pp. 49–72.

Gorton, Gary, and George Pennacchi (1990b), "Financial Innovation and the Provision of Liquidity Services," in Dan Brumbaugh (ed.), *Reform of Deposit Insurance and the Regulation of Depository Institutions in the 1990's* (forthcoming).

Gorton, Gary, and George Pennacchi (1990c), "The Opening of New Markets for Bank Assets," *Proceedings of a Conference sponsored by the Federal Reserve Bank of St. Louis on Recent Changes in the Market for Financial Services: Implications for Financial Institutions and Their Customers*. Boston: Kluwer Academic Publishers.

Gorton, Gary, and George Pennacchi (1991), "Banks and Loan Sales: Marketing Non-Marketable Assets," National Bureau of Economic Research working paper no. 3551.

Gorton, Gary, and Richard Rosen (1991), "Overcapacity and Exit From Banking," working paper.

Hannan, Timothy H., and Allen N. Berger (1991), "The Rigidity of Prices: Evidence from the Banking Industry," *American Economic Review 81*, pp. 938–45.

Hoshi, Takeo, Anil Kashyap, and David Scharfstein, 1990, "The Role of Banks in Reducing the Costs of Financial Distress in Japan," *Journal of Financial Economics 27*, pp. 67-88.

James, Christopher (1987), "Some Evidence on the Uniqueness of Bank Loans," *Journal of Financial Economics 19*, pp. 217–35.

James, Christopher, and Peggy Weir (1991), "Borrowing Relationships, Intermediation, and the Cost of Issuing Public Securities," *Journal of Financial Economics 28*, pp. 149–72.

Lummer, Scott, and John McConnell (1989), "Further Evidence on the Bank Lending Process and the Capital Market Response to Bank Loan Agreements," *Journal of Financial Economics 25*, pp. 99–122.

Lyon, Andrew B. (1984), "Money Market Funds and Shareholder Dilution," *Journal of Finance 39*, pp. 1011–20.

Neumark, David, and Steven Sharpe (1991), "Market Structure and the Nature of Price Rigidity: Evidence from the Market for Consumer Deposits," *Quarterly Journal of Economics* (forthcoming).

Pozdena, Randall (1991), "Is Banking Really Prone to Panics?" Federal Reserve Bank of San Francisco *Weekly Letter*, No. 91-35.

Rowe, Timothy D. (1986), "Commercial Paper," in T. Cook and T. Rowe (eds.), *Instruments of the Money Market*, Federal Reserve Bank of Richmond.

Smith, Clifford (1986), "Investment Banking and the Capital Acquisition Process," *Journal of Financial Economics 15*, pp. 3–29.

Swary, I. (1986), "Stock Market Reaction to Regulatory Action in the Continental Illinois Crisis," *Journal of Business 59*, pp. 451–73.

Tirole, Jean (1988), *Theory of Industrial Organization*. Cambridge, MA: The MIT Press.

Wall, Larry, and David Peterson (1990), "The Effect of Continental Illinois' Failure on the Financial Performance of Other Banks," *Journal of Monetary Economics 26*, pp. 77–100.

APPENDIX 3–A1: NONBANKS

The following nonbanking companies have traded common stock on NYSE, AMEX, or NASDAQ; the returns on their shares, as provided by CRSP, were used in Tables 3–6 and 3–7. The grouping of these companies into different categories follows COMPUSTAT.

1. Personal Credit Institutions (N=12)
    - Aristar Inc.
    - Advanta Corp.
    - Beneficial Corp.
    - Capitol Street Corp.
    - Cencor Inc.
    - Commercial Credit Company
    - Government Employees Financial Corp.
    - Household International Inc.
    - Mercury Finance Co.
    - Primerica Corp.
    - Surety Capital Corp.
    - Western Acceptance Corp.
2. Short-term Business Credit (except agriculture) (N=7)
    - Angeles Finance Tr.

C.I.T. Group Holdings
Highlander International Corp.
Interfund Corp.
Medmaster Systems Inc.
TFC International Inc.
Tecfin Corp.

3. Miscellaneous Business Credit Institutions (N=5)
   Ampal American Israel
   Bando McGlockin Capital Corp.
   First Conn. Small Business Investment
   Foothill Group Inc.
   Southwest Capital Corp.
4. Mortgage Bankers and Loan Correspondents (N=10)
   Commonwealth Mortgage
   Commonwealth Mortgage Company, Inc.
   Countrywise Credit Ind. Inc.
   Farragut Mortgage Co. Inc.
   First Financial Caribbean Corp.
   Green Tree Acceptance Inc.
   Hammond Co.
   Loan America Financial
   Lomas Financial Corp.
   Trust America Service Corp.
5. Loan Brokers (N=3)
   AFN Inc.
   Cal Star Financial Services Inc.
   TCS Enterprises Inc.
6. Financial Lessors (N=5)
   Airlease Ltd.
   DVI Financial Inc.
   Phoenix American Inc.
   Trans Leasing International Inc.
   Triumph Capital Inc.
7. Financial Services (N=10)
   Acton Corp
   Berkshire Hathaway Inc.
   Broad Inc.
   ITT Corp.
   Leucadia National Corp.

Loews Corp.
Midland Co.
RE Capital Corp.
Transamerica Corp.
Wesco Financial Corp.

APPENDIX 3–A2: FAILURE EVENTS

Lomas Financial Corporation, defaulted September 1, 1989.

Lomas was a diversified financial services company that included mortgage banking, life insurance, commercial leasing, and real estate companies. The company defaulted on senior notes due September 1,1989. Its commercial paper was rated Not Prime at that time.

Equitable Lomas Leasing Corporation, defaulted September 12, 1989.

Equitable Lomas Leasing is a separate legal entity from Lomas Financial. Equitable Lomas, partially owned by Equitable Life Assurance Society of the United States, was primarily engaged in commercial leasing. The company defaulted on $53 million of commercial paper on September 12, 1989. The paper was rated Not Prime by Moodys at the time of default. The parent company was unable to support Equitable Lomas.

Mortgage and Realty Trust, defaulted March 3, 1990.

Mortgage and Realty Trust was a self-administered real estate investment trust that defaulted on $160 million of commercial paper (unrated by Moody's) on March 3, 1990. Following Standard and Poor's March 1990 downgrade of the company's commercial paper, the company was unable to obtain short-term financing in the commercial paper market or from its banks to pay off its maturing debt. The company filed for Chapter 11 protection on April 12, 1990. Its revenues for 1989 were $66 million.

Washington Bancorp., defaulted May 11, 1990.

Washington Bancorp., a commercial bank holding company, defaulted on $36.7 million of commercial paper on May 11, 1990. The paper was unrated at the time.

COMMENT

William S. Haraf

According to one strand of literature, the theoretical rationale for banks is that it is efficient to finance nonmarketable loans with demandable debt. This combination, however, creates the possibility of panics and justifies deposit insurance and bank regulation. Gorton and Pennacchi conjecture that technology and lower information costs have made it possible to replicate these traditional bank products without combining them. The key issue in their paper is whether money market mutual funds and finance companies are not only efficient, but less prone to information asymmetries and panics than banks. The title of their paper is provocative, but I am afraid that the Federal Trade Commission would accuse the authors of false advertising.

The crux of the paper is a set of regressions purporting to test for evidence of panic in the markets for money market mutual funds and commercial paper. Let me briefly describe the regressions and the authors' conclusions.

In the first set of regressions, the spread between the Federal Reserve's weekly average three month commercial paper and Treasury bill yields is regressed on the Treasury bill yield and 12 dummies for weeks with commercial paper defaults. With only one exception, the authors find no statistically significant changes in default risk premiums.

They interpret this as supporting "the hypothesis that commercial paper investors are able to discriminate between the risks of different issuers and that 'contagion' effects from default are not prevalent."

In the second set of regressions, total assets of all money market funds excluding those investing only in government securities are regressed on commercial paper and Treasury bill yields and dummies for weeks with commercial paper defaults. The assets of funds investing only in government securities are then regressed on the same set of variables. Again, the dummies are not generally significant. These regressions are proposed as a test for "evidence of panic" by money market fund investors. They conclude: "significant flight-to-quality behavior following commercial paper defaults is unsupported."

In a third set of regressions, Gorton and Pennacchi examine the stock price response of portfolios of nonbank lenders to default announcements by two nonbank lenders: Lomas Financial and Lomas Leasing and two other financial firms: Mortgage and Realty Trust and Washington Bancorp. They conclude: "there is no strong evidence that nonbank lenders are subject to contagion effects that, historically, have affected U.S. commercial banks. We interpret this as evidence that these firms do not require government insurance or regulation in the way that banks may require."

Perhaps I've been away from academia too long, but it's hard to take the results of these regressions as serious support for their conclusions. The failure to reject a null hypothesis is not a very powerful result, and it could have many plausible explanations. Presumably, at least some money market fund, commercial paper, and finance company investors have "panicked" in response to defaults by individual companies. The fact that there was not a statistically significant response does not mean there was not an economically significant response to these events.

The more interesting question is whether money market funds and finance companies are somehow less contagion prone than banks. On this point, the paper provides no direct evidence, but the authors suggest that it is so. Yet I am willing to bet that the following regressions would also produce few statistically significant coefficients:

- a regression of the spread between the average large (uninsured) CD rate for the banking industry as a whole and the Treasury bill rate on a set of dummy variables representing bank failure dates;
- a regression of banking industry deposits (uninsured or total) on a set of dummy variables representing individual bank failure dates;
- a regression of the value of a large portfolio of bank stocks on a set of dummy variables representing bank failure dates.

These are the analogous regressions using banking industry data to those reported in the paper. Suppose I am correct in assuming that most of the coefficients in these regressions would not be significantly different from zero. I suspect I would be accused of overinterpreting results if I followed Gorton and Pennacchi in concluding that: (a) large depositors are "able to discriminate between the risks of different [banks] and that contagion effects from [bank failures] are not prevalent;" (b) "significant flight-to-quality behavior following [bank failures] is unsupported;" (c) "there is no strong evidence that [banks] are subject to contagion effects...these firms do not require government insurance or regulation in the way that banks [used to] require."

In sum, I believe that Gorton and Pennacchi's empirical results do not demonstrate very much, certainly not as much as they claim. Nonetheless, I do believe that technology, lower costs of information, and greater investor sophistication have made instances of panic or contagion less likely, not just for money market funds and finance companies, but also for banks.

The only evidence that Gorton and Pennacchi cite for contagion in banking is from Swary. He showed that when Continental Illinois failed, "questionable banks and liability-managed banks" experienced significantly negative returns. This is not evidence of panic, but a rational investor response to new information about a similarly situated institution. I believe that when Drexel, Burnham, Lambert failed, funding costs at other weak investment banks stuck with large amounts of bridge loans also increased. I doubt that the banking system as a whole experienced increased funding costs for uninsured instruments or an uninsured deposit drain when Continental Illinois failed.

George Kaufman, Anna Schwartz, Charles Calomiris, and others have, I believe, demolished the view that banks are generally prone to panic and contagion. There may be runs on individual banks, or groups of banks with common characteristics, but even in our own fragmented and vulnerable banking market, runs on the banking system as a whole are very unlikely.

Gorton and Pennacchi offer two reasons why nonbank lenders might not be subject to information asymmetries: First, they claim that most nonbank lenders, in addition to issuing putable debt and commercial paper, have traded equity. This is surely wrong. The vast majority of the top fifty finance companies in the United States are wholly owned subsidiaries of other companies. Second, they argue that information asymmetries between outsiders and loan creators have simply been reduced. This is true, but they admit that it also applies to banks. Indeed, my understanding is that the public disclosures required by bank regulators provide significantly more information about loan quality than the information the SEC requires of nonbank lenders, especially if they are wholly owned subsidiaries.

So, who will be the banks of the future? There is a good chance it won't be today's banks, at least not to a significant extent. The problem is not the nature of banking contracts; the problem is regulation. As Gorton and Pennacchi note, technology is making new products and delivery arrangements possible. Unfortunately, the banking industry is in the position that IBM would have been in today had Congress passed a law in the 1950s restricting its product offerings to mainframe computers. Banks simply cannot take advantage of market and technology changes as well as their competitors can. In Europe, banks and other financial services providers are combining to serve their customers better. This suggests that further integration, not further separation, of banking and financial activities could be more efficient absent regulation.

In addition, the cost burdens of bank regulation are considerable. It is interesting to note that, despite a tremendous expansion of the safety-net over the 1980s as a result of an increase in the official deposit insurance limit to $100,000, the articulation of the "too big to fail" doctrine, and the development of a sophisticated market in brokered deposits, insured institutions have lost market share to nonbanks. Indeed, the process appears to be accelerating. The mix of regulatory burdens and subsidies with which banks must operate has not been favorable for banks.

The rapidly growing separation of lending and liquidity services appears to be unique to the United State. Banks here are also uniquely burdened with uneconomic regulation. I conclude that the rapid growth of "alternative institutions" like money market funds and finance companies is primarily driven by the regulatory structure and that this separation is neither efficient nor necessarily desirable.

COMMENT

Robert E. Litan

I should confess at the outset that I like this paper, in significant part because it buttresses the case for narrow banking. Or more accurately, it helps rebut the principal criticism of the narrow banking concept that I have encountered since endorsing a version of the concept several years ago: Namely, that in a world in which more lending is channeled through uninsured lenders rather than deposit-insured banks, the financial system will be more exposed to systemic risk than it is now. Indeed, the recent failure by Congress to address the so-called "structural reform" issues in the 1991 banking bill makes this criticism and the narrow banking proposal to which it clearly relates of much greater interest than before.

Clearly, Congress in 1991 was in no mood to expand bank powers or to permit commercial firms to own banks at a time when it also was being asked to enable the FDIC to borrow up to $70 billion to bolster the resources of its beleaguered bank insurance fund (BIF). Congress was in this sour mood even though it called on the banks to repay the BIF. Imagine then how Congress is likely to react if as appears increasingly likely, in several years, additional funds must be poured into the BIF, not from the banks—who may be too weak to pay—but instead from *taxpayers*. If forced to swallow this castor oil, Congress almost surely will turn to even more drastic measures, and the one currently sitting on top of the shelf is some version of "core" or "narrow" banking. And any of these versions would have the effect of forcing more borrowing through the securities markets and uninsured lenders rather than through banks.

Indeed, even if Congress does not force to banks to narrow the range of their asset investments, the market has already done so. Having taken heavy losses on their loans to less developed countries, real estate developers, and leveraged buyout artists, a number of larger banks are turning instead to the "middle market," or medium sized companies, and to individuals for lending business. In the process, these banks are moving to become the "core banks" that Lowell Bryan, for one, would require them to become.[1]

In short, the issue that Gorton and Pennacchi address in their paper—the contagion risk in the commercial paper (CP) market and among noninsured lending institutions—is likely to become more important with time. What about their answers? I find them convincing. Based solely on the data points in their regressions, it certainly appears that the market is very capable of distinguishing bad from good CP and weak from strong nonbank lenders.

I would also add some anecdotal evidence to support these statistical results. I distinctly recall that during the week of October 19, 1987—or just days after the infamous 1987 stock market crash—Ford Motor Company, and perhaps other large corporate issuers, were easily able to sell medium-term unsecured debt, demonstrating that even in a financial panic buyers will buy good corporate paper. Similarly, the entire municipal bond market did not grind to a halt in the mid-1980s when the Washington Public Power System (WPSS) defaulted on its bonds. And the CP market did not go into a freefall recently when Drexel's security operations defaulted on its own CP.

Nevertheless, all of this evidence only takes one so far. The fact remains that the Gorton/Pennacchi data base necessarily does not include CP defaults from the largest issuers—such as GE Capital, GMAC, Salomon, or Merrill Lynch—whose potential failures are uppermost on the minds of those who worry most about the contagion risk inherent in the uninsured lending market. Put bluntly, are any of these large issuers like the large commercial banks that have been treated as "too big to fail"? If they are, so the critics of narrow banking argue, then there is little to be gained and conceivably much to be lost by shoving more of the nation's lending through nonbanks.

The honest answer to this question, of course, is that no one knows whether investors in CP would run from the market generally if one of the largest CP issuers defaulted. But I would argue that the Fed need not put itself in the position of having to bail out the creditors of any specific troubled or failed CP issuer in order to save the financial system from collapse. Instead, all the monetary authorities need to do when faced with such a situation is to pump reserves into the banking system by purchasing Treasury securities. Turning on the monetary spigot will bring Treasury yields down and thus widen any spread between CP and Treasury bills. At some point, the wider spread will bring buyers back to CP, and any contagion can be nipped in the bud. This, of course, is precisely what the Fed did in the wake of the October 1987 stock market crash. It injected much needed liquidity into the market *generally* without having to lend directly to any troubled company *in particular*.

Of course, the Fed also twisted the arms of some large commercial banks to continue lending to temporarily illiquid securities firms after the crash. Thus, some critics of narrow banking, and others who worry about the declining role of banks, are concerned that in a financial system dominated by lenders not under the Fed's direct control the Fed will not be in a position to use banks as a proxy for lending directly to illiquid, but presumably solvent, enterprises in the future—securities firms, insurance companies, or other types of enterprises that the Fed may deem essential to overall economic stability.

All of this is true, which means that if the Fed is truly worried about the viability of particular firms, it will have to lend to them directly (which it has long had the authority to do)—on good collateral of course. This does not mean, however, that the Fed needs to regulate all of the firms to which it may think it may have to lend. Such an open-ended reading of its potential responsibilities would give the Fed license to become a behind-the-scenes regulator of a good portion of the economy.

I want to conclude with an observation concerning discussion at this conference that seemed to put universal and narrow banking concepts at the opposite ends of a spectrum. In fact, the proposals are really much closer than might appear. At least under the version of narrow banking that I have advocated, narrow banks would have the right to affiliate with any other type of enterprise with a minimum of firewalls. Thus, I would envision a narrow bank's being able to sell other products in the same lobby and with the same personnel as may be engaged in other activities. The requirement that deposits in narrow banks be collateralized by marketable securities (actually they would be overcollateralized because of capital requirements) is what provides insulation to the FDIC, not the firewalls.

In short, a narrow bank affiliated with many other types of enterprises differs only from a universal bank in that the narrow bank's funding of its "nonbank" operations must come from uninsured funds. But both narrow and universal banks would still be able to enjoy operational economies.

To summarize, Gorton and Pennacchi have provided important findings about the lack of contagion risk in the nonbank lending market. These findings are especially important to advocates of core or narrow banks, for reasons I have mentioned. And while the authors (fortunately) do not have the opportunity to include the failure of large uninsured lenders in their statistical analysis, the monetary authorities have it well within their power to curtail contagion risk without lending directly to the troubled lenders.

NOTES

1. There has been much confusion about the content of the various narrow and core banking proposals. In the original version I proposed in 1987, the narrow requirements applied only to banks that wanted to affiliate with other nonbanking enterprises; these banks could then invest only in government or quasi-governmental securities. See Robert E. Litan, *What Should Banks Do?* (Brookings, 1987). Two years later, a Brookings task force of seven authors also proposed a conditional narrow bank or collateralization requirement (only for banks wanting to affiliate with other enterprises), but in this version the permissible asset list was expanded to include any security with a well-developed secondary market and the bank was required to mark its assets to market. See *Restructuring America's Financial Institutions* (Brookings, 1989). Since then, others—notably James Burnham, James Pierce, and James Tobin—have suggested applying a narrow banking requirement to *all* banks, whether or not they choose broader affiliations. Finally, Lowell Bryan—who originally supported a conditional narrow bank proposal—has lately urged a "core banking" requirement for all banks; in his scheme, the core banks would face steadily tighter loan-to-one-borrower restrictions as their assets grew and all would be subjected to a new Regulation Q deposit interest rate ceiling that floated with the Treasury rate.

COMMENT

Robert C. Pozen

In my comments, I will concentrate on money market funds as potential substitutes for bank deposit accounts. Gorton and Pennacchi examine this issue of substitution by testing whether money market funds (with uninsured deposits) are subject to information externalities (contagion effects) as a result of defaults on commercial paper held by money market funds. They find that such information externalities do not exist.

While their findings seem correct to me, I am struck by the narrowness of their test. To evaluate substitutability of money market funds for bank deposit accounts, I will explore a broader array of indicators from the viewpoint of the consumer. I will compare these two vehicles as to their financial returns and non-financial benefits relative to downside risks. I will then try to relate this comparative analysis to the policy debate about the proposal for a narrow FDIC-insured bank.

FINANCIAL RETURNS

I have done "in-depth research" on the financial returns of money market funds (MMFs) versus bank deposit accounts by reading the *Wall Street Journal* over the last few weeks. This research shows that the average 7-day yield on MMFs consistently exceeds the average interest rates on money market deposit accounts and 3-month CDs, but that the 7-day yield on

MMFs may be higher or lower than the average interest rate on 6-month CDs. While relative return obviously will vary depending on the level of interest rates and the shape of the yield curve, it seems fair to conclude that MMFs are good substitutes only for short-term deposits of 6 months or less, at least for instruments that yield taxable returns.

But MMFs do have one significant advantage over bank accounts in terms of after-tax return. Money market funds can produce tax-free yields by investing in short-term tax-exempt paper. Such funds have become quite popular, especially the double tax-free version (no federal or state tax in a particular state). To the best of my knowledge, no bank deposit currently provides a tax-free yield because a bank is not a true pass-through intermediary as a mutual fund is. A bank could provide a tax-free yield only through a personal trust or agency account, both of which are off the balance sheet of the bank and would not constitute an insured deposit.

ACCESS TO ACCOUNTS

If we look at convenience of withdrawing cash, bank deposits have a significant edge over MMFs. Banks allow cash withdrawals, not only at a multitude of branches but also through a broad array of ATMs. By contrast, most MMFs do not permit cash withdrawals even at investor centers. Investors typically receive a check from the MMF that must be cashed at a bank. While a few MMFs have allowed ATM access, the fees for ATM access to MMFs have typically been higher than those for ATM access to bank deposits.

MMFs do have one big advantage over bank accounts in terms of account access: It is very easy to switch from a MMF to an equity or bond fund within a complex. This usually can be done by phone in a matter of seconds. By contrast, it is relatively complicated to transfer out of a money market deposit account at a bank to an equity or bond account, unless this is done by a pre-authorized automatic sweep.

CHECKING PRIVILEGES

Most MMFs have limited checking privileges, with a minimum of $250 or $500 per check, but do not charge customer fees for checks. These checks are usually drawn on the bank serving as the MMF's custodian or transfer agent. Banks usually allow checks of any amount and usually do not charge customer fees per check. But banks usually charge an account fee unless the customer maintains a minimum balance.

Gorton and Pennacchi ask whether MMFs would provide more or cheaper checking if they were allowed to access directly the Fed payment system. The answer is that the costs of direct access to that system would probably not be worth the benefits for most MMFs. As Gorton and Pennacchi explain, MMFs are pass-through vehicles that lack the ability to build up equity capital. Yet the Federal Reserve requires substantial amounts of capital to back daylight overdrafts by any institution with access to the payment system.

The other relevant consideration is that MMFs generally charge expenses against the whole pool rather than individual accounts. As a result, there is little constraint on high checking volume by a few investors, who can spread the expenses across the pool. Some MMFs (e.g., Fidelity's Spartan Funds) have tried to solve this problem by externalizing transaction costs—i.e., charging the individual investor who writes a check or exchanges, rather than charging the pool. This pricing strategy has significantly reduced the transaction expenses and increased the yields of the Spartan Funds.

DOWNSIDE RISK

A comparison of downside risk must distinguish between accounts above and below $100,000. For accounts above $100,000, MMFs are generally less risky than bank deposits. The only exception is a large account in a bank that is "too big to fail." But this exception has been under severe attack from Congress and will likely be restricted.

For accounts below $100,000, the bank deposit is clearly less risky than the MMF account because the bank deposit is insured. The SEC has tightened the restrictions on MMFs by requiring that 95 percent of their assets be rated A_1P_1, imposing tough diversification limits, and setting 90 days as the maximum average maturity. Also, as pointed out by Gorton and Pennacchi, the advisers to MMFs have purchased at face value paper held by MMFs if the default on such paper would have forced a "breaking of the dollar." More could be done to decrease the risk of MMFs by changing SEC regulations to allow MMFs to establish loss reserves and/or to purchase private insurance.

POLICY IMPLICATIONS

In short, I would conclude that for many purposes MMFs are good substitutes for bank deposits, but that MMFs are inferior to bank deposits in two main respects:

1. Bank deposits provide individual consumers with better access to cash and better check-writing privileges for small amounts than MMFs.
2. Banks are better structured than MMFs to meet the requirements of direct access to the payment system and the services associated with that system.

On the assumption that government intervention should be limited to situations involving deficiencies in private market institutions, these two disadvantages of MMFs suggest two possible rationales for FDIC insurance of bank deposits. First, since MMFs do not provide ready access to cash and small checks, FDIC insurance might be justified on the ground of protecting relatively small deposits and withdrawals. Second, since MMFs are not in a good position to access the Federal payment system, FDIC insurance might be justified to support bank access to the payments system.

These two rationales for FDIC insurance are consistent with the narrow bank proposal that has been put forth by Robert Litan and others. Under this proposal, FDIC insurance would be limited to relatively small deposits (e.g., one $50,000 account per customer) at a bank whose assets would be limited to investments that are relatively liquid and that can be marked to market daily. Such a narrow bank would also be the only type of institution with access to the Federal payment system. The other types of the liabilities and assets now held by what we currently call banks would be allowed in non-insured bank affiliates of the FDIC-insured narrow bank as well as different kinds of financial institutions (e.g., finance companies, mortgage companies, etc.).

CHAPTER 4

SECURITIZATION, RISK, AND THE LIQUIDITY PROBLEM IN BANKING

Allen N. Berger
Gregory F. Udell

INTRODUCTION

The 1980s was a decade of dramatic change for depository institutions. Toward the beginning of the decade, geographic and product barriers were significantly reduced, and the deposit side of banks' balance sheets was substantially deregulated. By the end of the decade, the thrift industry had virtually collapsed, and commercial banking was plagued by a wave of failures unprecedented since the Great Depression. It is not surprising, then, that with the 1990s came a widespread feeling that the regulatory apparatus for the financial services industry was in need of a major overhaul. The title of the 1991 Treasury Department Report symbolizes this view: "Modernizing the Financial System—Recommendations for Safer, More Competitive Banks."

Restructuring the regulation of depository institutions, however, re-

The opinions expressed do not necessarily reflect those of the Board of Governors of the Federal Reserve System or its staff. The authors would like to thank Larry White for suggesting the topic of this research and making valuable comments. The authors also thank George Pennacchi, Sanford Rose, Ken Scott, and Lew Spellman for very helpful comments, and Jalal Akhavein for exceptional research assistance.

quires a clear understanding of the essence of banking and the relationship between banking and other financial markets. It has been argued that the essence of banking may have changed during the 1980s with the explosive growth of securitization, in which assets that formerly were on the balance sheets of banks are now held directly by individual investors. More than any other artifact of the decade, this growth of securitization challenges our understanding of the banking industry and the boundaries of financial intermediation. If the essence of banking is liquidity transformation, what are the implications of a process that redefines the liquidity of bank assets? Further, if the role of banks was delegated monitoring, what is their new role if investors are now directly holding many of the same types of assets? Thus, securitization tests our notions of the theory of financial intermediation, and it may force us to reexamine the way we regulate financial institutions. For instance, a justification that has often been made for government-provided deposit insurance is based on the costs associated with bank panics and the inherent illiquidity of a banking system that cannot easily sell its assets.

The purpose of this chapter is to examine both theoretically and empirically the relationships among securitization, risk, and liquidity in banking. In doing so, we attempt to expand the literature on securitization in several dimensions. We first present an extension to the modern information-based theory of financial intermediation that explains securitization as a reaction to improvements in monitoring and information technology. This "monitoring technology hypothesis" has a number of empirical implications and forms the basis for most of our empirical tests. We also summarize eight other plausible theories of securitization, most of them taken from the literature, and their empirical implications. We then explore the data on securitization behavior, risk, and liquidity in banking over time from a number of sources.

The centerpiece of our empirical analysis is an exploration of the relationships between several types of securitization and numerous measures of risk and liquidity using over 400,000 quarterly observations on banks from 1983 to 1991. This is the first paper to include the three main types of securitization—loan sales, standby letters of credit, and loan commitments—in the same regressions. This avoids the potential problem of picking up the effects of excluded types of securitization in the coefficient estimates of the included types. This procedure also allows us to test a variety of interesting hypotheses, including whether loan sales and standbys are treated identically in the market. We also explore the extent to which securitization activity represents a downsizing of the banking industry or an expansion of the industry into a form of securities underwriting.

Before embarking on this examination, it is important to define what we mean by securitization. For our purposes, it will be useful to view securitization as two distinct, but related, phenomena. By *disintermediation-type securitization,* we mean a movement away from intermediated bank loans towards direct financing of debt by capital markets. This may involve the sale of bank loans without recourse, or it may simply involve a shift in borrowing patterns away from bank-held debt and towards other forms of finance. In either case, the bank no longer acts as the principal monitor to ensure that the loan is repaid.

The second type of securitization involves shifting assets from on the balance sheet to off the balance sheet through a loan sale with recourse, a standby letter of credit, or a loan commitment that backs up a third-party loan. Under *off-balance-sheet securitization,* the bank retains the credit risk of the loan without supplying the funds directly and continues its role of monitoring because of its credit exposure. Off-balance-sheet securitization allows a bank to downsize its on-balance-sheet assets, reducing regulatory taxes such as reserve requirements, deposit insurance premia, and (in some cases) capital requirements, while continuing the traditional roles of monitoring and bearing credit risk [see Benveniste and Berger (1986), Greenbaum and Thakor (1987), Pennacchi (1988), and Berlin (1992)]. The fundamental economic distinction between disintermediation-type securitization and off-balance-sheet securitization is that only the former results in disintermediation in a meaningful economic sense.

Both types of securitization may be related to bank risk and liquidity. Benveniste and Berger (1987) and James (1988) presented models in which securitization is associated with relatively risky banks that wish to segregate the claims to risky and safe loans among investor pools. In these models, the relatively high quality assets are securitized, leaving the lower quality assets on the balance sheet for the depositors and the insurer. In contrast, Benveniste and Berger (1986), Avery and Berger (1991a), Boot and Thakor (1991), and Gorton and Pennacchi (1991) argued that securitization may be associated with safer banks because the value of bank guarantees is higher for safer banks or because the selection processes underlying securitization may favor safer borrowers. Moreover, the securitization phenomenon itself may change bank risk by altering the liquidity of bank assets and changing the probability and cost of bank runs. To the extent that the movement toward securitization has made bank assets remaining on the balance sheet more marketable in an emergency, bank liquidity risk may have been reduced. However, it is also possible that the process of securitization has already removed most of the liquid bank assets, leaving the remaining assets less liquid on average than previously. Thus, there is no consensus on the relationships among securitization, risk, and liquidity in banking and therefore little guidance in how to alter the regulatory system to meet the needs of the new financial services industry.

In order to investigate the net effect of securitization on bank risk, we turn to the theoretical literature on the theory of the banking firm. There has recently developed an extensive information-based literature on the theory of financial intermediaries as delegated monitors [e.g., see Diamond (1984), Ramakrishnan and Thakor (1984), Millon and Thakor (1985), Boyd and Prescott (1986), and Allen (1990)]. Unfortunately, this literature does not directly address the issue of securitization. Nevertheless, by extension this modern theory of the banking firm may yield valuable insights into the securitization process.

In the second section, we explore the logical extension of the modern theory to the securitization phenomenon. As noted above, the "monitoring technology hypothesis" will form the basis for our empirical tests of the relationships among securitization, risk, and liquidity in banking. The principal implication of this hypothesis is that securitization by itself is not likely to have a significant impact on bank risk or liquidity. Disintermediation-type securitization is predicted to be essentially independent of risk and liquidity. The intuition behind this prediction is that banks are essentially repositories for information-problematic, illiquid, risky loans. While this type of securitization may change the number or composition of borrowers whose loans are illiquid, it does not alter the basic fact that relatively illiquid, risky securities remain intermediated, while relatively liquid, safe securities do not require intermediation. The monitoring technology hypothesis provides no motive for off-balance-sheet securitization, although off-balance-sheet securitization is not inconsistent with the hypothesis; this type of securitization is likely driven by factors other than changes in monitoring technology. Under this hypothesis, off-balance-sheet securitization simply represents a segregation of bank assets between on- and off-balance-sheet accounts, and banks continue to bear the associated credit risk and to monitor the borrowers as if they remained on the balance sheet. The association between off-balance-sheet securitization and bank risk will be determined by whatever is the causal factor motivating this securitization.

The monitoring technology hypothesis contrasts sharply with the empirical predictions of some of the competing hypotheses noted above. In the third section, we outline these competing hypotheses and their respective empirical implications and also summarize the extant empirical literature on the topic. In the fourth section, we introduce the data on securitization, risk, and liquidity used to test the competing hypotheses and examine the aggregate behavior from 1983 to 1991 of several of the key variables. The fifth section presents our empirical analysis of the relationships among the variables using over 400,000 individual bank observations. The final section offers our conclusions.

SECURITIZATION AND THE THEORY OF THE BANKING FIRM

In this section, we informally extend the paradigm of the contemporary information-based theory of financial intermediation to encompass the phenomenon of securitization. The resulting "monitoring technology hypothesis" and its empirical implications will form the basis of most of our empirical analysis.

As noted above, we make an important distinction between disintermediation-type securitization (e.g., loan sales without recourse) and off-balance-sheet securitization (e.g., standby letters of credit that back up third-party loans). Our "monitoring technology hypothesis" argues that disintermediation-type securitization is a result of changes in the technology of monitoring, which has shifted the boundary between intermediated debt and direct investor debt in a direction that is unfavorable to banks. But these same technological changes have likely also shifted the boundary between insider debt and intermediated debt in a direction that is favorable to banks. The net effect may be either an increase or a decrease in the size of the banking sector, but banks will remain as specialists in lending to borrowers with information problems. If our hypothesis is the dominant explanation of disintermediation-type securitization, then this type of securitization should be essentially independent of bank risk and liquidity. However, our hypothesis has no empirical prediction about the relationship between off-balance-sheet securitization and risk, since under this hypothesis, off-balance-sheet securitization is motivated by factors other than changes in monitoring technology.

The modern theory of the banking firm rests on the assumption that contracting between borrowers and lenders is problematic because borrowers have informational advantages over lenders.[1] If lenders do not monitor borrowers and produce information about their payoff characteristics and actions, it is likely that borrowers will renege on their commitments to repay their loans. However, monitoring can be extremely costly. If every lender were to monitor each borrower, the duplication of effort could make the total monitoring cost prohibitively high and introduce degenerative free rider problems. Under these circumstances, financial intermediation arises as an organizational solution in which lenders (i.e., depositors) delegate responsibility for borrower monitoring to a bank.

Delegating monitoring responsibility, however, engenders its own set of incentive problems. That is, how can depositors be assured that the bank won't shirk its responsibility as a delegated monitor? Diamond (1984) and Ramakrishnan and Thakor (1984) demonstrated the importance of diversification in solving this delegated monitoring problem. In particular, Diamond rationalized the existence of banks as delegated monitors with economies of scale in monitoring borrowers on the asset side of the balance sheet and the ability to minimize signalling costs through diversification.

Bhattacharya and Thakor (1991) generalized the information-based theory of financial intermediation in a setting that specifies the conditions under which intermediary monitoring dominates direct monitoring by individual lenders. That is, they formalized the conditions under which intermediated debt dominates nonintermediated debt. In a market characterized by informational asymmetries, financial intermediation arises when the benefits of intermediary economies of scale in monitoring exceed the signalling costs incurred in convincing investors or depositors of the value of the intermediary's asset portfolio.[2]

By extension, it follows that the conditions under which the use of an intermediary dominates direct lending could exist for some borrowers and not for others, thereby permitting the theoretical coexistence of both intermediated markets and direct investment capital markets. That is, for high quality borrowers with minimal information problems, direct lender monitoring and capital market financing may dominate, while for low quality, information-problematic borrowers, intermediated financing may dominate. The boundary between the two groups is where the monitoring cost advantage of the intermediary is just offset by the costs associated with the intermediary's signalling its own quality.

Consistent with this line of reasoning, it may be useful to view borrowers as lying along a continuum with the most information-problematic borrowers at one end and the borrowers with the fewest information problems at the other end. In this setting, the location of a borrower along the information continuum will determine the type of financing that the borrower can obtain. This continuum is shown in Figure 4–1. At the far left are borrowers whose information problems are so acute that they cannot borrow from any outsiders because of the absence of any cost-effective monitoring technology. Next along the continuum are borrowers who fund in the intermediated markets through banks, thrifts, commercial finance companies, insurance companies, or other intermediaries. Finally, the borrowers with relatively few information problems lie along the far right of the continuum. The debt of these borrowers is held by direct investors who monitor the borrowers themselves.[3] As discussed below, included in the latter set of borrowers are those who contract with a bank, but whose loans are sold to direct investors without any explicit or implicit recourse to the bank.

Viewing borrowers as lying along this information continuum leads to a potential explanation for disintermediation-type securitization. If information/monitoring technology improved significantly in the past decade, as seems likely given the improvements in data processing and communications technologies and increased use of statistical techniques in credit analysis, then the boundaries between these types of funding sources are likely to have changed. Under the monitoring technology hypothesis, innovations in direct lender monitoring technology would move the boundary between intermediated debt and direct investor debt in Figure 4–1 to the left, other things equal. The highest quality, least information-problematic of bank borrowers would shift to the capital markets through disintermediation-type securitization, as the monitoring cost advantage of the bank fell below the level of the signalling costs of intermediation for these borrowers.[4, 5]

The boundary between intermediated debt and insider debt in Figure 4–1 may also be changed by improvements in monitoring technology. Innovations in intermediary monitoring technology would move the boundary between intermediated debt and insider debt to the left, as banks gain enough information to lend to previously "unbankable" borrowers. This encroachment of banks into insider debt territory may be augmented if there are also reductions in bank signalling costs. Thus, under our monitoring technology hypothesis, banks may lose some of their highest quality borrowers to disintermediation-type securitization because of improvements in direct lender monitoring technology, but they may gain some new borrowers at the low quality end because of improvements in intermediary monitoring of borrowers. The size of the banking sector could either decrease or increase, depending upon which of the boundaries moves further leftward on the continuum in Figure 4–1.

FIGURE 4–1
The Borrower Information Continuum

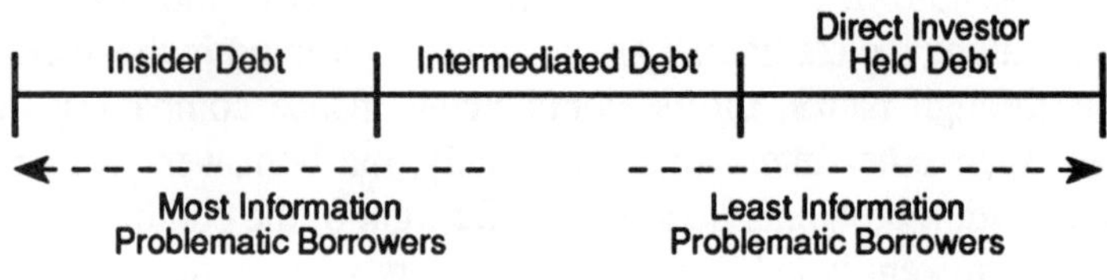

It follows from this line of reasoning that bank liquidity will be essentially unchanged by disintermediation-type securitization if the monitoring technology hypothesis is correct. Within this paradigm, banks continue to specialize in funding those borrowers who, because of their information problems, require bank monitoring and whose loans are therefore illiquid. That is, both before and after an innovation in monitoring technology, banks fund borrowers in the middle of the continuum for whom the bank has an information advantage over direct lenders that exceeds the marginal costs of the bank in signalling bank quality, but for whom the information problems are not so severe that the bank cannot fund them. Thus, either before or after the improvement in monitoring technology, the loans that a bank funds are in its portfolio *because* they are difficult to securitize—i.e., because the increase in monitoring costs if they were sold exceeds the bank's marginal signalling costs, so that sale of these assets could only be made at a loss.[6] Unfortunately, it is very difficult to test empirically for changes in bank liquidity because bank balance sheets report changes in the quantities of broad categories of assets, but not changes in the liquidity or marketability of the assets within these categories. In part for this reason, we also look to the implications of the monitoring technology hypothesis for changes in bank risk, which are more easily observable.

Similar to the implications for the size and liquidity of bank loan portfolios, the monitoring technology hypothesis implies some mutually offsetting changes in bank risk associated with the improvements in monitoring technology and changes in bank portfolios. The simultaneous egress from the banking sector of the least information-problematic borrowers through disintermediation-type securitization and ingress of relatively problematic, previously unbankable borrowers would increase intermediary risk, assuming that risk and information problems are strongly positively related. However, improvements in intermediary monitoring technology may also be expected to reduce risk in two ways. Improved monitoring enables intermediaries to sort borrowers better at the origination stage of lending, reducing *ex ante* borrower risk by reducing adverse selection problems in the pools of borrowers who receive bank funding. Similarly, improved monitoring technology also reduces *ex post* risk by improving the ability of intermediaries to observe borrower behavior after a loan is issued, allowing for better management of deteriorating credits and increased collections on nonperforming loans.[7] Both types of improvements should not only decrease the riskiness of the new set of borrowers (i.e., the formerly "unbankable" borrowers), but of the entire bank loan portfolio, i.e., over the entire intermediary lending portion of the continuum. It is assumed here that these decreases in risk will approximately offset the presumed increases in risk from the shifts along the information continuum. To the extent that bank information and liquidity problems perfectly predict differences in borrower risk, the offset will be complete, and the monitoring technology hypothesis predicts no change in risk associated with the increase in disintermediation-type securitization.

We next discuss the implications of the monitoring technology hypothesis for off-balance-sheet securitization, which are quite different from the implications for disintermediation-type securitization. Off-balance-sheet securitization, such as loan sales with recourse and standby letters of credit, differs from disintermediation-type securitization in that under off-balance-sheet securitization the bank maintains its exposure to the credit risk of the borrower and therefore has the full incentive to continue monitoring the loan. Under the monitoring technology hypothesis, off-balance-sheet securitization is essentially the same as on-balance-sheet intermediation and remains in the intermediated portion of the continuum.[8] This is consistent with Greenbaum and Thakor (1987), whose model showed that the amount of off-balance-sheet securitization is driven by a number of factors. A simple extension of their model suggests that the level of disintermediation-type securitization is driven by the difference between the bank's cost of monitoring and direct lenders' costs of monitoring.[9] Thus, the monitoring technology hypothesis does not by itself provide a motive for or predict the existence of off-balance-sheet securitization, although there is no inconsistency with the hypothesis. Rather, under the monitoring technology hypothesis, off-balance-sheet securitization is a rearrangement of claims, and its motivation must be the product of other theories of securitization, such as those described in the third section below. The monitoring technology hypothesis predicts essentially no causal effect of this type of securitization on bank risk or liquidity, since the bank continues to maintain the credit risk of illiquid loans. This does not, however, rule out an empirical correlation between off-balance-sheet securitization and risk where the causation runs in the other direction, i.e., from risk to securitization. Such a correlation would derive from whatever theory is the one motivating the off-balance-sheet securitization activity.

Before turning to the competing hypotheses explaining securitization in the third section, we deal with two issues regarding bank loan sales without explicit recourse, an important form of securitization and the focus of much of our empirical work. The first issue is whether these sales have some form of implicit recourse against the selling bank. There is a regulatory incentive to make any recourse on loans sold implicit, because loans sold with explicit recourse bear the "taxes" of capital and reserve requirements. This issue is particularly important when examining the monitoring technology hypothesis, since a loan sold with no explicit or implicit recourse is a form of disintermediation-type securitization and a loan sold with full recourse is a form of off-balance-sheet securitization, virtually identical economically with a standby letter of credit. As noted above, these two types of securitization have very different empirical implications under the monitoring technology hypothesis. This motivates the additional empirical implication that if there is full implicit recourse, loan sales would have virtually the same relationship with risk as standby letters of credit, while if there is no recourse, loan sales would be independent of risk.

The second issue is, to the extent that loan sales do not have implicit recourse and represent disintermediation-type securitization, are they "pure downsizing" or "underwriting"? "Pure downsizing" refers to a complete disintermediation and disentanglement between the bank and the borrower who now has direct access to the capital markets—i.e., the borrower who has shifted sides of the boundary from financial intermediaries to direct lenders. To the extent that pure downsizing dominates empirically, one would expect to see a large number of loan sales just after an improvement in direct lender monitoring technology as banks downsize their existing portfolios, followed by a curtailment of sales and a reduction in bank originations as these borrowers go directly to capital markets for future refinancings.

"Underwriting" refers to a disintermediation process in which the bank no longer provides the funding (except very temporarily), but continues to originate and sell loans that it previously would have funded. This origination activity may represent a vehicle through which banks can compete in the securities underwriting business by originating a security that is much more akin to traded debt than to an intermediated loan. That is, in the absence of the bank's origination activity, the loan might otherwise be conventional traded debt underwritten by an investment bank. Commercial banks may have a comparative advantage in underwriting/originating this type of loan over investment banks to the extent that the loan sales borrower represents the inframarginal borrower who formerly borrowed from the bank but has now migrated to the capital market because of an innovation in direct lender monitoring technology. Again, this represents disintermediation-type securitization, since direct lenders bear the risk and monitor the borrower (unless there is an implicit bank guarantee). To the extent that this category dominates empirically, one would expect to see persistently large loan sales numbers after an improvement in direct lender monitoring technology as commercial banks first downsize their existing portfolios and then continue to originate and sell loans for their former borrowers.

Several pieces of empirical evidence shown elsewhere suggest that the underwriting category of disintermediation-type securitization may empirically dominate pure downsizing. First, the time pattern of loan sales indicates that these sales were large and increasing over the latter half of the 1980s. This suggests that banks may have kept originating and selling loans for many of the borrowers they used to fund, rather than terminating the relationships with a one-time downsizing loan sale. Second, the contracts for loans that are sold have been changed in ways that make them more resemble underwritten debt. According to Gorton and Haubrich (1990), commercial bank loans that are sold are structured so as to eliminate the explicit long-term relationship between the bank and borrower, often implying reduced maturity length. Similarly, El-Gasser and Pastena (1990) studied large loans originated by both banks and insurance companies and found that syndicated loan contracts (i.e., contracts that have multiple lenders because they are syndicated, participated, or partially sold) often differ from intermediated loan contracts where a single institution is the sole investor. Specifically, they found that syndicated loan contracts tended to have less restrictive covenants than contracts where a single lender is involved and thus are more like the contracts for conventionally underwritten traded debt. Presumably the reason is that a single lender has a cost advantage in renegotiation and is therefore able to write tighter covenants and maintain more control over the borrower, while syndicated loans and conventionally underwritten debt must have looser covenants because of the high coordination costs in renegotiating the covenants.

THE COMPETING HYPOTHESES AND THE EXTANT EMPIRICAL LITERATURE

The previous section outlined our monitoring technology hypothesis and its empirical implications for the associations among securitization, risk, and liquidity. In the first part of this section, we much more briefly summarize some competing hypotheses of securitization, mostly from the literature, and their empirical implications. Together, the monitoring technology hypothesis and these eight competing hypotheses form the basis for our empirical analysis in the two following sections. In the latter part of this section, we briefly discuss some of the relevant empirical literature to date on securitization. For the reader's convenience, Appendix Table 4–A1 gives a brief description of all of these hypotheses, their empirical implications, and our main associated empirical results.

The Competing Hypotheses

The Regulatory Tax Hypothesis As noted earlier, the regulatory tax hypothesis suggests that regulatory taxes on on-balance-sheet assets or liabilities will tend to result in banks' substituting into off-balance-sheet activities. These increased activities include both disintermediation-type securitization, such as loan sales without recourse, and off-balance-sheet securitization, such as standby letters of credit. The regulatory taxes on on-balance-sheet entries include reserve requirements, deposit insurance premia, and capital requirements. As discussed in the literature, capital requirements were significantly increased in the 1980s, and they applied only to on-balance-sheet assets, encouraging loan sales, standbys, and commitments designed to back up third-party loans. Risk-based capital requirements are currently being implemented. These new requirements tax standbys equally with loans and also put fairly heavy taxes on long-term commitments, largely reversing the regulatory tax incentive to engage in off-balance-sheet securitization [see Avery and Berger (1988,1991a, b)]. However, the risk-based capital requirement does not tax loan sales without recourse nor does it tax loans made outside the banking sector, leaving in place the regulatory incentive to engage in disintermediation-type securitization.[10]

Securitization may be either positively or negatively associated with bank risk under the regulatory tax hypothesis, depending upon which of a number of theories of bank behavior is correct. Several papers explore theoretically how banks might alter their portfolio risk in response to an increase in capital requirements [e.g., Kim and Santomero (1988), Furlong and Keeley (1989), Gennotte and Pyle (1991), and Avery and Berger (1991b)]. We may generalize the spirit of these papers to cover the broader case of how banks might change their on- or off-balance-sheet risks in response to an increase in regulatory taxes. Unfortunately, these theoretical papers do not agree with one another on the effects of capital increases, so it is difficult to draw general conclusions about the implications of increasing regulatory taxes on overall risk-taking behavior. However, we would expect a positive cross-sectional relationship between *leverage risk* and securitization because highly leveraged banks would have been forced to move assets off the balance sheet to avoid increased capital requirements.

The Collateralization Hypothesis Benveniste and Berger (1986, 1987) argued that securitization provides a Pareto-improving mechanism for shifting risk from risk-averse to risk-neutral investors. Without securitization, banks are forced to pool these investors on the deposit side of the balance sheet while funding both high and low risk loans on the asset side. They demonstrated that the Pareto-improving effects of securitization obtain when banks securitize their safest assets and retain their riskiest assets on the balance sheet. The securitized (safe) assets are sold to the risk averse investors, and the risk neutral investors purchase the bank's deposits. The incentives to securitize are accentuated when the risk-neutral on-balance-sheet investors are essentially replaced by the FDIC through its backing of insured deposits, since the FDIC does not even charge the actuarially fair premium for additional risk that risk-neutral investors do. James (1988) obtained a similar result in a model motivated by the underinvestment problem. In his model, the separation of safe assets off the balance sheet from risky assets on the balance sheet is needed because the interest rates promised to on-balance-sheet investors are fixed and cannot respond when safe assets are added to the balance sheet. Both the Benveniste and Berger and James models predict a positive relationship between securitization and bank risk because the pooling problem or the underinvestment problem is more acute in riskier banks.

One difference in predictions between these two models is that the James model has essentially the same prediction about risk for *both* disintermediation-type and off-balance-sheet securitization. Loan sales without recourse and standby letters of credit solve the underinvestment problem equally by separating the investments. However, the Benveniste and Berger model predicts that standbys will provide a better solution to the pooling problem, because recourse against the bank adds extra value for the risk-averse investors by creating a safer investment vehicle than even the bank's safest asset. Therefore, the James model predicts a positive association between risk and both types of securitization, while the Benveniste and Berger model predicts this association only for off-balance-sheet securitization.

To examine in a rough way whether the two forms of the collateralization hypothesis could explain the increase over time in securitization activity, we note that bank risk did increase over the 1980s. The number of bank failures rose from 10 or fewer per year at the beginning of the decade to over 200 per year at the end of the decade. A number of arguments have been made for why this risk increase may have occurred. Keeley (1990) argued that a loss of franchise value over the 1980s may have triggered moral hazard incentives. Berger and Humphrey (1992) argued that the elimination of Regulation Q and related deregulation of deposit accounts reduced bank monopsony power on the deposit side of the balance sheet. The annual value of paying below-market rates on deposits declined from $61 billion to $4 billion. Berger and Humphrey argued that risk-averse bank owners or managers may have chosen to take part of this loss as a decline in expected returns and part of it as an increase in risk by choosing loans with both more risk and higher expected return without necessarily involving any moral hazard. It is also plausible that banks got riskier simply because the world got riskier due to various sectoral shocks. Regardless of the cause, if banks got riskier, then the incentive to securitize under the collateralization hypothesis should have increased.

The Moral Hazard Hypothesis Benveniste and Berger (1986) and Thomas and Woolridge (1991) suggested as a competing hypothesis that securitization may be motivated by the moral hazard problem associated with fixed-rate deposit insurance, which encourages banks to become riskier. Banks can increase their risk while retaining their comparative advantage in loan origination either by selling relatively safe loans or by issuing standbys, which are economically equivalent to loan sales with recourse. In addition, accounting rules allow income from loan sales and standbys to be booked immediately, which is important to banks with high failure probabilities, whereas income from on-balance-sheet loans cannot be booked until the interest has accrued. Consequently, under the moral hazard hypothesis, securitization would be positively related to bank risk to the extent that differences in bank risk reflect differences across banks in terms of exploiting the FDIC. This hypothesis may be empirically distinguished from the monitoring technology hypothesis by examining the behavior of banks whose moral hazard incentives are likely to be high. For example, banks that are about to fail should have significantly greater moral hazard incentives and therefore should securitize more than other banks under this hypothesis.

The Market Discipline Hypothesis[11] Benveniste and Berger (1986), Boot and Thakor (1991), Koppenhaver and Stover (1991), and Berger (1991b) argued that off-balance-sheet securitization may occur in larger quantities for safe banks or induce riskier banks to become safer. The intuition behind these arguments is that standbys and commitments are uninsured contingent future claims on the bank that are subordinate to most of the other claims. For example, a standby may simply be dishonored when a bank fails, while the uninsured depositors and subordinated debt holders may receive partial or full repayment. Therefore, the value of these claims increases with the safety of the bank, providing an incentive for banks that issue these claims to increase their safety and encouraging exogenously safer banks to issue more of these claims. Both phenomena would tend to make off-balance-sheet securitization negatively related to risk. Gorton and Pennacchi (1991) showed that this same type of argument may apply to loan sales activity *if* these loans are partially implicitly guaranteed by the bank—i.e., *if* they are somewhat more like off-balance-sheet securitization and somewhat less like disintermediation-type securitization.

To date, no one to our knowledge has modeled reputation effects, where banks that sell loans that turn out to have fewer problems would have a more valuable franchise for selling loans in the future. Reputation might work much like the market discipline hypothesis, giving banks incentives to originate and sell safe loans and to retain a safe balance sheet as well, to take advantage of a loan sales franchise. In this way, the market discipline hypothesis may be extended to disintermediation-type securitization, as reputation replaces recourse.

The Borrower Moral Hazard Hypothesis Boot, Thakor, and Udell (1987) and Boot and Thakor (1991) showed that commitments may reduce borrower moral hazard through up-front commitment fees. Essentially, by paying a fee up front, the promised interest rate on the loan is reduced, which gives the borrower more of a stake in the project and less incentive to increase project risk. This same argument may be applied to standbys, in which the borrower also pays an up-front fee to the bank and has a reduced promised interest rate.

Related to the borrower moral hazard hypothesis is the theoretical finding of Avery and Berger (1991a) that commitments may be either positively or negatively associated with risk because of borrower moral hazard and adverse selection problems. Since a commitment is issued in advance of a loan, the bank has less information available for a commitment loan than for a spot loan. This lack of information may exacerbate the borrower's incentive to increase risk after the loan rate has been set. The lack of information may also allow a larger proportion of uncreditworthy borrowers to pool with creditworthy borrowers. Both of these problems would increase bank risk. However, the selection process determining which borrowers receive commitments may ration many of the borrowers with moral hazard and adverse selection problems, resulting in a negative association between commitments and bank risk.

The Liquidity Hypothesis There is also the possibility of a direct effect of securitization on bank liquidity risk if the associated technology enhances the liquidity of the loans remaining on the bank's portfolio. Specifically, if banks with high loan sales volume have superior ability to securitize the remaining assets on the balance sheet than low sales volume banks, then loan sales activity will be negatively associated with liquidity risk. This argument may be extended to the banking industry as a whole. To the extent that loan sales reflect a diminution of the special nature of banks, then the banking industry as a whole is more liquid [see Gorton and Haubrich (1990)]. This conclusion, however, depends on the assumption that the loans that remain on the balance sheet are not all that different from the loans that are sold—in contrast to the monitoring technology hypothesis, which assumes just the opposite.

The Comparative Advantage Hypothesis Finally, securitization may simply arise out of exogenous differences in comparative advantages across financial intermediaries. Securitization can rebalance portfolios among financial intermediaries who have different loan origination opportunity sets or different preferences at the margin for their loan portfolios. Pennacchi (1988) also argued that loan sales may be motivated by differences in marginal funding costs. Small banks and some foreign banks may have comparative advantages in raising funds in deposit markets in part because of regulation and in part because large money center banks must borrow in more expensive wholesale markets at the margin. To the extent that loan sales reflect these funding cost differences, these sales compete with the federal funds and interbank deposit markets for reallocating bank liabilities. Thus, under the comparative advantage hypothesis, securitization provides a means by which relatively inexpensive funds raised by some banks can be used to finance relatively profitable loans at other banks. The empirical implications are that loan sales should be concentrated in large banks with relatively large loan portfolios and large wholesale liabilities, reflecting relatively good loan opportunities and poor liability opportunities.

The Extant Empirical Literature

For expositional purposes, we divide the extant empirical literature into three categories. The first category includes tests of the relationship between loan sales without explicit recourse and risk. Some of these tests are designed to help determine whether or not there is implicit recourse, which for our purposes determines the extent to which these sales constitute pure disintermediation-type securitization (no recourse) or off-balance-sheet securitization (full recourse). The second category encompasses tests of the relationships between standbys or commitments and risk. Standbys are clearly off-balance-sheet securitization, since the bank bears all of the credit risk. Commitments are off-balance-sheet securitization to the extent that they are used to back up third-party loans and the bank cannot easily escape its obligation to lend to a credit-impaired account party. The third category of tests examine the consistency of the data with the regulatory tax hypothesis.

The Relationship between Loan Sales and Risk Several studies have empirically examined the relationship between loan sales and bank risk. Pavel and Phillis (1987) measured risk in several ways, including leverage, net charge-offs, and asset concentration. As noted below, there are problems of interpretation with the asset concentration variable. They found that higher risk as measured by all three of these measures increases the probability of entry into the loan sales market. However, of the three, only net charge-offs predicts a greater volume of loan sales, and even this relationship does not hold up for large banks. Pavel (1988) used as a measure of risk the fair deposit insurance premium calculated using Ronn and Verma's (1986) option-pricing methodology. She found that the riskiest 30 of 117 traded bank holding companies sold 3.5 times as many loans as a fraction of assets as the safest 30. However, the opposite relationship held when risk was measured by leverage. The Pavel study also reports that loan sales are unrelated to *changes* in bank risk for various definitions of risk, leaving an overall ambiguous picture. Gorton and Pennacchi (1991) regressed the fraction of a loan sold and the bond rating of the borrower on the riskiness of the bank as measured by the failure probability in order to test for the presence of implicit guarantees. The coefficients of bank risk are statistically insignificant, consistent with the hypothesis that there are no guarantees. However, it would be difficult to find statistical significance in their model, because they only have risk for a single bank, which likely does not change substantially and because they estimated two parameters simultaneously on their risk variable in a nonlinear model, making it difficult to find either statistically significant. Thomas and Woolridge (1991) examined the relationship between loan sales and bank risk using an event study methodology of sales announcements. They found a positive impact of the announcements on the value of bank debt and no effect on the value of equity in a sample of 25 banks who sold pass-through securities, suggesting that these loan sales are negatively related to bank risk. Timme, Kale, and Noe (1990), on the other hand, found loan sales announcements to have positive effects on the value of bank equity, which could be consistent with a number of theories. Given the contradictory results in this literature, there is need for additional work to clarify the relationship between loan sales and bank risk.

The Relationship between Standbys or Commitments and Risk Numerous studies have tested the relationships between standbys or commitments and risk. Looking first at standbys, Benveniste and Berger (1986, 1987) used a logit analysis and found a positive association between a bank's leverage and the likelihood that it will issue standbys. Large banks were excluded from this equation because all large banks issued standbys. They interpreted this result as support for their version of the collateralization hypothesis, at least for small to medium sized banks. They also found a negative relationship between the number of dollars of standbys and risk for those banks that issued standbys (including large banks). They interpreted this result as support for the market discipline hypothesis's playing a role in limiting the amount of standbys issued at the margin. Finally, they tested the moral hazard hypothesis by examining whether failing banks tended to increase their use of standbys as the moment of failure approached. They found the data to be contrary to the moral hazard hypothesis and more in line with the market discipline hypothesis: Failing banks tended to issue decreasing, rather than increasing amounts of standbys as failure approached. Avery and Berger (1988) tested the association between the standby-to-asset ratio and several measures of bank risk and performance. The standby ratio is inclusive of both the decision to issue standbys and the quantity issued. They found a positive association between standbys and bank risk, suggesting that the collateralization hypothesis may be stronger overall than the market discipline hypothesis. James (1988) also found a positive association between standbys and risk, with risk measured by leverage and by the variance of monthly holding company returns. Koppenhaver (1989), on the other hand, found no relationship between leverage and the decision to issue standbys. Avery and Berger (1991b) used a number of measures of risk and found that standbys were positively related to risk for small banks, but negatively related to risk for large banks. One possible explanation for these results is that the collateralization hypothesis dominates for small banks and the market discipline hypothesis dominates for large banks. Such an explanation would be consistent with the Benveniste and Berger results cited above, which showed some support for both hypotheses. Ingram (1991) used both a logit analysis for whether a bank issued standbys and a Tobit analysis for the level of standby activity. He found a positive relationship between leverage and standby issuance, and a negative relationship between portfolio risk (as measured by loan loss reserves) and standby issuance.[12] Ingram also related standbys to the risk of the account party and found that municipalities that purchased standbys have higher bond ratings than those that did not. This evidence favors the collateralization hypothesis, since the safer borrowers should be issued standbys. Koppenhaver and Stover (1991) provided evidence that the other studies of the relationship between standbys and leverage that used contemporaneous data on both variables were vulnerable to a simultaneous equations bias. Using Granger-causality tests, they found (1) that bank leverage has a negative predictive effect on standbys and (2) that standbys have a positive predictive effect on bank leverage. The former result supports the market discipline hypothesis for marginal standby decisions, while the latter result is very difficult to interpret.[13] Thus, the standby data as a whole support the collateralization hypothesis in most cases, but also provide some support for the market discipline hypothesis.

There are many fewer studies that have tested the relationship between commitments and risk. Avery and Berger (1988) found a slightly negative relationship between commitments and bank risk, using data on both used commitments (i.e., loans taken down under commitment) and unused commitments (i.e., lines that have not been taken down) and relating them to several bank performance measures. Koppenhaver (1989) found no relationship between the probability that a bank has positive unused commitments and the bank's risk. Berger and Udell (1990) found a negative relationship between used commitments and risk, where risk is measured by premium of the loan rate over the Treasury rate of comparable duration. Avery and Berger (1991a) found both used and unused commitments to be slightly negatively related to various risk measures. Avery and Berger (1991b) found that unused commitments are negatively related to several risk measures. Thus, the commitment data are fairly consistent, showing a small to moderate negative relationship to risk, consistent with the market discipline hypothesis.

Support for the Regulatory Tax Hypothesis Tests of the regulatory tax hypothesis of securitization focused on how loan sales, standbys, and commitments responded to the fixed-rate capital requirements of the 1980s. Benveniste and Berger (1986,1987) formed a capital constraint dummy variable equal to one when a bank would not meet its capital requirement if standbys were on the balance sheet. When this variable equals one, issuing standbys in place of loans helps the bank meet its capital requirement. Benveniste and Berger found that the likelihood that standbys are issued by small banks does not depend on the capital constraint variable. However, the standby proportion of the portfolio and the probability that standbys exceed 5 percent of the portfolio were both positively related to the capital constraint variable, consistent with the regulatory tax hypothesis. Pavel and Phillis (1987) found that a binding capital requirement was a significant determinant of loan sales, again consistent with the hypothesis. Baer and Pavel (1988) also found that the standby-to-asset ratio was positively related to the level of the regulatory capital tax. Koppenhaver (1989) found no empirical relationship between the tightness of the capital constraint and the likelihood of participation in either the standby or commitment markets. Jagtiani, Saunders, and Udell (1991) found evidence that capital requirements affect the growth of standbys but not loan sales. Overall, these results are consistent with the regulatory tax hypothesis, but also suggest that the influence of this hypothesis may be less for the decision to enter securitization markets than for the degree of participation and that the influence may differ by type of securitization.

THE SECURITIZATION, RISK, AND LIQUIDITY DATA AND THEIR BEHAVIOR OVER TIME

In this section, we introduce the data and the variables we use to measure securitization, risk, and liquidity in banking. The data are taken from quarterly Call Reports (Reports of Condition and Income) over the interval from 1983:Q2 to 1991:Q2, the period over which loan sales and loan commitment data are available. We include information for each of the over 12,000 U.S. commercial banks over the entire 33 quarters, so that our empirical analysis describes the state of the entire U.S. industry. The unusually large number of observations employed in the analysis, well over 400,000, also should provide for a relatively definitive empirical treatment of the relationships among securitization, risk, and liquidity in banking.

We also examine here the aggregate behavior over time of several of the key variables. Examination of how these variables have changed over time for the industry as a whole may give some insight into the interrelationships among the variables and may also shed light on the question of how securitization activity has responded to changes in the regulatory environment over time. In addition, the direction and sheer size of the securitization figures may shed some light on the question of whether, as some have argued, securitization is becoming so widespread that the traditional bank function of funding illiquid assets is becoming extinct. We reserve econometric tests of the relationships among these variables across individual banks for the following section.

Table 4–1 defines the variables and gives the industry mean values. The securitization variables include commercial and industrial (C&I) loan sales without recourse (including participations), C&I loan purchases, standby letters of credit, and unused loan commitments, denoted by LS, LP, SLC, and COM respectively. The LS and LP data are quarterly flows of sales and purchases respectively, while the SLC and COM data are outstanding stocks. Performance-type standby letters of credit PSLC and short-term commitment STCOM are included in the analysis because they may bear a different relationship to risk than other standbys and commitments respectively.[14] We measure these variables as ratios to total bank assets (TA) in order to evaluate how these instruments of securitization have cut into the conventional bank business of funding assets on the balance sheet. Dividing by TA also helps control for differences across banks and time in the size of bank portfolios. The industry mean values of securitization shown in the table are weighted by assets, the denominator of each ratio, in order to indicate industry proportions of securitization. The use of unweighted means would be distorted by equal weights given to small banks who often have little participation in securitization activity. All other industry means shown in the table are also weighted by their respective denominators.

TABLE 4–1
Variable Definitions and Sample Means (1983:Q2 through 1991:Q2, except as noted)

Symbol	*Definition*	*Industry Means*
	Securitization Measures	
LS/TA	Ratio of quarterly flow of C&I loan sales without recourse (including participations) to total assets.	4.90%
LP/TA[a]	Ratio of quarterly flow of C&I loans purchased to TA.	0.54%
SLC/TA	Ratio of outstanding stock of standby letters of credit to TA.	4.86%
PSLC/TA[a]	Ratio of outstanding stock of performance-based standbys to TA.	0.34%
COM/TA	Ratio of outstanding stock of unused loan commitments (excluding credit cards) to TA.	20.59%
STCOM/TA[a]	Ratio of outstanding stock of short-term (< 1 year) COM (excluding credit cards) to TA.	2.25%
	Overall Risk Measures	
FAIL	Dummy, equals 1 if the bank fails in the current quarter.	0.28%
ROA	Ratio of net income to TA. When FAIL=1, ROA = –(equity in previous period + FDIC's estimated outlay) / (TA in previous period). Thus, failed banks are assumed to lose their previous equity plus the FDIC's expected losses.	0.13%
σ_{ROA}	Standard deviation for each bank of ROA (cross-section variable).	0.62%
z-score	(Mean of ROA + mean of equity/asset ratio)/ σ_{ROA} (cross-section).	56.32%
	Portfolio Risk Measures	
NPERF/TA	Ratio of nonperforming loans (past due and nonaccruing) to TA.	3.11%
CHRGF/TA	Ratio of net charge-offs (charge-offs less recoveries) to TA..	0.15%
RWA/TA[b]	Ratio of risk-weighted on-balance sheet assets to TA.	70.50%

TABLE 4–1, continued

Symbol	*Definition*	*Industry Means*
	Portfolio Risk Measures, continued	
TACONC	Sum of squares of the asset shares of C&I loans, real estate loans, consumer loans, and other assets.	51.54%
ROC&I	Ratio of net income on C&I loans (including pro rata share of loan loss provisions) to total C&I loans. When FAIL=1, includes pro rata share loss of equity and FDIC outlay as in ROA definition.	1.15%
$\sigma_{ROC\&I}$	Standard deviation for each bank of ROC&I (cross-section).	1.47%
	Leverage Risk Measures	
NEWCAP[b]	Ratio of Tier 1 plus Tier 2 capital to total risk-weighted assets (including off-balance-sheet items).	10.85%
OLDCAP	Ratio of primary plus secondary capital to TA.	8.23%
FAILNEW[b]	Dummy, equals 1 if bank fails to meet the new capital guidelines.	4.34%
FAILOLD	Dummy, equals 1 if bank fails to meet the old capital guidelines.	3.77%
	Liquidity Risk Measures	
C&I/TA	Ratio of C&I loans to TA.	20.23%
LN/TA	Ratio of total loans to TA.	60.76%
(LN+OBS)/(TA+OBS)	Ratio of (LN + SLC + COM) to (TA + SLC + COM).	68.72%
HOT/TA	Ratio of "hot" funds (deposits over $100,000, brokered deposits, foreign deposits, federal funds purchased) to TA.	31.23%
(HOT+COM)/(TA+COM)	Ratio of (HOT + COM) to (TA + COM).	42.97%
	Regression Control Variables	
BHC	Dummy, equals 1 if bank is in a holding company.	65.05%
UNIT	Dummy, equals 1 if bank is located in a unit banking state.	13.93%

TABLE 4–1, concluded

Symbol	Definition	Industry Means
	Regression Control Variables, continued	
LIMIT	Dummy, equals 1 if bank is located in a limited branching state.	19.85%
SIZE 2-9	Dummies, equal 1 for banks with $25 million < TA < $50 million; $50 million < TA < $100 million; $100 million < TA < $500 million; $500 million < TA < $1 billion; $1 billion < TA < $5 billion; $5 billion < TA < $10 billion; $10 billion < TA < $25 billion; $25 billion < TA, respectively, all in constant 1987 dollars. Banks with TA < $25 million are in the base group.	
TIME 3-32	Dummies, equal 1 for third,..., 32nd quarter. The first quarter is excluded because of lags, the second quarter is considered to be the base case.	

[a] Loan purchases, the breakout of standby letters of credit into financial versus performance types, and the breakout of loan commitments by maturity are available only since 1990:Q1. These are entered as zeros for earlier periods.

[b] Risk-weighted assets were estimated from Call Report data based on a number of assumptions. The estimates are considerably improved by the addition of some items in the Call Report beginning in 1990:Q1.

Source: Call Reports.

C&I loan sales without recourse are particularly interesting and important in our study. Unlike SLCs and COMs, loan sales may be a form of disintermediation-type securitization, provided that banks do not provide any implicit recourse or guarantee on these sales. To the extent that LS are implicitly guaranteed, however, they perform essentially the same intermediation role as SLCs and are a form of off-balance-sheet securitization. In the following section, we test the hypothesis that LS are fully guaranteed by seeing whether they bear the same relationship to risk and liquidity as SLCs. Another interesting aspect of these sales is that C&I loans are generally considered to be the most information-intensive of bank assets, so that disintermediation of these loans, if it is pure disintermediation without guarantees, would be most indicative of the loss of comparative advantage by banks in information acquisition and monitoring. In addition, these loan sales really constitute a new market of the 1980s. As noted by Gorton and Haubrich (1990), loan sales prior to the 1980s were mainly participations of overlines, or loans that exceeded legal lending limits to single borrowers.

Table 4–2 shows the aggregate behavior over time of the main

TABLE 4–2
Selected Securitization Variables Over Time (Industry Proportions Measured in Percentages)

Time Period	*LS/TZ*	*LP/TZ*	*SLC/TZ*	*COM/TA*
1983:Q2	1.22%	0.00%	4.41%	18.24%
1983:Q3	1.36	0.00	4.55	19.27
1983:Q4	1.56	0.00	4.71	18.66
1984:Q1	1.42	0.00	4.78	19.71
1984:Q2	1.41	0.00	4.94	19.79
1984:Q3	1.58	0.00	5.17	20.26
1984:Q4	2.01	0.00	5.23	19.96
1985:Q1	2.08	0.00	5.40	20.45
1985:Q2	2.35	0.00	5.35	20.24
1985:Q3	2.97	0.00	5.44	20.39
1985:Q4	2.80	0.00	5.78	20.08
1986:Q1	2.36	0.00	5.77	19.99
1986:Q2	2.89	0.00	5.48	20.09
1986:Q3	3.23	0.00	5.42	20.41
1986:Q4	3.71	0.00	5.19	19.46
1987:Q1	5.56	0.00	5.13	19.94
1987:Q2	6.56	0.53	5.13	20.30
1987:Q3	6.29	0.72	5.06	20.44
1987:Q4	6.43	0.55	5.06	20.63
1988:Q1	7.66	0.58	4.91	20.96
1988:Q2	7.99	0.56	4.88	20.89
1988:Q3	8.38	0.57	4.74	20.83
1988:Q4	9.00	0.62	4.85	21.04
1989:Q1	8.56	0.53	4.80	20.86
1989:Q2	8.47	0.58	4.76	20.80
1989:Q3	8.89	0.56	4.76	21.01
1989:Q4	7.66	0.59	4.85	20.92
1990:Q1	6.35	0.49	4.11	22.75
1990:Q2	5.55	0.48	4.02	22.54
1990:Q3	5.03	0.47	4.20	21.84
1990:Q4	4.86	0.51	4.26	21.53
1991:Q1	3.95	0.39	4.14	21.16
1991:Q2	3.72	0.50	4.08	20.93

securitization variables, LS/TA, LP/TA, SLC/TA, and COM/TA. Figure 4–2 shows these data graphically. The loan sales and purchases data shown in columns (1) and (2) of Table 4–2 reveal several interesting facts. First, the market is clearly substantial in magnitude. The LS/TA ratio reached a peak of 8.89 percent in 1989:Q3, with total sales of $285.1 billion. Unfortunately, this figure is somewhat difficult to interpret because, as noted above, the sales data collected on the Call Report are in the form of flows rather than

FIGURE 4–2
Selected Securitization Variables Quarterly Over Time (Measured Relative to Total Assets in Percentage)

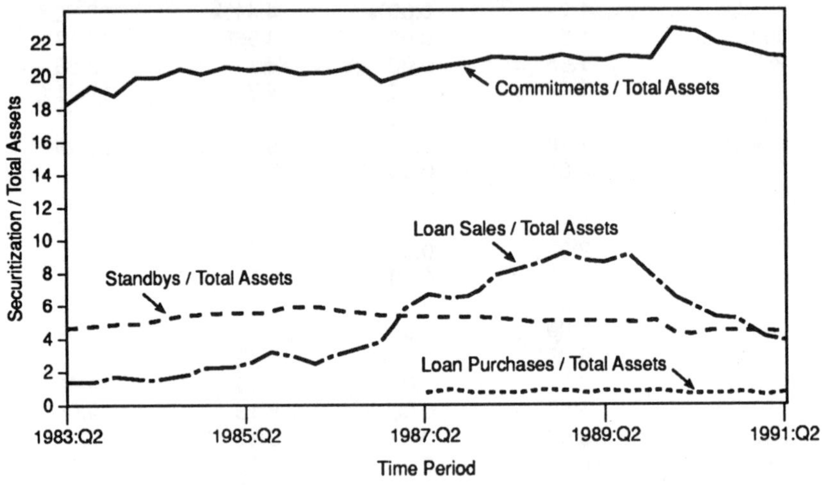

stocks. The quantity that these sales would represent in terms of a stock of assets that might otherwise remain on the balance sheet depends on the duration of the loans sold, since the same funds could in principle finance many very short-term loans originated and sold within a single quarter. Fortunately, some supplementary information is available. The Federal Reserve's Senior Loan Officer Opinion Survey on Bank Lending Practices occasionally surveys some relatively large banks on their stock of outstanding C&I loans sold and provides some additional information on this point. As of June 30, 1989, the virtual peak of this market, the total stock of outstanding loans sold for the survey banks was $72.2 billion. These banks are estimated to cover 90 percent of all U.S. loans sold, which would give a total of $80.2 billion in outstanding loan sales stock for all banks. Dividing this $80.2 billion figure for the LS stock by $3,188.3 billion in total bank assets yields an estimated 2.52 percent for the true stock-valued LS/TA ratio. Given that total C&I loans remaining on the balance sheet were $613.8 billion, this suggests that about 11.56 percent of all C&I loan dollars were off the balance sheet as of the peak of the market, a very substantial proportion.[15, 16]

An estimate of the dollar-weighted average duration of loans sold is obtained by calculating the LS turnover ratio—i.e., by dividing the $80.2 billion estimated outstanding stock as of June 30, 1989, by the flow figures from the Call Report for the quarter leading up to that date. Given that the total LS flow by all banks for 1989:Q2 was $270.0 billion, or $1,080.0 billion on an annual basis, the estimated dollar-weighted average duration is .074 years or 27 days. This corresponds closely with the 28 days average maturity (unweighted) found by Gorton and Pennacchi (1991) for a sample of loans sold by a money center bank. In addition, Gorton and Pennacchi's longest maturity was 277 days. This information suggests that C&I loans sold are much shorter-term on average than those remaining on the balance sheet, given that domestic C&I loans originated have average durations (unweighted) of about 5 months [see Berger and Udell (1990,1992)]. The relatively short terms for loans sold is consistent with the monitoring technology hypothesis, given that information problems generally increase with the duration of a loan, other things equal, as events further in the future are more difficult to forecast.

Additional evidence in favor of the dominance of short-term loans in the loan sales market is the dominance of a few firms. Security Pacific National Bank, the leading seller of loans, had a quarterly flow of $110.5 billion in loans sold as of 1989:Q2, or 40.9 percent of all sales. The fact that this bank's annual flow of $442.0 billion is eight times its assets of $55.1 billion strongly suggests that the vast majority of this large piece of the market is short-term. If the average duration of loans sold were as long as one year, its outstanding stock of C&I loans sold would be eight times its total assets and even larger relative to its on-balance-sheet C&I loans—figures that are hard to believe. Similarly, Bankers Trust Company, the second largest loan seller, had a 1989:Q2 quarterly flow of $44.8 billion in sales, yielding annual sales of more than three times its assets. Thus, the two banks that account for more than half of the entire loan sales flow almost surely specialize in selling short-term loans.

There are also some data on the maturity of the outstanding stock of loans sold. Senior Loan Officer Survey respondents were also asked for the rough distribution of loans sold by original maturity. The responses indicated that an estimated 62.6 percent of the outstanding stock had maturities of over one year and only an estimated 15.6 percent had maturities of 30 days or less. These data showing long average maturity of the stock are corroborated by information in the Asset Sales Report, which gives weekly figures for the combined outstanding stock of C&I loans sold without recourse for 10 major banks, including both Security Pacific and Bankers Trust. The Asset Sales Report data indicate that the majority of outstandings have maturities of greater than one year. The findings that most of the outstanding stock is long term, while most of the flow is short term, are not inconsistent. Rather, they reflect the fact that the outstanding stock figures are effectively duration-weighted. That is, loans sold that are short term are less often reflected in outstanding stock data because they have more often expired.

Some additional discussions with bankers suggest that loan sales markets are segmented into separate short- and long-term markets. The market for short-term business loans essentially amounts to a surrogate for commercial paper. Developed in the early 1980s, this market provides an alternative to commercial paper for "Fortune 1,000-type" borrowers with short-term paper ratings, although the average maturity and the average draw may be a bit longer and a bit smaller respectively in the loan sales market than the commercial paper market.

Much of the long-term loan sales market appears to be similar to the loan syndication business, although the sales component is distinct from primary distributions to syndicate members. Much of this activity is related to LBO/merger and acquisition activity. Unlike the private placement market, many transactions involve unfunded loans and floating rate pricing. Again, this business substantially involves "Fortune 1,000-type" borrowers, although the transactions are generally more complicated than capital market debt issues. There is also a significant secondary market for long-term loan sales. A transaction in this category involves the sale of a loan by an original investor at some point after the loan was funded. Somewhat related to secondary asset sales are arbitrage-driven loan trades. A typical loan trade might involve an original LBO investor who subsequently purchases additional pieces of the deal from other original investors and then resells these pieces at a positive spread.

A second important fact about aggregate loan sales volume is that the market appears to have become mature by 1989 and then went into a substantial decline. Nominal sales volume dropped by more than half from $285.1 billion in 1989:Q3 to $124.8 billion in 1991:Q2. The LS/TA ratio fell by a slightly greater (relative) amount from 8.89 percent to a level of 3.72 percent during the same seven-quarter interval. This decline is of particular interest since it comes as the Basle Accord risk-based capital standards are being implemented. The regulatory tax hypothesis would have predicted an increase, rather than a decrease in C&I loan sales. This is because the new capital requirements raise the amount of regulatory capital that must be held against each dollar of C&I loans from 6 cents to 8 cents and because the new standards represent a significant increase in required capital on large banks, who are the market makers in loan sales [see Avery and Berger (1991b)]. One might have expected these large banks to have increased their sales volume drastically as an alternative or significant supplement to raising additional capital or making other portfolio changes. Thus, the aggregate LS data are at least somewhat in conflict with the regulatory tax hypothesis, suggesting that these sales may be principally driven by other factors.

Some additional evidence sheds more light on the nature of the decline. About 76 percent of the drop in the flow from 1989:Q2 to 1991:Q2 is due to Security Pacific and Bankers Trust giving up most of their loan sales business. Security Pacific's flow went from $110.5 billion per quarter to $30.3 billion, and Bankers Trust's flow went from $44.8 billion to $14.8 billion.[17] The decline in the market was not nearly so great for the other large players. The outstanding stock of loans sold, according to the respondents to the Senior Loan Officer Survey (which includes Security Pacific and Bankers Trust), fell by a much smaller percentage over the same time interval, from $72.2 billion to $65.5 billion. This suggests that the decline was concentrated in the short-term market, which would be consistent with our conclusions regarding the specialization of the two dominant banks given above. In addition, the estimated proportion of the outstanding stock of loans sold by the respondents to the Senior Loan Officer Survey that were related to merger and acquisition (M&A) activities dropped from 44.5 percent in 1989:Q2 to 35.1 percent in 1991:Q2. In terms of dollar amounts, the M&A-related loan sales stock fell by $9.1 billion, more than the fall in the overall stock of $6.7 billion. This suggests that much of the decline in the loan sales market may be due to exogenous reductions in M&A activity, rather than changes in financing modes.[18]

A third set of important facts about the loan sales market concerns the types of buyers of these loans. The loan purchase (LP) data shown in Table 4–2, which are only available beginning in 1987:Q1, indicate that most of the loans are not sold to other domestic commercial banks. LPs are generally only about one-tenth as large as LS. This confirms the Gorton and Haubrich (1990) observation that loan sales are no longer primarily overlines that are participated within correspondent bank networks, but are sold outside the domestic banking industry. The more detailed data on the largest banks reveal that some of them are above average and some are below average in terms of LP/TA, but there is no great concentration of purchased loans as there is sold loans. The outstanding stock data from the Senior Loan Officer Survey yields some further information about the holders of this stock. The 1989 Survey showed an estimated 34.0 percent of sold loans outstanding at other domestic commercial banks, 45.2 percent at foreign banks, and only 6.6 percent at nonfinancial corporations. Presumably, the vast majority of the remaining 13.7 percent are at other nonbank financial institutions. The corresponding numbers for 1991 are 27.6 percent domestic banks, 39.5 percent foreign banks, and only 4.8 percent at nonfinancial corporations.

One implication of these data is that the relatively small figures for the *flow* of loan purchases shown in Table 4–2 may understate the *stock* of purchased loans in domestic bank portfolios. The approximately 30 percent of the stock versus about 10 percent of the flow purchased by U.S. banks suggests that the loans purchased by these banks have durations on the order of three times those of other loans sold. An even more important implication of the Senior Loan Officer Survey data is that the majority of the loan sales outstanding are held by other banks (foreign or domestic) or other financial institutions. The finding that only 4.8 to 6.6 percent of sold loans are on the portfolios of nonfinancial corporations raises significant questions about the extent to which loan sales truly represent disintermediation-type securitization that is funded by direct investors. It suggests that instead, much of the loan sales volume may represent a simple rebalancing of portfolios among financial intermediaries who have different loan origination opportunity sets or different preferences at the margin for their loan portfolios, consistent with the comparative advantage hypothesis. However, contrary to the comparative advantage hypothesis implication that small banks with deposit rate advantages would purchase many of the loans, the outstanding stock of loans sold are concentrated in large banks. The Senior Loan Officer Survey respondents reported that of the outstanding stock of loans sold to domestic banks, 85 to 90 percent were held by banks with assets in excess of $2 billion. An alternative explanation of these figures is that loans purchased by commercial banks may represent a liquidity reserve of traded debt that banks use as a substitute for corporate debt underwritten by investment banks.

The standby letters of credit data shown in Table 4–2 also show evidence of market maturity. The early literature on SLCs showed that they grew very rapidly in the 1970s and then slowed to about a 15 percent growth rate in the mid-1980s [see Benveniste and Berger (1986)]. The data in Table

4–2 suggest that this growth rate has been arrested and slightly reversed since the mid-1980s. The SLC/TA ratio slowly declined from 5.78 percent at the end of 1985 to 4.85 percent at the end of 1989. The sudden drop to 4.11 percent in 1990:Q1 is almost surely due to the change in reporting forms as of that date, given that the figures were quite steady before and after the change in forms. In addition to separating financial and performance SLCs, other instructions were changed as well. This and other changes in the reporting forms will be controlled for in the micro-bank empirical analysis through the use of time dummies. In part, the decline over the last half of the 1980s may be due to a fall-off in overall bank C&I business, since, as shown below, the C&I/TA ratio declined over this interval as well. These data are consistent with an hypothesis that the SLC market matured in the mid-1980s.

However, the SLC data are not particularly consistent with the regulatory tax hypothesis. If banks' SLC decisions were strongly affected by capital standards, then there should have been accelerated SLC growth in the early 1980s when formal capital requirements that did not tax SLCs were implemented. There should also have been a sharp decline from trend as 1990:Q4 approached, the first date at which risk-based standards that tax SLCs were implemented. Neither of these events appear in the data.[19]

The one way in which the SLC data are consistent with the regulatory tax hypothesis is their empirical dominance over loans sold *with* recourse. In 1986:Q1, SLCs were $157.7 billion, while respondents to the Senior Loan Officer Survey reported C&I loan sales with recourse of only $0.7 billion at that time. As noted above, an SLC is economically equivalent to securitization with recourse, since the bank bears all the credit risk for a loan or other contractual agreement between two other parties. However, SLCs had lower regulatory taxes, since SLCs were not subject to reserve requirements and were not subject to capital requirements before implementation of risk-based capital, while loan sales with recourse were subject to both regulatory taxes.[20]

The last category of securitization activity we analyze is loan commitments (COM). It should be noted that the COM data are noisy indicators of securitization activity, since many COMs do not closely resemble securitization (e.g., COMs that simply improve the convenience of borrowing from the bank). The COM data shown in Table 4–2 are similar in nature to the SLC data and again suggest a mature market that has not changed significantly over a number of years. COMs have steadily changed at about the same rate as bank assets, so that the COM/TA ratio has stayed near 20 percent for the entire time interval studied here. The reported jump from 20.9 percent in 1989:Q4 to 22.7 percent in 1990:Q1 is almost surely due to a change in reporting forms, which asked for much more detailed information than previously and encouraged the reporting of some COMs that simply went unreported earlier.[21] While the COM/TA ratio has remained nearly unchanged, it should be noted that the ratio of COM to C&I loans has increased somewhat, since C&I/TA has decreased over time.

The commitment data do not particularly support the regulatory tax hypothesis. Under this hypothesis, COMs of greater than one year (not shown separately in table) should be reduced as risk-based capital takes effect, since such COMs receive a fairly heavy capital tax [see Avery and Berger (1988, 1991b)]. Similarly, short-term commitments STCOM (not shown separately), which receive no capital tax under risk-based capital, should be increasing under the regulatory tax hypothesis as banks substitute these for long-term commitments and perhaps standbys. To the contrary, STCOM are decreasing over the 1990:Q1 to 1991:Q2 interval over which these data are available.

Thus, the securitization data shown in Table 4–2 suggest that a large amount of what formerly might have been bank assets have been securitized. However, the markets for securitized debt may have reached or come close to reaching maturity in the 1980s, suggesting that traditional bank on-balance-sheet intermediation may not be in imminent danger of disappearing. Moreover, given that most of the outstanding stock of loans sold is held by other banks, and only about 5 percent of this stock is estimated to be on the portfolios of nonfinancial corporations, it is questionable whether direct investors are wresting away from banks their traditional role of funding C&I loans. Finally, while the regulatory tax hypothesis undoubtedly plays a significant role in securitization decisions, the aggregate securitization data show little of the predicted reactions to changes in capital requirements.

In order to determine whether banks that tend to engage in more securitization activities are relatively risky or safe and liquid or illiquid, we also include in the analysis a relatively large number of measures of bank risk and liquidity. We measure variables that are descriptive of overall bank risk, portfolio risk, and leverage risk, as well as conventional measures of liquidity.[22] It is expected that all of the risk measures may yield valuable information about bank liquidity risk. The overall risk measures, like bank failure, directly include liquidity risk. The measures of portfolio risk and leverage risk are also related to liquidity risk, since the probability of a liquidity crisis or bank run is directly dependent upon outside perceptions of a bank's risk. In addition, it has been shown elsewhere that banks that take on more of one type of risk tend to take on more of other types of risk [see Keeton and Morris (1987), Berger (1991a), McAllister and McManus (1991), and McManus and Rosen (1991)].

As indicated in Table 4–1, we calculate four measures of overall bank risk. Bank failure risk (FAIL) is a very complete measure of bank risk, since failures incorporate every type of bank risk, including portfolio risk, leverage risk, interest rate risk, and liquidity risk, as well as their interactions. Unfortunately, FAIL also reflects some supervisory discretion, since not all banks are closed when their book capital reaches zero. Perhaps a better way to measure overall risk is through examining the likelihood of book-value insolvency, when equity is exhausted by a sufficiently negative earnings performance. This likelihood depends on both leverage and the probability distribution of earnings. ROA is the return on assets measured for each time period for each bank, and σ_{ROA} is the standard deviation of ROA for each bank, computed from the 33 (or fewer) quarterly observations for the bank. Note that unlike most studies, we include the bank-specific losses of the FDIC in the ROA data to avoid the problem of censoring out very large negative returns. The likelihood of insolvency is measured by the cross-section variable z-score, which puts the earnings data in a form that is inclusive of leverage risk: It is the mean ROA plus the mean equity/asset ratio divided by the standard deviation of ROA, and it measures the number of standard deviations that ROA could go below its mean before the bank would reach book-value insolvency.[23] This avoids the problem of supervisory discretion that is incorporated in FAIL.

Table 4–3 gives the behavior over time of some of the risk measures, beginning with FAIL and ROA. The FAIL data show what is commonly known, namely that the number of bank failures skyrocketed in the 1980s and continues at relatively high levels, over 1 percent per year (.25 percent per quarter). By this measure of risk, securitization could be related to risk, but less than perfectly so. The aggregate SLC and COM data in Table 4–2 show little relation with FAIL. Loan sales do increase with bank failures until 1989, but then fall off in a way that does not seem be related to this measure of risk. The ROA data shows an increase in volatility of earnings that began in 1987 and remains today. Some of the unusual down-and-up volatility beginning in 1987:Q2 is likely due to the Citicorp loan loss reserve announcement of 1987 and its aftermath [see Musumeci and Sinkey (1988) and Grammatikos and Saunders (1990)]. Again, there is no overriding rela-

TABLE 4–3
Selected Overall Risk, Portfolio Risk, and Leverage Risk Variables Over Time (Industry Proportions Measured in Percentages)

Time Period	*FAIL*	*ROA*	*NPERF/ TA*	*CHRGF/ TA*	*NEWCAP*	*OLDCAP*
1983:Q2	0.12%	–0.02%	2.85%	–0.42%	10.20%	6.98%
1983:Q3	0.08	0.16	2.97	0.09	10.31	7.08
1983:Q4	0.06	0.12	2.93	0.13	10.15	6.95
1984:Q1	0.08	0.18	2.94	0.07	10.67	7.03
1984:Q2	0.17	0.13	2.82	0.11	10.54	7.11
1984:Q3	0.15	0.18	2.81	0.12	10.78	7.29
1984:Q4	0.13	0.14	2.93	0.14	10.78	7.28
1985:Q1	0.14	0.19	2.98	0.09	11.06	7.52
1985:Q2	0.21	0.18	2.83	0.11	11.37	7.77
1985:Q3	0.22	0.19	2.86	0.12	11.44	7.84
1985:Q4	0.22	0.13	2.75	0.18	11.39	7.77
1986:Q1	0.20	0.18	2.98	0.11	11.59	8.01
1986:Q2	0.26	0.14	2.79	0.14	11.54	8.05
1986:Q3	0.33	0.17	2.84	0.15	11.67	8.15
1986:Q4	0.23	0.11	2.78	0.18	11.43	7.94
1987:Q1	0.33	0.18	3.49	0.11	11.73	8.26
1987:Q2	0.37	–0.37	3.23	0.13	10.96	8.46
1987:Q3	0.36	0.19	3.23	0.13	11.12	8.57
1987:Q4	0.33	0.07	3.25	0.19	11.00	8.50
1988:Q1	0.41	0.13	3.33	0.14	10.92	8.55
1988:Q2	0.37	0.17	3.09	0.17	10.98	8.54
1988:Q3	0.63	0.19	3.06	0.14	11.26	8.60
1988:Q4	0.29	0.19	2.88	0.19	11.35	8.57
1989:Q1	0.34	0.23	3.14	0.11	11.42	8.62
1989:Q2	0.48	0.21	2.98	0.16	11.48	8.62
1989:Q3	0.50	–0.04	3.12	0.14	11.24	8.78
1989:Q4	0.29	0.06	3.06	0.30	11.17	8.65
1990:Q1	0.27	0.19	3.22	0.20	9.67	8.75
1990:Q2	0.42	0.16	3.05	0.25	9.73	8.71
1990:Q3	0.47	0.11	3.31	0.18	9.74	8.75
1990:Q4	0.24	0.03	3.72	0.25	9.97	8.98
1991:Q1	0.25	0.17	3.96	0.19	10.22	9.19
1991:Q2	0.30	0.12	3.70	0.21	10.46	9.19

tionship between securitization and risk, except that loan sales and risk are both generally higher over the past several years than over the previous years.

Portfolio risk is measured by nonperforming loans (past due and nonaccrual), net charge-offs (charge-offs less recoveries), risk-weighted on-balance-sheet assets (where the risk weights are taken from the new risk-based capital standards), and the sum of squares of portfolio shares—NPERF/TA, CHRGF/TA, RWA/TA, and TACONC respectively. The return and risk on the C&I loan portfolio are given by ROC&I and $\sigma_{ROC\&I}$, which are measured the same way as ROA and σ_{ROA}, except that they focus on the part of the portfolio most directly affected by C&I loan sales and the other securitization measures. NPERF/TA and CHRGF/TA are standard measures of portfolio risk, and RWA/TA has been shown elsewhere [see Avery and Berger (1991b)] to be related to risk. TACONC is a measure of concentration or inequality in portfolio shares among investments—it is the sum of squares of the asset shares invested in C&I loans, real estate loans, consumer loans, and other assets. This variable is included because a similar measure was a key measure of risk in the Pavel and Phillis (1987) study of the relationship between loan sales and risk. Unfortunately, while Pavel and Phillis simply assume that their TACONC variable is positively related to portfolio risk, the relationship could very easily be negative, depending upon the moments of the joint distribution of returns on the various portfolio items.[24] Further problems arise in efforts to determine the effect of loan sales on TACONC. The only way for LS to affect TACONC directly is through a reduction in the C&I portfolio share; consequently, the effect on the C&I share (used as liquidity measure below) may be a better measure of this phenomenon. Moreover, a reduction in C&I could have either a positive or negative effect on TACONC, depending upon whether C&I has a relatively large or small share.

The behavior over time of NPERF/TA and CHRGF/TA are shown in Table 4–3. NPERF/TA increases substantially in 1987 and in 1990, but shows no other trends. CHRGF/TA is a very noisy series, with a slight upward trend and a bias toward reporting more of the charge-offs at the end of the year. RWA/TA (not shown) remains relatively constant over 1983–89 and over 1990–91. This variable jumped in 1990:Q1 because additional information was made available as of that date that made RWA more easily measured. TACONC seems to have increased in the mid-1980s and then returned to earlier levels. None of these portfolio risk measures seems to be strongly related to the trends in loan sales. Note that all reporting changes over time, as well as any end-of-year reporting effects, will be controlled for in the empirical tests in the next section by including dummy variables for each time period.

Leverage risk is measured by risk-based and nonrisk-based capital ratios, NEWCAP and OLDCAP. NEWCAP is the ratio of total Tier 1 plus Tier 2 capital to total risk-weighted assets used in the new capital standards.

This measure is inclusive of both leverage risk and portfolio risk, since risk-weighted assets is the denominator. OLDCAP is the ratio of primary plus secondary capital to unweighted assets used in the old capital guidelines. Both of these measures reflect regulatory considerations as well as leverage risk, and both are directly affected by the treatment (or non-treatment) of securitization in the denominators. We also transform these ratios into the dummy variables FAILNEW and FAILOLD, which measure whether the bank fails the capital standards.

As shown in Table 4–3, both NEWCAP and OLDCAP increase over time, suggesting a secular decrease in leverage risk. Similar to RWA/TA, NEWCAP changes abruptly in 1990:Q1 because of changes in reporting. The rather sharp rise in NEWCAP in the last few quarters may reflect a reaction to the implementation of the risk-based guidelines. The increases in capitalization during earlier periods may be also be due to increased regulatory pressure, as argued elsewhere [Wall and Peterson (1987), Keeley (1990)]. Since leverage risk appears to move in the opposite direction over time from portfolio risk and overall risk, there seems to be no consistent relationship between securitization and risk over time.

Liquidity risk is perhaps the most difficult type of risk to measure because it depends on the degree of marketability of bank assets, and this marketability is not always easy to discern from the data. As a result of securitization, some types of loans have become more marketable and liquid over time, but they are reported in the same manner as illiquid loans. For example, C&I loans to large corporate customers that may be relatively easily sold today appear identically in the Call Report as both (1) loans to these same customers in the past when they were not marketable, and (2) loans to small customers, which are still are not easily marketed. On the other hand, under our monitoring technology hypothesis, the highly marketable securities are already off the balance sheet, so that the conventional definitions of liquidity, such as the loan/asset ratio, are applicable. We measure the loan/asset ratio LN/TA, but we also measure another variable (LN+OBS)/(TA+OBS) in which we add off-balance-sheet SLCs and COMs to the the numerator and denominator, since these contingent obligations could be turned into loans at the sole discretion of the borrower. We also examine the ratio of C&I loans to total assets, C&I/TA. More than the TACONC variable above, changes in C&I/TA may reveal whether the composition of the loan portfolio has changed. C&I/TA may also help distinguish between the two types of disintermediation-type securitization, "pure downsizing" and "underwriting" by commercial banks. We also examine the liability side of the ledger for liquidity risk, by trying to capture the portion of funds that might be runnable in a crisis. HOT/TA is the ratio of uninsured "hot" funds to assets, including deposits over the $100,000 insurance limit and federal funds purchased. The proportion of hot funds also may yield insight into the comparative advantage hypothesis, since the rates paid on hot funds include risk premia and are therefore more costly than insured deposits of comparable terms. We also add COMs to the numerator and denominator of this portfolio, forming (HOT+COM)/(TA+COM), on the presumption that some commitment customers, particularly those with revolving lines, might "run" on these lines in the event of a liquidity panic and create the need to raise additional hot funds or liquidate other assets.

Table 4–4 shows the evolution over time of these liquidity risk measures. The LN/TA ratio increased from about 55 percent to about 62 percent from 1983 to 1991, with most of the growth occurring in the early part of the period. This suggests that banks may have become somewhat less liquid, although not because of loan sales, which would be expected to reduce the LN/TA ratio. Rather, the increase is from real estate and consumer loans, which grew from a combined 22.83 percent of assets to 36.55 percent over the period. The inclusion of off-balance-sheet items in (LN+OBS)/(TA+OBS) does not change the pattern, since SLC and COM volumes were fairly steady over time, as indicated above. The C&I/TA ratio decreases fairly steadily over time, from about 23 percent to 16 percent. This decline of more than one-fourth over an eight year period suggests an increase in liquidity, on the assumption that any other investment is at least as liquid as C&I loans, although there is the possibility that the remaining C&I loans may be less liquid than in the past. In part, the C&I/TA ratio decline reflects the secular movement away from C&I loans and toward real estate and consumer loans noted above. To some extent it also likely reflects disintermediation either through loan sales or through some other method not involving banks. However, the degree to which this disintermediation has occurred is difficult to determine until we examine the individual bank data in the next section to determine whether banks that sold off more loans had a greater decrease in C&I loans than other banks. The HOT/TA ratio shows a decline from about 34 percent to 27 percent, indicating a reduction over time in the proportion of funds that might run in the event of a liquidity panic. The (HOT+COM)/(TA+COM) ratio declines similarly from about 44 percent to 40 percent. Thus, most of the measures suggest a reduction over

TABLE 4–4
Selected Liquidity Risk Variables Over Time (Industry Proportions Measured in Percentages)

Time Period	*LN/TZ*	*(LN+OBS)/ (TZ+OBS)*	*C&I/TA*	*HOT/TA*	*(HOT+COM)/ (TA+COM)*
1983:Q2	54.99%	63.30%	22.68%	33.98%	44.16%
1983:Q3	55.50	64.06	22.56	33.92	44.60
1983:Q4	55.61	64.02	22.49	33.82	44.22
1984:Q1	58.64	66.77	20.44	34.15	45.00
1984:Q2	59.60	67.61	20.64	33.78	44.72
1984:Q3	60.47	68.48	20.56	33.60	44.79
1984:Q4	60.27	68.26	20.23	32.52	43.75
1985:Q1	60.74	68.80	20.55	33.20	44.54
1985:Q2	60.53	68.57	20.06	32.22	43.63
1985:Q3	60.64	68.72	19.77	32.10	43.60
1985:Q4	59.85	68.10	19.15	31.73	43.14
1986:Q1	60.21	68.36	19.37	32.49	43.73
1986:Q2	60.32	68.40	19.09	31.07	42.60
1986:Q3	60.15	68.33	18.60	31.27	42.92
1986:Q4	59.82	67.77	18.69	30.06	41.45
1987:Q1	60.08	68.08	18.56	31.19	42.63
1987:Q2	60.83	68.77	18.43	30.85	42.52
1987:Q3	61.22	69.10	18.18	31.38	43.03
1987:Q4	61.09	69.05	18.15	31.35	43.09
1988:Q1	61.43	69.35	18.39	31.49	43.36
1988:Q2	61.77	69.61	18.25	30.69	42.67
1988:Q3	61.52	69.36	17.80	31.11	42.99
1988:Q4	61.75	69.62	17.74	30.13	42.28
1989:Q1	61.90	69.68	17.88	31.61	43.41
1989:Q2	62.08	69.80	17.79	31.18	43.03
1989:Q3	62.82	70.44	17.83	31.17	43.12
1989:Q4	62.42	70.12	17.48	30.38	42.43
1990:Q1	62.06	70.09	17.60	30.86	43.67
1990:Q2	61.95	69.94	17.31	30.12	42.98
1990:Q3	62.25	70.05	17.20	29.83	42.41
1990:Q4	62.25	69.99	16.99	27.91	40.68
1991:Q1	62.36	69.96	17.00	28.28	40.81
1991:Q2	61.43	69.15	16.28	27.17	39.78

time in liquidity risk for the banking system that is more or less coincident with the increase over time in loan sales activity. Nevertheless, the aggregate relationships over time are less precise tools for examining the relationships among the variables than are the individual bank data, to which we turn next.

MICRO-DATA ANALYSIS OF THE RELATIONSHIPS AMONG SECURITIZATION, RISK, AND LIQUIDITY

In this section, we present regression results that examine the relationships among the variables described in the previous section. As noted above, the 33 quarters of data on over 12,000 banks per quarter allow for an unusually large data set of over 400,000 observations with which to test the implications of the various theories. We also include a relatively large list of variables to measure risk and liquidity in order to offer a thorough analysis.

As shown in the summaries in Appendix Table 4–A1, some of the theories predict that securitization causes changes in risk and liquidity, while other theories predict that the causation runs in the other direction, with risk and liquidity differences causing banks to choose securitization. Ideally, we would like to develop a structural model in which we could model causality as going in both directions and have the data distinguish the relative effects of each set of variables on the other set. In practice, however, the building of such a structural model from which confident conclusions could be drawn is not possible with the data available. Such a model would require data on variables that directly affect risk but do not affect securitization, plus data on other variables that directly affect securitization but do not affect risk. The exogenous control variables described below—bank holding company affiliation, state branching laws, bank size, and time period—can all be thought of as affecting *both* securitization and risk. It is also doubtful that any other readily available data that would qualify as exogenous variables (i.e., variables that are not caused by securitization or risk) could reasonably be determined to cause either securitization or risk, but not the other.

We choose to put the risk and liquidity variables on the left-hand side of the regressions and the securitization variables on the right-hand side for several reasons. First, this causal ordering is consistent with the main theory being tested, the monitoring technology hypothesis. Under this hypothesis, risk does not affect either type of securitization, but off-balance-sheet securitization may affect risk for other reasons (e.g., the collateralization hypothesis). Second, in this regression, all six of our securitization measures are specified in the same regressions, allowing us to perform some cross-coefficient tests and to control for variables that often move together. In particular, we are able to test the hypothesis that LS are fully guaranteed by examining whether they bear the same relationship to the risk and liquidity variables as SLCs. Moreover, since the various types of securitization are so highly correlated, neglecting to control for all of them in the same equation could lead to significant estimation bias. Finally, since some of the measures of risk are performance indicators that reveal past risk-taking behavior (e.g., bank failure), we estimate the equations with the risk and liquidity measures as left-hand-side variables observed one quarter later than the right-hand-side variables.

Despite this preferred ordering, we cannot rule out feedback effects because the estimated equations do not come from a structural model that incorporates all of the hypotheses—it is only fully consistent with the monitoring technology hypothesis and other hypotheses that have causation running from securitization to risk and liquidity. To the extent that other theories may explain the data, these results can be viewed as measuring gross statistical associations in the data between securitization and the risk and liquidity measures. It may be noted that the key regressions were also run with the securitization variables on the left-hand side and lagged risk and liquidity variables on the right-hand side (not shown in tables), and there was no material change in the results.

As indicated in Table 4–1, we also include a number of other control variables in the regressions. Our purpose is to reduce the possibility of estimation bias by controlling for exogenous factors that might be correlated with both the risk or liquidity left-hand-side variables and the securitization right-hand-side variables. The dummy variable for bank holding company affiliation (BHC) may be correlated with bank risk or liquidity for a number of reasons, including recourse to the holding company for a source of strength. BHC also likely controls for the possibility that affiliated banks may sell loans within the holding company or issue SLCs for tax or other regulatory reasons unrelated to securitization. For example, a number of Delaware affiliates of large BHCs issue disproportionately large quantities of SLCs and sell disproportionately large quantities of loans, presumably as within-BHC transactions [see Benveniste and Berger (1986) and Gorton and Haubrich (1990)]. The dummy variables for state branching laws UNIT and LIMIT (statewide branching is the base group) control for differences in competitive conditions that may be related to risk (e.g., the difficulty of diversifying the loan portfolio in a UNIT state). These variables may also be related to securitization to the extent that the sales and purchases of securitized assets is a partial substitute for branching to gain geographical diversification. The size class dummies SIZE 2-9 are standard control variables that account for the many differences in bank risk and liquidity opportunities for large versus small banks, as well as the opportunities to enter securitization markets. The time dummies TIME 3-33 account for the many

TABLE 4–5
Regressions Using Overall Bank Risk Measures as Left-Hand-Side Variables[a] (1983:Q2 through 1991:Q2)

	FAIL		*ROA*		σ_{ROA}		*z-score*	
Variable	*Parameter*	*t-stat*	*Parameter*	*t-stat*	*Parameter*	*t-stat*	*Parameter*	*t-stat*
				All Banks				
LS/TA	.00002	0.07	.00002	0.08	.0168	0.99	–17.5091	1.27
LP/TA	–.0102	2.26	–.0017	0.28	.4030	3.56	–176.6901	1.93
SLC/TA	.0684	7.66	.0435	3.67	.3949	2.72	–821.4875	6.98
PSLC/TA	–.0342	0.95	–.3279	6.86	.4025	0.47	1381.3418	1.97
COM/TA	–.0065	4.30	.0027	1.32	–.0380	1.40	–8.1557	0.37
STCOM/TA	–.0004	0.10	.0057	1.00	–.0393	0.34	–352.5371	3.75
R^2	.002		.002		.027		.115	
Num. Obs.	432,000		432,000		16,364		16,364	
				Large Banks (TA > $1 billion)				
LS/TA	—	—[b]	.0007	1.33	.0003	0.07	–15.8005	0.06
LP/TA	—	—	.0027	1.14	.0034	0.33	–309.9324	0.45
SLC/TA	—	—	–.0155	8.09	.0207	2.04	–656.0874	0.97
PSLC/TA	—	—	–.0160	2.02	–.2970	3.50	15546.4642	2.75
COM/TA	—	—	–.0005	1.58	–.0005	0.30	117.1791	1.00
STCOM/TA	—	—	–.0017	1.26	.0250	2.62	–1684.7443	2.64
R^2	—		.040		.579		.462	
Num. Obs.	—		10,454		466		466	

[a] Not shown, but also included in all of these regressions are an intercept and the following control variables: BHC, UNIT, LIMIT, SIZE 2-9, TIME 3-33.
[b] The FAIL regression could not be run for large banks (over $1 billion in assets) because the data set contained more right-hand-side variables than failures for this subsample of banks.

differences over time in regulation and macroeconomic environment that affect bank risk and liquidity, the evolution of securitization markets, and several changes in the reporting forms over time.[25, 26]

The regressions that involve the left-hand-side variables representing overall risk, portfolio risk, and leverage risk are shown in Tables 4–5, 4–6, and 4–7, respectively. More detailed securitization information for failing banks is shown in Tables 4–8a and 4–8b, and the regressions with conventional liquidity measures on the left-hand side are shown in Table 4–9. We

TABLE 4–6
Regressions Using Portfolio Risk Measures[a]
(1983:Q2 through 1991:Q2)

	NPERF/TA		*CHRGF/TA*		*RWA/TA*	
Variable	*Parameter*	*t-stat*	*Parameter*	*t-stat*	*Parameter*	*t-stat*
			All Banks			
LS/TA	.00005	0.40	–.00001	0.04	.0051	8.72
LP/TA	–.0219	9.62	–.0024	0.43	.1840	17.43
SLC/TA	.1962	43.48	.0773	7.18	2.0438	97.87
PSLC/TA	.1244	6.85	–1.2669	29.20	.0912	1.09
COM/TA	.0008	1.04	.0063	3.43	.3522	99.01
STCOM/TA	.0246	11.22	.0202	3.87	.2983	29.46
R^2	.022		.006		.149	
Num. Obs.	431,000		431,000		431,000	
			Large Banks			
LS/TA	.0002	0.06	.0007	2.00	.0259	1.79
LP/TA	–.0615	5.09	–.0018	1.29	.1670	2.70
SLC/TA	.0789	8.01	–.0002	0.16	.3502	6.94
PSLC/TA	.0318	0.78	.0003	0.07	1.5482	7.38
COM/TA	.0026	1.49	–.0006	2.91	.1364	15.16
STCOM/TA	–.0029	0.42	–.0011	1.37	.1600	4.51
R^2	.064		.052		.178	
Num. Obs.	10,454		10,454		10,454	
	TACONC		*ROC&I*		$\sigma_{ROC\&I}$	
			All Banks			
LS/TA	.0019	1.91	.0017	0.09	.5180	0.40
LP/TA	.0799	4.41	–.0490	0.14	–2.4113	0.28
SLC/TA	–1.3589	37.63	5.4360	8.59	–33.0971	2.98
PSLC/TA	.3885	2.69	–19.7762	7.74	235.7584	3.54
COM/TA	–.0800	13.00	.0076	0.07	1.5336	0.74
STCOM/TA	.0049	0.28	.0130	0.04	–37.7204	4.09
R^2	.120		.002		.029	
Num. Obs.	430,000		427,000		16,189	
			Large Banks			
LS/TA	.0524	3.41	–.0007	0.21	.0050	0.15
LP/TA	.3503	5.40	–.0058	0.37	–.0138	0.15
SLC/TA	–.1326	2.47	–.0559	4.57	–.1608	1.86
PSLC/TA	–.9504	4.32	–.0091	0.18	–.5522	0.76
COM/TA	–.1341	13.97	–.0055	2.50	–.0236	1.57
STCOM/TA	–.2613	7.02	.0094	1.08	.0198	0.23
R^2	.089		.066		.072	
Num. Obs.	10,124		10,283		458	

[a] Not shown, but also included in all of these regressions are an intercept and the following control variables: BHC, UNIT, LIMIT, SIZE 2-9, TIME 3-33.

TABLE 4–7
Regressions Using Leverage Risk Measures[a]
(1983:Q2 through 1991:Q2)

Variable	NEWCAP		OLDCAP		FAILNEW		FAILOLD	
	Parameter	*t-stat*	*Parameter*	*t-stat*	*Parameter*	*t-stat*	*Parameter*	*t-stat*
			All Banks					
LS/TA	–.0018	2.91	–.0001	0.75	.0014	1.51	.0003	0.42
LP/TA	–.0780	7.02	.0126	4.24	–.0260	1.50	–.0260	1.58
SLC/TA	–.8306	37.81	–.0563	9.61	1.6262	47.45	.5983	18.47
PSLC/TA	.6796	7.68	.4300	18.23	–1.1249	8.14	–.9090	6.96
COM/TA	–.1313	35.10	.0032	3.25	.2296	39.27	.0124	2.24
STCOM/TA	–.1367	12.83	–.0034	1.20	–.2081	12.51	–.0966	6.15
R^2	.072		.087		.0412		.008	
Num. Obs.	431,000		431,000		431,000		431,000	
			Large Banks					
LS/TA	–.0055	0.40	.0038	1.34	.1799	3.88	–.0810	2.60
LP/TA	.0181	0.31	.0814	6.79	–.2895	1.46	.1239	0.94
SLC/TA	–.2320	4.86	–.0666	6.81	2.1963	13.62	.5025	4.65
PSLC/TA	–.5842	2.94	–.0417	1.02	–1.2385	1.85	–1.6375	3.65
COM/TA	–.0173	2.03	.0134	7.67	.4482	15.58	–.0511	2.65
STCOM/TA	–.2178	6.49	–.0481	6.98	–.2597	2.29	.0456	0.60
R^2	.035		.102		.173		.123	
Num. Obs.	10,454		10,454		10,454		10,454	

[a] Not shown, but also included in all of these regressions are an intercept and the following control variables: BHC, UNIT, LIMIT, SIZE 2–9, TIME 3–33.

display for each regression six securitization variables, LS/TA, LP/TA, SLC/TA, PSLC/TA, COM/TA, and STCOM/TA. However, in our analysis, we only focus on the main variables LS/TA, SLC/TA, and COM/TA. The other three variables, which are of less general interest and are available only for the end of the sample time interval, are not discussed here. The coefficients of the other control variables are not shown in order to conserve table space.

Each of the regression forms is run twice, once for all banks and once for the subsample of banks with over $1 billion in total assets (constant 1987 dollars). The large bank regressions focus more on the banks that hold lion's shares in the securitization market. Over our sample, these banks account for

TABLE 4–8a
Tests of the Moral Hazard Hypothesis: LS/TA and SLC/TA for Banks that Failed in 1989:Q2 and Those that Did Not Fail

LS/TA by Size Class[a] as Failure Quarter Approaches (percent)

Bank Asset Size Class ($ millions)	*Fail or Control Group*	*Number of Banks*	*Quarters Before Failure* 1	2	3	4	5	6	7	8
0-25	Fail	22	0.31%	0.69%	0.74%	1.08%	0.67%	0.84%	0.86%	0.88%
	Control	3,533	0.64	0.69	0.64	0.72	0.70	0.65	0.58	0.64
25-50	Fail	7	0.63	0.84	0.96	1.35	0.68	0.86	0.57	0.70
	Control	3,140	0.53	0.57	0.51	0.53	0.51	0.52	0.47	0.52
50-100	Fail	2	0.65	0.22	0.41	0.91	1.34	0.38	1.76	0.07
	Control	2,627	0.42	0.63	0.57	0.60	0.53	0.57	0.64	0.69
100-500	Fail	1	0.00	0.00	0.00	0.00	0.00	0.00	0.00	0.00
	Control	2,181	0.52	0.62	0.58	0.62	0.63	0.64	0.60	0.69
500-1000	Fail	0	—	—	—	—	—	—	—	—
	Control	207	0.89	1.26	1.54	1.88	0.67	1.47	1.69	1.68
1000-5000	Fail	0	—	—	—	—	—	—	—	—
	Control	259	0.59	0.69	0.68	0.74	0.77	1.45	1.02	1.36
5000-10000	Fail	0	—	—	—	—	—	—	—	—
	Control	58	1.07	1.01	1.03	1.24	1.21	0.98	1.12	1.27
10000-25000	Fail	0	—	—	—	—	—	—	—	—
	Control	25	5.89	4.80	4.46	3.99	2.42	2.24	1.98	1.67
>25000	Fail	0	—	—	—	—	—	—	—	—
	Control	12	30.69	33.78	30.03	28.35	26.99	22.09	20.97	21.77

			SLC/TA by Size Class[a] as Failure Quarter Approaches (percent)							
0-25	Fail	22	0.43%	0.45%	0.43%	0.46%	0.46%	0.64%	0.66%	0.83%
	Control	3,533	0.18	0.18	0.20	0.19	0.24	0.25	0.25	0.24
25-50	Fail	7	0.25	0.21	0.30	0.26	0.39	0.38	0.45	0.58
	Control	3,140	0.31	0.30	0.31	0.30	0.30	0.30	0.31	0.30
50-100	Fail	2	0.04	0.08	0.16	0.52	0.66	0.55	0.54	0.53
	Control	2,627	0.47	0.44	0.45	0.43	0.42	0.43	0.43	0.41
100-500	Fail	1	0.02	0.02	0.06	0.12	0.12	0.12	0.00	0.09
	Control	2,181	0.85	0.83	0.85	0.83	0.81	0.80	0.81	0.78
500-1000	Fail	0	—	—	—	—	—	—	—	—
	Control	207	1.80	1.77	1.88	1.79	1.92	1.84	2.00	1.97
1000-5000	Fail	0	—	—	—	—	—	—	—	—
	Control	259	2.70	2.66	2.69	2.70	2.71	2.74	2.72	2.85
5000-10000	Fail	0	—	—	—	—	—	—	—	—
	Control	58	4.06	3.87	3.88	3.74	3.74	3.86	3.86	3.82
10000-25000	Fail	0	—	—	—	—	—	—	—	—
	Control	25	6.06	5.89	5.80	5.87	5.74	5.96	6.07	6.01
>25000	Fail	0	—	—	—	—	—	—	—	—
	Control	12	11.21	11.96	11.12	11.69	11.56	12.09	11.69	11.96

[a] All ratios to total assets are size class averages weighted by total assets.

TABLE 4–8b
Tests of the Moral Hazard Hypothesis: LS/TA and SLC/TA for Banks that Failed in 1991:Q2 and Those that Did Not Fail

LS/TA by Size Class[a] as Failure Quarter Approaches (percent)

Bank Asset Size Class ($ millions)	*Fail or Control Group*	*Number of Banks*	*Quarters Before Failure* 1	2	3	4	5	6	7	8
0-25	Fail	7	1.09%	1.04%	1.02%	1.36%	0.71%	0.80%	1.68%	1.30%
	Control	3,255	0.73	0.66	0.61	0.63	0.58	0.76	0.60	0.62
25-50	Fail	4	0.00	0.00	0.00	0.29	1.39	0.34	0.88	0.64
	Control	3,065	0.52	0.55	0.52	0.58	0.55	0.61	0.50	0.52
50-100	Fail	3	0.21	0.20	0.13	0.41	0.25	0.10	0.67	0.28
	Control	2,575	0.35	0.39	0.37	0.42	0.39	0.41	0.40	0.45
100-500	Fail	7	0.00	0.28	0.13	0.35	10.19	14.80	10.53	7.46
	Control	2,213	0.38	0.50	0.52	0.51	0.52	0.60	0.59	0.58
500-1000	Fail	0	—	—	—	—	—	—	—	—
	Control	232	1.45	1.33	1.30	0.80	0.74	0.98	1.22	0.79
1000-5000	Fail	1	0.00	0.00	0.00	0.00	0.00	0.00	0.00	0.03
	Control	243	0.51	0.75	0.81	0.69	0.64	0.75	0.56	0.72
5000-10000	Fail	0	—	—	—	—	—	—	—	—
	Control	56	2.02	2.17	1.94	2.10	1.80	1.97	1.42	1.31
10000-25000	Fail	0	—	—	—	—	—	—	—	—
	Control	28	3.62	4.71	3.98	4.78	7.33	7.21	7.58	6.93
>25000	Fail	0	—	—	—	—	—	—	—	—
	Control	12	12.62	15.55	16.20	17.84	20.11	26.14	31.91	29.93

SLC/TA by Size Class[a] as Failure Quarter Approaches (percent)

0-25	Fail	7	0.38%	0.26%	0.48%	0.45%	0.63%	0.64%	0.48%	0.44%
	Control	3,255	0.14	0.15	0.16	0.15	0.15	0.18	0.19	0.19
25-50	Fail	4	0.02	0.08	0.10	0.02	0.08	0.25	0.20	0.20
	Control	3,065	0.28	0.26	0.26	0.26	0.27	0.32	0.32	0.32
50-100	Fail	3	0.23	0.26	0.22	0.34	0.55	0.53	0.67	0.76
	Control	2,575	0.37	0.37	0.40	0.40	0.38	0.39	0.46	0.45
100-500	Fail	7	1.98	2.11	2.50	2.64	2.81	3.46	3.94	3.73
	Control	2,213	0.74	0.73	0.77	0.78	0.78	0.87	0.88	0.86
500-1000	Fail	0	—	—	—	—	—	—	—	—
	Control	232	1.27	1.33	1.32	1.35	1.35	1.54	1.58	1.56
1000-5000	Fail	1	0.00	2.59	2.65	2.91	0.00	2.13	2.21	1.94
	Control	243	2.50	2.53	2.59	2.53	2.42	2.79	2.73	2.65
5000-10000	Fail	0	—	—	—	—	—	—	—	—
	Control	56	3.69	3.76	3.63	3.62	3.74	4.21	4.10	4.05
10000-25000	Fail	0	—	—	—	—	—	—	—	—
	Control	28	5.32	5.13	5.34	5.02	5.14	6.35	6.10	6.00
>25000	Fail	0	—	—	—	—	—	—	—	—
	Control	12	9.78	10.27	9.57	9.04	9.31	11.35	10.91	10.94

[a] All ratios to total assets are size class averages weighted by total assets.

TABLE 4–9
Regressions Using Liquidity Risk Measures[a]
(1983:Q2 through 1991:Q2)

	C&I/TA		*LN/TA*		*(LN+OBS)/ (TA+OBS)*	
Variable	*Parameter*	t-*stat*	*Parameter*	t-*stat*	*Parameter*	t-*stat*
			All Banks			
LS/TA	.0030	7.61	.0046	6.95	.0047	7.19
LP/TA	.1561	21.80	.1127	9.34	.1273	10.65
SLC/TA	2.5691	181.33	2.0544	86.07	2.2544	95.36
PSLC/TA	–.7863	13.78	–.3989	4.15	–.6323	6.65
COM/TA	.2447	101.40	.3653	89.83	.5554	137.91
STCOM/TA	.0519	7.55	.2245	19.39	.2526	22.04
R^2	.192		.108		.167	
Num. Obs.	431,000		431,000		431,000	
			Large Banks			
LS/TA	–.0429	4.56	–.0140	0.86	–.0040	0.27
LP/TA	.5228	13.00	–.1432	2.07	–.1584	2.52
SLC/TA	1.1230	34.43	–.0717	1.27	.1951	3.80
PSLC/TA	.5355	3.93	.1687	0.72	.1756	0.82
COM/TA	.2076	35.41	.1337	13.27	.2951	32.20
STCOM/TA	–.0253	1.10	.0221	0.56	.0413	1.14
R^2	.373		.081		.188	
Num. Obs.	10,454		10,454		10,454	

	HOT/TA		*(HOT+COM)/(TA+COM)*	
		All Banks		
LS/TA	.0038	8.32	.0041	8.93
LP/TA	.1179	14.20	.1366	16.42
SLC/TA	1.9900	121.15	2.0473	124.42
PSLC/TA	–1.3641	20.62	–1.3464	20.32
COM/TA	.1505	53.78	.5824	207.96
STCOM/TA	–.0170	2.14	.0495	6.20
R^2	.173		.335	
Num. Obs.	431,000		431,000	
		Large Banks		
LS/TA	.0837	4.19	.0749	4.15
LP/TA	.5440	6.38	.4704	6.11
SLC/TA	1.6180	23.27	1.4710	23.44
PSLC/TA	–.2888	1.00	–.2595	1.00
COM/TA	.1179	9.51	.4398	39.29
STCOM/TA	–.3632	7.43	–.2257	5.11
R^2	.223		.402	
Num. Obs.	10,454		10,454	

[a] Not shown, but also included in all of these regressions are an intercept and the following control variables: BHC, UNIT, LIMIT, SIZE 2–9, TIME 3–33.

94, 95, and 91 percent of all LS, SLCs, and COMs, respectively, while they account for only 67 percent of all on-balance-sheet assets. However, small banks are still important to include in the analysis: Banks with under $1 billion in assets participate more than half as often as large banks in all three securitization markets, even though they have much lower ratios of securitization to assets. Of all small banks, 38, 54, and 55 percent have LS, SLCs, and COMs respectively, while the corresponding figures for large banks are 75, 95, and 96 percent.

In the tables, the regressions in which the risk variables are 0-1 dummy variables (FAIL, FAILNEW, FAILOLD) are run as linear probability models because the computational costs of limited dependent variable estimation with over 400,000 observations are prohibitive. However, logit models were also run using subsamples in which 10 percent of the "0"s and 10 percent of the "1"s were randomly chosen (not shown in tables), and no material changes in the results were evident. The regressions in which the risk variables are based on the standard deviations of bank returns (σ_{ROA}, z-score, and $\sigma_{ROC\&I}$) were run as cross-section regressions on bank-specific averages of all the right-hand-side variables, yielding a sample of just over 10,000 observations.

The results shown in Tables 4–5, 4–6, and 4–7 embody two very clear findings that bear on our hypotheses of interest: (1) Loan sales have virtually no association with risk, and (2) standby letters of credit are strongly positively related to bank risk. To see these findings, we first examine the ALL BANKS regressions using overall risk measures on the top of Table 4–5. Despite the large number of observations, none of the LS coefficients is statistically significantly different from zero at the 5 percent level, using a two-sided test (i.e., the t-statistics are less than 1.96). At the same time, banks with more SLCs had higher failure rates (FAIL), higher variance of returns (σ_{ROA}), and a higher risk of book-value insolvency (lower z-score). Banks with higher SLCs also had higher earnings, which could reflect either a positive risk-return tradeoff or the extra fee income earned on SLCs.

The ALL BANKS data on portfolio risk and leverage risk in Tables 4–6 and 4–7, respectively, tell virtually the same story. Banks with higher LS, other things held equal, do not show any statistically significant differences in loan performance (NPERF/TA and CHRGF/TA), C&I loan return or variance (ROC&I and $\sigma_{ROC\&I}$), or equity to asset ratio (OLDCAP and FAILOLD). The only equations in which LS is statistically significant or nearly significant are the RWA/TA, TACONC, and NEWCAP regressions. As noted above, these variables are largely functions of portfolio composition, rather than direct measures of risk. As will be shown below in the liquidity measures, banks with more C&I loans tend to sell more C&I loans. The variables here that include risk-weighted assets (RWA/TA and NEWCAP) and asset concentration (TACONC) likely capture this liquidity association, rather than portfolio risk or leverage risk, since banks with high loan sales do not have significantly different failure probabilities, earnings, loan performance, or leverage than other banks. In sharp contrast, SLCs are significantly positively related to risk as measured by all the variables except for TACONC and the ROC&I variables. TACONC, as discussed, may be more of a measure of liquidity than risk. The coefficients of the ROC&I variables may represent a feedback effect on the C&I portfolio if the safest loans are sold, as in the collateralization hypothesis. Nevertheless, the banks that issue more standbys still have greater risk overall.

Examination of the LARGE BANKS regressions reveals few important changes in the results. The LS variable becomes statistically significant in the CHRGF/TA equation and in the regressions involving the two capital guideline dummy variables (FAILNEW and FAILOLD). The coefficient in the CHRGF/TA equation is barely statistically significant (*t*-statistic = 2.00), and the capital guideline variables move in opposite directions, suggesting a regulatory, rather than a risk effect. The SLC variable loses statistical significance in the LARGE BANKS sample in the CHRGF/TA and *z*-score equations, but overall, SLC is still strongly positively related to risk.

There are five important sets of implications of these findings that LS are not meaningfully related to risk and SLCs are positively related to risk. First, these findings strongly suggest that LS are not bearing anything like full implicit recourse to the selling bank. As discussed above, a loan sale with recourse is virtually economically identical to a standby—the only real difference is the regulatory treatment. Therefore, one would have expected similar correlations with risk for LS and SLC if the sales were fully or nearly fully guaranteed, and this is not found in the data.

Second, the virtual independence of LS and risk suggests that the James (1988) version of the collateralization hypothesis—the underinvestment problem—is not the primary motivation LS. Recall that the underinvestment problem is equally solved by either LS or SLCs, so both variables should bear the same positive relationship to risk under this version of the hypothesis. That is, if the underinvestment problem were an important motivating factor behind LS, they should be positively related to risk, as are SLCs, since riskier banks would tend to sell more loans under this version of the hypothesis. Rather, other factors that do not depend upon risk, such as improvements in information technology, regulation, or a desire to compete in securities underwriting by offering a bank-originated substitute for traded debt, are likely to be associated with loan sales.

Third, the findings are consistent with the Benveniste and Berger (1986,1987) risk-shifting version of the collateralization hypothesis as an explanation of off-balance-sheet securitization: Banks with higher risk stand to gain the most by separating the claims to their portfolio returns and therefore issue more SLCs. Of course, given that the primary residual claimant for banks' portfolios is the FDIC, which does not explicitly charge for risk, it is difficult to tell from the data whether this version of the collateralization hypothesis holds because SLCs reallocate claims between relatively risk-averse and relatively risk-neutral investor pools or because SLCs reallocate relatively risky claims to the FDIC. We also note that the slightly weaker relationship between risk and SLCs for the LARGE BANKS subsample may suggest that virtually all large banks issue SLCs for reasons other than risk. This may be because most large banks have been close to or below the old capital to asset ratio guidelines, giving a powerful regulatory incentive to issue SLCs.

Fourth, the result that SLCs are positively related to risk runs contrary to the predictions of the market discipline hypothesis. Recall that under that hypothesis, bank guarantees like SLCs should be negatively related to risk because there should be greater demand for guarantees from safer banks and because banks that issue guarantees should be motivated to become safer in order to increase the price they can charge for these guarantees.

Fifth, the absence of an association between risk and LS is consistent with the monitoring technology hypothesis as an explanation of disintermediation-type securitization, which predicts LS to be virtually independent of bank risk and liquidity. We take these risk findings to have implications about the liquidity of the loans of the selling banks. As discussed above, risk is our only indicator of liquidity *within* the loan portfolio. The conventional liquidity variables analyzed below measure the proportions of the banks' asset and liability portfolios in certain categories, but do not suggest how easily the loans remaining on the balance sheet could be sold. The fact that we can find virtually no relationship between LS and risk suggests that there likely is no significant difference in the liquidity of the C&I loans held by banks that sell a substantial portion of their loans from other banks, other things being equal, since the liquidity and risk of a loan are closely related. This finding is consistent with the monitoring technology hypothesis—banks continue to specialize in keeping essentially illiquid loans for which their monitoring comparative advantage is important. However, the types of loans that fall into this set may shift over time as monitoring technology improves.

Turning to the results for loan commitments, we find that COMs have an ambiguous relationship with risk. For some risk measures (e.g., FAIL) the COM coefficient indicates less risk for banks with more commitments, for other risk measures (e.g., CHRGF/TA) COM is associated with greater risk, and for several other risk measures (e.g., NPERF/TA) the results are statistically insignificant. These findings are somewhat at variance with the empirical literature, which generally finds commitments to be associated with lower-risk banks. As indicated above, it is difficult to draw general conclusions about securitization from COM data, since many commitments are merely convenient ways to arrange loans, rather than true forms of securitization.

Tables 4–8a and 4–8b give some additional information on the securitization activity of failing banks in order to provide additional evidence on the moral hazard hypothesis. If banks increase their securitization activity as a result of moral hazard, this should occur most often when banks are about to fail, since failing banks presumably have high and increasing risks. Thus, under the moral hazard hypothesis it is expected that as banks approach failure, securitization activity would be higher than and increase at a faster pace than that of peer groups that are not failing. Table 4–8a shows the LS/TA and SLC/TA data for the eight quarters prior to failure for banks that failed in 1989:Q2, near the peak of the loan sales market. Data are also shown for control groups of banks that did not fail and had continuous data reported over the same eight quarters. The data are grouped by size class in the quarter before failure to maintain comparability in the peer groups since small banks tend to fail more often and large banks tend to securitize more often. The analysis is repeated in Table 4–8b for banks that failed in 1991:Q2, the current trough in the market.

In most cases, the data in Tables 4–8a and 4–8b show that securitization activity is lower and falling faster for banks that are about to fail than for their peer groups of nonfailing banks, contrary to the implications of the moral hazard hypothesis. The lower and declining SLC data for failing banks is consistent with the implications of the market discipline hypothesis, suggesting that the market may devalue the guarantees of failing banks. However, neither hypothesis appears to be very important in explaining the data, which seem to vary significantly for other reasons. The overwhelming majority of securitization activity appears to be related to bank size, rather than to bank risk, with large banks selling most of the loans and issuing most of the standbys.

The regressions with the conventional measures of liquidity on the left-hand side are shown in Table 4–9. The ALL BANKS sample generally indicates that LS are associated with less liquid banks on the asset side—i.e., banks that have more loans per dollar of assets. Since loan sales can reduce, but cannot increase the loan ratios, this finding suggests that less liquid banks may be selling more loans in an effort to increase their liquidity, which would be consistent with the comparative advantage hypothesis. However, examination of the LARGE BANKS subsample shows that this result appears to be at least partially reversed for the large banks that do most of the loan sales. LS/TA is associated with slightly smaller than average C&I/TA ratios and the other two loan ratios are negative, but not statistically significant. The LS coefficient in the LARGE BANKS C&I/TA regression suggests that for each dollar of sales, C&I loans remaining in the portfolio is reduced by only 4 cents. If the sales were measured in terms of their stock value instead of the flow, this figure would likely be even smaller, given that the discussion above suggests that the average duration of loans sold is much shorter than one year. These LARGE BANKS results suggest two conclusions. First, for large banks, there is very little evidence that LS is associated with liquidity, either by the conventional asset liquidity measures here or by the risk measures above. Second, for either small or large banks, the data are consistent with banks' using LS as a vehicle for underwriting new securities as opposed to pure downsizing, since C&I loans do not decline or do not decline much when LS increase. Both of these findings are consistent with the monitoring technology hypothesis.

LS/TA is, however, consistently negatively related to the liquidity of bank liabilities, having positive coefficients in all the HOT ratio regressions. This finding is consistent with Pennacchi's (1988) comparative advantage argument regarding deposit costs, since hot funds are more costly than other deposit funds, giving greater incentives for banks with hot funds to raise financing through loan sales.

The SLC and COM data suggest that both types of off-balance-sheet securitization are more often issued by banks that are illiquid by either asset or liability measures. All of the coefficients except the SLC coefficient in the LARGE BANKS LN/TA equation are consistent with this proposition. These findings may indicate that illiquid banks partially mitigate their liquidity problem by issuing SLCs and COMs rather than on-balance-sheet loans, reducing the need for funding, and collecting some up-front fees. In addition, banks with relatively high costs of funds tend to reduce their cost disadvantages by raising funds through securitization activity. All of these results are consistent with the comparative advantage hypothesis.

CONCLUSIONS

This chapter examines the theoretical and empirical relationships among securitization, risk, and liquidity in banking. We make an important distinction between disintermediation-type securitization, such as loan sales without recourse, and off-balance-sheet securitization, such as standby letters of credit. Under disintermediation-type securitization, there is a movement of intermediated debt to capital market financing, and banks no longer perform their traditional function of monitoring borrowers. Under off-balance-sheet securitization, the bank continues its traditional role of monitoring and bearing credit risk, but alters the distribution of claims against the proceeds of the loans.

Under our extension of the modern theory of the bank as delegated monitor—the monitoring technology hypothesis—disintermediation-type securitization may change the size of the banking sector, but not the fundamental role of intermediaries as holding risky, illiquid, information-problematic loans. The disintermediation associated with this type of securitization changes the set of loans that require the assistance of an intermediary, but not the fundamental nature of intermediation. This theory predicts that disintermediation-type securitization will be virtually empirically independent of bank risk and liquidity.

The monitoring technology hypothesis also has predictions about off-balance-sheet securitization, although this hypothesis does not by itself motivate the existence of this type of securitization. The hypothesis predicts that off-balance-sheet securitization will simply rearrange the claims to bank returns, but will not affect bank monitoring behavior nor bank risk and liquidity significantly. However, off-balance-sheet securitization may be correlated with bank risk, depending upon which concomitant theory explains the existence of this securitization.

The aggregate data suggest that securitization markets are relatively mature, with volume remaining constant or declining in recent years.

Most of the outstanding stock of C&I loans sold are held by other banks or intermediaries (especially foreign banks), suggesting that this activity may often reflect a rebalancing of portfolios among intermediaries with different comparative advantages as opposed to true systemic disintermediation. Alternatively, loans traded among banks may represent a liquidity reserve of traded debt that substitutes for corporate debt underwritten by investment banks.

Our empirical results confirm the importance of distinguishing between the two types of securitization. In particular, the data embody two clear findings: (1) that loan sales without recourse are virtually independent of risk, and (2) standby letters of credit are strongly positively related to bank risk. These findings suggest five important implications. First, loan sales without explicit recourse apparently do not carry anything close to full implicit recourse—otherwise they would have behaved essentially like standbys. Second, the independence between loan sales and risk does not support the underinvestment problem version of the collateralization hypothesis. Third, the positive relationship between standbys and risk does support the risk-shifting version of the collateralization hypothesis as an explanation for off-balance-sheet securitization. Fourth, the relationship between standby letters of credit and risk runs contrary to the predictions of the market discipline hypothesis. And fifth, the absence of a relationship between loan sales and risk supports the monitoring technology hypothesis as an explanation of disintermediation-type securitization.

Analysis of the conventional asset liquidity measures, such as loan/asset ratios, confirms the result that banks that sell most of the loans are no more liquid than other banks. These and additional results suggest that loan sales may represent a securities activity in which banks underwrite a substitute for traded debt. To the extent that these "underwritten loans" are held by direct investors, it is a form of disintermediation consistent with the monitoring technology hypothesis. To the extent that these loans sold are held by other banks, it may be as a substitute for other liquid assets, as opposed to disintermediation. Analysis of the liquidity of bank liabilities suggests that banks with uninsured, "hot" funds tend to have more securitization activities of all types, consistent with these banks' using securitization to offset a funding cost disadvantage. Overall, the data suggest that, contrary to the arguments of some, securitization is not likely to eliminate the role of banks as delegated monitors that hold illiquid loans anytime soon.

NOTES

1. See Bhattacharya and Thakor (1991) for a comprehensive summary of the contemporary information-based theories of the banking firm.
2. See Acharya and Udell (1992) for a more extensive discussion of the problems associated with depositors' delegating responsibility for borrower monitoring to the bank, or the problem of "who monitors the monitor." They argued in a more general setting than Diamond (1984) that depositors/taxpayers must simultaneously solve this delegation problem and the problem of bank runs. One solution is to designate the government as both the "super monitor" and the deposit insurer. The government guarantee solves the runs problem and provides the incentives necessary for the government to insure that the bank does not shirk its monitoring responsibility. In this setting, the signalling costs associated with intermediated debt include the costs incurred by the government and would be reflected in fairly priced deposit insurance premia charged by the government regulator/insurer.
3. This abstracts from the fact that as part of their monitoring activities, individual investors may utilize information produced by credit agencies, brokerage firms, etc. Here we view the level of access to this type of information as part of the monitoring technology available to individual investors.
4. Note, however, that the leftward movement of this boundary will be offset somewhat by any coincidental improvements in bank monitoring technology or reductions in bank signalling costs, both of which help retain the advantages of intermediation.
5. The importance of technical innovation in direct lender monitoring as a determining factor in securitization has been suggested elsewhere [see Kareken (1987)]. To the best of our knowledge, however, this argument has not been fully developed within the analytics of modern banking theory.
6. The only exception to this would be if banks chose to keep some liquid loans on the balance sheet as a secondary reserve for asset management purposes instead of other assets, such as government securities or tradable corporate bonds. However, even in this case, the overall liquidity of the bank would remain constant, with banks' simply choosing a different way to offset some of their illiquidity.
7. For an analysis of the distinction between information production at the loan origination stage and information production on the extant portfolio (i.e., "loan review"), see Udell (1989).
8. See Boot, Thakor, and Udell (1991) for a formal model in which financial intermediaries emerge as the optimal issuers of off-balance-sheet commitments.
9. Greenbaum and Thakor (1987) did not explicitly analyze the coexistence of intermediated and nonintermediated debt. Instead, they formally analyzed an environment in which there is no direct lending—all loans are originated by banks in either a traditional deposit funding mode (DFM) or a securitized funding mode (SFM), the latter essentially being off-balance-sheet securitization. In their model, relatively low direct lender monitoring costs leads to DFM banking. This paradoxical result is an artifact of two assumptions. First, they assumed that as depositors, direct lenders can only monitor the bank by monitoring each of its individual loans. That is, there are no economies of scale in delegated monitoring of the kind found in models like Diamond (1984). Second, they did not permit lending outside of the banking sector. We suspect

that if their model were extended to a more general framework in which banks emerge endogenously and borrowers have access to the capital markets, sufficiently low direct monitoring costs would lead to disintermediation-type securitization without qualitatively altering the model's other predictions regarding DFM versus SFM. For one of the few models in which both capital markets and intermediated markets are explicitly modeled, see Diamond (1991). Unfortunately, it is difficult to draw any implications from the Diamond model regarding securitization because he assumes that only banks, and not direct lenders, are endowed with a monitoring technology.

10. Note that the regulatory tax hypothesis does not necessarily imply less intermediation even when borrowers leave the banking sector. The banking industry could simply lose borrowers to other financial intermediaries such as insurance companies and finance companies where the regulatory taxes differ.
11. We refer here to discipline in securitization markets, rather than the more general topic of market discipline in banking, which includes discipline from bank equity and debt holders.
12. A potential problem of interpretation in Ingram's results is that his leverage variable, the ratio of primary capital to total assets minus the regulatory minimum ratio, included loan loss reserves, which was also his portfolio risk variable. In addition, his results may have been confounded with regulatory tax effects, since the leverage variable depended on the capital standard.
13. Koppenhaver and Stover interpreted the latter result as evidence that standbys are safe relative to on-balance-sheet loans and therefore require less capital. However, if one attributes the marginal amounts of capital to the market's requirements of what must be held against standbys, the nonsensical conclusion must be drawn that the market requires negative capital against standbys. What is more likely is that the quantity of standbys is positively correlated with quality of the overall on- and off-balance-sheet portfolio.
14. The Basle Accord risk-based capital guidelines, which set risk weights in accordance with perceived credit risk, assign performance standbys half the weight of financial standbys and assign short-term commitments a zero weight.
15. The 11.56 percent may be somewhat overstated, because some unknown proportion of the $613.8 billion in C&I stock were actually bought from other U.S. banks. This will be discussed further below.
16. Note that in many cases, the associated commitment lines are assigned along with the loans sold. This is because loan under a commitment that extends beyond the date the loan matures is considered as being under recourse for regulatory and reporting purposes, since the borrower has some claim (albeit imperfect) against the selling bank.
17. For neither Security Pacific nor Bankers Trust does it appear that the decline in loan sales resulted in significantly more loans' being kept on their balance sheets, since total assets for these both of these banks declined slightly over the same time period.
18. The fact that M&A loans comprise a substantial proportion of loan sales is consistent with the monitoring technology hypothesis, since these are loans about which important information is not completely private to the bank. At a minimum, the acquirer has had to do a credit analysis of the acquiree, and under normal circumstances numerous other parties involved in the financing have also done credit

analyses of the merging firms.

19. The SLC/TA ratio also did not appear to increase significantly in reaction to the increase in capital requirements against on-balance-sheet assets for large banks in 1985, as would have been predicted by the regulatory tax hypothesis. Primary capital requirements for large banks were raised from 5.0 to 5.5 percent of total assets, and total primary plus secondary capital standards were set at 6.0 percent of total assets in April 1985. The growth in SLC/TA slowed from 11.0 percent in 1984 to 10.5 percent in 1985 to –10.2 percent in 1986.
20. Even without any difference in capital requirements, SLCs have an estimated 21 basis point advantage over loans sold with recourse because of differences in reserve requirements [see Benveniste and Berger (1986)].
21. The forms now ask for separate information on lines for residential real estate, credit cards, commercial real estate, securities underwriting, and other, while before 1990, only a single category for essentially all lines other than credit cards was included. We exclude credit card lines from the reported data, but apparently some banks did not include all the other commitment types in their earlier reports.
22. Interest rate risk is not separately measured because it cannot be computed from information on the Call Report. However, since the vast majority of commercial loans are now either floating-rate or well under a year in duration, it is unlikely that many banks have significant interest rate risk [see Berger and Udell (1990,1992)].
23. Mean ROA is added to the equity/asset ratio in the numerator of z-score because we are measuring how far below the mean actual ROA would have to fall before insolvency.
24. For example, if we assume that all assets have the same mean return, an equally weighted portfolio of two assets with uncorrelated returns would have lower risk and higher TACONC than an equally weighted portfolio of three assets, where the returns on the first and third were perfectly correlated.
25. TIME 1 is excluded because the other right-hand-side variables are lagged one quarter, and TIME 2 is excluded as representing the base group.
26. One potentially important control variable that is not included is the typical size of borrower for each individual bank. Loan sales primarily involve large loans because such loans are more liquid. Unfortunately, the Call Report does not contain information about the individual borrowers or loan size.

REFERENCES

Acharya, Sankarshan, and Gregory F. Udell, "Monitoring Financial Institutions," *The New Palgrave Dictionary of Money and Finance* (1992), forthcoming.

Allen, Franklin, "The Market for Information and the Origin of Financial Intermediation," *Journal of Financial Intermediation* (March 1990), pp. 3–30.

American Banker, "Asset Sales Report," various issues.

Avery, Robert B., and Allen N. Berger, "Risk-Based Capital and Off-Balance Sheet Activities," *Proceedings of the Conference on Bank Structure and Competition*, Chicago: Federal Reserve Bank of Chicago (1988), pp. 261–87.

Avery, Robert B., and Allen N. Berger, "Loan Commitments and Bank Risk Exposure," *Journal of Banking and Finance, 15* (February 1991a), pp. 173–92.

Avery, Robert B., and Allen N. Berger, "Risk-Based Capital and Deposit Insurance Reform," *Journal of Banking and Finance, 15* (September 1991b), pp. 847–74.

Baer, Herbert L., and Christine A. Pavel, "Does Regulation Drive Innovation," *Economic Perspectives*. Chicago: Federal Reserve Bank of Chicago (March/April 1988), pp. 3–16.

Benveniste, Lawrence M., and Allen N. Berger, "An Empirical Analysis of Standby Letters of Credit," *Proceedings of the Conference on Bank Structure and Competition*. Chicago: Federal Reserve Bank of Chicago(1986), pp. 387–412.

Benveniste, Lawrence M., and Allen N. Berger, "Securitization with Recourse: An Instrument that Offers Uninsured Bank Depositors Sequential Claims," *Journal of Banking and Finance 11* (September 1987), pp. 403–24.

Berger, Allen N., "The Relationship Between Capital and Earnings in Banking," Board of Governors of the Federal Reserve System working paper (April 1991a).

Berger, Allen N., "Market Discipline in Banking," *Proceedings of the Conference on Bank Structure and Competition*. Chicago: Federal Reserve Bank of Chicago (1991b), pp. 419–27.

Berger, Allen N., and David B. Humphrey, "Measurement and Efficiency Issues in Commercial Banking," in Zvi Griliches (ed.), *Measurement Issues in the Service Sectors*. Chicago: National Bureau of Economic Research, University of Chicago Press (1992), forthcoming.

Berger, Allen N., and Gregory F. Udell, "Collateral, Loan Quality, and Bank Risk," *Journal of Monetary Economics, 25* (January 1990), pp. 21–42.

Berger, Allen N., and Gregory F. Udell, "Some Evidence on the Empirical Significance of Credit Rationing," *Journal of Political Economy, 100* (October 1992), pp. 1047–77.

Berlin, Mitchell, "Securitization," *The New Palgrave Dictionary of Money and Finance* (1992), forthcoming.

Bhattacharya, Sudipto, and Anjan V. Thakor, "Contemporary Banking Theory," Indiana University working paper (September 1991).

Board of Governors of the Federal Reserve System, *Reports of Condition and Income: Senior Loan Officer Opinion Survey on Bank Lending Practices*. Washington, DC, various issues.

Boyd, John and Edward C. Prescott, "Financial Intermediary Coalitions," *Journal of Economic Theory* (April 1986), pp. 211–32.

Boot, Arnoud W. A., and Anjan V. Thakor, "Off-Balance Sheet Liabilities, Deposit Insurance and Capital Requirements," *Journal of Banking and Finance, 15* (September 1991), pp. 825–46.

Boot, Arnoud W. A., Anjan V. Thakor, and Gregory F. Udell, "Competition, Risk Neutrality and Loan Commitments," *Journal of Banking and Finance 11* (September 1987), pp. 449–71.

Boot, Arnoud W. A., Anjan V. Thakor, and Gregory F. Udell, "Credible Commitments, Contract Enforcement Problems and Banks: Intermediation as Credibility Assurance," *Journal of Banking and Finance* (June 1991), pp. 605–32.

Diamond, Douglas W., "Monitoring and Reputation: The Choice between Bank Loans and Directly Placed Debt," *Journal of Political Economy* (1991), pp 689–721.

Diamond, Douglas W., "Financial Intermediation and Delegated Monitoring," *Review of Economic Studies* (July 1984), pp. 393–414.

El-Gasser, Samir, and Victor Pastena, "Negotiated Accounting Rules in Private Financial Contracts, *Journal of Accounting and Economics* (1990), pp. 381–96

Furlong, Frederick T., and Michael C. Keeley, "Capital Regulation and Bank Risk-Taking: A Note," *Journal of Banking and Finance 13* (December 1989), pp. 883–91.

Gennotte, Gerard, and David Pyle, "Capital Controls and Bank Risk," *Journal of Banking and Finance 15* (September 1991), pp. 805–24.

Gorton, Gary B., and Joseph G. Haubrich, "The Loan Sales Market," in George Kaufman (ed.), *Research in Financial Services*, Vol. 2, (1990), pp. 85–135.

Gorton, Gary B., and George G. Pennacchi, "Are Loan Sales Really Off-Balance Sheet?" *Journal of Accounting, Auditing and Finance 4* (1989), pp. 125–45.

Gorton, Gary B., and George G. Pennacchi, "Banks and Loan Sales: Marketing Non-Marketable Assets," Universities of Pennsylvania and Illinois working papers (August 1991).

Gorton, Gary B., and Richard Rosen, "Overcapacity and Exit from Banking," Federal Reserve working paper (October 1991).

Grammatikos, Theoharry, and Anthony Saunders, "Additions to Bank Loan-Loss Reserves: Good News or Bad News?" *Journal of Monetary Economics 25* (1990), pp. 289–304.

Greenbaum, Stuart I., and Anjan V. Thakor, "Bank Funding Modes: Securitization versus Deposits," *Journal of Banking and Finance* (September 1987): 379-401.

Ingram, Marcus A., "Securitization and Signalling: Evidence From Standby Letters of Credit," Clark Atlanta University working paper (September 1991).

Jagtiani, Julapa, Anthony Saunders, and Gregory F. Udell, "The Diffusion of Off-Balance Sheet Innovations in the Banking Industry," New York University working paper (August 1991).

James, Christopher, "The Use of Loan Sales and Standby Letters of Credit by Commercial Banks," *Journal of Monetary Economics* (November 1988), pp. 395–422.

Keeley, Michael C., "Deposit Insurance, Risk, and Market Power in Banking," *American Economic Review 80* (December 1990), pp. 1183–1200.

Keeley, Michael C., and Frederick T. Furlong, "A Reexamination of Mean-Variance Analysis of Bank Capital Regulation," *Journal of Banking and Finance 14* (March 1990), pp. 69-84.

Keeton, William R., and Charles S. Morris, "Why Do Bank Loan Losses Differ?" *Economic Review*. Kansas City, KS: Federal Reserve Bank of Kansas (May 1987).

Kim, Daesik, and Anthony M. Santomero, "Risk in Banking and Capital Regulation," *Journal of Finance 43* (December 1988), pp. 1219–33.

Koppenhaver, Gary D., "The Effects of Regulation on Bank Participation in the Guarantee Market," in G. Kaufman (ed.), *Research in Financial Services: Private and Public Policy*. Greenwich, CT: JAI Press, Inc. (1989), pp. 165–80.

Koppenhaver, G.D., and Roger D. Stover, "Standby Letters of Credit and Bank Capital: Evidence of Market Discipline," *Proceedings of a Conference on Bank Structure and Competition*. Chicago: Federal Reserve Bank of Chicago (1991), pp. 373–94.

McAllister, Patrick H., and Douglas A. McManus, "Risks in Banking: Evidence from ex post Returns," Board of Governors of the Federal Reserve System working paper, Washington, DC (November 1990).

McManus, Douglas A., and Richard J. Rosen, "Risk and Capitalization in Banking," Board of Governors of the Federal Reserve System working paper, Washington, DC (October 1990).

Millon, Marcia, and Anjan V. Thakor, "Moral Hazard and Information Sharing: A Model of Financial Information Gathering Agencies," *Journal of Finance* (December 1985), pp. 1403–22.

Musumeci, James J., and Joseph F. Sinkey, Jr., "The International Debt Crisis and Bank Security Returns Surrounding Citicorp's Loan-Loss-Reserve Decision," *Proceedings of the Conference on Bank Structure and Competition*. Chicago: Federal Reserve Bank of Chicago (1988), pp. 436–59.

Pennacchi, George G., "Loan Sales and the Cost of Capital," *Journal of Finance* (June 1988), pp. 375–96.

Pavel, Christine, "Securitization," in *Economic Perspectives*. Chicago: Federal Reserve Bank of Chicago (July/August 1986), pp. 16–31.

Pavel, Christine, and David Phillis, "Why Commercial Banks Sell Loans: An Empirical Analysis," *Economic Perspective*. Chicago: Federal Reserve Bank of Chicago (May/June 1987), pp. 3–14.

Ramakrishnan, Ram T.S., and Anjan V. Thakor, "Information Reliability and a Theory of Financial Intermediation," *Review of Economic Studies* (1984), pp. 415–32.

Ronn, Ehud I., and Avinash K. Verma, "Pricing Risk-Adjusted Deposit Insurance:

An Option-Based Model," *Journal of Finance* (September 1986), pp. 871–95.

Thomas, Martin, and J. Randall Woolridge, "The Wealth Effects of Asset-Backed Security Issues," The Pennsylvania State University working paper (September 1991).

Timme, Stephen G., Jayant R. Kale, and Thomas H. Noe, "The Impact of Loan Sales and Securitization on Bank Shareholders' Wealth," Georgia State University working paper (October 1990).

Udell, Gregory F., "Loan Quality, Commercial Loan Review and Loan Officer Contracting," *Journal of Banking and Finance* (December 1989), pp. 367–82.

Wall, Larry D., and David R. Peterson, "The Effect of Capital Adequacy Requirements on Large Bank Holding Companies," *Journal of Banking and Finance 11* (December 1987), pp. 581–600.

APPENDIX TABLE 4A–1 Securitization Hypotheses

Hypothesis	*Description*	*Empirical Implications*	*Main Empirical Results Found*
Monitoring Technology Hypothesis	Borrowers lie on information continuum. Borrowers with "high," "medium," and "low" levels of information problems borrow from insiders, intermediaries, and direct lenders, respectively. Innovations in monitoring technology shifts boundaries between these supplier categories.	Disintermediation-type securitization (LS) will be empirically independent of bank risk and liquidity. Off-balance-sheet securitization (SLC) does not cause differences in risk or liquidity, but may be correlated with them as a result of other theories.	LS are generally unrelated to measures of bank risk and liquidity of the asset portfolio, consistent with the hypothesis.
Regulatory Tax Hypothesis	Regulatory taxes drive a wedge between effective prices of on-balance-sheet and off-balance-sheet activities.	LS, SLC, and COM quantities should react to changes in capital requirements.	Raw data show a decrease in LS coincident with introduction of Basle Accord risk-based capital standards, which increased tax on C&I loans, inconsistent with the hypothesis. SLC and COM raw data are also inconsistent with the hypothesis.
Collateralization Hypothesis (Benveniste and Berger version)	Securitization provides Pareto-improving mechanism for allocating risk between risk-averse and risk-neutral investors. SLCs superior to LS as a collateralization mechanism.	Bank risk causes more SLCs because higher risk banks have greater pooling problems. Bank risk does not cause more LS, because SLCs dominate for solving the problem.	SLCs are positively related to risk and negatively related to liquidity. LS generally not related to risk and liquidity. Both results are consistent with the hypothesis.

APPENDIX TABLE 4A–1, concluded

Hypothesis	*Description*	*Empirical Implications*	*Main Empirical Results Found*
Collateralization Hypothesis (James version)	Securitization provides a solution to the underinvestment problem. Either SLCs or LS solve the problem equally.	Bank risk causes more SLCs and LS because higher risk banks more often have the underinvestment problem.	Same results as previous hypothesis. Therefore, data more consistent with Benveniste and Berger version of collateralization hypothesis.
Moral Hazard Hypothesis	Moral hazard problem encourages banks to be riskier. Banks should remove safer loans through LS or SLCs.	Banks with greater propensity to exploit FDIC are riskier and should have higher LS and SLCs.	Failing banks engage in less LS and SLCs than their peers, inconsistent with the hypothesis.
Market Discipline Hypothesis	SLCs introduce market discipline because safer banks have more credibility in issuing guarantees.	Safer banks will issue more SLCs (i.e., low risk causes SLCs), and banks with more SLCs will become safer (i.e., SLCs cause low risk).	SLCs are generally associated with riskier banks, inconsistent with the hypothesis. However, failing banks engage in fewer SLCs, consistent with the hypothesis.
Borrower Moral Hazard Hypothesis	Pricing menu on SLCs and COMs may reduce borrower moral hazard.	Borrowers will be safer than they otherwise would have been without guarantees.	SLCs are generally associated with riskier banks, *weakly* inconsistent with hypothesis (only weak evidence because the risks from different types of borrowers cannot be empirically distinguished). Empirical association between risk and COMs is ambiguous.

Hypothesis	*Description*	*Empirical Implications*	*Main Empirical Results Found*
Liquidity Hypothesis	Acquisition of LS technology enhances ability of banks to securitize assets remaining on balance sheet.	LS will cause bank assets to be more liquid.	LS are generally unrelated to measures of bank risk (which proxy for liquidity within the loan portfolio) and only ambiguously related to conventionally measured liquidity of the asset portfolio, inconsistent with the hypothesis.
Comparative Advantage Hypothesis	Securitization arises out of exogenous comparative advantages across banks in loan origination and deposit funding.	Banks with relatively large loan portfolios and relatively large wholesale liabilities should have higher LS.	Most of the outstanding stock of loans sold was bought by other banks, consistent with the hypothesis. LS are ambiguously related to conventional measures of asset liquidity measures, inconsistent with the hypothesis. LS are positively related to wholesale funds ratios, consistent with the hypothesis.

COMMENT

Jonas Prager

Berger and Udell suggest that "disintermediation-type securitization," whereby banks' role in financing economic activity is replaced by direct finance, does not reduce either the riskiness or liquidity of banking institutions. Their "monitoring technology hypothesis" proposes that although some debtors who previously relied on banks for their financing needs are, because of innovations in debtor monitoring, able to obtain direct finance, the same technology enables banks to lend to individuals and firms that were previously excluded from bank financing. Hence, the new loans in the new monitoring environment are qualitatively no different from the ones lost to direct finance. Berger and Udell test the plausibility of their hypothesis against a number of competing hypotheses with a massive data set consisting of more than eight years of quarterly Call Report data for over 12,000 banks. Having found disintermediation securitization and risk to be unrelated, they are satisfied that the monitoring technology hypothesis cannot be rejected.

There are, however, some problems with the monitoring technology hypothesis that stem from the underlying model of delegated monitoring. The model postulates that for the lending market to function efficiently potential lenders must offset the advantage that accrues to potential borrowers from asymmetric information. Because banks specialize in information monitoring, they are able to level this playing field and can do so more cheaply than can nonspecialized lenders. Knowing that banks are efficient monitors, depositors and other bank liability holders have entrusted banks with their assets and delegated to the banks the monitoring of the assets that ultimately represent their security.

All this may be true in the abstract. It is more difficult to reconcile delegated monitoring theory with the actual banking environment. Certainly, depositors covered by deposit insurance are unlikely to be especially concerned with the care with which banks monitor their assets. That may be equally true for all depositors, and some bondholders as well, in all those banks deemed "too large to fail." A large share of the public has really delegated monitoring not to the banks, but to the regulatory authorities. Yet, the record of the regulators in recent years hardly invites confidence in their monitoring effectiveness. Bankers are clearly aware of their operating environment and, consequently, may not be as careful monitors as the public would wish.

In essence, bank liability holders face a principal-agent problem, a point alluded to in the Berger-Udell paper. While the banker as agent may well be a more efficient monitor, it is not evident that the agent need comply with the desires of the principals. The ultimate control vehicle of the liability holders is withdrawal, a rather blunt instrument, especially for depositors who benefit from the transaction function of deposits as well as borrowers who profit from the customer relationship. The more tenuous commitment of other liability holders such as CD owners may cause the agent to serve the principals better. But they, too, are unlikely to be affected by the marginal change that securitization represents in the risk portfolio of an individual bank.

The inherent principal-agent conflict between bankers and depositors, as it plays out in securitization, combined with the reality that the public has delegated monitoring to regulatory agencies of questionable effectiveness, suggests that bankers have little to lose and much to gain by increasing their profitability through securitization, even at the expense of increased risk. If this is true, then Berger and Udell's monitoring technology hypothesis rests on a flawed foundation.

The second part of the Berger-Udell paper deals with "off-balance-sheet securitization," in which bank assets are moved off the balance sheet. When a bank issues standby letters of credit, for example, it continues to monitor the borrower, because the bank remains subject to credit risk. Berger and Udell do find a strong positive correlation between standby letters of credit and bank risk, a result consistent with a number of theories of bank behavior.

With banks' facing increased competition from nonbank financial intermediaries, will they survive the added challenge from direct finance as well? Berger and Udell are confident that banks will continue to fill a niche as purveyors of informational services.

COMMENT

Sanford Rose

The title of Berger and Udell's paper, "Securitization, Risk, and the Liquidity Problem in Banking," is, in my view, a misnomer. There is no liquidity problem in banking. Banks fail because of asset-quality problems, which, in the case of large banks, sometimes manifest themselves in the inability to roll over large deposits. While illiquidity may be the proximate cause of failure, the ultimate cause is the market's perception that the value of the bank's assets is less than that of its liabilities. No bank that is market-value solvent has ever failed because it couldn't borrow, at least not since the Great Depression. The oft-quoted statement by pop authors that illiquidity rather than insufficient capital is the cause of bank failure is a canard. Illiquidity is just a symptom arising at the fastigium of a bank illness brought on by asset-value deterioration.

The real question is whether securitization can contribute to solving the asset quality problem. As near as I can determine from reading the Berger-Udell paper, its view is that disintermediation-type securitization—loan sales without recourse—has not been associated with measurable reductions in bank risk. This is a little like arguing that the past record of bank mergers shows no impact on the rationalization of bank costs. The reason for this is that much of the merger activity of the 1980s did not have cost reduction as an object. Merger activity was designed as an interest rate speculation. Banks overpaid for other banks' future cash flows in the confident expectation that a decline in the rate at which these flows would be discounted to their present value would bail out their shareholders, which sometimes occurred. Cost savings do not show up because most acquirers weren't seeking them.

Similarly, securitization has not reduced bank risks because there haven't yet been meaningful attempts at the securitization of C&I portfolios, where most of the risk resides. C&I securitization is held to be infeasible because of information assymmetries: Most C&I borrowers are information problematic, to use the phrase of Berger and Udell. They thus are condemned to fund themselves in the intermediated market.

Clearly, however, there is a need for broad-scale C&I loan securitization. It can be reasonably argued that every sizable bank failure of the past decade has been a failure of underdiversification. The big Texas banks failed because they weren't properly diversified. So did Continental Illinois and the Bank of New England. And Bank of America very nearly failed because its managers, by their own confession, did not realize that most California borrowers shared a common vulnerability to disinflation.

The underdiversification of the major banks can be established prima facie by comparing their loss standard deviations with that of the banking industry as a whole. In the 1980s, the top ten banks had a loss standard deviation of about 45 basis points; for the entire bank industry this measure was only 16 basis points.

Further evidence comes from an experiment performed a few years ago. A group of California consultants calculated the improvement in the asset-efficiency ratios of the top 50 banks that would result from exchanging 25 percent of their C&I loans for an equivalent dollar amount of proportional shares in a hypothetical pool of loans to investment-grade national companies. The asset-efficiency ratio was defined as economic return—that is, loan spread over the riskless rate, minus average losses, divided by risk (proxied by the loss standard deviation).

The results of the exchange raised this asset-efficiency ratio for the 50 banks by an average of 30 percent. Although economic return fell because of a decline in spread, the overall efficiency ratio rose because the decline in risk outweighed the fall in economic return. And this came about because of the weak correlation between the losses in the pool of nationwide companies and those in the portfolios of the 50 banks. Thus, participation in the pool reduced the losses in the hypothetically restructured portfolios by decreasing the simultaneous defaults that would normally have resulted from local downtowns and regional economic shocks.

This experiment showed that (1) large banks are starved for quality assets; (2) despite their size and reach, the top 50 institutions are predominantly local; and (3) it was, and probably still is, possible for them to reduce their loss potential by participating in the securitization of paper of nonlocal borrowers who, being well known and investment grade, are not information problematic. That is, there is probably no agency problem blocking this type of securitization, although there may be other types of problems.

Let me advance the notion that the agency problem in securitizing the paper of noninvestment-grade or nonrated publicly traded C&I borrowers can now be surmounted through the use of a new technology developed by the KMV Corporation of San Francisco, with whom my firm, Oliver, Wyman, has recently formed a joint venture. If I am right, banks can in the near future sell the loans of at least their publicly traded borrowers, whose paper currently accounts for between 30 percent and 40 percent of the face amount of the C&I loans on the industry's balance sheet. And they can also buy back proportional shares in the nationwide pools their sales activity would create, thereby enormously improving their diversification and reducing short-term risks. The implications of this development for long-term profitability are, however, slightly less benign.

The technology permits remote assessment and monitoring of the expected and unexpected loss risk of any given loan and pool of loans—that is, the likely loss means and variances. The starting point is the observable stock price movement of 5,000 publicly traded firms. What concerns any lender is whether the market value of its borrower's assets is greater than the face amount of the bank debt. It is of course difficult to assess directly the market value of a company's assets. But that value is definitionally equal to the market value of the firm's liabilities plus liquidity. The KMV model measures the value of the assets by tracking the value of the stock and using this information to infer a market value for the over-one-year debt. Adding the face amount of the current debt to the market value of the equity and the noncurrent debt gives us the value of the assets.

Let us assume that a company has a mean stock price of $50 and that the standard deviation of the equity-price movement equals 10 percent. There are thus two chances in three that the stock price will range between $45 and $55, with a complementary probability of one in three that it will move outside this range. Also there is a 95 percent chance that the price will range between, roughly, $40 and $60, with a one-in-twenty probability of moving outside this range. The model measures the amount of stock volatility, or number of standard deviations, that would be needed to reduce the value of the equity to the point where, together with the imputed reduction in the value of the noncurrent debt, the market value of the assets is just equal to or less than the book value of the bank debt.

In the example just cited, assume that a fall in the company's equity price in excess of $10 is sufficient to drive the value of the liabilities, and therefore that of the assets, below the face amount of the bank debt. As noted, stock volatility equal to two standard deviations suggests that the stock price will move more than $10 to either side of its mean of $50 with a probability of one chance in twenty, or 5 percent. However, the lender is only interested in the downside volatility, which is equal to half this overall range of movement. Therefore, he concludes that the probability of this company's equity value's deteriorating sufficiently to bring it to default amounts to one in forty, or 2.5 percent. This, then, is the expected loss probability, which we then adjust for by multiplying it by one minus the likely recovery rate.

We believe that unexpected loss frequencies are formulaically linked to expected loss frequencies. As a result, so are unexpected and expected losses. Suppose that the recovery rate on the loan with a 2.5 percent loss probability is such that the expected loss is 50 basis points. Then the unexpected loss possibility amounts to 99.5 percent. That is, the variance of losses equals the expected loss times one minus the expected loss. And so, in the above example, the loss standard deviation equals the square root of 50 basis points times 99.5 percent. Otherwise put, if this loan was the only one the bank had, the amount of capital that would be needed to protect against unforeseen losses—at least at the level of one standard deviation—would be the square root of about 49, or 7 percent.

But of course loans are part of a portfolio. And the unexpected loss of a portfolio is a function of the expected losses of the pieces (from which we derive their stand-alone unexpected losses), the pairwise coefficients of loss correlation, and the weight of each piece in the portfolio.

The obvious problem is: How does the model compute pairwise loan loss correlations? It starts with the observable pairwise correlation of total stock returns. It assumes that these stock-return correlations are good proxies for asset-value correlations. And having arrived at asset-value correlations, it computes debt correlations using derivative asset-pricing, or options pricing, theory.

We have run a number of tests on this model and have found that it is far superior to anything in the marketplace. It may even be good enough to allow future credit enhancers of loan pools to price their letters of credit with a reasonable degree of accuracy. If it is, C&I loan securitization, with its attendant risk-reducing impact on the industry, is imminent.

In the long run, the availability of methods like this, particularly if they can be extended to nonpublic borrowers (which we believe is more than possible), will determine the role of banks as delegated monitors and thus circumscribe their income potential. It is of surpassing irony that the bank problem in the United States, which at bottom is traceable to a decline in the credit opacity of some classes of borrowers, should stimulate a search for short-term palliatives whose long-term effect will be to reduce the credit opacity of many other classes of borrowers and thus permit them to flee the confines of the intermediated sector of the economy.

COMMENT

Kenneth E. Scott

Berger and Udell, working with eight years of quarterly bank balance sheet data, undertake to examine the relationships among the growth in securitization activities of banks and various measures of their risk and liquidity. Their objectives seem to be both general and particular. In general, they wish to understand better in a descriptive sense where securitization, an important trend in the 1980s, is taking the banking industry. In particular, they wish to shed light on some theories about the essential functions performed by banks as financial intermediaries.

One theory about why banks exist is that they perform a liquidity transformation function, bridging a gap between demand and supply of short-term and long-term financial assets. Another theory is that banks perform the role of bridging the information asymmetry between borrowers and lenders. In effect, the bank acts as a monitor delegated by all its depositors to assess borrower risk and oversee borrower performance. The bank in turn signals the quality of its own performance by issuing to its depositors a demandable debt claim backed up by its own equity.

These theories of why we have banks are familiar from the literature, but exactly how do they relate to bank securitization activities? Berger and Udell do not spell out in detail whatever links they may have in mind. Instead, they launch into an exploration of a variety of hypotheses, most of which were put forth to deal with other issues. But fundamentally, Berger and Udell seem to be examining two possible hypotheses in relation to their implications for the growth of securitization in the 1980s:

(1) ***The Monitoring Technology Hypothesis*** There has been significant improvement over this period in the technology, and a concomitant reduction in the cost, of gathering and processing information about borrowers in order to evaluate and monitor them. This in turn has shifted the boundaries between traded debt, intermediary-held debt, and owner-held debt. Disintermediation securitization occurs in response to and reflects that shift, by transferring assets from bank portfolios to the portfolios of investors who purchase financial assets in the market. Loan sales without recourse would be the prime example.

(2) ***The Regulatory Tax Hypothesis*** Regulatory taxes (particularly capital requirements) have gone up during the 1980s, causing banks to engage in added efforts to lower these taxes by getting assets and liabilities off their balance sheets while continuing to play their traditional role of evaluating and bearing risk. The prime example of off-balance-sheet securitization would be loan sales with recourse, or the issuance of standby letters of credit and loan commitments that are used to back up customers' debt so that this debt may be traded on the public securities markets. But regulatory taxes would encourage disintermediation-type securitization also.

There are several difficulties with the inquiry Berger and Udell wish to undertake. First, the foregoing explanations are of course not mutually exclusive, for both may have been at work in the 1980s. The operational distinction between them is that they imply, to a limited extent, the growth of different kinds of securitization at different points in time. Second, the two different kinds of securitization, unfortunately, are not cleanly measured or separated. Loan sales that are made formally without recourse may nonetheless bear some implicit understanding as to possible recourse. Loan commitments combine both debt backups and arrangements based merely on administrative convenience, and the data on loan commitments do not reflect the borrowers' motivations in obtaining commitments. Third, the underlying causal forces are not closely examined. What are the technological changes Berger and Udell have in mind—what cost elements of information and monitoring and renegotiation were affected, by how much, and when were they introduced? What were the changes in regulatory taxes through the data period—how large were they, and when were they effected? The time series aspects of the data are not really exploited.

Leaving aside the various possible reasons for the growth in bank securitization, Berger and Udell are primarily interested in how the trend affected bank risk and liquidity. The problem in making that inquiry is that the effects will not be direct and simple, because feedback loops are involved. Securitization may affect risk, but the bank risk level may also affect further efforts at securitization.

When it comes to the empirical side, I have both some comments on the Berger and Udell results and some suggestions as to how they might carry their results further. They begin with a description of trends in the 1983–91 period for both disintermediation securitization and off balance sheet securitization. In both cases, although at different times, there is a period of fairly rapid growth, which then tapers off. These patterns cannot really be used to test either their regulatory tax hypothesis or their monitoring typology hypothesis, because neither hypothesis is sufficiently developed. During the relevant time period, when did changes occur in the structure of taxes or technology, and when were their effects felt? It may be possible to extract more from the time series data on the growth of loan sales, standby letters of credit, or loan commitments than the paper achieves.

The central concern of Berger and Udell, however, is the association of these trends with changes in bank risk and liquidity. I shall omit the liquidity side of their findings and concentrate on the risk aspects, where Berger and Udell reach their two main conclusions: (1) Loan sales without recourse are independent of risk, and (2) standby letters of credit are strongly positively related to bank risk.

Preliminarily, Berger and Udell find that the loan sales as reported appear to be genuinely without recourse, since they do not perform in the regressions like standby letters of credit, which are clearly claims on the bank. For my purposes, I will take that proposition as established. Then, as proof that loan sales are unrelated to risk, they run a variety of regressions of risk variables on securitization variables and come up with no significant coefficients.

But, for several reasons, I am skeptical of the strength of that finding. First, on econometric grounds: Their regressions (as shown in Tables 4–5 and 4–6) generally have very low R-squared numbers—several as low as .002. That suggests a very incomplete specification of the determinants of bank risk, and so does their model, which has only securitization variables on the right hand side. Second, on a priori grounds: The monitoring technology hypothesis would lead me to quite a different expectation. The loans that would be sold off without recourse would be the larger loans to larger borrowers, implying that the bank is left with a portfolio of smaller loans to smaller borrowers, and smaller firms have on the average higher betas. So loan sales should be positively associated with risk, holding other factors constant.

But a bank's commercial loan portfolio, of course, is not the sole determinant of its risk. One would have to take into account the composition of other assets, the level of bank capital, and so on. The way to test the foregoing observations, and perhaps to strengthen the support for Berger and Udell's conclusion, would be to put additional variables on the right hand side of their regressions to control for these other factors.

For the second main conclusion, that standby letter of credit activity is strongly related to risk, Berger and Udell offer as proof the fact that its coefficient in the Table 4–5 and Table 4–6 regressions is in general highly significant. Again, I have some econometric reservations. The problem already mentioned of low R-squares and inadequate specification applies here as well. The high degree of statistical significance of the coefficients is not all that surprising, given the 430,000 observations.

I would also offer a competing hypothesis with respect to the expected effects of off balance sheet securitization. By itself, growth in sales of standby letters of credit implies an increase in a bank's contingent liabilities and risk. But an increase in a bank's risk should have an adverse effect on the quality of and demand for its guarantees. If a bank is to continue in that line of business and preserve its fee income, it may move to offset the increased risk by, for example, raising additional capital. The net effect of these processes for the riskiness of the banking industry seems something that could only be determined empirically. One would have to examine a bank's changes and responses in a time series, again introducing other variables that affect risk.

It should be evident that Berger and Udell have put together a stimulating paper. At least it certainly stimulated me to a fresh effort to think about the relationships they are examining; whether my effort bore any fruit I will leave to the authors and to the readers of this book.

But in conclusion let me return to a fundamental issue with which this volume is concerned. Will securitization render banks extinct, because there is no useful function that they perform better than others? That strikes me as unlikely. Information intermediation, at some level, will continue to be needed. It presents savers with moral hazard and adverse selection problems, which have to be addressed by credible guarantees or ownership retention on the part of the intermediary. Are banks going to be the information intermediary, or at least one among others? The answer should be yes, unless regulatory costs and taxes on banks are raised to the point that they are left with no advantage over other intermediaries.

COMMENT

Lewis J. Spellman

In my view Berger and Udell have undertaken an heroic task. They have attempted to sort out the many influences that both theoretically and empirically shape the securitization activities of commercial banks. In their analysis of the literature they have shed some light on the following questions regarding bank securitization:

1. Is there a meaningful dichotomization of possibly different "types" of securitization activities?
2. Why do bank securitize?
3. Which banks are more apt to securitize?
4. What is the effect of the securitization activity on the bank's risk and liquidity profile? This question is addressed at both the theoretical as well as the empirical level.

This is clearly a highly ambitious and worthwhile undertaking, as there is relatively little known about banks' involvement in the securitization process, and this is a useful beginning. I would like to elaborate on their framework.

1. ***Are there different types of securitization?*** Berger and Udell classify securitization on the basis of whether the bank has a continuing financial guarantee of either the security or the assets in the securitized package of loans. The existence of the guarantee implies a continuing obligation on the part of the bank to monitor the loans in the securitized package. If securitization is accomplished without a credit enhancement or

financial guarantee by the bank, it has been termed a "disintermediation" type of securitization.

In general, the disintermediation type is viewed as a shedding of the bank's assets without further recourse. The presumption is that the securitization activity was the result of an attempt to develop a liquidity mechanism or a down-sizing mechanism for the bank.

The disintermediation type of securitization has been differentiated from the securitization activity in which the bank continues to be at risk through guarantees, letters of credit, or other third party guarantees. Presumably the latter type of securitization requires credit judgment, continuing risk, and monitoring services. It is presumed that this is a profit-related business rather than a mechanism to shed bank assets.

2. ***Why banks securitize?*** Berger and Udell examine the financial literature for clues or implications as to why securitization by banks might take place. First, they examine the implications of the information-based theories of financial intermediation in which banks are presumed to possess economies of scale in the monitoring of credit especially among problematic and relatively small corporate borrowers.

In a similar vein they cite the bank lending officers' capability to underwrite business loans. That is, the banker's ability to judge "the five C's of lending" is a skill that banks develop; with modest additional staff outlay the bank could exploit securitization as a joint product.

Another motivation for securitization is the possibility that banks might wish to shed loans that they believe are more risky than those held in portfolio. This is what has been called the "moral hazard" hypothesis for securitization. This of course would be in direct contrast to another view that banks wish to exploit their "reputational capital" and in effect sell their reputation for making sound investments for a fee. Because a bank's reputation continues to be on the line whether or not there is an explicit guarantee, securitization causes a bank to be subject to the "discipline" of the market. Hence, the bank lays off only those assets that are superior.

But perhaps the most important motive for securitization cited by Berger and Udell is the desire to avoid regulatory taxes. If one presumes that bank regulators and the FDIC have imposed taxes on banks in the form of high capital requirements, cash reserve requirements, or insurance premiums for on-balance sheet activity, then moving activities off the balance sheet presumably would free them of the taxes that are imposed for on-balance sheet activities.

3. ***Which banks securitize?*** The question of which banks is not a

matter of large versus small, city versus regional. Rather, the variable is quality. On this there is both an *ex ante* and an *ex post* observation. The literature indicates that *ex ante* the safer banks engaged in the activity and *ex post* they have become less safe for having engaged in the activity. This is understandable for securitization cum guarantees as compared to securitization for the purpose of disintermediation.

4. ***What is the effect of securitization on the bank's risk and liquidity?*** Berger and Udell cite studies in which the consensus is that securitization removes high quality assets from banks' balance sheets, suggesting more risk. However, the very process that allows banks to shed assets reduces another dimension of risk: the risk of illiquidity. Again, there are cross-currents to sort out, making it difficult to assess how either the market or the regulators would view banks engaged in securitization. As previously noted, banks could become less risky by shedding risky assets; or they could become more risky because of an urge to cash in on their reputational capital and lay off the better assets. With no general consensus on the effect of securitization activity on the bank's residual risk and liquidity, the authors test the null hypothesis of no relationship between securitization and variables they believe to measure risk and liquidity.

Empirically their heroic attempts to relate securitization activities to bank variables associated with either liquidity or risk can be summarized in a nutshell: Securitization without guarantees appears to be unrelated to any of the measures of bank liquidity and risk, whereas securitization with guarantees appears to be related to variables that ostensibly measure bank risk.

However, because these inferences are drawn from the bank's entire balance sheet, which in itself is an aggregation of many activities, it is difficult to isolate securitization effects alone. If it were possible to isolate the securitization data, a framework that associates securitization with the returns from securitization would be a more fruitful approach for the empirical investigation.

Basically, from the bank's perspective, securitization is a product that is generated for fee income. The securitization process of gathering assets and packaging those assets for the purpose of selling pro rata shares of the package only makes sense when the proceeds from the sale of the package exceed the costs of the raw material loans placed in the package as well as the expenses associated with the packaging and sale. In the process of the bundling of loans to sell off pro rata shares of the bundle, the market value of the whole must be greater than the value of the sum of the parts.

In the production of the securitization product there are many layers of value added, with each value added activity deserving a fee. A commercial bank could engage in many of the valued added activities itself, but it is quite possible that, because of regulatory fire walls or comparative advantage, some of the stages in the process of producing securitization bundles might be subcontracted to others such as investment banks, insurance companies, or other commercial banks.

There are nine elements of value added that can be identified in creating the securitized package. The first would be the value added from underwriting bank loans typically found in a bank's securitization package. The bank is presumed to have developed an expertise in the five C's involved in the underwriting of a business loan, but there is no reason that other financial firms might not similarly develop that expertise.

The second element would be the origination of the loan intended for the bundle, which a bank could either undertake for its own securitization packages or for other banks.

Third is the administrative function of providing the documents, including SEC registration, etc. Again, this is hardly a strata of value added that would be unique to banking.

A fourth fee generating activity in the production of the securitization package is the design of the bundle of assets in order to maximize the revenues from the sale of the pro rata shares of the bundle. The designer of the package maximizes the value of the bundle by selling specific attributes to the markets willing to pay a premium for that attribute. The example that comes to mind are the interest-only (IO) and principal-only (PO) splits of mortgage securities or other structures that separate the bundle by maturity or risk.

A fifth element of value added and hence the ability to charge a fee is risk-taking. The risk occurs because the bundle could change in value in the market while the bundle is being assembled, either because interest rates change or because the credit risk of the elements in the loan package changes.

Sixth, there is the separate business risk requiring a fee in the event the bundle will have been poorly constructed so that the sales price of the pro rata shares of the bundle is disappointing and less than the costs of assembling the bundle.

Seventh, there is the interim financing fee of the package. This activity is likely a joint product with the design and risk-taking activities.

Eighth, there is the fee associated with the sale of the pro rata shares of the bundle.

Finally, having designed and assembled the bundle for sale there is the ninth activity of making the package understandable to investors at low costs, since there are informational asymmetries. Providing information to the investors is necessary to the pricing of the bundle. The information could be conveyed in the form of a credit rating and/or a financial guarantee. Hence, in viewing the Berger-Udell dichotomization by type, the question of providing the financial guarantee might come down to the economics of whether the fee associated with the guarantee is worth the additional risk to the bank. This, like other elements in the value added of the package, could be supplied by the banks or in some cases by other entities such as insurance companies. Undoubtedly, the designer will shop the guarantee market and determine whether or not there is good value in the financial guarantee; if not, the asset bundle could be credit rated instead. Hence securitization as a fee-driven business by commercial banks could result in either guarantees or a rating, depending on the economics of the marketplace at the time the bundle comes to market.

Berger and Udell's disintermediation type or guarantee type of securitization are likely to be generated from the same process, with the economics of the marketplace determining the extent of the bank's involvement at any point in time. If the above is correct, banks can engage in several of the elements of value added in producing the securitization bundle and might also subcontract for various activities.

In conclusion, Berger and Udell delve into an extraordinarily murky area, for which only tangential theory exists. To the extent that financial or economic theories provide superstructures to analyze the financial mechanism, they are far better suited for examining marginal changes in a given paradigm. What we have witnessed is a metamorphosis of commercial banks' delving into off-balance-sheet activities. Attempts to extrapolate from received theory to explain structural change are likely to be very difficult.

But the first step in developing superstructures to analyze problems is often excursions into the raw data for inferences as to what theoretical structures need be created. The Berger-Udell findings are a useful starting point, which could lead to theoretical developments.

CHAPTER 5

SECURITIZATION: ITS EFFECT ON BANK STRUCTURE

Tamar Frankel

INTRODUCTION

Securitization of debt has emerged, part, as a response to the problems of banks. In addition, the securitization phenomenon has a substantial effect on banks. Therefore, proposals to restructure the banking system must include securitization.

What is securitization? The term "securitization" refers to the massive movement that began in the 1970s to transform illiquid debt into securities.[1] "Securities" and "loans" have much in common; both are obligations by one party to pay money or cash equivalent to another. Both can be viewed as evidence of money claims[2] and as financial assets. For the purpose of this discussion, the main distinction between them is that loans are less amenable to trading than are securities. The form, amounts, and terms of loans do not meet the conditions necessary to create active markets in them. For efficient financial markets to develop, the instruments traded must be standardized and available in a sufficient number and denominations, and the public must be able to receive relatively low-cost information about the borrowers.[3] Loans lack these attributes.[4]

The difference between "loans" and "securities" affects the kind of channels through which savers' money flows to issuers or borrowers. Issuers sell, and investors buy and trade in, securities with the help of securities firms.[5] When the conditions necessary for the creation of markets are absent—for example, when savers prefer terms or require information that borrowers cannot or will not provide—financial intermediaries bridge the gap between the parties. These intermediaries may be able to borrow on terms acceptable to savers and lend the proceeds on terms acceptable to borrowers.[6] Some borrowers can raise funds both by issuing securities and by borrowing from institutions; some investors can invest both by purchasing securities and by lending through intermediaries. But not all have the luxury of choice; small borrowers must usually resort to institutional intermediaries.

For over fifty years, the financial system in this country consisted basically of these two investment channels: financial intermediaries and securities markets. The channels were kept more or less separate, and banks functioned as the primary intermediary.[7] Since the early 1970s, however, the securities market channel has been widening, and the separation between the two channels has been blurred.[8] Securitization has emerged as a new investment channel that substitutes markets for financial intermediaries, or combines parts of both in new ways. Although banks have securitized loans for decades (e.g., loan participations[9]), the "new" securitization has been so pervasive and different as to change the whole financial system qualitatively and structurally.

Forms of securitization Securitization, broadly defined, has taken three forms. The first form is a substitution of securities for loans. Large borrowers have chosen to increase the portion of funds they raise by issuing securities (e.g., commercial paper and "junk bonds") and to reduce their bank loans. Similarly, investors have increased the securities portion of their investments and reduced their bank deposits. By 1990, nonfinancial firms had issued $130 billion in commercial paper, approximately 20 percent of the $642 billion in bank commercial and industrial (C&I) loans outstanding.[10] Small investors flocked to investment companies (money market funds) and reduced their bank deposits.[11]

Second, securitization of large loans has taken the form of "loan participations" ("LPs")—the sale of relatively standard portions in such loans. The enormous development of the LP markets is illustrated in the international financial markets. Since the 1970s, the Euro-markets in LPs have become an efficient and inexpensive source of capital for sovereign states and large borrowers. While in 1981, $147.7 billion out of $200.5 billion (73.7%) raised in the international markets was in the form of syndicated (direct) bank loans, in 1985 only $42.0 billion out of $256.5 billion (16.4%) raised in these markets was in loan form; 79.5% was in the form of LPs and securities.[12] In the United States LPs are sold to large- and medium-sized banks, insurance companies, credit unions, and pension funds. In 1989, estimates of the amount of LPs outstanding in the United States range from $26 billion to more than $35 billion.[13]

For small loans, a third, more complicated, form of securitization has emerged. These loans are transferred to an entity (a "pool") that holds the loans and issues its own securities. Financial institutions then develop secondary markets for these securities. Usually, the credit risk and other risks that these small loans pose are directly or indirectly (fully or partially) underwritten by U.S. government-sponsored enterprises (GSEs), the original lenders, or third-party banks, or insurance companies. These institutions provide "credit enhancement" to the pool or to the investors in pool securities directly. Through this pooling technique, GSEs have propelled mortgage loans into a huge secondary market in mortgage-backed securities. This process served as a model for securitizing other types of loans made by the government and the private sector. In a relatively short period, the value of securitized loans has grown tremendously. By 1990 $1.34 trillion of mortgage-backed securities were outstanding.[14] In 1986, the U.S. Government began planning to securitize its loan portfolio (valued at more than $800 billion) starting with a $5 billion public offering in the late 1980s.[15] During 1987 and through July of 1988, the U. S. Government sold $7.3 billion of loans for $4.7 billion, and planned to sell $6.5 billion worth of its loans in 1988 and $7.7 billion worth in 1989.[16]

The variety of securitized loans has also increased. After residential mortgages came auto[17] and light truck loans, credit card and trade receivables, computer leases, and insurance premiums loans.[18] Loan-backed securities issued by the private sector amounted to almost $270 billion in 1986, up from $25 billion in 1980.[19] The amount of outstanding asset-backed securities (in addition to mortgage-backed securities) was estimated in 1990 at $107.5 billion.[20] There also exists a limited market in securitized third world loans, and attempts are being made to extend and deepen this market.[21] Markets in whole loans are also developing. In sum, the movement to securitize loans is sweeping the U.S. financial scene and is on its way to world markets.[22]

Securitization is not a passing fad

Some forms of securitization have been practiced by banks for decades. However, new content was poured into these old forms in the 1970s, and this "new" securitization is affecting the whole financial system. Why did the "new" securitization appear only in the 1970s? I believe that it was triggered by unstable economic conditions, a new technology, and a different government policy, all of which emerged only in the 1970s.

Arguably, what the government has created, the government can undo. If public policy is re-oriented toward bolstering banks and traditional banking activities, will not securitization die a natural death? For a number of reasons I conclude that it will not; securitization is not a passing fad.

First, although still in its infancy, there are indications that securitization is a better intermediation process than the traditional processes. It may be an innovation that better utilizes markets, financial intermediaries, and new technologies, especially in an unstable economic environment. Securitization unbundles the traditional banking functions of originating loans, holding loans to maturity, and managing or servicing the loans. Banks are efficient loan originators because their cost of information about their borrowers and the localities in which they operate is comparatively low. Banks, however, are not the most appropriate holders of long-term or medium-term loans because most of the banks' own liabilities are short-term. More appropriate institutions to invest in such loans are insurance companies and pension funds, whose liabilities are long-term.

The most appropriate institution to hold such loans is an institution that passes to its investors only those funds that it receives and provides investors with liquidity through secondary markets rather than by undertaking to redeem its own obligations. Securitization creates such an institution through pooling. A pool holds illiquid loans but has no liabilities. It offers either pass-though securities or different classes of equity securities among which the pool divides the cash flow from its assets. The pool provides its security holders with liquidity because its securities can be traded in secondary markets. The pool does not offer to redeem the securities directly.

Moreover, even though pool assets are not diversified because they are the same type of assets, these assets are more diversified geographically than a typical bank's assets. Pool sponsors can choose loans; they buy them from lenders nationwide rather than competing for borrowers locally. Furthermore, investors in pool securities can further diversify their own portfolios by buying securities of pools that hold different types of loans. In addition, the sponsors of such pools can impose standards (including underwriting standards) on the originating lenders.

Securitization by pooling allows banks to perform the functions they are most suited for—originating loans. It allows other, more suitable, institutions to hold these loans. By converting illiquid loans into liquid instruments, securitization enables the investing institutions to hold liquid long-term and medium-term loans. These institutions will accept a lower return in exchange for this liquidity. In addition, not all banks have the personnel and automated information systems to service numerous small loans. Securitization fosters a market for the loan-servicing function. Therefore, this function can be performed by the more efficient servicers.[24]

Second, securitization is driven in part by technology. Technology cannot be regulated away, and its benefits continue to give incentives to securitize and create markets.

Third, even though securitization's design and development have been heavily influenced by GSEs, a policy decision to reverse the process would be difficult to implement. The larger banks and financial institutions continue to restructure internally. Money market banks trade in securities abroad, and other financial institutions and others have entered the lending and "near deposit" business. Money center and regional banks are engaged in creating asset-backed securities. Such changes would not be easily undone by law. The higher the investment that institutions make in restructuring themselves, the harder it will be to force them to go back to the status quo ante.

Fourth, as technology links financial markets globally, no one country can regulate its banks and financial markets, except in cooperation with most other countries. The alternative of closing the country's doors to fleeing capital is rarely, if ever, effective. Thus, even though the government had a substantial role in introducing securitization, the government may find it hard to reverse the process.

Fifth, although not all debt can be securitized today, it is likely that by the end of the decade most debt could be securitized. Some believe that by the year 2000 at least 80 percent of all new loans will be securitized.[25] Loans that meet the conditions for creating a market, such as commercial paper, can be securitized by substitution. Loans to well-known borrowers in amounts that are sufficiently large can be securitized by participation. Other types of loans may be securitized by pooling, depending on a number of factors.

The first factor is information about the borrowers. The lower the information costs (to investors or guarantors of the pool securities), the easier it will be to securitize the loans. As the saying on Wall Street goes, "if it's gradable, it's tradable." Since pools hold a large number of small loans, information costs about pools' assets are relatively high. Therefore, the more standard and simple the terms of the loans and the more predictable their cash flow and maturity, the more easily they can be priced and securitized. The second factor is servicing costs, which depend on the number of loans in a pool and the frequency of the borrowers' payments and defaults. The third factor is the level of credit risk, and the corresponding collateral and guarantees attached to the securitized loans. The more risky the loans, the more costly it will be to securitize them. However, risk can be reduced by guarantees and insurance and by diversification of the pools' portfolios.

Loans to medium-size commercial and industrial companies have not yet been securitized because they lack many of the attributes described here. Some predict, however, that these loans are next in line to be securitized.[26] Entrepreneurs are seeking ways to standardize these loans for trade, gathering information and developing techniques, using statistics and computerized modeling, for pricing these loans[27] and thus preparing for the securitization of these loans.

Markets in whole loans are also developing. Trade in large, whole commercial and industrial loans of large corporations has increased substantially;[28] if these trends continue, we may see trading in loans of small companies. Perhaps the time will come when a small company, fitting a particular profile, could borrow by signing a round-figure note or an arrangement in a standard form. A rating agency will prepare the company's profile for a fee, which will be lower than the lenders' information costs today. Regulated professional appraisers would evaluate the collateral. The rating, appraisal, price, and terms of the loan could give sufficient information to the buyer about the risk level posed by the borrower and a comparison with other similar loans. The originator may then sell such a loan to a pool or sell it directly in a secondary market for similar loans. Currently, however, this scenario is only a twinkle in someone's eyes.[29]

I conclude that securitization is here to stay.[30] The extent to which it will be developed by the private sector may depend in part on the new infrastructure that is being established for the process: relaxing the current laws to remove legal barriers to the process, and providing adequate protections to investors in securitized loans by regulating the new intermediary institutions. The extent to which securitization will help the banks may depend on what functions they will be allowed to perform in the process, and, most important, on what assets they will be allowed to hold.

What is the effect of securitization on banking? In part, the answer depends on what the benefits and disadvantages of securitization to banks are and on how we view the problems of banks. Therefore, the first part of this paper discusses the conditions that enabled traditional banks to remain stable for over fifty years, and the conditions since the 1970s that destabilized the banks. This discussion focuses mainly on the problems of banks that securitization can affect and also explains why the new forms of securitization appeared in the 1970s and not before.

The second part of the paper examines the effects of securitization on the traditional functions and structure of banks.[31] Securitization changes some of the banks' functions and can resolve some of the banks' structural problems; it also creates new problems and brings to the fore old ones that were previously less apparent. These new and old problems can be reduced by amending the current banking laws.

The third part of the paper compares the law of securitization applicable to banks with the law applicable to other market actors. It is difficult to evaluate the competitive position of banks because the regulatory costs are higher on some activities and lower on other activities. Even if we could calculate the aggregate regulatory costs for the whole securitization process, the results are not conclusive because regulatory costs are but one item in the decision of banks and their competitors to engage in certain activities and their starting base line is not the same. Further, securitization allows institutions to choose some but not necessarily all securitization activities. Besides, apart from serving as a payment system, bank businesses differ greatly among themselves. One kind of bank may bear heavy regulatory costs, and another may bear low costs.

I conclude that securitization is transforming our financial system, including the banking system. Securitization allows market actors more freedom to choose their future business niche. To be sure, law and regulation play a role in reshaping the system. Institutions might choose activities in accordance with the regulatory burdens or limitations that are currently in place. Law and regulation should play a role in transforming the system. Like any system in transformation, the financial system is now more vulnerable. Therefore, regulators have a crucial and difficult role: allow the markets and the institutions to experiment, select their future businesses, and restructure, and at the same time monitor closely the sensitive areas that historically require regulation. Hopefully, when the dust settles we will find out which institutions do what activities best and also which activities should be addressed by regulation. We will also discover the institutions into which the traditional banks will evolve.

THE PROBLEMS OF TRADITIONAL BANKS

The inherent weakness of bank structure

The main weakness of traditional banks is rooted in their usefulness as intermediaries. In addition to serving as a payment system, the great contribution of traditional banks to the economy is that they intermediate between savers and borrowers whose preferences are very different. Depositors usually desire a liquid and safe place for a portion of their transaction balances, while borrowers usually offer riskier, longer-term obligations. However, these benefits for the parties and the economy make the traditional banks' structure highly risky, and because this structure is the source of bank profits, bank profits are also risky. Admittedly, there is risk involved in every economic activity. But the structure of banks need not be as risky.

Bank liabilities and assets do not match with respect to liquidity and maturity.[32] On the liability side, most banks' liabilities are short-term and liquid, while on the asset side, most bank assets are longer-term and less liquid. Banks' profits are tied to, and depend on, this risky structure. Their profits depend largely on the spread between the cost of the banks' funding.[33] If they reduce the structural risk, they would reduce the spread. With the exception of reducing expenses, they can do little to increase profits otherwise. In addition, the substantial and costly capital "cushions" that banks must keep to increase their safety and soundness[34] reduce their profitability. Under current law, the "cushions" must remain stable while banks' spreads narrow, and that reduces the banks' profitability even more.

Yet banks do not use the one risk reduction technique that does not affect the spread; they do not diversify their loan portfolios effectively. Under the traditional view of banking, banks must develop a stable customer-base that is usually limited to particular localities and businesses.[35] It is true that information about the borrowers helps the lender assess credit risk. But there are other risks that are independent of the creditworthiness of the borrowers, such as industry and locality risks. A stable borrower base severely limits the freedom of banks to design a fully diversified portfolio. Loans cannot be picked like securities in the secondary markets. If the bank customer-base is steady and limited, the fortunes of bank loan portfolios rise and fall with business cycles of the borrowers' industries and the localities in which the banks and their customers are situated.

Second, although banks are allowed to invest in a large menu of securities, and in asset-backed securities, some of these securities are not sufficiently liquid, and not all asset-backed securities are available to all banks.

Third, banks and their regulators apparently do not think in terms of a diversified portfolio but in terms of the credit risk involved in each loan. The current law limits loans to one borrower to 15% of capital and surplus. The limit does not necessarily preclude a portfolio of loans to borrowers in the same industry and locality. Banking regulation and its enforcement is also focused on the credit risk of each loan rather than on risks involved in a loan in relation to the portfolio.

Fourth, banks can diversify by lending outside their charter state through loan production offices. However, the legal limitation on interstate banking hampers interstate lending because customers seek full financial services, not only loans, and deposit taking (which is now prohibited interstate) is important to secure the loans.

In addition to problems that stem from the banks' unique unbalanced structure, banks are also vulnerable to the universal problem caused by negligent and incompetent management.

In sum, bank problems and losses stem mainly from an inherently risky structure; a risky source of profits; illiquid loan portfolios; constraints on full diversification of non-systemic credit risk in their loan portfolios; and transactions made negligently and incompetently.[36]

If traditional banking is so frail, how did banks remain stable and healthy for fifty years?

The survival of banks during the past fifty years can be attributed to a number of factors: the legal system of monopolies for banks, government support for the banks, depositors' patterns of behavior, banks' practices, and (until the late 1970s) the relative stability of interest rates in the United States.

Traditional banks were granted a legal monopoly on bank deposits. The law prohibited competition for deposits by nonbanks and inhibited competition for deposits among banks by setting maximum interest rates. Further, a fixed amount of each deposit was insured by the government, adding value to no-interest or low-interest bank deposits.

The pattern of depositors' behavior also helped the banks' stability. Depositors behaved in a fairly predictable manner; amounts of deposits that were withdrawn nearly matched the amounts deposited. Furthermore, since 1913, banks could borrow from the Federal Reserve System (the "discount window") to alleviate temporary liquidity problems. Thus, banks were assured of inexpensive and stable funding.

Banks' dominance of lending was also substantial. Few borrowers could raise funds abroad. Competition among banks for borrowers was largely limited to geographical areas in which they had branches. Except for the large automobile manufacturers, few companies, if any, could profitably enter the lending business. Consumer banks, credit unions, mortgage brokers, and factoring companies remained small because their cost of funds was higher than the cost of deposits for banks. Since these lenders had to charge borrowers more, they offered little competition to banks.

Bank practices also helped reduce their riskiness. Rather than make long-term loans to risky enterprises, banks made mostly short-term loans to seasoned enterprises. These prudent lending policies reduced the banks' interest rate and credit risks. The privilege and duty of long-term financing for housing was bestowed on savings and loan associations; this activity rendered their structure even less rational than that of banks. However, since 1966, they were granted a competitive advantage over banks in attracting savings because the interest rate that they were allowed to pay on savings accounts was higher than the rate that banks were allowed to pay on the savings accounts they accepted.

Paradoxically, illiquid loan portfolios enhanced the apparent bank stability. Banks' financial statements were insulated to a great extent from the fluctuations in the markets. Their liabilities were independent of market interest rates because regulations capped these rates, and their loan portfolios were carried on the books at face value, regardless of fluctuations in credit risk or in market interest rates. This legal regime made banks appear stable and profitable.

In addition, the banking business was designed to a large extent by regulation. Banks could issue only few specific types of obligations. This non-competitive and highly regulated environment attracted to banks a cautious and conservative type of manager; banks conducted business and loaned "by the book." Even losses from conflict of interest transactions remained low and predictable.

The changing environment

The historical regime worked—at a price. That price became too high when the environment in which banks operated changed. Economic pressures, most notably, inflation, made banks unattractive to depositors.[37] Government exemption from the interest rate ceiling for large depositors made these monopolies most unattractive to small depositors. Banks deposits became uncompetitive as the money market funds appeared, savers withdrew their money, and the sources of funding for bank and thrifts dried up.

Further, new technology provided automated information systems, which enhanced direct investment at the expense of bank intermediation. In addition, a fundamental change occurred in the philosophy underlying government regulation of banking. Social and political attitudes militated against the monopoly of banks and against overregulation of business generally. The government increased its intermediation functions and developed the securitization process. Competition eroded banks' profitability, as the interest that they paid on deposits increased and the interest charged to borrowers decreased.[38]

While historically much of the banking business was designed by regulation, the new regime encouraged competition, and competition breeds variety, to distinguish competing products. This environment brought pressures for an aggressive and innovative management approach (though not as aggressive as that of the securities industry) and required banks to change their culture. It also required a new type of regulatory surveillance. These changes brought about tensions: Neither a new institutional culture nor a new regulatory approach is established easily or even willingly.

The federal government played a crucial role in eliminating bank monopolies and paving the way to securitizing debt. By allowing banks to issue negotiable certificates of deposits the government gave banks incentives to develop sales departments. By tightening bank capital requirements, the government gave the banks incentives to sell their loan portfolios, instead of raising new capital (which was prohibitively expensive) and to utilize the sales departments not only to sell certificates of deposits but also to sell loans. The need to sell loans generated pressure to securitize these loans in order to obtain a better price (because investors value liquidity, for which they are willing to sacrifice some return). Pressures to securitize also produced incentives to reduce the cost of securitization to increase the banks' net benefits from securitizing their assets.

The government also actively initiated and developed the process of securitization by pooling. It created and financed GSEs to securitize mortgage loans as a way to channel more credit to the housing capital market. Thus, securitization became a form of intermediation that provided an alternative to both banks and securities markets by combining both.

EFFECTS OF SECURITIZATION ON TRADITIONAL BANKS

Securitization can reduce or resolve some of the problems of traditional banks but may create other problems. I discuss here both the solutions that securitization offers and the new problems that it brings, as well as proposed solutions to these new problems.

Securitization enhances competition

Securitization helps eliminate the banks' monopolies and exposes them to competition with other banks and nonbanks, on both funding and lending. Now banks must compete in the market for funds and pay similar rates as those paid by nonbanks with similar credit risk. On the lending side, with equal cost of funds, nonbanks can compete with banks. In addition, securitization helps some borrowers and investors resort to the markets directly, through commercial paper, bonds, and investment companies that hold such securities. Thus, banks have become less special.[39]

Securitization opens the flood gates for bank competitors. Because it separates banking functions, it allows many and different actors to engage in different parts of the banking and securities business and provide alternatives to bank functions and products: originating and buying loans, sponsoring pools of loans to securitize them, underwriting pool securities and acting as market makers, issuing commercial paper as a substitute for large bank deposits and loans, and money market fund shares as a substitute for small bank deposits.

Because securitization splits banking activities, banks compete on each specific activity with those for whom the particular activity is most advantageous. Thus, at each juncture of the process, banks must compete with the best positioned competitors.[40] Although the law of securitization does not treat banks and nonbanks alike, it seems that banks are not at great disadvantage vis-à-vis most of their competitors.[41]

The effect of competition on the banks is serious. It shrinks the banks' spread by reducing the return on bank loans and increasing the cost of bank funding. But banks' structure remains as risky as before. In addition, while competitors may securitize loans by engaging in their traditional activities, banks that engage in securitization must change (at least some of) their traditional activities and culture. Change for older institutions such as banks can be costly because it involves replacing obsolete property and technology, and overcoming individual and organizational habits. Thus, losses to some banks from reduced spreads and adjustment costs can be attributed in part to securitization.

There are small, medium, and large banks that have fared well in this changing environment. Many community banks that operate in more isolated communities have done well; they have maintained a more stable base of depositors and borrowers, and their spreads have remained comfortably high, perhaps because they are less exposed to competition. These banks may be operating in an environment that resembles the past environment. Whether they could overcome competition in the future, the growth of securitization, and their risky structure remains to be seen. They might find a niche in the emerging new financial system and serve as a distribution network for financial products designed by others.[42] Perhaps growth is not the answer for banks.[43] Banks that have maintained high underwriting standards but did not grow have weathered economic downtrends. Financial institutions that recruited talented personnel, changed their business strategies, and specialized have also fared well. Whether these banks will continue to be successful in the future is an open question.

Securitization helps banks to specialize

Securitization allows each bank to specialize in activities that are suitable for it; for example, a bank can invest in information retrieval systems and specialize in custodial and servicing activities; or a bank can develop a securities sales force and engage in dealing and underwriting securitized loans.[44]

More important, banks have an advantage in originating loans because their cost of information is comparatively low, but they have a disadvantage in holding illiquid loans. Securitization enables banks to maintain their advantage and lend to a stable customer-base in their localities, and to overcome the disadvantage by selling the loans they originate.[45]

Securitization enables banks to reduce their structural risk with respect to liquidity

Securitization enables banks to hold liquid securitized loans and thereby reduce if not eliminate their liquidity problem. However, although current law allows banks to hold securitized loans and select debt securities, not all of these instruments are liquid.[46] Arguably, liquidity may be accompanied by volatility and instability. But volatility should not be attributed to securitization. When market interest rates rise, bank assets with fixed lower interest rates fall automatically. In the past, banks appeared to be somewhat insulated from the markets. They raised insured funds independently of market rates, they did not sell their assets, and the regulatory accounting framework did not (and still does not) require them to reflect the market values of their assets on their balance sheets. Today, banks must pay market rates on their deposits, and many banks originate loans for sale. The effect of interest-rate volatility on bank assets and liabilities is thus more visible, regardless of how the assets appear on the books.

Unless the liquidity and maturities of a bank's assets and liabilities coincide, the latent structural problems of the banks will remain. But banks can and do protect against maturity mismatches by hedging instruments such as swaps, options, futures, or combinations of these instruments. Options and futures contracts protect buyers against price variations in particular financial assets or in a "basket" of such assets. Banks can also adjust their capital. Currently, capital requirements are tied to the risk attached to classes of assets in the bank's portfolio. Interest-rate risk is treated as a matter of safety and soundness. I believe that this risk should be factored into the capital requirements instead.[47]

Securitization enables banks to diversify their portfolios

Securitization allows banks to retain their relationships with borrowers and at the same time diversify credit risk. Although the Glass-Steagall Act restricts the amount and type of securities that banks may hold, asset backed securities are treated as loans for this purpose.[48] Thus, banks can invest in securitized financial assets available in secondary markets and thereby diversify their assets; they can focus on the whole portfolio and eliminate or substantially reduce nonsystemic risk.

However, the existing banking law is not geared to portfolio management or diversification and ignores the portfolio theory that has been developed in the past 50 years. The law today still adopts the arcane view of diversification held at the beginning of this century. In essence the law limits the amount that banks may lend to one borrower[49] and requires that banks invest in low risk loans in most cases. Bank regulation and enforcement focuses on the risk from each bank loan and less on the portfolio as a whole. A similar view of diversification was imposed in traditional trust law[50] and other laws passed at that time.[51] Yet, any fixed percent of the capital and surplus, or of assets, or of any other amount, may be too much or too little for diversification, and "safe investments" (e.g., first mortgages) may be very risky, depending on the composition of the whole portfolio.

Securitization reduces information costs about bank assets

Securitization distributes and reduces the costs of valuing banks' portfolios, for the banks, the markets, and the regulators. Banks gather information about small borrowers and monitor them; both banks and the markets monitor large borrowers who also issue securities. Markets factor in bank loans, and banks take the market prices of the borrowers' securities into account.

Banks and other loan originators that make loans for sale and securitization evaluate each borrower. But once the loans are pooled and loan-backed securities are issued, the performance of the whole portfolio is evaluated by the markets. This reduces valuation cost for the banks that hold securitized loans and the cost of valuing bank assets that consist of securitized loans. Today, bank assets are valued periodically. Market valuation of bank assets can help the banks and the regulators to evaluate the safety and soundness of banks and help control the level of risk of the banks' portfolios. If banks hold securitized loans, valuation of their assets and obligations will be more timely, less expensive, and arguably more accurate.[52]

However, if bank portfolios are valued more often and marked to market, a temporary disparity between the assets and liabilities can render banks insolvent. Banks may resolve the problem either by hedging or by maintaining capital in the form of a "margin" that fluctuates with this disparity and compensates for it.[53]

In sum, securitization reduces bank liquidity and interest-rate risk, but brings to the fore the volatility problem; that problem may be reduced by compensating reserves. Securitization helps banks diversify their portfolios, but to do so effectively, banks should be guided to focus on portfolio design. Finally, securitization helps evaluate the banks' portfolios, the banks' obligations, and their safety and soundness.

SECURITIZATION LAW: ARE BANKS AT A COMPETITIVE DISADVANTAGE?

General

To determine whether banks and their competitors play on a "level playing field" in the securitization business one can compare the laws and market discipline governing their securitization activities. That is the easy part. Since the laws are not identical, the harder part is to determine whether these differences affect the banks' competitive position, and this question is outside the boundaries of this discussion.[54] However, I hope that the comparison made here may lead to more work on the issue. This comparison follows the process of securitization: raising funds, making or buying loans, selling loans and providing credit enhancement to the buyers, establishing pools of loans, issuing and distributing participations in loans or pools of loans and making secondary markets in these participations, and managing the pools and servicing the loans.

Raising funds

Depending on market demand, anyone can raise funds by issuing securities (equity, and long-term or short-term debt). But banks also can raise funds in two ways that are not available to their competitors. First, banks can obtain short term loans from the Federal Reserve System.[55] Second, banks can take deposits. Although banks must now compete with other institutions that offer "near deposits," such as commercial paper and shares in money market funds, bank deposits have advantages. For a start, they provide unlimited checking privileges. To offer such low cost money-transfer mechanisms, other financial institutions must use banks. However, for a particular bank, the cost of providing checking services could offset the benefits of the funds raised by such deposits. For example, if the funds are immediately withdrawn in cash or invested in securities, the particular bank may lose, even if the whole banking industry is not affected.

Another advantage of bank deposits is that a certain amount of deposits is covered by the FDIC insurance, although some bank competitors have a similar coverage. For example, customers of broker dealers are covered under certain conditions by the Securities Investor Protection Corporation; policy holders of insurance companies may be covered by special state funds; pensioners of some types of pension funds are covered by the Pension Benefit Guarantee Corporation. A third advantage for bank deposits is that deposits can be used as collateral without limitation. The use of "deposits" at some bank competitors—for example, pensions and insurance companies—may be restricted by law because these "deposits" involve tax advantages that serve as incentives for savings, or because withdrawals of these "deposits" would eliminate the pooling and distribution of risk which they offer. Finally, most bank deposits establish clear debt relationships between the bank and its depositors. Therefore, banks may use the funds raised by such deposits freely, while most types of "deposits" taken by other institutions are subject to conditions and fiduciary duties.[56]

Bank deposits are partially designed by law. Demand deposits are payable on demand; savings accounts are payable on 7 days' notice; the number of withdrawals per month from money market accounts is limited. Bank competitors' deposits may be subject to similar legal limitations. For example, money market funds must redeem their shares within 7 days of demand (in practice, they honor the customers' demands even sooner). Nonetheless, as compared to banks, their competitors, including money market funds that offer redeemable securities, have greater flexibility to design the other terms of the "near deposits" that they offer.[57]

The regulatory burdens on raising funds by issuing securities are uneven. Banks' securities (but not securities issued by their holding companies or their nonbank subsidiaries) are exempt from registration under the Securities Act of 1933[58] and from the Trust Indenture Act of 1939.[59] Banks are regulated by their own regulators under the Securities Exchange Act of 1934, although the substance of the regulation is similar.[60] As compared to banks' securities exemption, thrift securities are exempt from registration under stricter conditions.[61] Although insurance policies and annuities are exempt from registration,[62] the securities issued by insurance companies are not exempt.

Making or buying loans

Anyone can make and buy loans, depending on whether he can raise funds or sell these loans in advance. However, the law limits the amounts banks can lend to one borrower. Similarly, the law limits the amount of securities issued by one issuer that diversified investment companies (which claim to be diversified[63]) may hold. In addition, banks, thrifts, pension funds, and insurance companies are subject to legal prudence restrictions in making loans, including some measure of diversification. Registered investment companies must establish their investment policies, which may be changed only with the approval of a majority of their shareholders.[64] Investment companies must also comply with prudence rules. In addition, by definition, investment companies are issuers that engage primarily in investing or trading in securities.[65]

While the portfolios of banks, thrifts, and insurance companies are valued periodically by government examiners, the portfolios of investment companies that offer redemption must be marked to market daily, and the securities of investment companies that do not offer redemptions are usually traded and priced in the secondary markets.

Market buyers can affect the underwriting standards and terms of loans made for sale. But if these buyers are regulated, lenders are likely to comply with the regulations of potential buyers (e.g., the Office of the Comptroller of the Currency).

Selling loans and providing credit enhancement

Anyone can sell the loans that he makes or buys. However, for banks, the accounting treatment and implications of loan sales differ from those for bank competitors. The difference affects the capital requirements imposed on banks and their ability to offer credit enhancement to the buyers of their loans.

Banks must maintain a minimum amount of capital.[66] To increase their capital, banks can reinvest profits, issue securities, or sell assets and apply the proceeds to reduce their fixed obligations. Since the 1970s, when long-term capital became very costly, numerous banks have chosen to increase their capital by selling their portfolio loans. In this context, the definition of sale in the banks' accounting becomes crucial. If bank regulations do not deem a loan transfer to be a "sale," the selling banks' ratio of capital to assets would not increase. The Regulatory Accounting Principles (RAP), which apply to banks, provide that (with few exceptions) a transfer of a loan in which a bank retains risk is not a sale.[67] In contrast, the Generally Accepted Accounting Principles ("GAAP"), applicable to many bank competitors, provide for a more liberal definition that recognizes the transaction as a sale even though the transferor retains substantial risks under the transferred loan.[68]

Under the strict definition of a sale under RAP, banks that desire to increase their capital cannot offer credit enhancement to the buyers of their loans. This impedes a bank from reducing its assets and increasing its capital ratio.[69] Bank competitors (e.g., insurance companies and large corporations with good credit) may sell loans coupled with credit enhancement under a GAAP accounting treatment and remove the loans from their books. These bank competitors have an advantage.

Establishing pools of loans

Small loans are securitized by transferring them to a pool and issuing securities representing a pro rata share of, or another type of claim to, the pool's assets. If a pool is not an excepted entity, the Investment Company Act applies to them.[70] Therefore, banks and most of their competitors are treated equally under the Act.

Issuing and distributing participations in loans or pools of loans and making secondary markets in the participations

With a number of exceptions, the Glass-Steagall Act prohibits banks from issuing, dealing in, and underwriting securities. In addition, banks and entities engaged in these securities activities may not be affiliated with banks.[71] However, the prohibition does not apply to securitized loans and has been greatly relaxed with respect to affiliation with securities firms generally. The Comptroller of the Currency has viewed securitization as sale of loans, in which banks may engage.[72] Although securitized loans possess the features of securities, they are backed by traditional bank loans (or by securities backed by such loans). By ignoring the pool that issues the securities, the securities attain the classification of the underlying loans. The Second Circuit affirmed the Comptroller's "pierce through" approach and held that a bank may underwrite and deal in asset-backed securities of loans that the bank has made.[73] This decision was based also on the "incidental powers" of banks to carry out their express powers. Specifically, the power to securitize mortgage loans was "convenient and useful," and thus "incidental," to the express power of banks to sell such loans.[74] The Second Circuit left open the question whether a bank may invest, underwrite, and deal in securitized loans made by other banks (or other lenders), but the Comptroller has long approved such transactions. Thus, banks may securitize the loans they make or purchase from inception to fruition of the process.[75]

Further, as stated above, the Securities Act of 1933 exempts banks from registering securities that they issue or guarantee. Disclosure to buyers of loan participations is prescribed by bank regulators. Since it is treated as an issue of prudence, regulators are less concerned about protecting nonbank buyers. Banks are exempt also from regulation under the Securities Exchange Act of 1934, for example, from registration as broker–dealers.[76] Moreover, courts have generally held that loan participations and bank certificates of deposits are not securities subject to the antifraud provisions of the act (in particular Rule 10b-5 promulgated under the act).[77]

Managing the pools and servicing the loans

Banks may act as financial advisers to individuals and as managers of common trust funds[78] and pension funds. With respect to common trust funds, banks are regulated by bank regulators,[79] but with respect to pension funds, they are subject to the Employee Retirement Income Security Act of 1974 ("ERISA"). However, banks are excepted from the definition of an investment adviser under the Investment Advisers Act of 1940.[80] Nonexempt actors must register under that act and comply with the Act's limitations on fees.[81] Other substantive differences are not great, because regulation follows the principles of fiduciary law.

With respect to custody of assets, banks have an advantage under the Investment Company Act of 1940. They qualify as custodians for investment companies including unit investment trusts.[82] Broker dealers qualify as custodians for investment companies excluding unit investment trusts.[83]

Holding securitized loans

While banks, thrifts, and insurance companies may hold securitized loans,[84] investment companies may be prohibited from holding securities of pools that are investment companies, unless they obtain an exemption.[85]

General regulatory environment

Banks and their competitors may not engage in conflict of interest transactions.[86] The prohibition protects savers' interests directly and also indirectly, by promoting the safety and soundness of the institutions. Securities regulation focuses mainly on protecting securities traders and advisees; institutional regulation focuses mainly on protecting the safety and soundness of the regulated institutions. Which focus is more restrictive in a competitive environment may depend on the particular institutions and on the business environment.

A comparison of the black letter law suggests that banks today are not at a great competitive disadvantage in the securitization business. But to evaluate the banks' competitive position we must consider the banks' business environment. In addition to losing the legal protections they enjoyed, banks are undergoing radical changes in their business, culture, and image. This process is costly. Further, banks must satisfy the needs of the public and serve as a tool for implementing fiscal policy. These services have prompted some legislators to view banks as "public utilities." If that is so, when bank public utility functions conflict with profitability, banks should be awarded some competitive advantages by law.

CONCLUSION

What is the impact of securitization on banking? First, securitization has helped dismantle the monopolies that enabled banks to appear stable notwithstanding their risky structure. Second, securitization can help banks overcome their structural deficiencies, by enabling them to hold a diversified portfolio of liquid securitized loans. Banks should be encouraged to diversify and evaluate the risk of their whole portfolio rather than of each loan or securitized loan they hold. Risk-based capital requirements should also shift to a view of the banks' whole portfolio. The legal diversification formula in banking law should be revamped to reflect a more sophisticated portfolio design. That design may be less quantified and specific, but safer for banks.

Third, it is difficult to determine whether banks are competing on a "level playing field" because the laws of securitization applicable to banks and other market actors are not identical. It seems that the main regulatory burden imposed on banks relates to the definition of "sale" of loans in accounting standards and the provision of credit enhancement. In any event, a comparison of black letter law is not sufficient to evaluate the competitive position of banks because the cost of the same activities and regulation may differ for banks and their competitors. Even if we could calculate the aggregate regulatory costs for the whole securitization process, the results are not conclusive because regulatory costs are but one item affecting the profitability of banks and their competitors; not all competitors start at the same baseline, and not all engage in the whole securitization process. Besides, banks are not homogeneous. One kind of bank may bear heavy regulatory costs while another bears lower regulatory costs.

Fourth, securitization is helping to transform our financial system, including banking, by allowing market actors substantial freedom to choose their business niche. The process has reduced the role of law in designing the financial system. To be sure, the market forces unleashed by securitization are affected by the law. Business strategies of institutions factor in regulatory burdens, limitations, and protections that are currently in place. Law establishes the ground rules for the market players, including the financial markets. However, securitization as a method for bank restructuring allows market actors to initiate change and places the regulators in a more reactive role. Today policymakers do not define banks. The banks are designing themselves. Competitors offer alternatives to bank products, and banks offer alternatives to competitors' products.[87] Hopefully, when the dust settles, we will find out which institution does what best.

We have no accurate account of what the 12,000 banks in this country really do. We know their size, but that is not enough. Institutions called "banks" are doing very different things, and have and pose very different problems. We should start not by debating what banks should do, but by finding out what they are actually doing: their products and financial structures, their profitability and long-term viability. Only then can we propose legislation that addresses problems that stem from market failures. So, if you ask: What is the main impact of securitization on the financial system and the banks? I would answer: Securitization helps the banks of the past and other financial institutions evolve into a rich variety of entities that will constitute the financial system of the future.

NOTES

1. See T. Frankel, *Securitization* (1991). For other definitions of securitization that focus on the process, see Schenker and Colletta, "Asset Securitization: Evolution, Current Issues and New Frontiers, *Texas Law Review 69* (1991), pp. 1369–73.
2. Money claims can arise from various transactions, for example: obligations to repay loans, obligations to repay deposits, compensation for services, price for commodities, proceeds of insurance, or commitments to make loans.
3. See J. Guttentag and R. Herring, "Financial Innovations to Stabilize Credit Flows to Developing Countries (Brookings Discussion Papers), *International Economics 33* (1985), pp. 4–6; and Murray and Hadaway, "Mortgage-Backed Securities: An Investigation of Legal and Financial Issues," *Journal of Corporate Law 11* (1986), pp. 203–4. Since there is no generic term for less tradable instruments evidencing money claims

and because most securitized debts arise from loans, I use the word "loans" interchangeably with "debts."

4. The parties to loans and securities are even described by different words. These names highlight the different features of loans and securities. The parties to loans are called "borrowers" or "debtors" and "lenders" or "creditors," respectively. The parties to securities transactions are called "issuers" and "investors." Loans are named by the transaction and the relationship they create. Securities are named by the instruments that are traded.
5. Underwriters distribute securities from issuers to investors; broker-dealers may participate in this distribution network. Broker-dealers also maintain secondary markets in which investors trade among themselves in securities.
6. Intermediaries include banks, thrifts, mortgage bankers, and consumer banks ("banks"), and insurance companies, pension funds, and investment companies (collectively, "intermediaries"). Intermediaries also provide other services. Banks provide access to a payment system and serve as a tool to control the money supply; insurance companies pool and distribute risk; investment companies diversify investment portfolios and provide economies of scale for small savers. Industrial and marketing enterprises act as intermediaries when they borrow and sell to customers on credit. The federal government and state governments act as intermediaries when they borrow in the capital markets and lend the proceeds for particular purposes—for example, housing.
7. See J. Gurley and E. Shaw, "Financial Intermediaries and the Savings-Investment Process" (Brookings Institute Reprint No. 13, 1956), [the share of nonbank institutions (insurance companies, investment companies, pension funds) in lending services has been slowly increasing since their appearance more than a hundred years ago]; Robert E. Litan, *What Should Banks Do?* (1986)
8. For example, an innovation that encouraged the movement from intermediaries to markets is "swaps." Like a do-it-yourself kit, the instruments enable one party to a loan agreement, in effect, to change the terms of a loan for *it,* without a change for the other party, by contracting with a third party. The instruments enable borrowers to bypass intermediaries, even when the borrowers' preferences do not match those of the lenders.
9. Report by G. Alger, Moreland Commissioner, to H. Lehman, Governor of the State of New York, on the Management and Affairs of the Insurance Department (October 5, 1934), pp. 9–10; Perlstein, "What the 1920s Tell Us About Mortgage Backed Securities Today," *Problems and Probabilities,* January–February 1987, pp. 19–21; Lance, "Balancing Private and Public Initiatives in the Mortgage-Backed Securities Market," *Real Property Probabilities and Transactions Journal 18,* pp. 426–30; Knight, "Loan Participation Agreements: Catching Up with Contract Law," *Columbia Business Law Review 21,* pp. 587–92; Threedy, "Loan Participations—Sales or Loans? Or Is That the Question?," *Oregon Law Review 68* (1989), pp. 649–50.
10. Robert E. Litan, *The Revolution in U.S. Finance* (1991), p. 17.
11. For the composition of bank demand deposits and money market deposit accounts in comparison to money market funds, see Robert E. Litan, *The Revolution in U.S. Finance* (1991), pp. 9–10 [in 1990 bank demand deposits held approximately $260 billion; bank money market deposit accounts held approximately to $510 billion;

money market funds held approximately to $480 billion]; see also Investment Company Institutions News Release ICI-89-45 (December 28, 1989).

12. T. Congdon, *The Debt Threat* (1988), p. 200.
13. See Weiner, "As Bank Loan Market Comes of Age, Sellers Pursue Nonbank Purchasers," *American Banker* (September 30, 1986), p. 1, col. 2 [purchasers of loan participations include thrifts, pension funds, insurance companies, and even other corporations. Banks in depressed areas where lending is weak may buy loans to diversify and fill their portfolios. Foreign banks buy loans to enter the United States markets. Currently, most loan participations are sold to other banks—94%, according to a study by the Federal Reserve Board]; see also Albert "Loan Sales Twice as High as a Year Ago," *American Banker* (September 15, 1987), p. 1, col. 4 [in the first quarter of 1986, bank loan sales amounted to $42.9 billion. In the first quarter of 1987, they leaped 99% to $85.4 billion].
14. *Inside Mortgage Capital Markets,* Washington DC: Financial World Publications (December 21, 1990), p. 2; Robert E. Litan *The Revolution in U.S. Finance* (1991), p. 14.
15. See "Concurrent Resolution on the Budget for Fiscal Year 1988: Hearings Before the Senate Committee on the Budget," 100th Congress, 1st Session (1987), pp. 93–275; "Loan Asset Sales: OMB Policies Will Result in Program Objectives Not Being Fully Achieved," GAO/AFMD (1986), pp. 86–79, reprinted in Staff Representatives House Committee on Small Business, 100th Congress, 1st session, *Government Loan Asset Sales* (1988), pp. 74–88; and "Bank Letter," *Institutional Investors* (July 1, 1986).
16. *American Banker* (October 12, 1988), p. 18, col. 2.
17. "A Driving Business, Thrift Steers Its Way to Profits in Secondary Market," *American Banker* (March 6, 1987), p. 22.
18. Neustadt, "Hanover Tries New Approach to Securitization," *American Banker* (October 6, 1987), p. 2, col. 2.
19. See Robert E. Litan *The Revolution in U.S. Finance* (1991), pp. 14–15 [securitized consumer loans have grown from $29 billion in January 1989 to more than $70 billion in November 1990—nearly 10% of all consumer installment credit]. Note-issuance facilities, under which banks undertake to lend money to a borrower if its note issue cannot be placed, rose to $33 billion in 1986. There are today outstanding about $300 billion in interest-rate swaps and $680 billion of open positions in financial futures and options; Miller, "Commercial Loan Securitization—Review and Outlook," *Loan Pricing Report,* vol. VI, no. 4 (September 1991), p. 2 [in the past three years, $9 billion worth of highly leveraged obligations have been securitized through collateralized loan obligations].
20. Dean Witter Reynolds, Inc., *Asset-Backed Securities Reference Guide A–14* (January 1991), cited in Schenker and Colletta, "Asset Securitization: Evolution, Current Issues and New Frontiers," *Texas Law Review 69* (1991), pp. 1369–72.
21. Puchala, "Securitizing Third World Debt," *Columbia Business Law Review* (1989), p. 173; Park, "Legal Policy Conflicts in International Banking," *Ohio State Law Journal* (1989), pp. 1067, 1089–92.
22. "Thoughts from the Ministry," *Economist* (September 24, 1988), p. 107; Basch, "Mortgage Securities Get Slow Start in Europe, Catch on in Japan," *American Banker* (March 3, 1987), p. 8, col. 1 [while securitized loans have not yet caught on in England,

they are becoming very popular in Japan]; see "Annual Report: Structured Finance 1988 Review and 1989 Outlook," *Structured Finance* (March 1989) [discusses developments and projections in in the U.S. markets].

23. As defined by J. Schumpeter, an innovation includes "a new form of organization" and "combines factors in a new way" *Business Cycles* (1st ed. 1939), pp. 87–8. Securitization fits this definition both by introducing new processes of intermediation and by producing new financial instruments. See also T. Podolski, *Financial Innovation and the Money Supply* (1986); Baer and Pavel, "Does Regulation Drive Innovation?," *Economic Perspective* (March/April 1988), p. 3; Campbell "Innovations in Financial Intermediation," *Business Horizons* (November/December 1989), p. 70; Smith and Taggert, "Bond Market Innovations and Financial Intermediation," *Business Horizons* (November/December 1989), p. 24, cited in Schenker and Colletta, "Asset Securitization: Evolution, Current Issues and New Frontiers," *Texas Law Review 69*, pp. 1369–70, note 2 [dealing with recent financial innovations including securitization].
24. See T. Cohone and R. Rafferty (eds.),*Servicing Mortgage Portfolios, Strategies, and Applications for Buying, Selling and Managing Mortgage Loan Portfolios* (1991) [on the process of assembling mortgage [on the process of assembling mortgage portfolios for sale and transfer of the servicing rights].
25. "Changes in Our Financial System: Globalization of Capital Markets and Securitization of Credit," *Hearings Before the Senate Committee on Banking, Housing, and Urban Affairs*, 100th Congress, 1st session (1988), p. 137 [statement of Lowell L. Bryan, McKinsey & Co.]; Miller, "Commercial Loan Securitization—Review and Outlook," *Loan Pricing Report*, vol. VI, no. 4 (September 1991), p. 2.
26. Weiner, "Securitization: What Will They Package Next?," *American Banker* (January 7, 1987), p. 1; Silver and Axilrod, "Pushing Technology to Its Limits: Securitizing C&I Loans," *Bankers Magazine* (May-June 1989), pp. 16–17; *Loan Pricing Report No. 7* (July-August 1990), pp. 19–20; "Changes in Our Financial System: Globalization of Capital Markets and Securitization of Credit," *Hearings Before the Senate Committee on Banking, Housing, and Urban Affairs*, 100th Congress, 1st session (1988), p. 137 [statement of Lowell L. Bryan, McKinsey & Co.]; Miller, "Commercial Loan Securitization—Review and Outlook," *Loan Pricing Report*, vol. VI, no. 4 (September 1991), p. 2 [describing the techniques for securitizing short-term commercial loans in 1991. These are joint programs established by banks. A separate entity makes direct loans to customers referred by participating banks. The banks provide credit enhancement to their customers. So long as there are no capital requirements on such credit enhancement, this technique helps banks reduce their capital requirements. Another form of securitization is by pooling loans, especially highly leveraged loans. The loan portfolio can be fixed or managed].
27. A current specialized publication is providing information about these loans and their terms nationwide. See *Loan Pricing Reports*, published by Loan Pricing Corporation, 810 Seventh Avenue, New York, NY 10019.
28. See "Problems in Mortgage Packaging," *Hearings Before the Subcommittee on General Oversight and Investigation of the House Committee on Banking, Finance, and Urban Affairs*, 99th Congress, 1st session (1985), p. 89 [testimony of Laurance D. Fink, Managing Director, First Boston Corporation].

29. A similar development has occurred in the life insurance field. Whereas in the past each insured had to pass a medical examination, now most insureds are classified according to information provided in their application and are pooled. I am told by an expert that this technique is possible and can be applied to commercial and industrial medium-sized borrowers.
30. See Robert E. Litan, *The Revolution in U.S. Finance* (1991), p. 36 [expressing a similar opinion].
31. I include savings and loan associations in the discussion of traditional banks.
32. Even though banks hold some liquid assets, such as government securities and transferrable notes, most of their assets consist of illiquid loans. Historically, the assets of thrifts were even less liquid because the loans they held had longer maturities than those of banks.
33. Regardless of how prudent their lending decisions may have been, banks are nevertheless vulnerable to the credit risk of their customer-borrowers. Prudence is not prescience; loans made prudently can turn sour. Of course, banks may charge sufficient interest to cover (in the aggregate) their losses, provided they set aside sufficient amounts as loan loss reserves at the outset with respect to each loan and do not consider these amounts to be profits. If bank profits were high enough in the past to cover the deficiency, they are not high enough in today's competitive environment. Furthermore, banks could charge interest on the basis of a statistical default rate, as insurance companies do with respect to the risks they cover. However, it is doubtful whether banks' interest rates were tied to the statistical default rate of the loans they hold.
34. These "cushions" consist of equity and long-term debt securities on which return to investors is higher than on short-term debt, and reserves that reduce retained earnings. When retained earnings are low, the dividends paid to the equity security holders are reduced, and the cost of equity securities for the banks is increased.
35. Even if bank branches could develop a nationwide, diversified stable borrower-base, their ability to do so is limited by law. Banks may establish "loan production offices" outside their charter state, but may not offer other services nor take deposits there. Since customers often expect full service, this limitation restricts banks from effectively attracting customers. Therefore, for big banks the cost of interstate lending is high; for small banks the cost is even higher.
36. Arguably, FDIC deposit insurance adds incentives for bank managements to engage in excessively risky business. This issue has been extensively debated elsewhere.
37. While they charged borrowers real interest, banks paid depositors nominal interest.
38. This process hastened the dismantling of the traditional bank monopoly. Securitization and competition were not the only available solutions. During the initial period of inflation, the government could have maintained the old system and merely increased the specified interest on demand deposits and savings accounts to reflect the rate of inflation, instead of allowing banks to issue certificates of deposit and pay market rates (although, arguably, this approach would not have helped the thrifts). Similarly, the government could have strengthened the banks' monopoly by prohibiting banks from providing shareholders of money market funds with checking privileges, which helped the funds reduce the costs of redeeming their shares. Instead, the government opted for innovation and a decreased share for bank intermediation.
39. Robert E. Litan, "The Revolution in U.S. Finance" (1991), pp. 25–27 [showing a

reduction in banks' and thrifts' profits and increased risk].

40. See Linda Aguilar, "Banks and Nonbanks: The Competition Heats Up," *Bankers Magazine 175* (May/June 1992), pp. 31–37 ["Are commercial banks losing market share? The answer is 'yes,' but not just to other intermediaries offering banklike services."]
41. Ibid.
42. See Bird, "Community Banks, Ask Not for Whom Restructuring Tolls," *American Banker* (March 18, 1991), p. 4, and Bird, "'Super-Community' Banks Service Rich Middle Ground," *American Banker* (February 13, 1991), p. 4.
43. It seems that banks with assets between $25 million and $1 billion achieve the optimal economies of scale because their noninterest expenses remain relatively constant as a percentage of their assets; the expenses of larger banks grow without commensurate gains. Watt, "Adding Branches May Not Yield Big Profits," *American Banker* (July 8, 1991), p. 4 [a 1991 study by S. A. Thoads and D. T. Savage of the Federal Reserve Board found that banks with assets of $25 million to $5 billion are most likely to obtain the highest profits on investment].
44. See Thompson, "Securities Activities of National Banks Recent Regulatory, Judicial, and Legislative Developments," in *Eleventh Annual Institution Securities Activities of Banks* (1991), p. 18. To choose appropriate activities, banks should seek fees rather than spread, yet many banks still focus on spread. I can understand why. Spread is, or used to be, higher than fees. The answer is that in the new environment spread can be risky and unreliable while fees can be more profitable and stable.
45. Wall, "Recourse Risk in Asset Sales," (Federal Reserve Bank of Atlanta) *Economic Review 76*, No. 5 (September/October 1991), p. 1 [even if banks sell their loans with recourse, the risks banks retain may be partially offset indirectly].
46. Securitization also helps banks to sell their loans quickly, but the market for whole loans is not as liquid nor as efficient as a market for securities.
47. See 55 Federal Regulation 251, at 53,529 (December 31, 1990) [The Office of Thrift Supervision proposed rule to factor interest risk in the capital requirements].
48. See Letter of Robert L. Clarke, Comptroller of the Currency (June 16, 1987).
49. The legal limit on the amount lent to one borrower or issuer is 15 percent of the bank's paid-up capital and surplus. 12 U.S.C. §84 (1988); 12 C.F.R. §32; Reg. K, 12 C.F.R. §212 (1991).
50. In the trust area these notions have recently been revamped by the American Law Institute. See *American Law Institute Restatement of the Law Trusts (Third), Prudent Investor Rule* (1990).
51. See, for example, *I*nvestment Company Act of 1940, §5(b)(1), 15 U.S.C. §801–5(b)(1) (1988).
52. Even though market valuation is a "black box" and includes speculative information, it may be more accurate than valuation based solely on individual credit risk assessments of illiquid loans. See "Blueprint for Restructuring America's Financial Institutions," *Report of a Task Force* (The Brookings Institution, 1989), p. 26 [task force members are G. J. Benston, R. D. Brumbaugh, Jr., J. M. Guttenberg, R. J. Herring, G. G. Kaufman, R. E. Litan, and K. E. Scott].
53. In fact, margins are loan loss reserves for losses from portfolio volatility rather than for losses on particular loans.

54. The issue is more complex. The purposes of regulation extend beyond parity among competitors and may outweigh disadvantages to any player. After all, if a bank desires relief of regulatory burdens, it can surrender its charter and engage in another business.
55. 12 C.F.R. part 201 (1991).
56. By law, broker dealers may pool and hypothecate the securities of customers that bought securities on margin and use these securities as collateral to raise funds. See L. Loss and J. Seligman, Securities Regulation 3264 (1991), pp. 3179–83.
57. The funds usually impose a minimum amount that shareholders can redeem, and reserve the right to redeem the rest of the shares if the shareholders hold below a certain amount. Presumably, these terms reduce the cost for the funds, because the cost of servicing small accounts is the same as servicing larger ones.
58. 15 U.S.C. §77a (1988).
59. 15 U.S.C. §77aaa–77bbb (supp. 1990).
60. See Securities Exchange Act of 1934, §§3(a)(5), 3(a)(6), and 12, and 15 U.S.C. §§78c(a)(5), 78c(a)(6), 781(i) (1988).
61. See Securities Act of 1933, §§3(a)(5), 4(5), and 15 U.S.C. §§77c(a)(5), 77d(5) (1988).
62. 15 U.S.C. §§77a(3), 77c(8) (1988).
63. 15 U.S.C. §80a–5(b), (c) (1988).
64. 15 U.S.C. §80a–13 (1988); 15 U.S.C. §80a–26 (1988) [investment companies that are unit investment trusts have fixed portfolios, which they may not change].
65. 15 U.S.C. §80a–3(a) (1988). For exceptions from the definition of an investment company, see 15 U.S.C. §80a–3(c) (1988).
66. Other competitors are subject to various capital requirements. Insurance companies must support their policies with reserves. Broker dealers must maintain net capital. L. Loss and J. Seligman, Securities Regulation 3128 (3d ed. 1991), p. 3137; 17 C.F.R. §240.15c3–1 (1991). Parents of finance companies that guarantee their subsidiaries' obligations may be subject to market discipline.
67. T. Frankel, "Securitization" §7.14.3 (1991); Federal Financial Institute's Examination Council, *Instruction for Preparation of Reports of Condition and Income for a Bank with Domestic and Foreign Offices* (FFIEC 031) A–48 to A–49 (1989).
68. Op. cit., §7.14.4; Reporting by Transferors for Transfers of Receivables with Recourse, Statement of Financial Accounting Standards No. 77 (Financial Accounting Standards Board, 1983), reprinted in 3 Securities Regulation (P-H) ¶8577.24.
69. Op. cit., §7.13.4.1.
70. Investment Company Act of 1940; 15 U.S.C. §§80a–1 to 80a–64 (1988); §3(c)(1), 15 U.S.C. §80a–3(c)(1) (1988); [exception for small investment companies with less than 100 shareholders] and §3(c)(5), 15 U.S.C. §80a–3(c)(5) (1988); [exceptions for factors, lenders for consumer loans and pools holding real estate and interests in real estate].
71. 12 U.S.C. §78 (1988).
72. Letter from Robert L. Clarke, Comptroller of the Currency (June 16, 1987) ["the Glass-Steagall Act does not restrict the means by which national banks may sell or transfer interest in, among other assets, their mortgages and mortgage-related assets"]. The Glass-Steagall prohibition has been slowly eroded. For example, in the 1970s, bank regulators held that banks may engage in private placements of securities. Federal Reserve Board, Commercial Bank Private Placement Activities (1977), pp. 29–31; see

generally, 2 Malloy, "The Corporate Law of Banks" §7.3.6 at 658–69 (1988). Rule 144A, which has broadened the secondary market in unregistered securities, has also broadened the securities activities in which banks may engage.

73. Securities Industries Association *v.* Clarke, 885 F.2d 1034 (2d Circuit, 1988), *vacating* 703 F. Supp. 256 (S.D.N.Y. 1988), *cert. denied,* 110 S. Ct. 1113 (1990).
74. Ibid., at 1050.
75. Ibid.
76. 15 U.S.C. §78c(5), (5) (1988) [excepting banks from the definition of a broker and a dealer]. The Securities and Exchange Commission promulgated rule 3a–9 in an attempt to exclude from the exception bank departments that engage in securities activities. The rule was struck down by the court. See American Bankers Association *v.* SEC, 804 F.2d 739 (1986).
77. See T. Frankel, Securitization §9.2 (1991).
78. 12 U.S.C. §92a (1988); E. Symons and J. White, *Banking Law* (3d ed., 1991), p. 284.
79. See 12 C.F.R. §9 (1991) [regulation of national banks by the Comptroller].
80. Investment Advisers Act of 1940, §202(a)(11)(A), 15 U.S.C. §80b–2(a)(11)(A) (1988).
81. Investment Advisers Act of 1940, §§203, 205, 15 U.S.C. §§80b–3, 5 (1988).
82. Investment Company Act of 1940, §17(f), 15 U.S.C. §§80a–17(f), 26 (1988).
83. Ibid.
84. See Letter of Brian W. Smith, Chief Counsel, No. 257 (April 12, 1983), [1983–84 Transfer Binder] Federal Banking Law Report (CCH) ¶85,421.
85. See Investment Company Act of 1940, §§12, 17, 15 U.S.C. §§80–12, 17 (1988).
86. These prohibitions are similar to those in fiduciary law. See, for example, Investment Company Act of 1940, §§17, 36, 15 U.S.C. §§80a–36, 36 (1988) [applicable to investment advisers of investment companies]; Employee Retirement Income Security Act of 1974, §406, 29 U.S.C. §1106 (1988); Internal Revenue Code, 26 U.S.C. §4975 (1988) [applicable to fiduciaries]; Federal Reserve Act, §§23A, 23B, 12 U.S.C. §§371c, 371c–1 (1988) [applicable to banks and thrifts].
87. As an example, banks developed an alternative to the insurance "guaranteed investment contract" (GIC), in the form of a unique bank deposit serving the same purpose. An alternative to a security is a loan participation serving a similar purpose. See T. Frankel, Securitization §9.4 (1991).

COMMENT

James P. Holdcroft, Jr.

Reading Professor Frankel's paper, "Securitization: Its Effect on Bank Structure," I was reminded of the fable about the three blind men who attempted to describe an elephant. In addition to the obvious lesson on the risks of over-generalization that this story teaches, this fable illustrates the problem with undertaking a task when physical restrictions significantly limit one's chances for success. In "Securitization: Its Effect on Bank Structure," Professor Frankel attempts the mammoth undertaking of condensing all topics related to securitization and bank structure into one comparatively short paper. Unfortunately, the effort fails to give the reader a proper appreciation for the considerable expertise of Professor Frankel in the area of securitization.[1] More importantly, in attempting to cover such a broad scope, Professor Frankel fails to deliver much in the way of convincing evidence for her assertions. "Securitization: Its Effect on Bank Structure" raises many questions but gives few persuasive answers.

I also was reminded of the fable about the three blind men because securitization as a concept is very much like the elephant in the fable: Securitization can mean quite different things to different people. In the past few years there have been numerous articles written about "securitization." Unfortunately, many of these articles refer to a variety of very different financial products and processes with little attempt at definition. The success of any effort to assess the probable effect of securitization on bank structure requires in the first instance a clear definition of securitization.

Professor Frankel starts off with good intentions by defining "securitization" as the transformation of debt into marketable securities. These good intentions' however, are forgotten quickly as Frankel immediately abandons this definition when she attempts to identify three forms of securitization. Two of the three forms identified—the creation of loan participations ("LPs") out of large loans and the creation of interests in pools of small loans—fit the suggested definition and involve a transformation of debt into more marketable instruments;[2] however, the remaining form of securitization identified by Professor Frankel does not.

The third form of securitization identified is simply the direct issuance of debt securities by entities that might otherwise have borrowed from banks. Frankel is correct to note that a significant number of large creditworthy entities that formerly borrowed from banks in recent years have begun to access the securities markets directly. Frankel is equally correct to observe that a number of persons who formerly saved only with banks in recent years have begun to invest in securities either directly or indirectly through mutual funds and similar investment vehicles. No one is likely to argue that either of these trends bodes well for the financial prospects of traditional banks. However, these trends reflect the development of the securities markets generally and are not closely associated with the concept of transforming bank debt into securities.[3] Professor Frankel never returns to discuss this form of "securitization" or to her definition generally in what follows. At times it appears as if Professor Frankel abandons this earlier definition of securitization in favor of one that is limited to a process involving only small business loans. This is unfortunate, as Professor Frankel's paper depends upon the reader's maintaining a clear understanding of what is meant by securitization.

After reciting statistics on the tremendous growth in the market for LPs and "pool" securities, Frankel sets forth an outline to guide the reader through the remainder of her analysis. Frankel first promises a review of the conditions that enabled banks to remain stable for "the past 50 years" and the conditions since the 1970s that "destabilized" the banks (presumably, the "golden age of banking" does not include the years of destabilization beginning in the 1970s, or alternatively, the 1929–1934 period). As if this were not enough to address in one paper, Professor Frankel also promises to explain at the same time why securitization was able to develop during the 1970s and not before.

Frankel's second area of focus is the future of securitization. The third general topic of Frankel's ambitious undertaking, namely, "the effects of securitization on the traditional functions and structure of banks" (including savings and loan associations), is essentially the paper's topic as well as this volume's central issue. Finally, Professor Frankel tells the reader that she will compare the law of securitization applicable to banks with the law applicable to other market actors. At this point the reader is on notice that if Frankel is to adhere to this self-imposed outline in a total of 28 pages, the analysis and conclusions that will be offered will be either self-evident or quite general.

Frankel begins her explanation of how banks were able to survive and prosper during the 1920–1970 period with a discussion of the inherent weakness of the traditional bank structure. This weakness we are told is rooted in the role of banks as financial intermediaries. Traditional banks have liabilities and assets that do not match with respect to liquidity and maturity. In addition, we are told that the inability of banks to offer full service branches in all states combines with the desire of banks to develop a stable customer base for loans to result in the creation of potentially risky loan concentrations and higher interstate lending costs. For good measure we are also told that banks are inherently weak because they are subject to the "universal" problem of bad or negligent management. If Professor Frankel is attempting to distinguish actively managed financial intermediaries such as banks, finance companies, and mutual funds on the one hand from self-liquidating and limited management securitization vehicles such as grantor trusts, Real Estate Mortgage Investment Conduits ("REMICs"), and special purpose corporate issuers of Collateralized Mortgage Obligations ("CMOs") and Asset Backed Securities ("ABSs"), the point is made rather obliquely.

With respect to the assertion that loan origination requires full service branches to be efficient (presumably "efficient" means profitable), Professor Frankel's thesis needs further work. Even if one were to assume the validity of the proposition that efficient loan origination requires the offering of full banking services, Professor Frankel's analysis fails to give proper weight to the use of the bank holding company structure and the existence of regional banking compacts. These factors allow banks to offer a broad array of banking services in many of the potentially most desirable geographic areas. More importantly, the proposition fails to address the tremendous growth in the origination of consumer loans (i.e., mortgage loans, student loans, automobile, truck, and boat loans and credit card loans by nonbanks) originated by a variety of nonbank financial intermediaries. Ironically, it is the development of this nonbank market for consumer loans that has sparked the interest in securitization as an alternative to traditional banking. If Professor Frankel intends to limit her observations to small business loans, the proposition may have greater merit.

Professor Frankel goes on to suggest five reasons why banks prospered despite their inherent weakness during the 1920–1970 period. Frankel contends that banks prospered because (1) banks enjoyed a legal monopoly on deposit taking; (2) government policy supported banks while governmental regulation promoted safe practices; (3) deposit and withdrawal patterns limited liquidity demands on banks; (4) bank's cautionary management limited credit risk; and (5) interest rates were comparatively stable throughout the 50-year period. Although Frankel's assertions are undoubtedly reasonable and may in fact be correct, the reader is given no support for the validity of these claims. Instead the reader is left to infer the validity of these assertions when Frankel offers five separate reasons for the destabilzing of banks. For unknown reasons, there is no attempt to link the previously identified inherent weaknesses of banks to the subsequent destabilization of banks. Frankel's five reasons for destabilization are (1) inflation triggered an outflow of deposits to money market mutual funds; (2) "technology" improved (presumably this means computer and information processing technology, although it may also refer to the "technology" of "financial engineering") thereby allowing others to compete with banks for presumably both deposits and loans; (3) deregulation presumably allowed bank mangers (who, we have been told, used to be cautious, but are now weak and/or negligent) to do all those things that inept managements are prone to do if they are not closely supervised; (4) the creation of government-sponsored mortgage securitization programs; and (5) changes in regulatory policies such as allowing the sale of negotiable certificates of deposit and raising minimum capital requirements for banks.

Frankel's points are once again plausible explanations for what caused banks to lose customers and profits to securities businesses of various types and are very plausible explanations for describing what happened to the thrift industry during this same period; however, little in the way of support is offered to the reader for these propositions.

The most interesting aspect of Frankel's paper is addressed in the section, "Effects of securitization on traditional banks." Here, Frankel suggests that securitization requires that we look at "unbundling" the traditional roles of banks. Although Frankel primarily focuses on unbundling the functions associated with loans, the concept is a good one and should be extended to other bank functions as well.

Frankel identifies three functions relating to loans: (1) origination, (2) servicing, and (3) portfolio investing.

Frankel asserts without any support that banks are best suited to originate loans. Is this because banks offer "full service" branches and the rating agencies are not yet rating small business loans? Frankel is willing to concede that not all banks are the best servicers of small loans. She also concedes that banks may not be the best holders of all loans; indeed, in her brief history of banking Professor Frankel argues that banks are unstable because they have assets and liabilities (largely loans) that have different credit, liquidity, and other risks. Why then are all banks better at origination? The development of the mortgage and asset backed securities markets strongly suggests that at least with respect to certain types of loans, banks have no special advantage in origination over nonbank originators. Loans that are suitable for standardized documentation and underwriting procedures can be, and are, originated by many different types of entities. Origination and servicing criteria and procedures are largely standardized (following the lead of the federally sponsored mortgage agencies), with price as major distinguishing factor. As a result, maintaining low operating costs becomes a key to profitable competition. Marketing expertise and convenience also contribute significantly to success in the origination of these loans.

It is far from clear that every bank is in a preferred position relative to, say, Ford Motor Credit in making an automobile loan, AT&T or American Express in making an unsecured consumer loan, or GMAC in making a mortgage loan. It is similarly improbable that every bank is better than GECC at originating business loans. Familiarity and convenience also are important factors for borrowers. In this regard it appears that banks may have an advantage over nonbanks, at least for the time being. Banks have existing customer relationships and presumably convenient branch locations to originate loans.

On the other hand, other financial institutions, including those mentioned above, are actively working to develop direct access to bank customers. Many of these institutions are excellent marketers and comparatively low cost providers of financial services. In addition, as the competition for underwriting debt issues of large corporations has significantly reduced the profitability of that business, investment banking firms are pursuing financing assignments from smaller companies.

There is no doubt that while some banks will continue to do very well in the face of this competition, others will not. Simply put, it is unlikely that banks have a structural advantage over all others in the origination of loans.

Professor Frankel offers the reader a few observations regarding the impact of securitization on investment portfolio management. Frankel correctly points out that securitization will improve the opportunities of banks to invest in more liquid instruments with credit characteristics with which banks are comfortable (i.e., loans). Frankel's thoughts on liquidity and price volatility are less clear. The concepts are related, but different. In the context of securitization and banking, liquidity reflects how quickly a security or loan can be sold and turned into cash, while price volatility reflects how the price of an instrument changes in relation to another factor such as an index, other prices, or interest rates. Liquidity reflects demand and to that extent will influence price volatility. Price volatility, on the other hand, will also reflect supply and the cash flow characteristics of the instrument.

Professor Frankel's discussion of volatility and capital requirements for banks also is a bit confusing. At one point, Frankel argues that banks were more stable when they held illiquid loans. The reasoning goes something as follows: Illiquid loans could not be sold; hence there was no price volatility. True enough; however, the issue seems to have more to do with accounting and recognition than actual condition. One could argue that a bank with loans that it cannot sell at any price is actually less "stable" than a bank that can liquidate its loan portfolio even if at a loss. Later in her paper, Professor Frankel argues as much herself and, in fact, suggests that bank capital be adjusted to reflect fluctuations in liquidation value. It is rather difficult for the reader to reconcile these two points of view.

Professor Frankel's views on the interaction of the ability of banks to invest in securitized loans and to underwrite issues of securitized loans similarly need further clarification. Banks currently have considerable authority to invest in loans and securities collateralized by or representing interests in pools of loans. Professor Frankel builds on this observation to argue that banks should be allowed to employ more fully modern theories of portfolio management to diversify risk. Curiously, Frankel suggests that legislated loan concentration limits prevent banks from diversifying. One would think the opposite were true, that limiting exposure to any one borrower or type of obligation would serve to create a more diverse portfolio.

As an aside, I would note that current law does not present a significant restriction on the ability of banks to manage risk through diversification and investment in securities. My bank, Republic National Bank of New York, typically has between 75 percent and 80 percent of its assets in securities of one form or another. The application of modern portfolio theories to banks is not the dream suggested by Frankel's paper; it is a reality.

I began my comments with the observation that "securitization" could have different meanings for different people. Personally, I look at securitization as an evolving process of channeling cash flows from one or more sources through one or more intermediaries to investors. The securities can be in a variety of forms for a number of different reasons. The process of securitization involves matching as closely as possible the objectives of originator/servicers with investor preferences. If enough originator/servicers have the same objectives and enough investors have the same preferences, a marketable security is developed; otherwise the process results in a private placement.

My particular perspective causes me to conclude that a useful starting point for a discussion of securitization is an understanding of the microeconomics of securitization and the legal and practical hurdles associated with realizing the financial benefits that are generally available from securitization. To understand the likely effect of securitization on banks, one should have an understanding of the magnitude of the economic incentives that securitization presents to banks and nonbanks, respectively. One should also understand with a high degree of detail how each area of the law encountered in the securitization process treats banks and nonbanks.

Generally, securitization can offer significant financial advantages over traditional debt financing and portfolio investing to originator/servicers of loans. The principal source of this financial advantage is the accounting treatment of the typical securitization transaction. By removing the securitized loans from the balance sheet of the originator/servicer, capital requirements are reduced. When the cost of capital is high in relation to the cost of debt, this becomes a very significant factor in the analysis.

The following example illustrates how even a highly rated issuer with a comparatively low cost of funds can benefit from securitization.

	Traditional Funding	*Asset Backed Security*
Principal Amount (millions):	$100	$100
Interest Rate on Loans:	8.00%	8.00%
Loan Servicing Costs:	50 bps	50 bps
Average Life of Loans:	2 years	2 years
Pricing Reference:	2 yr. Trsy.	2 yr. Trsy.
Reference Rate:	4.65%	4.65%

Security (liability) Rating:	AAA	AA
Spread to Reference Rate:	45 bps	90 bps
Security (liability) Coupon:	5.10%	5.55%
Credit Enhancement Amount:	NA	10%
Cost of Credit Enhancement:	NA	.05%
Leverage Ratio:	10 to 1	NA
Cost of Capital:	15%	NA
Underwriting Cost:	10 bps	30 bps
All-in Cost (excluding Capital):	5.15%	5.76%
All-in Cost (including Capital):	6.05%	5.76%

In the example above, securitizing presents the originator/servicer with a savings of 29 basis points per annum on $100 million. That equates to $300,000 per year for two years when compared to traditional debt financing. In addition, securitization allows the originator/servicer of the loans to transform spread income into more stable fee income. In the example above, the originator/servicer can account for the 50 basis points servicing fee as fee income. More important, the originator/servicer can capitalize the present value of the remaining 195 basis points of "excess servicing fees." Discounted at the originator/servicer's cost of capital, this equates to approximately $3.2 million. Obviously, this represents primarily a timing advantage to the originator/servicer; however, for companies that have limited ability to raise additional capital, this can be significant.

Moreover, even for companies that can readily raise additional capital, this accounting treatment allows the originator/servicer to increase its capital base while simultaneously reducing its assets. The company's leverage ratio improves from both factors. As a practical matter, a significant portion of the capitalized excess servicing fee will be used to pay for losses and delinquencies on the newly created asset backed securities. Sometimes this will take the form of increased letter of credit or insurance premiums on the issue. Other asset backed security structures such as those typically used to securitize credit card receivables, use the excess servicing fee to cover credit loss and to allow for early redemption, if necessary.

Another benefit of securitization is the elimination of funding risk for the originator/servicer. Securitization allows the originator/servicer to achieve perfect asset/liability management with regard to the sold loans, while retaining a significant portion of the economic benefits of the loans and, perhaps more important, the customer relationship.

Finally, securitization lowers the barriers to entry into the loan origination and servicing businesses by virtually eliminating the need for capital.

As markets for securitized loans have developed, many originator/servicers now originate loans only for sale and only against forward delivery sales agreements. It is no wonder then that securitization presents a very strong trend in finance and a very real threat to bank profitability.

This leads to the second area that I suggest should be considered when attempting to determine the effect of securitization on banks—namely, the process itself. Securitization is a rather complicated process, not because it is inherently very difficult (to the contrary, securitization is conceptually very straightforward), but rather because most laws that touch on the process were drafted before securitization became a significant trend in finance. Professor Frankel indirectly makes this point in her discussion of investment limitations. Her paper would have been more informative if Professor Frankel had shared her extensive knowledge of the securitization process with the reader.

If one concludes that securitization presents a financing advantage to originators/servicers of loans, it seems reasonable to examine the securitization process to determine whether or not banks can securitize as easily or efficiently as nonbanks. Securitization allows nonbanks to do what previously only banks did. The effect of securitization on banks will depend in part upon whether banks can do what nonbanks can now do.

It is beyond the scope of these comments to provide a comprehensive review of each of the laws and regulations that are involved in securitization. Nevertheless, it is worth noting that banks must comply with all of the legal requirements generally applicable to nonbank originators/servicers plus the special rules bank regulatory laws. The most significant of these involve accounting treatment and capital requirements, which are of course the areas most critical to realizing the benefits of securitization. In addition, the general separation of banking and the securities industry presents additional hurdles for banks seeking to securitize loans. At a minimum, these issues and regulatory approvals add significantly to transaction costs.

On balance, securitization presents less of a benefit to banks than to nonbanks. In other words, securitization represents a significant competitive advantage to nonbanks in the originating and servicing of loans. To the extent that banks lose this profitable business to new competitors or increased competition reduces the profitability of originating and servicing loans, and banks cannot securitize as efficiently as nonbanks, securitization will adversely effect banks. Securitization will not, however, have a direct adverse effect of the financial structure or riskiness of banks. To the contrary, the direct effect of securitization on banks' financial structure and risk will be positive.

CONCLUSION

Professor Frankel has undertaken an enormous task in attempting to address all of the possible effects of securitization on banking in a comparatively short paper. Unfortunately, the enormity of the subject does not lend itself to simple generalizations. As a result the reader does not gain enough of Professor Frankel's extensive knowledge of either securitization or banking.

NOTES

1. Professor Frankel has written a comprehensive guide to securitization entitled *Securitization: Structured Financings, Financial Asset Pools, and Asset-Backed Securities* (1991).
2. Unfortunately, Professor Frankel gives the reader little insight into the nature of the securities created or the process of transforming loans into marketable securities.
3. Admittedly, some of the investments made by would-be borrowers are in securitized instruments and some of the issuances that have contributed to the increase in the new issue market are in the form of securitized instruments; however, these factors are addressed by the other two forms suggested by Frankel.

COMMENT

Martin E. Lowy

Our picture of a bank historically has been as a repository of financial assets that are funded by borrowed money (whether or not called deposits) and, to a far lesser extent, by "capital" (that is, money placed at risk more explicitly). The earnings of this "bank" come largely from "spread": the difference between what the bank earns on its assets and what it pays on its liabilities.

It is this model that has gotten into trouble over the last 15 years, as both interest rate risk and credit risk have caused unacceptable levels of loss to banking institutions. And it is these losses that impel thinking on "Structural Change in Banking."

It may be that, in order to solve the high-risk nature of the banking business, we will have to change not only our picture of what is insured but also our picture of what a bank is and how it makes its money. And here securitization takes center stage, potentially shaping the structure of banking for the future.

I believe that Professor Frankel understates the degree to which the banking world will be changed by securitization. Securitization already has made savings and loan associations substantially obsolete. (This fact has been obscured by all of the other causes of the savings and loan debacle.) Some savings and loans do continue to make money as portfolio lenders; but securitization (on both sides of the balance sheet) is likely to continue to squeeze even these efficient lenders and eventually to force them either to contract or to seek to be producers rather than holders of assets.

Securitization also has tended to drive banks from their dominant position in consumer lending. Both credit card lending and automobile lending once were practically private preserves of banks, at least in part because banks had funding advantages. Today those funding advantages are gone because nonbanks can securitize credit card debt and consumer paper as well as, or better than, banks.

Will various other types of loans be securitized in the future? Some experiments are beginning already. The outcomes depend upon how credit risk can be spread. Historically, we have thought of banks as the right place to make credit decisions. Bankers are trained in credit; they tend to be proud of their "credit cultures"; but in the last 15 years bankers have made too many bad credit decisions for policymakers to have very much belief in this system of credit culture.

Why do banks make bad credit decisions? Is credit analysis just too difficult? Or do banks have other priorities that interfere with their credit judgment?

Several reasons arise as to why bankers delude themselves about credit quality. First, they think they should develop "relationships." The market, by contrast, has no relationships; so it never makes this mistake. Second, lenders' jobs depend on their making loans. If too few loans are made, lenders get laid off. Market participants have a wide variety of securities from which to choose; they don't get laid off for failing to buy a particular type of security. Third, bankers think they are supposed to be creative in structuring credits to serve their "clients." The market has no clients. In addition, because banks are regulated, they react to government stimuli. They accept government suggestions to "recycle petrodollars," leading to excessive LDC lending; and in the case of savings and loans, they reacted to government housing policies, leading to excessive interest rate risk.

The "market" has none of these problems, as Professor Frankel points out. The market demands a minimum level of credit quality as judged by a rating agency (AA seems to be demanded for a truly liquid market), and with that level of credit quality, the market will trade the securitized loans based on their expected cashflow characteristics. The fact that the underlying loans are on cars or cards—or anything else—becomes practically irrelevant to the market. The market has no "customers."

This tells us that the market will buy securitized commercial and industrial loans—or even real estate-backed loans—if they are properly securitized; that is, if they are packaged in a way that provides no greater risk than that represented by a AA credit rating. No technological issues stand in the way of this securitization. We have learned to chop up very complex cashflows into readily marketable units; the problem is credit enhancement. Who is willing to take the pure credit risk and at what price?

Knowledgeable market participants have suggested that banks underprice credit risk on smaller commercial loans and that that is why these loans cannot be securitized. There simply isn't enough spread to pay for an independent credit enhancement. Therefore, they say, the originating bank has to hold the paper. On larger, syndicated credits the credit probably is more properly priced because several banks are accepting the same pricing. But in the smaller credits, it is typical that the originating bank cannot find a participant if it wants to lay off a part of the risk.

It appears to me that empirical work to determine whether the underpricing hypothesis is correct would be very useful. If the banks are underpricing smaller business credits, why are they doing so? Do they make up for the risk by supracompetitive profits in other parts of the business attracted from the customer? Is the funding advantage provided by deposit insurance a necessary condition to the decision to underprice? What banks do this? Should they be preserved? If so, how?

These questions take on significance if we proceed to the next logical level in the securitized world. Professor Frankel foresees a world in which banks will diversify their portfolios by holding securitized paper. By contrast, I see a world in which banks will shrink significantly because banks are not efficient holders of securitized paper. If a bank pays a market rate for its deposits, then there will be little spread between those deposits and a AA-rated security of similar duration. Cashflow and interest-rate-risk management through swaps and other derivatives may increase spreads slightly, since the bank's expertise then will be used, but it seems to me unlikely that this will generate sufficient spread to cover bank operations and the cost of capital.[1] A mutual fund will be a more efficient intermediary to hold the paper; a mutual fund that holds securitized loans should be able to offer higher yields than a bank that holds similar assets.

What kind of a banking world would this forecast of securitization of both sides of the balance sheet produce? It would be a world with quite a few very big banks that would have basically liquid portfolios. They would make their money not so much from spread as from trading, credit enhancing, originating for sale or securitization, and providing services. Nonbanks also would provide many of the same services. This world also would have some large banks (perhaps different ones) that provided consumer deposit and credit services on a national scale. And it would have quite a number of smaller, more local banks that provided a more intimate brand of services to local customers. I think an unanswered question is whether these local institutions would or should continue to hold local business loans and what kind of safety net they should have when those loans go bad because of local economic failures. Ideally, the smaller banks, too, will securitize their loans and divest themselves of this local credit risk; but whether they can do so and remain profitable is a question yet to be answered.

The small bank question needs to be addressed, it seems to me, in conjunction with an exploration of what small banks in fact do today. And along with that investigation we should address the question of whether additional government-sponsored enterprises (GSEs) should be formed to securitize additional types of loans with government backing.

We are all free market economists, of course, but government policies—tax policies, regulatory policies, etc.—do influence the allocation of resources among sectors of the economy and do seek to stimulate economic growth in general. If FNMA and FHLMC work in the housing sector to reduce costs and thereby to facilitate home ownership at an acceptable social cost, should they not be replicated for other specific sectors of securitized loans? Maybe it is cheaper to have a GSE with strict standards than to have deposit insurance that does not seem capable of strict standards. And maybe it is more realistic to have GSEs that are subject to specific government oversight buying specified types of credit risk than putting the credit risk into large institutions that realistically would have to be bailed out if they fail.

These thoughts about government guarantees are anathema to most banking theorists; but I believe that the people of the United States are not willing to accept whatever the market produces. If the market produces an economic contraction, that is not acceptable.

In conclusion, the process of securitization, combined with Federal policies that punish risk-taking by insured banks, probably mean drastic changes in the risk profiles of banks as we have known them in the U.S. for the last 50 years; but it does not mean the end of banks. A key policy goal will have to be to manage the transition to lower risk in the banking system so that the damage to the economy is as small as possible. The government so far has botched the S&L transition (at considerable cost to the economy) and didn't even see that the banks were already in transition by the early 1980s. The academic community needs to formulate a clear and fairly simple view of what banks will be and must figure out how to explain it to Congress. Only a simple and compelling view of the future that promises a better economy in the public interest will overcome the gridlock caused by the cacophony of raised voices that comes from the financial service lobbies.

Unfortunately, the ill-named bill enacted just before Thanksgiving 1991, which I have elsewhere called the Turkey Bill and which former FDIC Chairman William Seidman has dubbed the "Credit Crunch Enhancement Act," has already threatened to botch the transition by imposing draconian early intervention requirements on the regulators, prematurely deterring the taking of credit risk, and dooming banks that get into trouble. The 1991 Act will hasten the coming of the world that I have foreseen here, but the costs to the economy and existing banks will give us no joy.

NOTES

1. I assume for this purpose that these securities will have a 100 percent risk weighting. A 20 percent risk weighting would make a great deal of difference to the analysis, but I question whether the U.S. regulatory authorities are likely to treat securities that are not government guaranteed any better than loans.

COMMENT

Jonathan R. Macey

INTRODUCTION

Securitization removes assets from banks' balance sheets in one of two ways. Securitization may involve a shift in funding patterns from bank loans to direct financing of debt through the sale of securities. Alternatively, securitization may take the form of a sale by a bank of loans or other assets, backed by a guarantee of some kind by the selling bank. This second type of consideration differs fundamentally from the first in that the bank retains the ultimate credit risk on the loans or other assets it is selling.[1]

Despite this fundamental difference between the two types of securitization, both types of securitization have the same effect on bank structure, because both types of securitization diminish the extent to which banks serve as providers of capital in the economy. Under either type of securitization, commercial banks are not the first-line providers of capital to borrowers. That role is shifted from banks to other segments of the economy. Consequently, if we stick to the traditional definition of banks as institutions that take demand deposits and make commercial loans, the effect of securitization on basic bank structure is transparently clear: after securitization, banks will shrink as capital needs are met through the sale of securities rather than through traditional bank lending. Only by expanding the definition of what constitutes commercial banking beyond its traditional boundaries can we conclude that securitization will result in anything other than a major reduction in the role that banks and banking play in the economy.

Using the Conference papers by Berger and Udell, by Nakamura, as well as Frankel's paper as background, this comment explores the effects of securitization on the traditional business of commercial banks. The conclusions are simple. First, while there is no question that the securitization phenomenon is good for the economy generally because it lowers capital costs and improves the capital allocation process, securitization is very bad for the commercial lending business. The diminution in demand for commercial loans caused by securitization is not random. Only the best assets in a bank's portfolio will be securitized. After this "cream-skimming" inherent in the process of securitization is accomplished, the remaining assets in the banks' loan portfolio will be more costly to monitor and less liquid. Contrary to popular belief, this cream-skimming phenomenon is not solely due to the perverse incentives for excessive risk-taking caused by deposit insurance. Rather, this cream-skimming is, in fact, an efficient manifestation of the basic economic differences between the market for commercial loans and the market for securities. Consequently, securitization leads not only to a diminution in demand for commercial loans, but also to a decline in the average quality of the assets held by banks in their commercial loan portfolios.

Second, securitization leads to an uncoupling of the commercial lending function of banks and the deposit-taking function performed by banks. This uncoupling raises the costs to banks of taking deposits and leads to a further erosion in bank profitability. The implications of this phenomenon for deposit insurance are, in my view, misunderstood by Nakamura in his interesting and important paper. This Comment seeks to clarify this misunderstanding.

Finally, and perhaps most importantly, securitization brings into sharp focus the basic fact that the distinction between commercial banking and investment banking is a wholly artificial, legal fiction lacking in economic reality. The inability of banks fully to participate in the securities markets appears truly irrational in light of securitization and other phenomena that combine to make the traditional activities of banks increasingly unimportant.

THE CREAM-SKIMMING PHENOMENON

Perhaps the most singular characteristic of commercial banks is that they are in a unique position to analyze nonstandardized credit risks and to hold such credit risks in portfolio. As Berger and Udell observe, it is useful to view credit risks (borrowers) as lying on a continuum, with "information-problematic" borrowers at one end and borrowers with few information problems at the other end. At one end of this continuum are credit risks with such acute information problems that they are unable to obtain credit from any source, including banks. At the other end of the continuum are borrowers with few information problems, who "issue traded securities (along with commercial paper and medium term notes) and are monitored directly (and individually) by the investors who purchase these securities."

Berger and Udell are correct in their conclusion that firms and individuals with few information problems will utilize securitization. They also are correct in their conclusion that only firms and individuals with acute informational problems will continue to utilize the monitoring services of commercial banks. But Berger and Udell incorrectly characterize the processes through which these conclusions are reached. The investors who purchase securities are not the monitors that provide information about securitized credit to the market. The monitoring necessary to make the securities markets work is conducted by investment bankers and other professional financial intermediaries who act as rivals for commercial banks, not by the ultimate investors.

The monitoring conducted by investment bankers and other professional intermediaries takes place in two contexts. First, when a firm issues new securities, the issuing firm's affairs "will be reviewed by an investment banker or some similar intermediary acting as a monitor for the collective interest of (the ultimate investors)…. "[2] Thus, as Easterbrook has observed, firms that regularly turn to the securities markets in search of new capital regularly receive monitoring from the investment bankers and others who act as financial intermediaries.

The second source of monitoring for securitized assets is the investment professionals who have strong economic incentives to engage in monitoring of securities in the secondary market. If investment professionals can identify a mispriced security, they stand to profit by buying or selling that security until the price adjusts to reflect the appropriate price. Thus competition among market professionals to obtain arbitrage profits by buying and selling mispriced securities provides the second source of monitoring for traded securities.

Thus Berger and Udell mischaracterize the secondary market for securities by claiming that investors monitor the credit risks available in that market. This would be analogous to a claim that depositors (rather than bank managers) monitor banks' loan portfolios. But investment professionals, not investors, monitor the issuers of assets that have been securitized. Investors are able to rely on competition among investment professionals to create an incentive for monitoring that in turn leads to efficient securities markets that price securities accurately and reflect new information promptly.[3]

The problem with the way that Berger and Udell characterize the securities markets is that they leave no role for financial intermediaries. Everything is done by issuers and investors. This is inaccurate. Financial intermediaries play a role in monitoring assets that have been securitized just as they play a role in monitoring nonsecuritized assets such as commercial loans. The crucial distinction is that the financial intermediaries who monitor the securities markets are self-funding. Their compensation for monitoring securitized assets comes from their potential to obtain trading profits by identifying mispriced securities. By contrast, issuers of assets that lie on the low end of the information-continuum identified by Berger and Udell must pay directly (in the form of higher borrowing costs) to receive the monitoring from the commercial banks, thrifts and insurance companies that hold these nonsecuritized assets, since, by definition, these intermediaries cannot realize trading profits from holding such assets.

Thus, one characteristic of assets that are susceptible to securitization is that sufficient public information is available about them so that they can be traded in secondary markets, or at least distributed broadly at an initial public offering. And, as Berger and Udell observe, borrowers with acute information problems will not have access to this market.

As assets that are more easily susceptible to monitoring are stripped out of banks' assets and securitized, banks are faced with the following choice: They can either shrink by declining to replace securitized assets with new assets, or else they can go further out on the continuum described by Berger and Udell and make loans to borrowers with more severe information problems than previously had been made. Thus, the securitization phenomenon presents banks with a simple choice: shrink or become riskier.

One of the advantages of holding securitized assets instead of holding loans is that holders of securitized assets can free-ride on information processing capabilities of the secondary markets in ways that holders of nonsecuritized assets cannot. As noted above, holders of securitized assets benefit from the competition among market professionals to locate mispriced securities. By contrast, banks that hold nonsecuritized assets internalize all of the costs associated with monitoring the quality of those assets. As a result, a firm that owns a fully diversified portfolio of securities has lower costs than a bank that has a fully diversified portfolio of loans of exactly the same size because the firm with the portfolio of securities can rely on market processes to monitor those assets, while the bank cannot.

For banks to maintain their loan portfolios they need people (loan officers) who are experts in many areas of business and who are spread out geographically in order to perform on-site monitoring of the banks' loans. The skills that make a good loan officer are the same skills that make a good financial analyst. Unfortunately, the Glass-Steagall Act prohibits the same people from performing these functions simultaneously.

Because securitization is a low-cost substitute for bank lending, it must cause banks to shrink. And, while it is clear that there still could be a profitable lending market in an economy in which large numbers of assets are securitized, the fact remains that the rates set by banks for commercial lending for the assets remaining in their portfolios after securitization must be sufficiently high to compensate those banks both for the higher risks associated with those assets (relative to assets that have been securitized) as well as for the higher costs of monitoring those assets.

SECURITIZATION AND BANK DEPOSITS

Turning now from the asset side of the balance sheet to the liability side, I wish to refer to the interesting and important points made by Nakamura on the issue of the extent to which securitization affects the social desirability for federally sponsored deposit insurance. Nakamura argues that securitization undermines the need for deposit insurance because it makes banks' assets more liquid, thereby eliminating the basic justification for deposit insurance provided by Diamond and Dybvig.[4]

Diamond and Dybvig argue that banks and other depository intermediaries transform illiquid assets (loans) into liquid liabilities (deposit accounts). Bankers make some prediction about their depositors' normal demand for cash. Based on these predictions, bankers convert some of their depositors' money into loans and leave enough in liquid form to meet normal demands, allowing, of course for some cushion. The problem with this arrangement, according to Diamond and Dybvig, is that depositors are in a prisoners' dilemma. If any single depositor attempts to obtain her cash at any given time, the bank will have no problem meeting her needs. But if all depositors attempt to gain access to the funds in their demand deposit accounts simultaneously, the bank will have to convert its illiquid assets (loans) into cash at distress prices and will render itself insolvent.

According to Diamond and Dybvig, deposit insurance solves this collective action problem, by preventing these panics or runs. The problem with this analysis is that it ignores the facts that the collective action problem identified by Diamond and Dybvig can be solved by very simple contracts among the parties and that there is a central agency—the bank—that is fully capable of writing the contracts necessary to solve the problem. Most obviously, the problem can be solved by having banks issue certificates of deposit to customers rather than demand deposit accounts. Customers willing to wait longer to gain access to their money are compensated for the inconvenience in the form of higher rates of interest. If the interest rate differential between demand deposits and certificates of deposit of longer maturities grows large enough, the problem identified by Diamond and Dybig largely disappears.

But, of course, depositors do need immediate access to some of their money. As Diamond and Dybvig fully recognize, this is the case with or without deposit insurance. Certificates of deposit do not solve the entire problem. Something must be done to the asset side of the balance sheet. And, as Nakamura suggests banks can solve the collective action problem facing their depositors by keeping a larger portion of its assets in liquid investments.

Nakamura argues that securitization removes the need for deposit insurance for banks that are able to transform a large portion of their assets into more liquid investments. The problem here is that under *any* theory of banking, *some* of banks' assets must be kept in highly liquid form. The only question is how much. And banks could keep their assets in liquid form even without securitization if they could hold stock, government securities, and other sorts of assets. In other words, Nakamura's argument is that securitization enables banks to transform their assets into more liquid form. My argument is that securitization presents only one additional means for banks to transform their assets into more liquid form. There are other liquid assets that banks could hold besides securitized assets. Thus, securitization only presents one additional method for dealing with the problem identified by Diamond and Dybvig.

The most that can be said for securitization is that it lowers the marginal cost to banks of eliminating the collective action problem faced by their shareholders. My argument is that depositors and banks should bear the costs of dealing with this collective action problem because they enjoy the benefits of the banking relationship. Deposit insurance externalizes the cost of dealing with this collective action problem and therefore removes banks' incentives to solve the problem for themselves.

In a nutshell, then, deposit insurance creates the environment in which banks are free to mismatch their assets and liabilities in a socially suboptimal way, by externalizing the costs of this mismatch. Absent deposit insurance, banks would structure both their assets and their contractual arrangements with depositors, so as to eliminate this problem.

Nakamura's argument that securitization will have a more dramatic effect on large banks than on small banks does not seem well founded. Small banks, like large banks, can take the dollars contributed by depositors and buy securitized assets as easily as large banks. Nakamura argues that large banks have easier access to capital markets than do small banks. This is true, but not dispositive. Large banks' access to the securities markets enables them to attract funding from sources other than depositors. This funding can be long term in nature and therefore—unlike assets funded by deposits—need not be offset by securitized assets in order to solve the mismatch between the maturity structure of assets and liabilities.

Nakamura also argues that large banks can securitize a larger variety of their products than can smaller banks. Specifically, Nakamura posits that smaller banks have been successful only at securitizing mortgages, while large banks have been successful at securitizing auto loans, commercial loans, and credit card loans. But this does not mean that smaller banks are more in need of deposit insurance than larger banks. Instead it means that small banks either will have to find other ways to solve the asset-liability mismatch, such as reducing the proportion of their total portfolios devoted to loans or issuing more CDs and fewer demand deposits.

In other words, Nakamura's analysis suggests that smaller banks will have advantages over larger banks through lower funding costs because smaller banks obtain a larger proportion of funding from deposits, which are cheaper than other sources of funding. This means that smaller banks can earn competitive spreads at lower risk than large banks. This, in turn, suggests that large banks are likely to become more, rather than less risky as a result of their greater reliance on the capital markets. As Nakamura suggests, the securitization phenomenon offsets this tendency by enabling larger banks to reduce the costs of holding their liabilities.

My goal has not been to cast doubt on Nakamura's argument that the need for deposit insurance on the part of large banks has declined as a result of securitization. Clearly he is correct about this. Rather my goal has been to challenge his argument that small banks continue to need deposit insurance. And Nakamura's own example about how small banks use information is instructive in this regard.

Nakamura's example concerns a gas station that for a time has enjoyed a degree of market power as a result of being the only station located at a busy intersection. When a rival gas station sets up in business on another corner of the same intersection, the original gas station owner must decide whether to meet his rival's lower prices or to enter a price war in order to drive the newcomer out of business and regain his former status as a monopolist.

Nakamura correctly observes that, if the first gas station holds debt in its capital structure, some of the cost of losing the price war to the new station will be borne by the lenders, while the profits from winning the war will be enjoyed entirely by those who own the equity in the station. Commercial bankers, Nakamura argues, have methods of dealing with this phenomenon that give them information advantages over other types of lenders and thereby enable them to force the gas station to embark on the strategy that prevents suboptimally risky behavior by the gas station.

Let us move the analysis back a frame, however, so that we focus on the interests of the bank's equity claimants instead of the interests of the gas station's equity claimants. In this case a different picture emerges. Like the gas station, the bank has fixed claimants—i.e. depositors. But unlike the bank in Nakamura's example, these fixed claimants have no incentive to monitor the activities of the bank. And, like the gas station, all of the profits from engaging in riskier activities enure to the bank's equity holders, while losses are shared with the bank's fixed claimants—or, more accurately—the FDIC.

Thus, even if Nakamura has succeeded in making his point that small bankers are in a better position than other lenders to maximize the value of their loans *ex post*, by declaring loans to be in default or by using the threat of default to induce the borrower to engage in a workout, he fails to provide any explanation for why such banks should not be subject to the same moral hazard as might apply to gas station owners. In particular, he does not explain why banks will not engage in behavior that fails to optimize the gross value of the firm by engaging in suboptimally risky behavior that transfers wealth from the FDIC to the banks' equity claimants.

None of Nakamura's empirical results casts doubt on the analysis I have presented here. Nakamura's empirical results suggest four things: (1) that small banks have an informational advantage over large banks because the checking accounts kept as small banks are more readily comprehensible; (2) that banks do not have an informational advantage over nonbank lenders in lending to large borrowers; (3) that small banks do not have as good access to capital markets as large banks; and (4) that large banks lend to large borrowers while small banks lend to small borrowers. These conclusions all reinforce Nakamura's hypothesis that small banks may be in a good position to police small borrowers *ex post* (i.e., after the loans are made). But they do not provide any rationale for why banks would not make risky loans to such borrowers *ex ante*, in order to transfer wealth from the FDIC to their shareholders.

Of course, my argument about the moral hazard problem posed by FDIC insurance is not limited to small banks. The difference between small banks and large banks becomes relevant because securitization makes it easier for regulators to evaluate big banks than small banks.

For Nakamura, a major difference between small banks and large banks is that large banks find it easier to securitize their assets. The greater ability of large banks to securitize their assets relative to small banks results in a corresponding increase in the ability of outside regulators to monitor the quality of those assets, because they can look to the secondary trading markets in which those assets trade. Similarly, the fact that large banks have publicly traded debt and equity in their capital structure makes it easier for regulators to evaluate the financial status of banks by looking at the performance of that debt and equity in the secondary markets.

Thus data showing that there has been an increase in the rate of failures of large banks relative to small banks may be due more to the fact that—for reasons consistent with Nakamura's arguments—regulators are able to identify large problem banks more easily than they are able to identify small problem banks. After all, financial institutions generally do not enter insolvency proceedings voluntarily. They are forced into insolvency proceedings by regulators. For the reasons described above, it is easier for regulators to force large banks into insolvency than small banks because, as a legal matter, it is easier for regulators to establish that a large bank is insolvent than it is to show that a small bank is insolvent.

The data Nakamura adduces to show that smaller banks are more profitable than larger banks supports my arguments. If for the reasons given here: (1) it is harder to evaluate small banks than it is to evaluate large banks; and (2) small banks, like large banks, have an incentive to engage in excessive risk-taking due to the moral hazard problem posed by FDIC insurance, then small banks are likely to show higher profits than large banks.

This is because the profits of small banks will show up on the balance sheets of such banks in order to allow such banks to make dividend payments and other distributions to equity claimants. On the other hand, the loan portfolio of smaller banks is not likely to reflect the true asset quality of the banks' assets. And, for the reasons articulated by Nakamura, the quality of the assets of a small bank will be much more difficult to evaluate than the quality of the assets of a large bank. The very fact that a larger portion of the assets of large banks has been securitized means that it will be easier for regulators and market participants to evaluate the quality of those assets.

SECURITIZATION IN A LARGER CONTEXT

In her paper on securitization and bank structure, Tamar Frankel repeats the standard incantation that banks' are inherently risky because of the inevitable mismatch between the term structure of their assets and the term structure of their liabilities. The ability of banks to sell certificates of deposits and to purchase liquid assets reveals this incantation for what it is: sheer myth. But Frankel's error appears to be harmless because she gets to the right conclusion, which is that banks should be given expanded securities powers in order to permit them to alleviate the "inevitable" mismatch between assets and liabilities.

The problem with Frankel's analysis is that she imagines that unspecified "dangers" would accompany banks' entry into securities activities and fails to acknowledge that the only real danger lies in continuing to prevent banks from expanding their activities. Aside from some inaccuracies about the nature of the current regulatory regime that governs banks' activities, the basic flaw in Frankel's analysis is that she presumes that banks will never do anything unless guided to do so by regulators. So, for example she argues that banks should be "encouraged to diversify and evaluate the risk of their whole portfolio rather than of each loan or securitized loan they hold."

Similarly, Frankel suggests that current regulations that require banks to diversify their loan portfolios in minimal ways somehow are an impediment to diversification. Frankel says that current banking law is "not geared to portfolio management or diversification" because a bank's portfolio is deemed diversified if the amount lent to one borrower or issuer does not exceed 10 percent of the bank's paid up capital or surplus." But this rule does absolutely nothing to *prevent* a bank from diversifying more broadly if it should choose to do so.

Frankel looks at securitization as a regulatory phenomenon. But securitization should instead be viewed in the way it is presented by Nakamura and by Berger and Udell: as a market development made possible by a series of technological innovations. This market development puts new pressures on the existing regulatory equilibrium because it puts new competitive pressures on an industry that long had been insulated from such pressures by regulation. In this way, securitization is only one in a series of developments that threaten banks by rewarding new and more efficient ways of providing services that were once provided solely by banks. All of these developments are leading to an irreversible decline in the demand for the traditional, core services provided by commercial banks. Pension funds, life insurance products, annuities, and, of course, money market funds are all attractive substitutes for the traditional demand deposit accounts and savings accounts offered by banks. Even the stock market has emerged as an attractive substitute for investors, as portfolio theory has shown how depositors can hedge the risks associated with such investments and the rise of the options and futures markets has expanded the ability of investors to reduce certain kinds of risk and to eliminate other risks entirely.

Small borrowers can borrow from corporations such as General Motors, Ford, and Sears, not only through such vehicles as the General Motors Acceptance Corporation, but also through the credit cards accepted by virtually every retail store in America. Securitization has transformed banks from their traditional roles as lenders into their modern—and far more unprofitable role—as clearing agent for loans funded by others.

This transformation has reduced the need for bank lending officers, and for banks. As markets develop, it is only natural that intermediaries will suffer. Securitization, at its most fundamental level simply operationalizes the old adage "let's cut out the middleman." The middleman in the securitization story is the bank. In the wake of securitization, society's need for commercial lending is diminished. Securitization also facilitates the unbundling of deposit-taking and lending and thereby brings into sharp focus the fact that the line between investment banking and commercial banking is an artificial demarcation attributable not to economic reality but to regulatory fiat. Securitization is a low-cost substitute for bank lending. In the wake of securitization, banks have a simple choice: shrink dramatically, or expand the scope of their services beyond their traditional focus on deposit taking and commercial lending. If lending and deposit taking constitute banking, then banks inevitably are going to account for an increasingly small share of the GNP in years to come.

CONCLUSION

The phenomenon of securitization should bring into sharp focus the ineluctable reality that there is nothing "special" about banking other than the way it is regulated. People with cash can obtain highly liquid investments in a myriad of formats other than the traditional demand deposit at a bank. People in need of funds view the traditional commercial loan as only one of a number of sources of money, ranging from commercial paper for large issuers to consumer loans extended by finance companies and loans on life insurance policies extended by insurance companies.

Similarly, the securitization phenomenon brings into sharp focus the fact that there is nothing inherently risky about banking. The riskiness associated with the mismatch between the term structure of banks' assets and liabilities is perfectly avoidable. That banks have *elected* not to avoid this mismatch is a straightforward manifestation of the moral hazard problem posed by the maintenance of FDIC insurance.

Thus, in an age of securitization in which the capital markets are becoming increasingly efficient with respect to their ability to process and assimilate information, any justification that ever existed for federally sponsored deposit insurance has disappeared.[5] To be sure, it would be nice to have deposit insurance if such insurance could be provided at zero cost. But there is no such thing as a free lunch, and deposit insurance is no exception. Securitization, along with a host of other market forces, has had the effect of increasing the cost of the deposit insurance lunch as good assets on banks' balance sheets are replaced by assets that are both more risky and more difficult to evaluate. Securitization also has increased the costs of deposit insurance by making banking more competitive, and therefore more risky.

NOTES

1. Berger and Udell, 1991, p. 2.
2. Easterbrook, 1984, p. 654.
3. Macey and Miller, 1990, pp. 1089–90.
4. Diamond and Dybvig, 1983.
5. As Nakamura presciently observes, if there is a rationale for government sponsored insurance for the banking industry, it has to do with protecting the payments system. But there is no reason to link whatever regulatory system may (or may not) be needed to protect the payments system with deposit insurance. While Nakamura limits this point to his argument that large banks don't need deposit insurance, I believe the point applies with equal force to small banks.

REFERENCES

Diamond, Douglas B. and Philip H. Dybvig, "Bank Runs, Deposit Insurance and Liquidity," *Journal of Political Economy*, vol. 91 (June 1983), pp. 401–19.

Easterbrook, Frank H., "Two Agency Cost Explanations of Dividends," *American Economic Review*, vol. 74 (September 1984), pp. 650–59.

Litan, Robert E., *The Revolution in U.S. Finance*. Washington, DC: The Brookings Institution (1991).

Macey, Jonathan R., and Geoffrey P. Miller, "Good Finance, Bad Economics: An Analysis of the Fraud-on-the-Market Theory," *Stanford Law Review*, vol. 42, no. 4 (April 1990), pp. 1059–92.

Other books in the *New York University Salomon Series* from Business One Irwin . . .

RECENT DEVELOPMENTS IN FINANCE
Edited by ***Anthony Saunders***

An essential resource for anyone responsible for managing financial resources: portfolios, corporate funds, or deposits. Shows you how the reconfiguration of global financial markets, new approaches to issuing securities, continued introductions of new derivative securities, and threats to banking liquidity have completely changed the world of finance. (224 pages)
ISBN: 1-55623-706-5

THE BATTLE FOR CORPORATE CONTROL
Shareholder Rights, Stakeholder Interests, and Managerial Responsibilities
Edited by ***Arnold W. Sametz***

An enlightening pro and con account of recent takeover/defense activities and court decisions that describes the fiduciary responsibilities of the institutional investor, and argues the value-added issue of mergers and acquisitions. Includes strategies for surviving a takeover bid. (522 pages)
ISBN: 1-55623-305-1

CRASHES AND PANICS
The Lessons from History
Edited by ***Eugene N. White***

Offers new light on the causes of financial panics and recommends policy responses. (260 pages)
ISBN: 1-55623-361-2

FINANCIAL OPTIONS
From Theory to Practice
Edited by ***Stephen Figlewski, William Silver, and Marti Subrahmanyam***

Using little math, this complete reference explains option valuation theories and shows you how they apply to trading. (416 pages)
ISBN: 1-55623-234-9

BANKRUPTCY AND DISTRESSED RESTRUCTURINGS
Analytical Issues and Investment Opportunities
Edited by ***Edward I. Altman***

This unique book covers investment opportunities in distressed and defaulted securities, examines management and competitor behavior related to distress, and explains the determinants of successful distressed exchange issues and Chapter 11 proceedings. (417 pages)
ISBN: 1-55623-901-7